Argentina
& Uruguay

Perfect places to stay, eat & explore

D0377601

Published by Time Out Guides Ltd, a wholly owned subsidiary of Time Out Group Ltd.
Time Out and the Time Out logo are trademarks of Time Out Group Ltd.

© Time Out Group Ltd 2009

10 9 8 7 6 5 4 3 2 1

This edition first published in Great Britain in 2009 by Ebury Publishing
A Random House Group Company
20 Vauxhall Bridge Road, London SW1V 2SA

Random House Australia Pty Limited 20 Alfred Street, Milsons Point, Sydney, New South Wales 2061, Australia
Random House New Zealand Limited 18 Poland Road, Glenfield, Auckland 10, New Zealand
Random House South Africa (Pty) Limited Isle of Houghton, Corner Boundary, Road & Carse O'Gowrie,
Houghton 2198, South Africa

Random House UK Limited Reg. No. 954009

Distributed in USA by Publishers Group West
1700 Fourth Street, Berkeley, California 94710

Distributed in Canada by Publishers Group Canada
250A Carlton Street, Toronto, Ontario M5A 2L1

For further distribution details, see www.timeout.com

ISBN: 978-1-84670-127-6

A CIP catalogue record for this book is available from the British Library

Printed and bound by Firmengruppe APPL, aprinta druck, Wemding, Germany

The Random House Group Limited supports The Forest Stewardship Council (FSC), the leading international forest
certification organisation. All our titles that are printed on Greenpeace approved FSC certified paper carry the FSC
logo. Our paper procurement policy can be found at http://www.rbooks.co.uk/environment.

Time Out carbon-offsets all its flights with Trees for Cities (www.treesforcities.org).

While every effort has been made by the author(s) and the publisher to ensure that the information contained in this
guide is accurate and up to date as at the date of publication, they accept no responsibility or liability in contract, tort,
negligence, breach of statutory duty or otherwise for any inconvenience, loss, damage, costs or expenses of any nature
whatsoever incurred or suffered by anyone as a result of any advice or information contained in this guide (except to
the extent that such liability may not be excluded or limited as a matter of law). Before travelling, it is advisable to
check all information locally, including without limitation, information on transport, accommodation, shopping and
eating out. Anyone using this guide is entirely responsible for their own health, well-being and belongings and care
should always be exercised whilst travelling.

All rights reserved. No part of this publication may be reproduced, stored in a retrieval system, or transmitted in any
form or by any means, electronic, mechanical, photocopying, recording or otherwise, without prior permission from the
copyright owners.

Introduction

Welcome to *Time Out Argentina & Uruguay: Perfect places to stay, eat & explore*, one in a new series of guidebooks that picks out the very best places to go in a country or area. We've chosen the most inspiring destinations across Argentina and Uruguay, and for each of them singled out the most appealing hotels, shops and restaurants across all price brackets.

Argentina is the eighth biggest country in the world, and in terms of landscapes, it is one of the most diverse places imaginable, offering vibrant jungle, wildlife-packed wetlands, dramatic glaciers, mammoth mountains, sprawling pampas, dune-dotted beaches and shockingly turquoise lakes. It ticks boxes for every type of traveller, and this guide is designed to help pick what's right for you.

For added inspiration, we've also covered the best of Argentina's lesser-known neighbour, Uruguay. Savvy travellers are now realising that a side trip across the Río de la Plata offers more than just another passport stamp: this tiny country lays claim to South America's hippest beach resorts in José Ignacio and Punta del Este, as well as unspoiled countryside that provides the ultimate crowd-free escape.

Most of our writers are long-term residents of Argentina and have travelled extensively throughout their adopted country and its neighbour. We have tapped into their knowledge to bring you the inside track in the hope that you will come to share their passion for this special part of the world.

As well as featuring all the well-known must-see attractions – including the vineyards in Mendoza, the towering waterfalls of Iguazú and the awe-inspiring glaciers around El Calafate – we've uncovered many emerging destinations that have yet to build up an international following. Our 'watch this space' tips include the Andean oasis of Barreal, the palm forests of El Palmar de Colón and the prehistoric rock formations in Parque de las Quijadas.

A word about the listings. The £ symbols indicate the price bracket of a venue: £=budget, ££=moderate, £££=expensive and ££££=luxury. Unless otherwise stated, all venues accept credit cards.

All of our listings are double-checked, but businesses do sometimes close or change their hours and prices. In Argentina and Uruguay, management often has a very flexible approach, and opening hours are rarely set in stone. We recommend that you check the particulars by phone or online before visiting.

Contents

20

92

136

Cities

Rural Escapes

Rivers & Wetlands

Mountains & Lakes

174

226

278

Coast

Dramatic Landscapes

Argentina & Uruguay

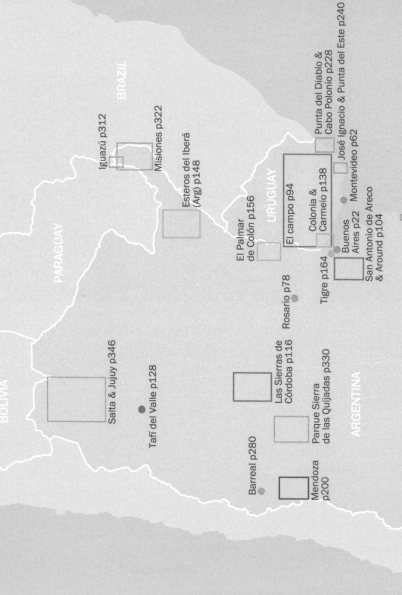

BOLIVIA

PARAGUAY

BRAZIL

CHILE

ARGENTINA

URUGUAY

PACIFIC OCEAN

Iguazú p312

Misiones p322

Esteros del Iberá
(Arg) p148

El Palmar
de Colón p156

Punta del Diablo &
Cabo Polonio p228

José Ignacio & Punta del Este p240

Montevideo p62

Colonia &
Carmelo p138

El campo p94

Buenos
Aires p22

Tigre p164

San Antonio de Areco
& Around p104

Pinamar, Cariló & Mar de las Pampas p266

Rosario p78

Salta & Jujuy p346

Tafí del Valle p128

Las Sierras de
Córdoba p116

Parque Sierra
de las Quijadas p330

Barreal p280

Mendoza
p200

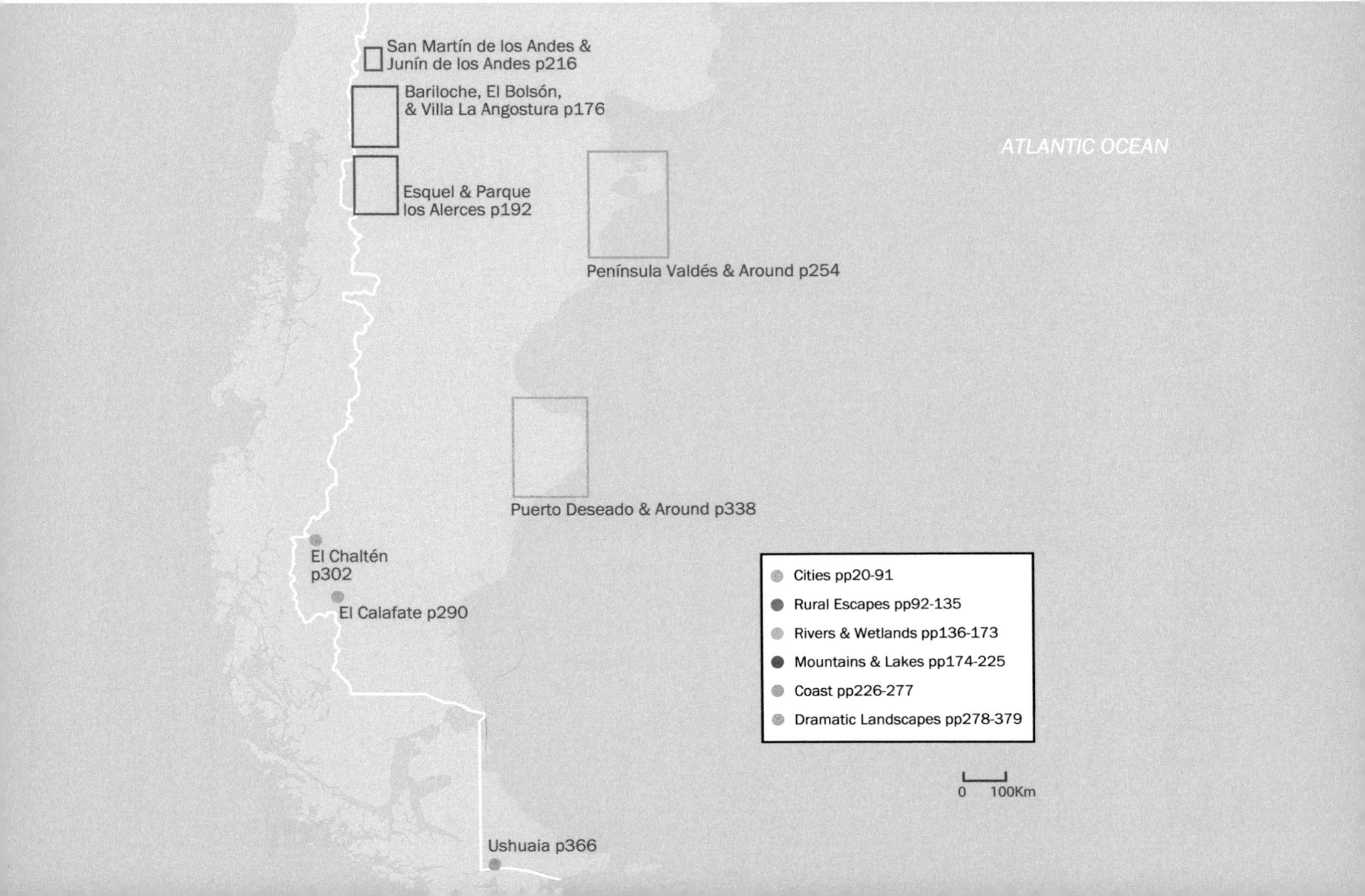
ATLANTIC OCEAN
San Martín de los Andes & Junín de los Andes p216
Bariloche, El Bolsón, & Villa La Angostura p176
Esquel & Parque los Alerces p192
Península Valdés & Around p254
Puerto Deseado & Around p338
El Chaltén p302
El Calafate p290
Ushuaia p366
Cities pp20-91
Rural Escapes pp92-135
Rivers & Wetlands pp136-173
Mountains & Lakes pp174-225
Coast pp226-277
Dramatic Landscapes pp278-379
0 100Km

Editor's Picks

FIVE-STAR DESTINATIONS

ART & ARCHITECTURE
Buenos Aires p22

EATING & DRINKING
Bariloche, El Bolsón & Villa La Angostura p176

Buenos Aires p22

José Ignacio & Punta del Este p240

Mendoza p200

HISTORIC SITES
Colonia & Carmelo p138

Puerto Deseado p338

HOTELS
Bariloche, El Bolsón & Villa La Angostura p176

Buenos Aires p22

El Calafate p290

José Ignacio & Punta del Este p240

Mendoza p200

NIGHTLIFE
Buenos Aires p22

OUTDOOR ACTIVITIES
Bariloche, El Bolsón & Villa La Angostura p176

Barreal p280

El Calafate p290

El Chaltén p302

Mendoza p200

San Martín de los Andes &
Junín de los Andes p216

Las Sierras de Córdoba p116

SCENERY
Bariloche, El Bolsón & Villa La Angostura p176

Barreal p280

Cabo Polonio & Punta del Diablo p228

El Calafate p290

El Chaltén p302

Iguazú p312

José Ignacio & Punta del Este p240

Mendoza p200

Parque Sierra de las Quijadas p330

San Martín de los Andes &
Junín de los Andes p216

Ushuaia p366

SHOPPING
Buenos Aires p22

ACCOMMODATION

LUXURY
Alvear Palace Hotel, Buenos Aires p47

Las Balsas, Villa La Angostura p187

La Becasina Delta Lodge, Tigre p171

Casa los Sauces, El Calafate p299

Los Cauquenes Resort & Spa, Ushuaia p375

Cavas Wine Lodge, Mendoza p213

Challhuaquen, Esquel & Parque los Alerces p354

Colomé, Salta & Jujuy p362

Estancia La Paz, Las Sierras de Córdoba p126

Estancia Rincón Chico, Península Valdés p264

Four Seasons Carmelo, Carmelo p146

Hotel Garzón, near José Ignacio p252

Jardín Escondido, Buenos Aires p51

Llao Llao, Bariloche p190

Posada de la Laguna, Esteros del Iberá p154

La Posada del Faro, José Ignacio p252

Río Hermoso Hotel de Montaña,
San Martín de los Andes p224

El Rocío, San Antonio de Areco & Around p115

Tipiliuke, Junín de los Andes p224

Yacutinga Lodge, Misiones p328

GOOD VALUE

La Aurora del Palmar, El Palmar de Colón p161

El Bordo de las Lanzas, Salta & Jujuy p360

Campo la Sierra, Parque Sierra de las Quijadas p337

The Cocker, Buenos Aires p49

La Confluencia Lodge, El Bolsón p188

Estancia las Carreras, Tafí del Valle p125

Estancia Paz, El campo, Uruguay p101

Hostería la Forêt, Mar de las Pampas p176

Hostería El Pilar, El Chaltén p310

Hotel Villa Victoria, Tigre p171

Lungomare Trieste, Rosario p90

Posada de los Corvinos, Cabo Polonio p238

El Rancho de Carmen, Barreal p288

SPAS

Casa Calma, Buenos Aires p47

Cavas Wine Lodge, Mendoza p213

Rumbo 90° Delta Lodge & Spa, Tigre p172

BODEGAS

Achaval Ferrer, Mendoza p204

Bodega Domingo Hermanos, Salta & Jujuy p353

Bodega La Rural, Mendoza p206

Bouza Bodega Boutique, Montevideo p66

Carinae, Mendoza p206

Carmelo Patti, Mendoza p206
San Pedro de Yacochuya, Salta & Jujuy p354

Viñedo de los Vientos, El campo, Uruguay p98

CHILDREN

La Cantina, El Palmar de Colón p160

El Colibri, Las Sierras de Córdoba p125

La Isla de los Inventos, Rosario p82

Jardín de los Niños, Rosario p82

Museo Paleontológico Egidio Feruglio (MEF), Trelew, Península Valdés p258

Viejo Barrio, Colonia p146

DRIVES

High-peaks route to Valle de Traslasierra, Las Sierras de Córdoba p121

Quebrada de Humahuaca, Salta & Jujuy p354

Ruta 40, El Chaltén p307

Ruta de los Siete Lagos, Bariloche, El Bolsón & Villa La Angostura p182

Salta to Cafayate via Cachi, Salta & Jujuy p353

EXCURSIONS

Día de campo, San Antonio de Areco & Around p108

Football match, Buenos Aires p26

Llama trekking, Salta & Jujuy p359

Moonlight tour of Iguazú Falls, Iguazú p316

Star-gazing, Barreal p284

HERITAGE

Colonia del Sacramento, p140

Cueva de las Manos, Puerto Deseado p343

Estancia Santa Catalina, Las Sierras de Córdoba p121

Jesuit ruins of San Ignacio Miní, Santa Ana and Loreto, Misiones p324

Las Ruinas de Quilmes, Tafí del Valle p130

La Trochita (Old Patagonian Express), Esquel p194

esplendor

COLECCIÓN DE HOTELES BOUTIQUE

Esplendor: (m.) Apogeo, intensidad, cualidad que ha alcanzado su máximo brillo.

Todos los hoteles de la cadena Esplendor ofrecen: habitaciones con caja de seguridad, TV con cable, minibar, camas queen size, colchones con pillow-top, chaise longue (silla lounge), teléfono, kit de baño, secador de pelo, aire acondicionado y calefacción. Habitaciones para fumadores y no fumadores. Desayuno Buffet. Room service. Restaurante y lobby bar. Salón para Eventos. Servicios de recepción y envío de fax, impresiones y fotocopias. Computadoras con acceso a Internet de alta velocidad sin cargo. Lavandería y tintorería con servicio de urgencia. Personal bilingüe con atención personalizada.

BUENOS AIRES - ROSARIO - EL CALAFATE - ASUNCIÓN - CIUDAD DE PANAMÁ
CENTRAL DE RESERVAS: (54-11) 5217-5700 I DESDE EL INTERIOR: 0810-345-5700
RESERVAS@ESPLENDORHOTELES.COM I WWW.ESPLENDORHOTELES.COM

Fën hoteles
Hotel Franchising & Management
www.fenhoteles.com

MUSEUMS

MAAM, Salta p350

Macro, Rosario p86

MALBA: Colección Costantini, Buenos Aires p29

Museo Nacional de Bellas Artes, Buenos Aires p29

Museo Paleontológico Egidio Feruglio (MEF), Trelew, Península Valdés p258

MUSIC

Calle Balcarce (folk), Salta p348

La Catedral (tango), Buenos Aires p43

Ciudad Cultural Konex, Buenos Aires p43

Notorious (jazz), Buenos Aires p40

La Trastienda, Buenos Aires p40

OUTDOOR ACTIVITIES

BOAT TRIPS

Canal Beagle, Ushuaia p370

Cruceros Marpatag, El Calafate p294

Lago Argentino, El Calafate p294

Lago del Desierto, El Chaltén p304

Lago Viedma, El Chaltén p306

Paraná Delta, Tigre p166

Ría Deseado, Puerto Deseado p340

DIVING

Península Valdés p260

FISHING

Barreal p284

Junín de los Andes p220

Lago Strobel, El Calafate p294

Parque Nacional los Alerces, Esquel p197

Pinamar p270

Salta & Jujuy p359

GOLF

Cariló p270

Punta del Este p244

San Martín de Los Andes p223

HIKING

El Chaltén p302

Esquel & Parque los Alerces p194

Parque Nacional Lanín, Junín de los Andes p220

Parque Nacional Nahuel Huapi, Bariloche p179
Parque Nacional Santa Teresa, Punta del Diablo p232

Parque Sierra de las Quijadas p332

Quebrada de los Cuervos, El campo, Uruguay p98

HORSE RIDING

Barreal p284

El Bolsón p184

Cabo Polonio & Punta del Diablo p235

El Calafate p294

El campo, Uruguay p101

Cariló & Pinamar p273

Estancia Huechahue, Junín de los Andes p224

Estancia Los Potreros, Las Sierras de Córdoba p123

José Ignacio & Punta del Este p244

Mendoza p209

San Antonio de Areco & Around p104

San Lorenzo, Salta p350

ICE TREKKING

Glaciar Perito Moreno, El Calafate p294

Glaciar Torre and Glaciar Viedma, El Chaltén p306

KAYAKING

Parque Nacional Tierra del Fuego, Ushuaia p370

Península Valdés p260

Río Paraná, Rosario p82

KITESURFING

Laguna Garzón, José Ignacio p243

ALL CONFORT. ALL DESIGN. ALL SUITES.

HONDURAS 4762 - PALERMO SOHO (C1414BML)
BUENOS AIRES, ARGENTINA - TEL. (5411) 4832 3000
info@sohoallsuites.com
www.sohoallsuites.com

SOHOALLSUITES

ULISES
RECOLETA
SUITES

HOTEL BOUTIQUE
BUENOS AIRES
ARGENTINA

The pleasure of feeling unique
El placer de sentirse único

Ayacucho 2016 (C1112AAL)
Recoleta.

Tel: (5411) 4804.4571 / 4572
Fax: (5411) 4806.0838
info@ulisesrecoleta.com.ar
reservas@ulisesrecoleta.com.ar

www.ulisesrecoleta.com.ar

LANDSAILING
Barreal p284

MOUNTAIN BIKING
El Bolsón p184

PARAGLIDING
Cuchi Corral, Las Sierras de Córdoba p122

Mendoza p209

San Lorenzo, Salta & Jujuy p356

RAFTING
Bariloche p184

Barreal p284

Mendoza p209

San Martín de los Andes p220

ROCK CLIMBING, MOUNTAINEERING
Cerro Aconcagua, Mendoza p209

Cerro Mercedario, Barreal p284

El Chaltén p306

SANDBOARDING
Punta del Diablo p235

SKIING
Cerro Castor and Cerro Martial,
  Ushuaia p370

Cerro Catedral, Bariloche p180

Chapelco, San Martín de los Andes p220

La Hoya, Esquel p197

Las Leñas, Mendoza p209

SURFING
Cariló p273

Punta del Diablo & Cabo Polonio p235

RESTAURANTS

STAND-OUT TREATS
1884, Mendoza p209

La Bourgogne, Punta del Este p247

Caleuche, San Martín de los Andes p223

La Huella, José Ignacio p247

Kaupé, Ushuaia p372

Olsen, Buenos Aires p34

Osaka, Buenos Aires p34

Tinto Bistro, Villa La Angostura p187

SUCCULENT STEAK
La Cabrera, Buenos Aires p33

Don Julio, Buenos Aires p33

La Estancia, Rosario p85

El Faro, Las Sierras de Córdoba p122

Mercado del Puerto, Montevideo p66

La Querencia, Misiones p325

VALUE & ATMOSPHERE
Las Cabras, Buenos Aires p33

La Casona de Carlos Keen, Luján p110

Comedor Balcarce, Rosario p85

La Cosquilla del Ángel, Colón p164

Dadá, Buenos Aires p33

Lo de Joselo, Cabo Polonio p235

VIEWS
Garganta del Diablo, Iguazú p316

Glaciar Martial, Ushuaia p370

Glaciar Perito Moreno, El Calafate p293

Miradores, Parque Sierra de las Quijadas p334

Onelli Bay, El Calafate p294

Teleférico, Salta p350

WILDLIFE
Antarctica p378

Esteros del Iberá p148

Península Valdés p254

Puerto Deseado p338

Ushuaia p366

home

↳ 14 ROOMS
↳ 4 SUITES
→ SPA
→ POOL
→ RESTOBAR
→ GARDEN

WWW.HOMEBUENOSAIRES.com

WWW.REMOLINO.ORG

HOTEL home BUENOSAIRES

Honduras 5860 (1414) Palermo Viejo Bs. As. Argentina
tel (5411) 4778 1008 • fax (5411) 4779 1006
info@homebuenosaires.com

www.homebuenosaires.com

1555
MALABIA HOUSE
hotel

HOTELES
CON ENCANTO DE
BUENOS AIRES
BUENOS AIRES CHARMING HOTELS
www.buenosairescharminghotels.com

WORLD TRAVEL AWARDS

World Luxury Hotel Awards
NOMINEE 2009

"... in an ancient convent, at the soho Buenos Aires..."

Malabia 1555 C1414 DME - Tel (5411) 4833 2410 rot - www.malabiahouse.com.ar
Palermo Viejo, Soho, Buenos Aires, Argentina

Contributors

Ismay Atkins spent two years living in Buenos Aires, making frequent escapades across the plains to Patagonia armed with a dome tent and a head torch. She now lives in west Cornwall, working as a freelance editor and writer.

Vicky Baker, the project editor, fell in love with Argentina six years ago. After numerous return visits, she is now using Buenos Aires as her base while continuing to write about South America for various newspapers and magazines.

Matt Chesterton found himself in Buenos Aires in 2002 after talking a *porteña* into marrying him; he has lived there happily ever since. Work on this guide took him from the ice fields of Antarctica to the jungles of Misiones.

Peter Dorrien Traisci spent several highly enjoyable months exploring and writing about Argentina. He currently lives by the sea in Newport, Rhode Island, where he's doing his best to become a character from a Fitzgerald novel.

Emily Anne Epstein is a photographer who writes and a writer who photographs. Some months ago, she came to Buenos Aires and is now grateful for her newfound addictions to *mate* and mountains.

Esme Fox is a freelance writer who lives wherever the wind blows her. Recently, she had an amazing time travelling around Argentina, falling in love with the breathtaking scenery, passionate tango dancing and the delicious ice-cream.

Elizabeth Gleeson has a love of enigmatic Buenos Aires that has kept her close to the Río de la Plata for the past three years. She works as an artist and journalist.

Amanda Guerrero has spent two years playing *porteña*, fine tuning her Spanish and discovering a passion for Argentinian football. She works and writes in Buenos Aires.

Jeremy Helligar is a former New York City magazine editor who traded celebrity photo shoots and interviews with Britney Spears and Christina Aguilera for Buenos Aires three years ago. His new life revolves around freelance writing and editing, blogging, pilates and siestas.

Maeve Hosea spent a delightful year living, working and exploring Argentina, finding a particular affinity with the landscapes of the Andes. She currently lives in London, where she contributes to a range of publications.

Eve Hyman wrote about New York City nightlife and street art until a couple of months in Buenos Aires convinced her to move south. Three years later, she has found herself writing about everything from *cumbia* music to polo.

Janine Israel spent five months switching between tango shoes and hiking boots as she travelled from the pampas to Patagonia, with a stint in between as a wannabe *porteña*. She works as a journalist in Sydney.

Rent your car from Avis and drive around Argentina

#1 in Customer Service
#1 in Vehicle Quality
#1 in Benefits for you!

Save 10% off on-line booking!

Visit our website and start enjoying your Avis rental experience getting this special discount.

avis.com.ar
Where your trip begins…

AVIS

We try harder.

Jonah Lowenfeld is a freelance writer who lives in New York, except when he doesn't, which is a lot of the time. Most recently, he has been resident in Córdoba, acquiring a taste for *cuarteto* music and fernet.

Sorrel Moseley-Williams had the difficult task of living amid pine trees and dune-surrounded beaches in Cariló for two years. She now has the equally complex job of entertainment journalist for the *Buenos Aires Herald*.

Layne Mosler is a food and travel writer who spent four years exploring Argentina's culinary scene via the recommendations of cab drivers and other assorted folks. She now writes, eats and taxis around New York City.

Chris Moss is travel editor of *Time Out* magazine, London, and the author of *Patagonia: A Cultural History* published by Signal/OUP. He lived in Argentina for ten years, from 1991 to 2001.

Sophie Parker arrived in Argentina in 2006 and hasn't been able to stay away since. When she's not writing about the capital's shopping scene for *Time Out Buenos Aires* magazine, she's hatching plans to escape to San Juan.

Catherine Quinn is a freelance travel journalist. When she's not being stunned into silence by the Iguazú Falls, or a similarly spectacular global attraction, she can be found planning her next trip from her hometown of Brighton.

Mark Rebindaine told his friends and folks that he was heading out to Buenos Aires on a three-month sabbatical. Some 12 years later, he's still there, having been won over by the succulence of the beef and the warmth of the locals.

Claire Rigby first lived in Buenos Aires in 1993. She's now married to a *porteño* artist and working as the editor of *Time Out Buenos Aires* magazine. She also edited Time Out's first-edition guide to Mexico City.

Carmen Roberts has reported from over 60 countries around the world as a television travel presenter. When she can, she escapes to her partner's house in Uruguay's Punta del Diablo, where she spends many a day running along the beaches and sipping cocktails.

Eric Rosenbaum is a New Yorker who has been living and travelling in South America for several years. His year in Argentina took him from Iguazú Falls to the southern stretches of Patagonia.

Leigh Shulman was born in South Africa and has lived in countries all over the world, including Israel, Panama and the US. After two years of travelling, she settled in Argentina's Salta, with her husband and daughter, where she writes a blog about expat life.

Philip Thompson is from Cork, Ireland. After spending a few years working in TV in London, he moved to Argentina to escape hectic city life. Following an enjoyable year in Salta, he now lives in the hectic city of Buenos Aires, which he strangely likes.

Julián Varsavsky is an Argentinian travel writer and editor who has travelled constantly in his home country for the last decade while working for the travel supplement of *Pagina 12* newspaper. He is also senior editor of *Recorriendo la Patagonia* magazine.

Additional contributions by Cintra Scott.

Contributors by chapter

Buenos Aires Jeremy Helligar & *Time Out Buenos Aires* staff; *A cut above* Sorrel Moseley-Williams; *Paint the town* Elizabeth Gleeson. **Montevideo** Claire Rigby; *It takes two to tango* Philip Thompson. **Rosario** Vicky Baker. **San Antonio de Areco & Around** Eve Hyman. **Las Sierras de Córdoba** Jonah Lowenfeld. **Tafí del Valle** Leigh Shulman; *Queen of the empanadas* Layne Mosler. **El campo** Elizabeth Gleeson. **San Martín de los Andes & Junín de los Andes** Eric Rosenbaum; *Coach class with a difference* Philip Thompson. **Cabo Polonio & Punta del Diablo** Mark Rebindaine & Carmen Roberts. **José Ignacio & Punta del Este** *Time Out Buenos Aires* staff; *Bed and barbecue* Matt Chesterton. **Península Valdés & Around** Esme Fox. **Pinamar, Cariló & Mar de las Pampas** Sorrel Moseley-Williams. **Colonia & Carmelo** Eve Hyman. **Esteros del Iberá** Matt Chesterton. **El Palmar de Colón** Philip Thompson. **Tigre** Elizabeth Gleeson. **Bariloche, El Bolsón & Villa La Angostura** Eric Rosenbaum with Esme Fox. **Esquel & Parque los Alerces** Emily Anne Epstein. **Mendoza** Maeve Hosea. **Barreal** Sophie Parker. **El Calafate** Julián Varsavsky; *translation* Claire Rigby; *Meanwhile in Chile...* Ismay Atkins. **El Chaltén** Janine Israel; *Road tripping* Chris Moss. **Iguazú** Catherine Quinn. **Misiones** Matt Chesterton. **Parque de las Quijadas** Philip Thompson. **Puerto Deseado & Around** Julián Varsavsky; *translation* Amanda Guerrero. **Salta & Jujuy** Philip Thompson. **Ushuaia** Matt Chesterton. **Festivals & Events** Amanda Guerrero. *Carnival time* Peter Dorrien Traisci.

Visit our website
today to start
planning
your abroad
program
in Argentina!

Spanish ◄
Semester ◄
Internship ◄
TEFL ◄
Volunteering ◄
Extracurriculars ◄

 R2A **ROAD2ARGENTINA**
immersion programs in argentina

www.road2argentina.com

info@road2argentina.com

MAG NOLIA
HOTEL BOUTIQUE
BUENOS AIRES

—A TRADITIONAL HOME IN A NEW HOTEL—
Palermo • Buenos Aires • www.magnoliahotel.com.ar
+ 54 11 4067 4900/01

Trees for Cities
Charity registration number 1092154

Offset your
flight with
Trees for Cities
and make your
trip mean
something for
years to come

www.treesforcities.org/offset

Time Out Guides Limited
Universal House
251 Tottenham Court Road
London W1T 7AB
Tel + 44 (0)20 7813 3000
Fax + 44 (0)20 7813 6001
Email guides@timeout.com
www.timeout.com

Editorial
Editor Vicky Baker
Copy editors Jeremy Helligar
Listings checkers Gaby Chesterton, Analia Kerman
Proofreader Emma Clifton, John Watson
Indexer Sophie Parker

Managing Director Peter Fiennes
Editorial Director Ruth Jarvis
Business Manager Dan Allen
Editorial Manager Holly Pick
Assistant Management Accountant Ija Krasnikova

Design
BA Designers Javier Beresiarte, Sofia Iturbe

Art Director Scott Moore
Art Editor Pinelope Kourmouzoglou
Senior Designer Henry Elphick
Graphic Designers Kei Ishimaru, Nicola Wilson
Advertising Designer Jodi Sher

Picture Desk
Picture Editor Jael Marschner
Deputy Picture Editor Lynn Chambers
Picture Researcher Gemma Walters
Picture Desk Assistant Ben Rowe

Advertising
Commercial Director Mark Phillips
International Advertising Manager Kasimir Berger
International Sales Executive Charlie Sokol
Advertising Sales (Argentina & Uruguay) Time Out Buenos Aires

Marketing
Marketing Manager Yvonne Poon
Sales & Marketing Director, North America Lisa Levinson
Senior Publishing Brand Manager Luthfa Begum
Art Director Anthony Huggins

Production
Group Production Director Mark Lamond
Production Manager Brendan McKeown
Production Controller Damian Bennett

Time Out Group
Chairman Tony Elliott
Chief Executive Officer David King
Group General Manager/Director Nichola Coulthard
Time Out Communications Ltd MD David Pepper
Time Out International Ltd MD Cathy Runciman
Time Out Magazine Ltd Publisher/Managing Director Mark Elliott
Group IT Director Simon Chappell
Marketing Circulation Director Catherine Demajo

Maps: All maps by E-Cartografia (www.e-cartografia.com), except Buenos Aires street maps, produced by Nexo Servicios Gráficos, (www.nexolaser.com.ar).

Photography by pages 16, 22 (top, middle left, bottom right), 27, 31 (bottom left), 73, 99, 104 (top), 107 (top left, middle left, middle right, bottom right), 116 (bottom), 167, 174, 176, 181, 185, 186, 192 (bottom right), 195 (top), 200 (middle), 216 (middle left, bottom left, right), 219 (top, middle left, bottom left), 221, 228 (middle right), 233 (top), 240, 246, 254 (top left, top right, middle left, bottom left, bottom right), 257, 259, 261, 278, 290, 295, 297, 302 (bottom left, bottom right), 312 (top left, bottom right), 315, 317 (top left, top right), 346 (middle), 349 (top, bottom left), 352 (bottom), 357 (bottom), 366, 369, 371, 373 (bottom left, bottom right) Marc Van der Aa; 22 (bottom left, middle right), 31 (bottom right), 35, 45,104 (bottom right), 164 (middle right), 183, 236 (bottom), 253 (bottom), 269, 300, 302 (top left, top right), 305, 312 (top right), 346 (top, bottom right), 361 (top, bottom left) Time Out archives; 31 (bottom left), 38 (top left), 192 (top, middle, bottom left), 195 (bottom), 196 (top right, middle left, middle right, bottom left, bottom right) Emily Anne Epstein; 41, 94 (middle left), 97, 100, 164 (bottom left), 228 (bottom right), 234 (bottom) Elizabeth Gleeson; 62 (top left, bottom left), 65, 67 (bottom), 71 (top left, top right), 138 (bottom left), 141 (bottom right), 231 courtesy of Ministerio de Turismo y Deporte de Uruguay; 62 (top right), 94 (bottom right), 104 (bottom left), 107 (bottom left), 109, 138 (bottom left), 141 (bottom left), 228 (bottom left), 234 (top), 239 (middle left), 336 (bottom left) Vicky Baker; 62 (middle left) Claire Rigby; 78, 87 courtesy of Ente Turístico Rosario; 92 courtesy of Estancia El Colibrí; 107 (top right) Christina Wiseman; 111 courtesy of El Metejón Polo; 123 courtesy of Los Potreros; 128 (top, middle right, bottom right), 131 courtesy of Ente Turístico Tucumán; 128 (middle left, bottom left), 138 (top), 141 (top, middle right), 200 (bottom left), 202, 207, 216 (top), 219 (middle right, bottom right), 312 (bottom), 330 (bottom left), 346 (bottom left), 349 (bottom left), 357 (top) Anna Katsnelson; 133 Ryan Bird; 148 (top left) courtesy of Posada de la Laguna; 148 (top right), 312 (middle left), 329 Matt Chesterton; 148 (bottom right, middle left) courtesy of Rincón del Socorro; 156 (top right, bottom), 159 Charlie Adamson; 156 (top left) courtesy of Refugio de Vida Silvestre La Aurora del Palmar; 338 (top, middle, bottom left), 342 (top, bottom left), 345 Julián Varsavsky; 164 (top left, top right) 330 (top, middle right, bottom right), 333, 336 (top, middle), 338 (bottom right), 341, 342 (bottom right) Ariel Mendieta; 169 courtesy of Posada Isla Escondida; 200 (top, bottom right) Charlie Whale; 226, 228 (top, middle left), 233 (bottom left, bottom right), 239 (bottom left) Stéphan San Quice; 245 courtesy of Artisan Books; 254 (middle right) courtesy of Faro Punta Delgada; 266 (top left, top right), 280 (bottom right), 288 (bottom right) Sophie Parker; 266 (bottom), 271, 272, 275 (bottom) Guido Piotrkowski; 280 (top, middle, bottom right), 283, 285, 287 courtesy of Turismo del Gobierno de la Provincia de San Juan; 302 (middle left) courtesy of Los Cerros; 307 Chris Moss; 355 courtesy of House of Jasmines; 378, 379 courtesy of Cox & Kings.

The following images were provided by the featured establishments/artists: page 31 (top), 38 (top right, middle, bottom left, bottom right), 48, 52, 67 (top left, top right, middle right), 71 (bottom), 83, 84, 89, 103, 112, 116 (top left, top right, middle left), 120, 124, 127, 134, 143, 145, 151, 152, 163, 170, 173, 189, 191, 196 (top right), 205, 211, 212, 215, 222, 236 (top, middle left, middle right), 239 (top, bottom right), 253 (top, middle), 262, 275 (top), 288 (top, middle, bottom left), 298, 308, 317 (bottom), 319, 322, 327, 336 (bottom right), 351, 352 (top), 361 (bottom right), 363, 364, 373 (top), 377.

The editor would like to thank: Jonathan Evans, Sara Hatchuel, Astrid Perkins at Think Argentina, Pablo Tañira.

© Copyright Time Out Group Ltd
All rights reserved

Clockwise from top: Buenos Aires skyline; Abasto; Club 69; Puerto Madero; Casa Rosada.

Buenos Aires

Argentina

A European-style metropolis where anything goes.

In ciudad de Buenos Aires, the possibilities are endless. Where else can you get your tango fix at practically any hour? (Dance it, or watch it – take your pick.) Here, there's enough beef to make the most ardent carnivore reach for a salad. Cups overflow with wine that's as piquant and full-bodied as it is inexpensive. And Boca Juniors and River Plate matches satisfy the football-obsessed. But even for teetotalling vegetarians with two left feet and no interest in spectator sports, the Argentinian capital is brimming with potential.

The metropolis with so much to offer was founded by a Spanish expedition in the 16th century in what is now the southern *barrio* of San Telmo. Today, San Telmo remains a favoured stomping ground for newcomers and visitors, with its antiques market, booming boutique hotel scene and old-world architecture.

The vintage aesthetic extends to much of Buenos Aires. It's the most European of all South American cities in look and in demographic profile, as the 19th and 20th centuries brought a massive influx of Spaniards and Italians, as well as other European, Jewish, Middle Eastern and Asian immigrants.

While BA may lack the iconic landmarks of Paris, London or Rome, its visual delights are numerous. Being in the city is like visiting the world's largest film set, filled with intriguing details (both period and contemporary), unforgettable scenery and a fascinating cast.

THEGLU
palermo soho

Godoy Cruz 1733 (C1414CYK) - Buenos Aires, Argentina
Tel/Fax: +54 11 4831 4646
info@thegluhotel.com - www.thegluhotel.com

N
NUSS
BUENOS AIRES SOHO

El Salvador 4916 - C1414BPP
Ciudad de Buenos Aires
Argentina
Tel: (54 11) 4833- 6222
Fax: (54 11) 4832-9939
info@nusshotel.com
www.nusshotel.com

THE SPIRIT OF SOHO

The latest premium accommodation option in Buenos Aires. The perfect fusion between traditional and modern components has created an eclectic style. 16 rooms and 6 suites. A Deli Lobby Lounge where snacks are served, a large roof garden, ideal for outdoor events, an outdoor swimming pool, a Business Library Space and a meeting room for corporate and social events.

Explore

Buenos Aires is divided into 48 *barrios*. The significant ones for sightseeing are downtown in the city centre (Microcentro, Congreso, Tribunales and Retiro), south of the centre (Monserrat, San Telmo and La Boca), north of the centre (Recoleta and Palermo), west of the centre (Abasto, Once, Almagro, Caballito, Villa Crespo and Chacarita) and along the river (Puerto Madero, Costanera Sur and Costanera Norte). When you're ready to hit the road, hang on to your map but forget the itinerary: BA offers rich rewards to the aimless wanderer who has an open mind and an open-ended game plan.

For those who prefer a bit of structure or even a theme to their visit, there are countless tours. Español Andando (011 5278 9886, www. espanol-andando.com.ar) combines sightseeing with Spanish lessons as you walk; Cicerones (011 5258 0909, www.cicerones.org.ar) offers free, tailor-made tours led by volunteer guides. The knowledgeable historians at Eternautas (011 15 4173 1078 mobile, www.eternautas. com) lead expeditions across town, exploring themes such as tango, politics and Jewish Buenos Aires, while Urban Biking's cycling tours include atmospheric night-time rides (011 4568 4321, 011 15 5165 9343 mobile, www.urbanbiking.com).

MICROCENTRO, CONGRESO & TRIBUNALES

Downtown BA, in particular the area around Avenida de Mayo and Plaza de Mayo, is perhaps the nexus of sightseeing in the capital, home to many of the city's most historically significant buildings. Here, you'll find the Casa Rosada ('pink house', Balcarce 50), the Argentinian president's ceremonial residence; the colonial Museo Histórico Nacional del Cabildo (Bolívar 65); and the Catedral Metropolitana (Avenida Rivadavia & San Martín), a neoclassical house of worship with a façade that dates back to the 1700s.

La Casa de la Cultura (Avenida de Mayo 575), with its impressive Salón Dorado, was inspired by the Palace of Versailles. It's used as a venue for free chamber music concerts on Friday and Saturday evenings at 7pm (call ahead on 011 4323 9669, as they don't take place every week, and days can change).

It's worth sparing some time for a walk down Avenida de Mayo. If you start at Plaza de Mayo and head away from the river, you'll pass Palacio Barolo (Avenida de Mayo 1370), a neo-Gothic allegorical tribute to the 100 cantos of Dante's *Divine Comedy*, and eventually you'll reach the Palacio del Congreso (Hipólito Yrigoyen 1849). Argentina's Constitution was inspired by the US model and likewise, the congress building is a dome-and-column affair deliberately resembling its Washington-based counterpart. The building's

Buenos Aires

Buenos Aires

Historic sites
● ● ● ●

Art & architecture
● ● ● ● ●

Hotels
● ● ● ● ●

Eating & drinking
● ● ● ● ●

Nightlife
● ● ● ● ●

Shopping
● ● ● ● ●

0   200 km

very extravagant interior can be visited on a free guided tour in English or Spanish on Monday, Tuesday, Thursday and Friday at 11am and 4pm (011 4010 3000).

The BA monument that stands out the most – perhaps not for all the right reasons – is the 68-metre Obelisco, which can be viewed in all its phallic glory by taking a walk or a taxi down Avenida 9 de Julio, said to be the widest avenue in the world. And no architectural buff should leave BA without admiring the Teatro Colón (Cerrito 618), the world-renowned opera house that has been closed for restoration work since 2006. The theatre is now scheduled to reopen in time for Argentina's bicentenary celebrations in 2010, marking 200 years since the revolution. Further downtown, at Avenida Leandro N Alem 339, the Palacio de Correos y Telecomunicaciones is also being transformed for the bicentenary, and will become the 110,000-square-metre Centro Cultural del Bicentenario.

RETIRO

Plaza San Martín in **Retiro** is grand, romantic and second only to Plaza de Mayo among BA's notable squares. Even more impressive is the architectural splendour that surrounds it: Palacio Paz, the largest private residence in the city; Palacio San Martín, which was built between 1909 and 1912 for the filthy rich Anchorena clan; Edificio Kavanagh, an art deco landmark that was once South America's tallest building; and the Torre Monumental, a clock tower that was a gift from the Anglo-Argentinian community to celebrate Argentina's 1910 centenary. All these structures stand in spectacular contrast to the three massive train stations located across from the plaza, all in various states of disrepair, and the nearby bus terminal.

> "San Telmo is bubbling over (or under) with a delightfully eclectic bar and restaurant scene."

MONSERRAT, CONSTITUCIÓN, SAN TELMO & LA BOCA

To the south of the centre, **Monserrat**, **Constitución**, **San Telmo** and **La Boca**, four of the oldest barrios in central BA, offer old buildings, colonial churches, antiques shops, crowds of wandering tourists and plenty of tango. Monserrat's Manzana de las Luces (Perú 272), or the 'Block of Enlightenment', is a complex of historical buildings that takes up an entire city block and includes the Iglesia de San Ignacio,

on the corner of Alsina and Bolívar, which dates from 1734 and is the oldest church in the city. The Manzana was, at various times, home to a Jesuit school and residence, a marketplace, a university library and the representative chamber from which Buenos Aires was governed until 1880.

San Telmo is best known for its myriad tango joints and the Sunday antiques market that extends from café-lined Plaza Dorrego along calle Defensa. Competing for attention with the street performers and peddlers are the tattered but still beautiful mansions that give the area a similar feel to New Orleans' French Quarter.

After the market closes, stick around for the weekly Sunday night *milonga* (tango party), when a mainly local crowd comes to dance tango in Plaza Dorrego. Beyond these obvious charms, working-class San Telmo is best known among locals as the city's original 'bohemian quarter'. True to form, it's bubbling over (or under) with an eclectic bar and restaurant scene, some of the best shops in the city for snapping up the work of hot young designers, and a vibrant arty undercurrent, with a handful of outstanding galleries and some striking street art.

La Boca, at the mouth of the Riachuelo, is the working-class *barrio* that the football team Club Atlético Boca Juniors calls home (Brandsen 805, 011 4309 4700, www.bocajuniors.com.ar). You can arrange a stadium tour of Estadio Alberto J Armando, also affectionately known as La Bombonera, or the chocolate box, via the Museo de la Pasión Boquense (Brandsen 805, 011 4362 1100, www.museoboquense.com). Tour companies can arrange escorted trips to football matches, including Tangol (011 4312 7276, www.tangol.com), with the most sought-after tickets being for the derby games between Boca Juniors and their arch rivals River Plate, who are based across town in Nuñez's Estadio Monumental (Avenida Presidente Figueroa Alcorta 7597), also a major concert venue.

Aside from football, La Boca is also known for the slightly garish tourist magnet Caminito (little walkway), a pedestrianised street full of souvenir stands, restaurants and busking tango dancers. Caminito is where you'll find the brightly coloured, corrugated zinc shacks that you see in all the tourist brochures. They owe their resplendent colours to the imaginative but impoverished *porteños* ('people of the port', as all BA residents are known) who begged incoming ships for excess tins of paint in the early 20th century.

Fundación Proa

Avenida Pedro de Mendoza 1929, between Magallanes & Rocha, La Boca (011 4104 1000/www.proa.org). Open 11am-8pm Tue-Sun. Admission AR$10; AR$3-$6 reductions.

The phenomenal Proa arts centre is even more of a joy since a makeover gave it expanded exhibition spaces, the city's

San Telmo.

FRENCH?
NO!
JAPANESE?
NO!
FRAPANESE

tô

tô FRAPANESE CUISINE
COSTA RICA AND AREVALO - T. 4772 8569
WWW.TORESTAURANT.COM

OPEN >
MON. TO SAT. 8 PM TO 1 AM
BUENOS AIRES - ARGENTIN

best art library and a third-floor gourmet café with a river view. The renovations ensure the centre continues to draw excellent international exhibitions, which in the past have included works by minimalist light sculptor Dan Flavin, Mexican archaeological artefacts, and work by French Modernist pioneer Marcel Duchamp.

RECOLETA & BARRIO NORTE

Tree-lined **Recoleta**, to the north of the centre, is where moneyed *porteños* buy their designer hats (on Avenida Alvear, the most expensive shopping street in town), lay them (in the numerous residences lining the Parisian-style streets), and are buried in them (in Cementerio de Recoleta, the city's most exclusive real estate, for dead VIPs only). Right next to the cemetery is the Basílica Nuestra Señora del Pilar, a beautiful colonial church, and Plaza Francia, which draws numerous tourists, students and hippies with its busy weekend handicrafts fair.

Barrio Norte is a less upper-crust subdivision of Recoleta that's dominated by restaurants, stores and middle-class apartment buildings.

Cementerio de la Recoleta
Junín 1760, between Guido & Vicente López (011 4803 1594). Admission free.
Originally conceived by Bernardino Rivadavia and designed by Frenchman Próspero Catelin, this splendid cemetery was opened in 1822. Its narrow passages and high walls make comparisons with the real city outside inevitable. The cemetery is home to hundreds of illustrious corpses, laid out in a compact yet extensive maze of granite, marble and bronze mausoleums – most of the materials came from Paris and Milan. A slow walk down its avenues and alleyways is one of BA's undisputed delights. Many Argentinian presidents are entombed here, but the most-visited resting place of all is that of María Eva Duarte de Perón, aka Evita.

Museo Nacional de Bellas Artes
Avenida del Libertador 1473, ar Pueyrredón (011 4803 8814/www.mnba.org.ar). Open 12.30-7.30pm Tue-Fri; 9.30am-7.30pm Sat, Sun. Admission free.
The Museo Nacional de Bellas Artes is home to 32 rooms, sculpture patios, an architecture display, studios, a library and an auditorium. It houses the country's biggest collection of 19th- and 20th-century Argentinian art, including outstanding works from Cándido López, Antonio Berni, Xul Solar and Guillermo Kuitca. The international collection on the ground floor includes works by El Greco, Rubens, Rembrandt and Goya.

PALERMO, PALERMO VIEJO & LAS CAÑITAS

You could easily spend your entire trip to Buenos Aires inside the bubble of Palermo; you certainly wouldn't run out of restaurants, bars and shops. The area is divided into sub-neighbourhoods – some official, some not – with its boundaries

constantly expanding as its hipness rubs off on neighbouring *barrios*, and as rising costs start forcing artists, bar owners and culinary upstarts to look a little further afield for their latest ventures.

The oldest part of Palermo is **Palermo Viejo**, with its cobblestone streets and (apart from some out-of-place anomalies) charming, low-rise buildings. It is unofficially, though commonly, divided into two parts: the southern part is dubbed Palermo Soho for its increasingly chic boutiques, while the marginally less-developed Palermo Hollywood is named in a nod to the resident television studios. The two central hubs in Palermo Viejo are Plaza Armenia and Plaza Cortázar (known locally as Plaza Serrano); the latter is more lively, with a weekend market and plenty of pavement cafés.

Palermo also has an abundance of green spaces and must-see sights. The Jardín Botánico Carlos Thays, the Jardín Japonés and the Jardín Zoológico (Avenidas Las Heras & Sarmiento, 011 4806 7412) are three of the most noteworthy outdoor sites; two of BA's most prominent museums, MALBA and Museo Evita, are also located in the *barrio*.

Heading towards Recoleta along Avenida Figueroa Alcorta in a taxi or *colectivo* (bus), you'll spot Floralis Genérica, a steel and aluminum flower sculpture with petals that open and close with the sun. For horse-racing fans, there's the Hipódromo Argentino on the edge of the massive Parque Tres de Febrero. The park has a huge fan base among lovers, loungers, in-line skaters, cyclists and joggers. **Las Cañitas** is a Palermo sub-*barrio* with a collegiate atmosphere that's filled mostly with restaurants and laid-back watering holes.

MALBA: Colección Costantini
Avenida Figueroa Alcorta 3415, between Salguero & San Martín de Tours (011 4808 6500/www.malba. org.ar). Open noon-8pm Mon, Thur-Sun; noon-9pm Wed. Admission AR$15; AR$5 reductions. Free for students on Wed.
Winning consistently rave reviews in both the local and foreign media, the MALBA would be many people's pick for best museum in the city. Frida Kahlo and Diego Rivera, Tarsila do Amaral and other ground-breaking painters share the walls with Argentinian modern masters such as Antonio Berni and Jorge de la Vega, who are respected but not very well known internationally. There's also a good café and a terrace restaurant, plus a small cinema that specialises in cult and arthouse retrospectives. The excellent museum shop has some great design items. The building itself is smaller than Eduardo Costantini originally wanted, and can accomodate only 40% of his collection. To solve this problem, he has funded a three-year expansion project that will add several new exhibition areas in an underground space beneath Plaza República de Perú.

Museo Evita

Lafinur 2988, between Gutiérrez & Las Heras (011 4807 9433). Open 1-7pm Tue-Sun. Admission AR$5.
Opened in 2001, this museum is housed in an aristocratic residence that President Juan Perón expropriated to convert into a women's shelter for his wife's quasi-governmental welfare agency. It's worth a visit, if only to see the range of myths that Eva Perón, aka Evita, has inspired in Argentina. Paintings, posters and busts are displayed alongside the outfits she wore on tours of Europe. The star exhibits are two dresses designed by Paco Jamandreu, which she wore for her audiences with the Pope, and her *libreta cívica* (ID card), no.0.000.001. The museum also has a lovely restaurant and outdoor terrace.

VILLA CRESPO & CHACARITA

Villa Crespo is a largely residential enclave that resembles the Palermo Viejo of 15 years ago – that is, before the hip boutiques and ethnic restaurants arrived. It's not a place for sightseeing, but it's the kind of quiet, pretty neighbourhood with tree-lined streets that makes for a very rewarding detour and offers the chance to catch a glimpse of slowed-down *barrio* life. Neighbouring **Chacarita**, which features BA's other must-see necropolis, is similarly old-school, its mainly middle-class residents served by weekend food markets, haberdasheries and late-night, strip-lit pizza parlours. **Abasto**, **Once**, **Almagro** and **Caballito** round out BA's western working-class *barrios*.

Cementerio de la Chacarita

Guzmán 630, at Federico Lacroze (011 4553 9034). Open 7am-6pm daily. Admission free.
More than ten times the size of Recoleta's exclusive cemetery and with car access to its thousands of vaults, Chacarita is largely for ordinary folk. Still, a number of popular heroes have wound up here, including tango king Carlos Gardel (look out for the smoking cigarette visitors often place between his statue's fingers). The tall columns of the entranceway lead to a web of numbered streets, which, in turn, lead to vaults and mausoleums with underground galleries, and typical graveyards with headstones and wooden crosses. Don't miss the bizarre Panteón de Actores, where the deceased have been immortalised in lively and sometimes comic poses.

PUERTO MADERO, COSTANERA SUR & COSTANERA NORTE

The dockside development of **Puerto Madero** is home to some of BA's grandest hotels, most expensive restaurants and, from the Puente de la Mujer (Woman's Bridge), the most stunning view of the city from the ground. Just beyond the docks sprawls the Reserva Ecológica Costanera Sur, a sort of wilderness on the edge of the city (moonlit tours are arranged one night per month; call 011 4893 1588 for details).
   Costanera Norte contains some of the city's hippest nightclubs (*see pp43-44*), as well as

what is perhaps its cheesiest attraction. Tierra Santa is a religious theme park, capped by an 18-metre statue of Jesus that rises from the dead every 40-45 minutes (Avenida Costanera Rafael Obligado 5790, 011 4784 9551, www.tierrasanta-bsas.com.ar).

FURTHER AFIELD

Out west, in an area that was once the heart of Argentina's slaughterhouse (*mataderos*) industry, gauchos show off their skills with guitars and horses, and day-trippers indulge in country food and browse at the crafts market at the Feria de Mataderos (011 15 6043 4233, www.feriade mataderos.com.ar), a rural-style weekend fair. The fair takes place from April to December, from 11am to 8pm on Sundays, and from January to March, from 6pm to 1am on Saturdays. Mataderos is a 30- to 45-minute bus ride from the city centre (buses 55, 80, 92 or 126), or you can take a taxi.
   For other easy day trips from Buenos Aires, consider a visit to the Paraná Delta in Tigre (*see pp164-173*), a *día de campo* in the pampas (*see pp104-115*) or a trip across the Río de la Plata to Colonia or Carmelo in Uruguay (*see pp138-47*).

Eat

Good things come to those who wait. And when it comes to dining out in BA, you're better off if you do. The average *porteño* doesn't eat dinner until at least 10pm, and it's not uncommon to see restaurants packed well after midnight, especially on the weekends. If you plan on playing *porteño* by arriving fashionably late, call in advance for reservations. For restaurants that don't take bookings, it's best to arrive just before 9pm (or before 1pm for lunch), or to arrive very late.
   Buenos Aires is renowned for its closed-door dining experiences, which see professional chefs, or keen amateurs, offering a multi-course, set-price menu in their home to anyone who calls ahead. Among the most established hosts are Casa Saltshaker (011 15 6132 4146 mobile, www.casasaltshaker.com), Casa Felix (011 4555 1882, www.diegofelix.com) and Casa Coupage (011 4833 6354, www.casacoupage.com). Newer kids on the block are A Little Saigon (www.alittlesaigon.com) and Cocina Discreta (011 4772 3803, www.lacocinadiscreta.com).

Almacén Secreto

Villa Crespo *Aguirre 1242 (011 4775 1271/ http://almacensecretoclub.blogspot.com). Open noon-4pm Tue, Wed; noon-4pm, from 8pm Thur, Fri; from 8pm Sat, Sun. ££. No credit cards. Traditional.*
This 'secret store' was never really a store and is no longer even a secret. Lucien Freud-esque portraits hang in a gallery

Clockwise from top:
Tô; La Cabrera;
Dada; Las Cabras.

PURA · VIDA

JUICE BAR

Experience the highest quality, most delicious
health food in Buenos Aires!
We specialize in natural and organic vegetarian
food as well as refreshing juices and smoothies.

SANDWICHES - WRAPS - SALADS - SOUPS
SMOOTHIES - WHEATGRASS - MACA - GOJI
FRUIT SALADS - BAGELS - JUICES - MUFFINS
VEGAN BROWNIES - COOKIES

MICRO CENTRO
Reconquista 516 - 43930093
RECOLETA
Uriburu 1489 - 48060017

Check out our website for more info
www.puravidajuicebar.com

MADE
THE WAY
THEY USED
TO.

28 SPORT

Gurruchaga 1481

www.28sport.com

OASISBA
BUENOS AIRES

LUXURY RENTALS

An Oasis for the modern traveler

www.oasisba.com

behind the restaurant, and animal gargoyles line the patio's inner wall. The menu is split into three divisions – 'El norte' (the north), 'El centro' (the centre) and 'El sur' (the south). From 'El centro', try the *carne al horno de barro* (meat slow-cooked in an adobe oven), and from 'El sur', the *cordero patagónico* (Patagonian lamb). Music nights and art workshops complete the Secreto experience.

Bio

Palermo Viejo *Humboldt 2199, at Guatemala (011 4774 3880). Open 10.30am-5pm Mon; from 10.30am Tue-Sun. ££. Vegetarian.*
Feeling a twinge of guilt after a week-long gorgefest of chorizo and fried cheese? There's no finer locale for detoxifying your system (and assuaging your conscience) than this organic bistro. Start your atonement with a pot of green tea and complimentary chunks of heart-healthy brown bread, then choose a starter suited to the season: quinoa risotto with seasonal vegetables and goat's cheese, tofu in a mustard reduction, and mushroom-topped bruschetta are just a few specialities of the house.

Las Cabras

Palermo Viejo *Fitz Roy 1795, at El Salvador (011 5197 5301). Open noon-1am daily. ££. No credit cards. Parrilla.*
This insanely popular parrilla has proven to be a great success on the overcrowded Palermo eating scene. The secret recipe? It's simple: cheap, good-quality food. It doesn't stray too much from the pasta-and-parrilla formula, but a mixed grill (enough for at least three), including two types of chorizo and all the offal you can think of, is very good value. Quesedillas and fish are also welcome additions to standard parrilla fare. The wine list ticks the value for money box too, with very little mark-up from supermarket prices; and crayons are provided so that you or your children can sketch away on the tablecloths. Reservations are not permitted, so get there early or very late, or expect to join the throngs queuing on the pavement.

La Cabrera

Palermo Viejo *Cabrera 5127/5099, at Thames (011 4832 5754/www.parrillalacabrera.com.ar). Open 8pm-1am Mon; 12.30-4pm, from 8pm Tue-Sun. £££. Parrilla.*
This is one of Buenos Aires' most talked-about parrillas – at least in recent times. In an attractive corner building that used to house a general store, tables are laden with extra-large portions of expertly prepared beef, grilled with a few sprigs of rosemary or sage. The steak-sized *mollejas* (sweetbreads) are among the best in the city, and easily justify the price. Don't order too much; half portions will be fine for even the hungriest of diners, especially as ten to 12 interesting side plates will also land on your table. The sister restaurant, La Cabrera Norte, half a block away, has helped cut waiting times a little, but a reservation made in advance pays dividends.

Café San Juan

San Telmo *San Juan 450, between Bolivar & Defensa (011 4300 1112). Open noon-4pm, 8.30pm-midnight Tue-Sun. £££. No credit cards. Traditional.*

The San Juan menu, a short list that changes daily, is scrawled on chalkboards that the waiting staff haul from table to table. Tapas and generously sized pasta dishes are built around seasonal vegetables. Homey dishes such as cured ham with mushrooms or the courgette-rich fettuccine are ideal for sharing. The dinner menu comprises more substantial fare, like *bife de chorizo* (sirloin steak), salmon, and pork loin in cream sauce. Reservations are more or less essential here, unless you're planning to slip in for a quick bite at noon sharp.

Café Tortoni

Microcentro *Avenida de Mayo 829, between Esmeralda & Suipacha (011 4342 4328/www.cafetortoni.com.ar). Open 7.30am-2am Mon-Thur; 7.30am-3am Fri, Sat; 9am-1am Sun. ££. Café.*
Argentina's oldest café is everything you would expect it to be: breathtakingly grand and charmingly ceremonial. Since opening in 1858, this glorious place has played host to a stellar cast, from the depths of bohemia to the heights of the literati and all across the political spectrum. Today, it's teeming with camera-wielding tourists, but don't be put off – Tortoni is a must, if only for its old-school BA atmosphere and visual splendour. Beyond the wooden tables and marble floor, a popular salon hosts jazz and tango shows, while in the back area, pool tables await. Order a glass of draught *cidra* (cider) and breathe in the history.

Dadá

Microcentro *San Martín 941, between Marcelo T de Alvear & Paraguay (011 4314 4787/www.dadabistro. blogspot.com). Open noon-2am Mon-Sat. ££. Modern.*
This highly-regarded bar and restaurant has a menu that is as colourful and imaginative as its lighting and furnishings. The chalkboard regularly changes, but it's the classics like the *lomo* Dadá (tenderloin), the *ojo de bife* (ribeye steak), the salmon with polenta and the delicious houmous and guacamole dips that continue to stand out.

Don Julio

Palermo Viejo *Guatemala 4691, at Gurruchaga (011 4831 9564/011 4832 6058). Open noon-4pm, 8pm-midnight daily. ££. Parrilla.*
This classic but outstanding parrilla prides itself on a meat menu that's a cut above the rest, and an outstanding wine list. Thanks to owner Pablo, who sends his waiters to wine school, your server will be able to help you choose the cabernet that best complements your *bife de chorizo*. Leather tablecloths and exposed brick walls add to the cosy, warmly lit atmosphere. Vegetarians should try the *soufflé de calabaza y espinaca con crema de verdeo* – a crispy squash and spinach creation.

El Federal

San Telmo *Carlos Calvo 599, at Perú (011 4300 4313/ www.barelfederal.com.ar). Open 8am-2am Mon-Thur, Sun; 8am-4am Fri, Sat. £. Bar.*
Built in 1864, El Federal is one of BA's most historic bars. It's also one of the best kept, with its magnificent cash registers, faded lamps hanging overhead and a collection of old advertising posters. There's a standard set of coffees,

beers and spirits, and a long list of snacks and sandwiches – the *lomo completo* beef sandwich comes with all, and we mean all, the trimmings. The *picadas* (cold meat and cheese platters) are a good way to go. If you're lucky, you'll be treated to an ad hoc performance of tango standards.

Gran Bar Danzón
Recoleta *Libertad 1161, between Santa Fe & Arenales (011 4811 1108/www.granbardanzon.com.ar). Open from 7pm Mon-Fri; from 8pm Sat, Sun. £££. Modern.*
The 'gran' is merited: this is a truly great wine bar and restaurant, and a banquet for the senses from the moment you climb up the candlelit and incense-scented stairwell. The main menu roams freely between Europe and Latin America, offering flawlessly executed fusion dishes such as confit of duck perched atop a banana blini, veal braised in port with potatoes and caramelised onions, and red salmon in a brioche crust served with a fig and tomato chutney. Or, if you think East is best, try the superb sushi – easily as good here as in most of BA's Japanese restaurants. A wine list of over 200 labels (some available by the glass) and great promotions make this an exceptional place for a drink, for dinner, or both. The people behind Gran Bar Danzón also run Bar Uriarte (Uriarte 1572) in Palermo Viejo and Sucre (Sucre 676) in Belgrano,which are also highly recommended.

> **"What to serve the listless palate that's tried everything? Why, Peruvian-Japanese food, of course – and that's the speciality at stylish, minimalist Osaka."**

Green Bamboo
Palermo Viejo *Costa Rica 5802, at Carranza (011 4775 7050/www.green-bamboo.com.ar). Open from 8.30pm daily. ££. International.*
This popular Vietnamese restaurant combines the five essential elements of sweet, salty, bitter, spicy and acidic tastes, which will keep the most sophisticated palate interested and, in accordance with Taoist philosophy, balanced. Tuck into a seafood-based menu of starters that includes prawns fried in sesame seeds and ginger and sweet chilli squid tentacles, then get stuck into the fish of the day – marinated with tamarind, basil and shallots, then wrapped up in a bamboo leaf and barbecued. For a refreshing aperitif, give the green grass cocktail a go.

Manolo
San Telmo *Bolívar 1299, at Cochabamba (011 4307 8743/www.restaurantmanolo.com.ar). Open noon-1am Tue-Sun. £. Parrilla.*

This friendly neighbourhood joint is buzzing most nights with a loyal clientele who come to feast on the excellent parrilla standards, and the standard with a twist – a ham and mozzarella-stuffed steak. There's a sprinkling of traditional *criollo* cuisine (try the hearty *locro* stew), and chicken prepared in a dozen different ways, including the Suprema Gran Manolo – a breaded chicken breast topped with ham, egg, cheese and olives.

Olsen
Palermo Viejo *Gorriti 5870, between Carranza & Ravignani (011 4776 7677). Open from noon Tue-Sat; from 10.30am Sun. £££. International.*
If your aim is purely to make an inroad into the 60-plus vodka shots on offer, you would be doing an injustice to Olsen's fabulous cured meat and fish menu. Lunchtime snacks include a modern Scandinavian *smørrebrød* (open sandwich) comprising smoked salmon, trout and blinis, while dinner delicacies of red tuna (nigh on impossible to get hold of in BA), slow-cooked lamb and smoked pork should keep your focus squarely on the food. Enjoy Naum Knop's sculptures in the outdoor lounge, over – you guessed it – a vodka shot, to the splish-splash of a relaxing water feature. Olsen's Sunday brunch is a local legend.

Osaka
Palermo Viejo *Soler 5608, at Fitz Roy (011 4775 6964/www.osaka.com.pe). Open 12.30-4pm, 8pm-1am Mon-Sat. £££. No credit cards. International.*
Even gourmands well-versed in black truffles and port wine reductions may sometimes find themselves, privileged as they are, bored by gastronomic repetition. What to serve the listless palate that's tried everything? Why, Peruvian-Japanese food, of course – and that's the speciality at stylish, minimalist Osaka. With a good range of more familiar Japanese dishes underpinning the menu, it takes flight with fusion creations and eclectic innovations such as duck confit-stuffed samosas and deep-fried Peruvian-style fish in Japanese mushroom sauce. Don't miss the chance to try Osaka's unusual South America meets Far East starters, which are substantial enough to share, or its exotic cocktails – sample the Thai Chi (a heady blend of saké, orange, cranberry and cinnamon), or the lemongrass-infused Pico Grass.

Oui Oui
Palermo Viejo *Nicaragua 6068, between Arévalo & Dorrego (011 4778 9614). Open 8am-8pm Tue-Fri; 10am-8pm Sat, Sun. ££. No credit cards. Café.*
Until recently, most of BA's French eateries were expensive, formal bistros, more the seventh than the fifth arrondissement. Oui Oui, by comparison, offers honest, down-to-earth Gallic fare of the kind the French actually eat, as opposed to just write about. Francophile Rocío García Orza works wonders in the kitchen with filled croissants, fresh baguettes, vichyssoise and pain au chocolat, which is all spelled out on chalkboards amid a colourful clutter of dried flowers and rosewood tables. The latest Oui Oui addition is the *almacén* Orza, which is just across the street and serves speciality foods as well as good-quality salads and sandwiches.

A cut above

From inside the most exclusive hotels to the kitchens of greasy cafés, the cow's deific status is reduced in one fell swoop of a knife to prime position on a fancy dinner plate or slapped between slices of bread and slathered with *chimichurri* sauce. But what's with Argentina's beef obsession?

Eating beef isn't just a pastime here: cooking it is a national compulsion. Unfamiliar with the disposable barbecue concept, families gather religiously at weekends to release their inner gaucho by sparking the fire and slapping some *tira de asado* (ribs) on the grill.

Although you might assume your steak will be served raw to bleeding without the need to specify, Argentinians often prefer it *bien hecho* (well done), so don't be embarrassed to ask the *asador* (your chef and meat expert) for *jugoso* (medium rare). But if your barbecue invites are on the thin side, the alternative is, of course, to sniff your way to a parrilla (steak house).

Pablo Rivero, whose family has run Palermo-based restaurant Don Julio (*pictured, see p33*) for ten years, goes back to basics. 'Let's start with breeds. Among others, we have the Hereford and Aberdeen Angus in La Pampa, and a cross-breed, Brangus, which is found in Entre Ríos province. These cows originated from the Netherlands and the UK. Like dogs, the breeds were imported here in the 19th century. The meat quality depends on how the cattle adapt to the land and climate, and the feed is paramount to that.

'There are two ways to fatten up cows: with grass, or with cereals from a feeder. Argentina is fortunate enough to have a lot of space with plenty of grass. If cows have to source their own food and exercise too much – for example, in Patagonia, which has a dry climate – their meat is tasty but tough because the muscles have worked excessively. But in the more humid pampa region where the grass is plentiful and high in nutrients, the quality of that animal is higher: less fibrous, tastier.'

Rivero sources his meat from Buenos Aires' Liniers cattle market, the largest in the world, and chooses La Pampa meat. 'Important buyers with their own slaughterhouses go to Liniers, but small-timers like us also send a guy there to make our purchases. We use certain cuts, not the entire cow, and in December when we're at our busiest, we sell 115 kilos of beef a day. Although *entraña* (skirt steak) is our house speciality, which Argentinians love, foreigners opt for *bife de chorizo* (sirloin) or *lomo* (tenderloin).'

Tira de asado and *vacío* (flank) aren't exported due to the Argentinian love affair with these cuts: try them for size, and remember to ask for them *jugoso*.

To advertise in the next edition of...

TimeOut

Argentina
& Uruguay

Perfect places to stay, eat & explore

Sightseeing
Restaurants
Hotels

E: guidesadvertising@timeout.com
C: +44 (0)20 7813 6020

America del Sur
H O S T E L
BUENOS AIRES & EL CALAFATE

www.americahostel.com.ar

EL CALAFATE
Calle Puerto Deseado N° 153
(Z9405CNE)
T./F: +54 (2902) 493525/3
calafate@americahostel.com.ar

BUENOS AIRES
Chacabuco N°718
(C1098AAN) - San Telmo
T./F: +54 (11)4300 5525
baires@americahostel.com.ar

Move in. Feel local. Live simple.

livin'
RESIDENCE

www.livinresidence.com
reservas@livinresidence.com
Viamonte 1815, T. (+5411) 5258 0300 / 01
Ciudad de Buenos Aires, Argentina

Pura Vida

Microcentro *Reconquista 516, between Lavalle & Tucumán (011 4393 0093/www.puravidabuenosaires. com). Open 9am-8pm Mon-Fri. £. No credit cards. Café.*
In a city famed for its lean, blemish-free inhabitants, there are surprisingly few places geared solely towards health-promoting food. But when the hearty steak, empanada and wine diet begins to take its toll, relief beckons at Pura Vida juice bar, with its 15 different smoothies, variety of fresh juices and wholesome array of soups, wraps and salads. The truly virtuous can even preface their midday meal with a shot of wheat-grass.

Status

Congreso *Virrey Cavellos 178, between Hipólito Yrigoyen & Alsina (011 4382 8531/www.restaurant status.com.ar). Open noon-4pm, 8pm-midnight daily. £. International.*
This cantina, owned by the friendly Valenzuela family, serves abundant platters of ceviche and lamb, as well as nicely spicy starters. Don't be put off by the fact that the ceviche is made from *tiburón* (small bonnet-headed shark): it's fresh – caught off the shore of Mar del Plata – well-seasoned and served under a heap of red onions, with potatoes, egg and toasted corn on the side. Busy during the day, the restaurant is usually packed by 9pm (expect to queue) with a chatty crowd of discerning backpackers, businessmen, artists and members of the local Peruvian community.

Tegui

Palermo Viejo *Costa Rica 5852, at Carranza (011 5291 3333). Open from 8.30pm Mon-Sat. ££££. Modern.*
This swanky new hideout is tucked discreetly behind a (deliberately) graffitied wall and unassuming black door. Owned by the same team that runs the equally high-end Olsen (*see p34*) and Casa Cruz (Uriarte 1658), this younger sibling is quickly making a name for itself. Ring the bell and saunter into the home-turned-restaurant, which dazzles with its contemporary decor, accented by all things black and white. A wine cellar spans the entire front wall, forming an impressive backdrop to the larger-than-life interior. A simple menu of three to four main courses typically includes meat or fish and changes weekly, depending on the season and availability of ingredients.

Thymus

Villa Crespo *Lerma 525, between Malabia & Acevedo (011 4772 1936/www.thymusrestaurant.com.ar). Open from 8.30pm Mon-Sat. £££. Modern.*
Set in a beautifully converted Villa Crespo house, this restaurant not only offers a warm atmosphere but outstanding food. There are no fusion dishes or fancy foaming thingamajigs on the menu, just the highest quality produce, prepared to a virtuoso standard. The Kobe beef with spicy *chimichurri* sauce and confit of orange is exceptional, while the rabbit and foie gras terrine with fig and Dijon mustard purée and the beef tartare are both expertly assembled. For dessert, there's molten-centered chocolate cake with orange blossom ice-cream, or vanilla soup with passion fruit mousse and almond macaroon.

Tô

Palermo Viejo *Costa Rica 6000, at Arévalo (011 4772 8569/www.torestaurant.com). Open 8pm-1am Tue-Sat; 12.30-4pm Sun. £££. International.*
Sashimi, meet foie gras. Tô presents Buenos Aires's first and only conveyer-belt sushi service, with a Gallic twist. Toufic Reda, a newcomer on the BA dining scene, directs a brawny team of sushi *shokunins*, chefs and mixologists in a slick loft space that is fast becoming a celebrity haunt. Grab a counter stool for California rolls and salmon sashimi while you choose from a long list of mains, including pork dumplings, prosciutto rolls and seafood tempura; the bento box will easily satisfy two. Drinks range from a spicy ginger take on the conventional cuba libre to a cucumber-infused saké concoction.

La Vinería de Gualterio Bolívar

San Telmo *Bolívar 865, between Independencia & Estados Unidos (011 4361 4709/www.lavineriade gualteriobolivar.com). Open 12.30-4pm, 9pm-midnight Tue-Sun. £££. No credit cards. Modern.*
This diminutive whitewashed restaurant has just a chalkboard menu to show what's on offer. But don't be misled by the low-key build-up and lack of visual frills: the food here is very special. Molecular gastronomy-style touches such as potato foams appear on the menu, as do scallops with stewed lamb's tongue and vanilla squash mash with a citrus vinaigrette. The slow-cooked egg dish is heated at 62°C for 50 minutes and served with white truffle, lamb stock and goat's cheese foam. There's also a 40-vegetable salad containing cooked and raw ingredients, flowers, roots, germinated seeds and shoots. Only set menus are available in the evening.

Shop

Shopping malls may have a bad reputation as being hopelessly mainstream elsewhere in the world, but here in BA, they feature some of the city's top shops. And in the case of the big five – Abasto de Buenos Aires (Avenida Corrientes 3247), Alto Palermo (Santa Fe 3253), Galerías Pacífico (corner of Florida and Avenida Córdoba), Paseo Alcorta (Jerónimo Salguero 3172) and Patio Bullrich (Avenida del Libertador 750) – the grand, ornate buildings are as much an attraction as what's for sale inside.

As for the rest of BA's retail scene, Avenida Alvear in Recoleta is the strip to head to for upmarket haute couture, while Palermo Viejo, especially around Plaza Serrano, features BA's hippest designers. Avenida Santa Fe and Avenida Córdoba are more hit and miss, but for the most part, the prices are right. For leather, the stretch of calle Murillo between Scalabrini Ortiz and Gurruchaga in Villa Crespo has plenty of outlets offering goods at below bargain-basement prices. Among the markets, the Mercado de las Pulgas flea market, in

Top left: Gil Antigüedades.
Top right: Balthazar.
Middle Juana de Arco.
Bottom left: Lo de Joaquin
Alberdi. Bottom right:
Autoría BsAs.

Colegiales (Avenida Dorrego 1650, 11am-7pm Tue-Sun), and Feria San Pedro Telmo (*see p26*) are two of the best.

28 Sport

Palermo Viejo *Gurruchaga 1481, between Cabrera & Gorriti (011 4833 4287/www.28sport.com). Open 11am-8pm Mon-Sat.*
Reinforced stitching, leather lining and bronze eyelets are hallmarks of a well-made shoe, and hark back to a long-gone era when footwear was made with practicality and durability in mind. And that's exactly the ethos of this company, which bases its designs on original sports footwear from the 1950s. With rubber soles and a multitude of colours, these leather shoes and lace-up boots will appeal to fans of Camper's classic 'Pelotas'.

Autoría BsAs

Microcentro *Suipacha 1025 (011 5252 2474/ www.autoriabsas.com.ar). Open 9am-8pm Mon-Fri; 10am-2pm, 4-8pm Sat.*
Located close to Plaza San Martín, this multi-space design boutique houses a varied array of clothing and objects created by talented local designers. Flip through carefully selected garments from clothing designers Vicki Otero, Spina, Vero Ivaldi and Min Agostini, and accessories and home decoration items from Nobrand, Guiño, Móviles and Andrea Cavaganaro, among others. A gallery section includes works from recognised artists as well as novices, and features not only paintings and photos, but also sculptures and installations. A brilliant shop for a browse, Autoría is a tasteful, well-executed fusion of art and design.

> "Fashion superstars such as John Galliano and Carolina Herrera have turned up on the doorstep of Gil Antigüedades."

Balthazar

Palermo Viejo *Gorriti 5131, between Thames & Uriarte (011 4834 6235/www.balthazarshop.com). Open 11am-8pm Mon-Sat.*
Balthazar is worth a visit if only to admire the decor. The Palermo branch is located in a beautifully restored townhouse, while the sumptuous San Telmo store (Defensa 1008) is an art deco dream, with blood red walls, Persian rugs and French antiques. An urban dandy's candy store, Balthazar offers a range of striking shirts in high-quality Italian fabrics. Multicoloured striped shirts are a popular choice, as are the sleek ties and blazers – and even the heat of a scorching *porteño* summer shouldn't put you off purchasing an alpaca scarf.

Bolivia

Palermo Viejo *Gurruchaga 1581, between Gorriti & Honduras (011 4832 6284/www.boliviaonline.com.ar). Open 11am-8pm Mon-Sat; 3-8pm Sun.*
For the fashion-conscious man, Bolivia offers an abundance of tempting items. From the striped or checked trousers to the Liberty-print shirts, there are plenty of stylish, distinctive garments. A new line of tailored dark jackets has been added, but Bolivia hasn't turned over a sombre new leaf: there are plenty of skinny jeans in red, yellow or fuchsia for trendy rocker types. Shopping is an enjoyable experience in the store, which is kitted out with kitsch magazines, vintage glasses and a collection of Faber Castell colouring pencils. There's another Palermo branch at Nicaragua 4908.

El Buen Orden

San Telmo *Defensa 894, at Estados Unidos (011 15 5936 2820 mobile/www.elbuenorden.com.ar). Open 11am-7pm daily. No credit cards.*
Strategically placed one block away from San Telmo's Plaza Dorrego, El Buen Orden is more than an average antiques shop: it's a vintage treasure trove. New items appear daily as stock is constantly rotated in a store that's more like a museum of all things retro than a shop. There's everything from clothing and bags to period-piece jewellery, hats and eyewear. Pick up a vintage pill box or a powder compact for some elegant old-school glamour, or browse through the buttons, buckles and lace trims. An essential stop on the city's shopping circuit.

Comme Il Faut

Recoleta *Arenales 1239, Rue des Artisans, apartamento M, between Libertad & Talcahuano (011 4815 5690/www.commeilfaut.com.ar). Open 11am-7pm Mon-Fri; 11am-3pm Sat.*
Hidden away in a peaceful lane off one of Recoleta's swanky streets, Comme Il Faut offers beautifully made tango shoes for *milongas* and more. The technical aspect of the design makes the footwear ideal for the most demanding dancer, and the aesthetic element ensures that these shoes are coveted by *tangueras* and tourists alike. They are also, in case a wedding is in the offing, perfect for brides.

Gil Antigüedades

San Telmo *Humberto 1º 412, at Defensa (011 4361 5019/www.gilantiguedades.com.ar). Open 11am-1pm, 3-7pm Tue-Sun.*
This jewel in the crown of San Telmo's antiques trade looks more like a costume museum than a shop, but amid the enormous collection of vintage fashion there's something to suit almost every taste – and every wallet. Fashion superstars such as John Galliano and Carolina Herrera have turned up on the doorstep, and a certain Miss Minogue popped in to browse the racks when she was in town. After 25 years in business, and with more than 6,000 pieces in stock, this store emphasises quality and variety. Its treasures include clothing, jewellery, footwear, fans, parasols and figurines. No one with even a passing interest in fashion should think of leaving San Telmo without paying this place a visit.

Juana de Arco

Palermo Viejo *El Salvador 4762, between Gurruchaga & Armenia (011 4833 1621/www.juanadearco.net). Open 10am-8pm Mon-Sat; 1-8pm Sun.*

Ten years ago, Mariana Cortés, the designer behind the Juana de Arco label, began creating her highly original designs from scraps of fabric. With a crafty, handmade aesthetic, every Juana de Arco garment is guaranteed to be colourful and individual. Underwear is something of a speciality here, as is the fun, feminine and comfortable collection of sleepwear: the mix and match separates include pedal-pusher sleep shorts and loose and lovely harem pants.

Lo de Joaquin Alberdi

Palermo Viejo *Jorge Luis Borges 1772, between El Salvador & Costa Rica (011 4832 5329/011 4831 7720/www.lodejoaquinalberdi.com.ar). Open 11am-9.30pm daily.*

If you're looking for a great bottle of wine in BA, you could probably find it at the *supermercado* across the street. So a trip to Lo de Joaquin Alberdi, a *vinoteca* in the middle of Palermo's retail heartland, is only partly about what's on sale – which would be all the usual wine suspects, organised museum-style so they are as appropriate for admiring as for drinking. The lovely Victorian building that Joaquin Alberdi calls home, all brown and golden tones on the outside, is as much of a draw, as are the weekly wine tastings held inside. Boutique bodegas are especially well represented here.

Sabater Hermanos

Palermo Viejo *Gurruchaga 1821, between Costa Rica & Nicaragua (011 4833 3004/www.shnos.com.ar). Open 10am-8pm Mon-Sat; 2-8pm Sun. No credit cards.*

Run by the third generation of Sabater family soap-makers, this funky shop and workshop is a soap version of a pick 'n' mix counter. With coloured soap flakes, cookie-cutter shapes, golf balls and soapy 'hundreds and thousands', there are plenty of choices way beyond the common or garden bar of soap. For rebels, there are Black Sabbath or marijuana leaf squares, and don't miss the designs with cheeky phrases in Spanish, such as 'Doesn't wash your conscience'. The no-nonsense, traditional blocks embossed with the company's name in a classy font should satisfy sophisticates.

Tramando, Martín Churba

Recoleta *Rodriguez Peña 1973, between Posadas & Avenida Alvear (011 4811 0465/www.tramando.com). Open 10.30am-8.30pm Mon-Fri; 11am-7pm Sat.*

Martin Churba is an established fashion mind and creative talent with a following in Japan and shops in New York and Tokyo, as well as in Buenos Aires. His signature silhouettes are loose and labyrinthine, with a variety of colour that allows for multiple combinations. Voluminous pleated trousers in silk reflect a mix of oriental and art deco influences, and the characteristic intertwining and wonky weaving feature on necklines and accessories. The hand-worked dresses in chalky tones are a highlight, but if you can't work up the nerve to don such daring designs, try some of the accessories or homewares.

Vicki Otero

Palermo Viejo *El Salvador 4719, between Armenia & Gurruchaga (011 4833 5425/www.vickiotero.com.ar). Open 10am-8pm Mon-Sat.*

Vicki Otero is considered a pioneer in the Buenos Aires fashion world. She opened her Palermo boutique in 2002, and has continued to produce flattering cuts in contrasting textures ever since. The signature look is prim but unconstrained; her recent collection features retro 1950s-style silhouettes and a strong use of black and white. Selected pieces are sold in San Telmo's Ffiocca (Perú 599).

Zivals

Tribunales *Callao 395, at Corrientes (011 4371 7500/www.zivals.com). Open 9.30am-10pm Mon-Sat.*

Claiming to stock the widest selection of music in South America, Zivals (also an excellent bookshop, with travel guides and selections in English) covers all genres but specialises in classical, jazz, folk, tango and hard-to-find independent local recordings. There's another store in Palermo Viejo at Serrano 1445.

Arts

Buenos Aires has a thriving theatre scene and a legendary opera house (Teatro Colón), which has been closed for renovations since 2006 and is now scheduled to reopen in 2010 to coincide with Argentina's bicentenary. Music fans should check out La Trastienda (Balcarce 460, 4342 7650, www.latrastienda.com) for cutting-edge local bands, established Latin American artists and international acts, or Notorious (Avenida Callao 966, 4815 8473, www.notorious.com.ar) for jazz and occasional new folk and world music recitals. ND/Ateneo (Paraguay 918, 4328 2888, www.ndateneo.com.ar) is a key venue for all musical genres, as well as the occasional film screening, theatre performance and poetry recital.

Then, of course, there's tango. Whether you're looking to take classes, check out a dinner show or dance the night away at a *milonga*, there's no reason to leave BA without getting your fix. Although most *milongas* offer pre-party classes, there are various other options, including Estudio La Esquina (4th Floor, Sarmiento 722, 011 4394 9898), which offers classes for all levels, and Argentina's very own 'university of tango', the Academia Nacional del Tango (1st floor, Avenida de Mayo 833, 011 4345 6968, www.anacdeltango.org.ar), which is an excellent source of information and tango lore, with weekday classes from 6pm to 8pm.

There are lively *milongas* for every night of the week. Monday is best at Salón Canning (Scalabrini Ortiz 1331) for the Parakultural *milonga*'s trendsetting MC; on Tuesday, the arty, grungy La Catedral (*see p43*) draws in a funky

Paint the town

Looking for the next big art thing? Chances are you might find it in Buenos Aires. From painters and sculptors to photographers and graffiti artists, the creative scene here is large, varied and impressive. So much so that international collectors are now flocking to BA to seek out the work of the biggest and brightest local art stars. The buzz starts here.

You can find your footing within the scene by first arranging an art-themed tour. Hop on to the Behind the Scenes art tour, led by the folks at **What's Up Buenos Aires** (www.whats upbuenosaires.com), for an excursion that's custom-crafted to include the work of both upmarket and underground artists. Or, for a street-side insider's approach, seek out Marina Charles and Jo Sharff, the masterminds behind **Graffiti Mundo** (www.graffitimundo.com), an energetic tour through the side streets, tunnels and artists' studios in the *barrios* of Palermo and Colegiales. If aerosol- and roller-wielding artists are your bag, you should also check out the latest and greatest works at **Hollywood in Cambodia** (www.hollywoodincambodia.com.ar), **Loveyou** (www.loveyouweb.com.ar) and **Turbo Galeria** (www.turbogaleria.com).

Buenos Aires Art Sight (011 4867 0095, www.buenosairesartsight.com.ar) offers full- and half-day tours of all things in contemporary art and design (think canvases, objects, architecture, interiors, fashion and jewellery), introducing clients to the works of such notable figures as the eccentric dressmaker Andrés Baño and the mural artist Diego Perrotta, whose Mexican pop-style street art adorns walls all over town.

Another excellent option is to make studio visits to meet the maestros themselves and get a glimpse of their work in the intimacy of their own work-space. Visitors who are up for total art immersion could try a customised trip arranged by **Blue Parallel** (+1 800 256 5307 US, +44 20 8819 3904 UK, www.blueparallel. com), a high-end concierge service that can plan a dawn-to-dusk-to-dawn-again itinerary of gallery and museum visits in the company of owners and curators, as well as exclusive meet-and-greets with major artists and collectors. If you plan to be in BA for the massively popular arteBA fair at the end of May, book your junket through Blue Parallel for VIP access to more arty events than you knew existed.

If you want to take a souvenir home, the original work on exhibition in galleries around town is usually on sale, and all galleries have back-room stock that is available for purchase. At the first hint of interest or, dare we say, a potential sale, gallery employees will trip over themselves to pull out canvas after canvas, photograph after photograph. Out of the hundreds of galleries scattered around town, which ones are worth your while? Seasoned local buyers such as Jean-Louis Larivière and Dudú von Thielmann, co-proprietors of Ediciones Larivière fine art photography books, point towards **Dabbah Torrejón** (El Salvador 5176, 011 4832 2332, www.dabbahtorrejon. com.ar) and **Ruth Benzacar** (Florida 1000, 011 4313 8480, www.ruthbenzacar.com) as being among the top galleries for serious collectors.

Remember, if you do decide to invest in a work of art while you're in town, be sure to hang on to the receipt – and, on on your way out of the country, be prepared to answer routine questions at customs about where and why you purchased your new find.

own customize your stay.

Cabrera 5556, Palermo Hollywood • T. (++54 11) 4772 8100
info@ownhotels.com • reservations@ownhotels.com

ownhotels.com
hotel + 16 suites + lounge + resto

10 AÑOS

ELEVAGE
BUENOS AIRES HOTEL

www.elevage.com.ar

ELEVAGE
GENERAL RODRIGUEZ RESORT

crowd. Wednesday is a good day to visit La Maldita Milonga (Perú 571), with great bands for those who just want to listen, while experienced dancers will enjoy the Niño Bien events, held on Thursday at Centro Región la Leonesa (Humberto 1462). On Friday, try the tourist-friendly Confitería Ideal (*see below*); on Saturday, La Viruta (Armenia 1366) has a young crowd and a disco vibe. Finally, San Telmo's Plaza Dorrego is the venue for a free, open-air *milonga* on Sunday.

"Based in a former factory, Ciudad Cultural Konex provides a gritty industrial backdrop to a wide array of original events."

Los Cardones

Palermo *Jorge Luis Borges 2180, between Paraguay & Guatemala (011 4777 1112/www.cardones.com.ar). Open from 7am Wed-Sat. Admission AR$15. Free on Fri. No credit cards.*
This is a great all-year-round *peña*, with a live *folklore* show where you can tune into the country sounds of Argentina's far-flung provinces. Los Cardones is particularly popular when the young gauchos descend on BA for La Rural, a country fair exhibition that is held close by at the end of July. The *peña* has its own restaurant serving *salteña* food – dishes from the northern province of Salta.

La Catedral

Almagro *Sarmiento 4006, at Medrano (011 15 5325 1630 mobile). Classes 8pm-midnight Mon-Sat. Milonga after classes. Admission AR$10-$15. No credit cards.*
The atmosphere at this formerly underground venue (now licensed and above board) is pitched somewhere between post-punk/neo-goth and circus/music hall. On Tuesdays, a young and funky crowd descends on to the wooden dancefloor. Musicians play here on selected nights, while *folklore* classes are offered on Sundays. The menu is entirely vegetarian.

Ciudad Cultural Konex

Abasto *Avenida Sarmiento 3131, between Jean Jaurés & Anchorena (011 4864 3200/www.ciudadcultural konex.org). Shows daily, times vary.*
Based in a former factory, this trendy complex provides a gritty industrial backdrop to a wide array of events. It's currently best known for Monday's regular Bomba de Tiempo, an improvisational musical show based on a group of percussionists who never fail to get the crowd moving. The show starts at 7pm; arrive early to beat the queue.

Confitería Ideal

Microcentro *1st floor, Suipacha 380, at Corrientes (011 4328 7750/www.confiteriaideal.com). Milonga 2-8.30pm Mon, 10.30pm-4am Tue; 10.30pm-4am, 2-8.30pm Wed-Sun. No credit cards.*
A gorgeous and historic café, Confitería Ideal hosts a full schedule of classes by day but really comes alive at night with the *milonga* and orchestra. Particularly good are Thursday evening's Tangoideal bash (www.tangoideal. com.ar) and Unitango Club's Tuesday and Friday night affairs (www.unitango.com).

Sabor a Tango

Congreso *General Juan Perón 2535, at Larrea (011 4953 8700/www.saboratango.com.ar). Dinner from 8.30pm daily. Shows 10pm daily.*
This is a glamourous setting for a tango show that features expert dancers, gaucho music and Argentinian *folklore* as well as an orchestra. Go on Saturday to catch the Italia Unita *milonga* in full swing.

Tango Cool

Palermo Viejo *Avenida Córdoba 5064, between Thames & Serrano (011 4383 7469/www.tangocool. com). Classes 9pm Fri. Milonga 10pm Wed; 11pm Fri. No credit cards.*
Drop by this friendly and informal *milonga* for good beginners' classes in English. Start the night with a lesson – no need to reserve, just turn up – and then dance the night away with an international crowd. Occasionally, the relaxed, tourist-friendly venue hosts bands and, on Fridays, shows. There is also a tango-themed art space to browse, and a restaurant and bar.

Nightlife

Whoever coined the cliché 'the early bird catches the worm' probably never went out in BA. Here, you're better late than, well, early. The top bars don't get going until after 1am, with the dancefloor action at the A-list discos peaking sometime around 4.30am. The crowds tend to be an anything-goes mix of boys and girls, gays and straights, and everything in-between, with *porteños*, expatriates and tourists all competing for precious elbow room at the bar and under the strobe lights. So pace yourself, and don't plan on going to bed until well after the sun comes up.

878

Villa Crespo *Thames 878, between Loyola & Aguirre (011 4773 1098). Open from 7pm Mon-Fri; from 8pm Sat, Sun.*
Once a 'word of mouth' bar, 878 has gone straight and business is quietly booming. Ring the bell at the still unmarked door, and you'll be invited into a slick, low-lit space with comfortable couches and more than a few reminders of its early days as a carpentry workshop. It's the perfect spot for a flirtatious dinner for two or a

comprehensive exploration of one of the best-stocked bars in the city. A chat with Julián, the ever-effervescent owner and in-house whisky specialist, should clear up any doubts you might have over which cocktail to choose, and you might, if you play your cards right, be granted entry to the VIP/smoking back room.

The Basement Club

Recoleta *The Shamrock, Rodríguez Peña 1220, between Juncal & Arenales, (011 4812 3584/www.the shamrockbar.com). Open from 9pm Thur; from 1am Fri, Sat.*

This unlikely combination of Irish pub/electro club in Recoleta attracts some of BA's best DJs in an ever-changing, roster focusing on electronica and deep house. It's always full, fun and wild, and is one of the few clubs that gets busy earlier on, especially on Thursdays. It's also one of the best places to be during the key nightlife hours of 3am to 7am, when the place is usually rocking with a mix of locals, tourists and some of BA's hardiest clubbers.

Carnal

Palermo Viejo *Niceto Vega 5511, at Humboldt (011 4772 7582/www.carnalbar.com.ar). Open from 7pm Tue-Sat.*

The big story at Carnal is the rooftop terrace. It's a hugely popular place to be in summer, and even manages to retain its happy crowd of punters through the winter. Add to this a reggae soundtrack, a bar decorated in lost-and-found knick-knacks and a fine collection of rum, and you have a laid-back and perennially hip place to spend an evening. Time it right and you may also get to experience the proposed extension, which will provide space for bands. Carnal also functions as the ideal warm-up bar for Niceto Club (*see below*), which is handily located across the street.

La Cigale

Microcentro *25 de Mayo 722, between Viamonte & Avenida Córdoba (011 4312 8275). Open from 6pm Mon-Fri; from 10pm Sat.*

At downtown's La Cigale, you're as likely to find the *Pink Panther* being shown on a giant screen as you are bands on the tiny stage, or a minimal-tech DJ tucked behind the blue mosaic bar. It all goes towards keeping weeknights kicking at this bar, which French expats prop up on Tuesdays. La Cigale's happy hour, from 6pm to 10pm, is one of BA's best, with white Russians, mojitos and pints of Heineken all two-for-one. Grab a drink from the friendly staff and take your pick of a booth or a bar stool to see out your evening.

Congo

Palermo Viejo *Honduras 5329, between Godoy Cruz & Juan B Justo (011 4833 5857). Open 8pm-4am Wed, Thur; 8pm-6am Fri, Sat.*

For all the laid-back charm of the leather-clad interior, the true magic of Congo resides in its garden, which ranks among the city's best summer drinking spaces. There's no better place to enjoy an icy Bossa Nova (rum, brandy, galliano, passionfruit and honey) as BA's sticky summer reaches boiling point. It's probably the most happening bar in town; lengthy queues to get in can form from midnight.

Crobar

Palermo *Paseo de la Infanta, Avenida del Libertador 3883, at Infanta Isabel (011 4778 1500/www.crobar. com). Open from 10pm Fri, Sat.*

Crobar – southern sister to the North American super clubs of the same name – is now firmly established on BA's dance music scene, drawing a regular crowd of devoted party people. A network of overhead balconies, walkways and VIP areas is cantilevered over the main dancefloor, with four well-attended bars serving up decent drinks at a premium. Saturdays can be a bit hit-or-miss: better to shell out the hefty entry fee on Friday nights for the international DJ sets. The new Friday night Rheo party in the side space is now one of the most happening gay events in town.

Milión

Recoleta *Paraná 1048, between Marcelo T de Alvear & Santa Fe (011 4815 9925/www.milion.com.ar). Open noon-2am Mon-Wed; noon-3am Thur; noon-4am Fri; 8pm-4am Sat; 8pm-2am Sun.*

Set in a sumptuously elegant mansion, Milión is as popular as ever, ten years after it reinvented itself as a swanky bar. Classical architecture is offset by dim lighting, cutting-edge art displays, projected visuals and arthouse movies. Milión's high-ceilinged rooms are often littered with reservation cards, making it hard to find a seat. But somewhere between the first-floor terrace, the lovely garden and the marble staircase, you're bound to find a place to rest your frozen cocktail. If you're peckish, there's the option of tapas by the bar or a full meal in the restaurant.

Niceto Club

Palermo Viejo *Niceto Vega 5510, between Humboldt & Fitz Roy (011 4779 9396/www.nicetoclub.com). Open from 12.30am Thur, Fri; from 1am Sat.*

At the enduringly popular Niceto, the two rooms, Side A and Side B, pump out an eclectic programme of local and international performers, together with shimmering party nights. Thursday's Club 69 bash is an anything-goes funhouse and one of the hottest club nights in town. Friday's multifaceted INVSN kicks off the weekend, and monthly reggaeton, dancehall, and indie-rock parties are crowd-pullers, with action generally peaking around 3am.

Pachá

Costanera Norte *Avenida Costanera Rafael Obligado, at La Pampa (011 4788 4280/www.pachabuenosaires. com). Open mid Feb-Dec from midnight Fri; from 1.30am Sat.*

Global club brand Pachá shot Buenos Aires on to the international scene a decade back, and this gleaming white brick of a venue overlooking the river remains a sure-fire destination for top-notch partying, especially on Saturday nights. The main room is sizeable and forms a regular sweaty pit of party-hard dance fiends, with several bars in easy reach. The patio DJ tends to push for softer, funkier tunes, while preening, sunglasses-clad clubbers get their groove on under the stars. Those pretty and rich enough to go VIP have more chill-out options, including an upstairs terrace and a downstairs open-air seating area.

Crobar.

AVANT-GARDE +
TRENDY +
BOHEMIAN

VITRUM
HOTEL

A LUXURY HOTEL IN THE HEART
OF PALERMO HOLLYWOOD

RESERVATIONS
Tel: (54 11) 4776-5030
www.vitrumhotel.com

MANSIÓN VITRAUX
BOUTIQUE HOTEL - WINE LOUNGE & SPA

Carlos Calvo 369 - San Telmo
(1102) Buenos Aires - Argentina
Tel: +54 11 43006886 - www.mansionvitraux.com

AIR CONDITIONING RELAX PARKING TERRACE
WI-FI INTERNET COOL ROOMS WEB
BREAKFAST
JACUZZI DESIGN INTERNET ROOM DVD ROOM

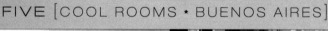

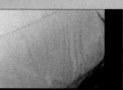

FIVE [COOL ROOMS ★ BUENOS AIRES]

Honduras 4742 . (C1424BJV) . Palermo Soho . Buenos Aires . República Argentina
Tel. 5411 5235-5555 . info@fivebuenosaires.com . www.fivebuenosaires.com   5.FIVE

Sugar

Palermo Viejo *Costa Rica 4619, at Armenia (011 15 6894 2002 mobile/www.sugarbuenosaires.com). Open from 12.30pm Tue-Sat.*

A lively, expat-run bar, Sugar is a comforting slice of home for disoriented Brits and other far-flung wanderers, and the rustic, bare-brick interior and low comfortable seating, make a welcome change from the area's penchant for the white and minimalist. It's great for a lazy evening's drink during the week, with happy hour from 9pm to midnight and selected drinks at dangerously bargain-basement prices. On weekend nights it gets very crowded; the music is an eclectic mix of predominantly US and UK classics.

Stay

Though BA is brimming with top-notch accommodation, including scores of trendy boutique hotels, more and more tourists are forgoing that option in favour of the 'home away from home' experience of renting an apartment. There are numerous short-term rental agencies throughout the city, including ApartmentsBA.com (011 5254 0100, 011 4800 1700, +1 646 827 8796 US, www.apartmentsba.com), OasisBA (011 4831 0340, www.oasisba.com) and International Nest (www.internationalnest.com). All three specialise in ultra-modern, state of the art luxury pads with five-star amenities – but alas, no 24-hour room service.

1555 Malabia House

Palermo Viejo *Malabia 1555, between Gorriti & Honduras (011 4833 2410/www.malabiahouse.com.ar). ££.*
Much imitated and arguably still not bettered, this establishment was at the vanguard of the boutique hotel wave in Palermo Viejo. It's set in a converted convent – although the sisters of San Vicente Ferrer would scarcely recognise its contemporary incarnation. Three small gardens combine to create a relaxed oasis; inside, the owner's inherent flair for design is evident in the use of colour and the play of natural light. Three of the 14 guest rooms are categorised as 'classic' and the remainder as 'modern', but all have queen-size beds, air-conditioning and private bathrooms.

Alvear Palace Hotel

Recoleta *Avenida Alvear 1891, between Callao & Ayacucho (011 4808 2100/www.alvearpalace.com). ££££.*
Still flying the standard for the fabulously rich, the sumptuous Alvear reeks of money and old-school class. Filling half a block of the lavish Avenida Alvear, the 210 rooms – 100 of which are suites and among the largest in the city – are an ocean of opulence in rich burgundies, with antique French furniture and Hermès bathroom goodies scattered around the jacuzzis (and in the huge spa). Among the hotel's bars and restaurants are two of the city's most illustrious establishments, both of which are open to the public. A buffet lunch or afternoon high tea in the

spectacular, bird-cage-like Orangerie is probably the best way for non-guests to soak up the hotel's ambience, while La Bourgogne restaurant is a gastronomic legend.

Art Hotel

Recoleta *Azcuénaga 1268, between Arenales & Beruti (011 4821 4744/www.arthotel.com.ar). ££.*
Modelled on the European *hôtel de charme* concept, this handsome establishment has no trouble living up to its name. A regularly changing art exhibition occupies the ground floor of this impeccably converted, century-old townhouse, and paintings by Argentinian artists adorn every room. A few of the 36 guest quarters are a little small, but six of them can be combined with adjacent rooms to create family-sized living quarters. The decor and fittings are a successful combination of neo-industrial modernity and classic designer chic.

Blue Soho Hotel

Palermo Viejo *El Salvador 4735, between Armenia & Gurruchaga (011 4831 9147/www.bluesohohotel.com). £££.*
No two suites are quite the same in this former youth hostel, a recent addition to the Palermo boutique hotel scene. Though the dormitories are now a distant memory, a playful and youthful spirit lives on in themed rooms such as the Oriental, Retro and Urban suites. There are nice, whimsical touches in the decor, and thoughtful amenities such as cordless phones and DVD players. In three of the suites, you can pull open wooden shutters to reveal a balcony overlooking the leafy street below.

Bo Bo Hotel

Palermo Viejo *Guatemala 4882, at Thames (011 4774 0505/www.bobohotel.com). £££.*
Bo Bo stands for bohemian-bourgeois and, true to its name, a sense of hip, affordable luxury runs throughout the property. Each of the boutique hotel's seven rooms represents a 20th-century art or design movement, and the top-priced Argentinian deluxe suite has a lagoon-sized jacuzzi. The friendly and efficient staff bring a wealth of international experience from five-star hotel chains, and with a top-notch contemporary restaurant downstairs and the perfect location from which to explore Palermo Soho's bar and boutique scene, Bo Bo is one of BA's best bets.

Casa Calma

Retiro *Suipacha 1015, between Santa Fe & Marcelo T de Alvear (011 5199 2800/www.casacalma.com.ar). ££££.*
If you feel the need to escape the big-city traffic and pollution, the headlines or the heat, then a few days' decompression in Casa Calma should more than do the trick. 'Wellness' suites and premium suites each come with their own sauna and jacuzzi, and the rooms themselves are bright and spacious, with a faintly Scandinavian air. The hotel is a new-age haven in which ambient forest sounds play softly in the hallways, and where you can order a massage as well as purchase items from the 'wellness boutique' gift basket. As a bonus, there's an honesty bar packed full of snacks and refreshments in the lobby.

Top left: Bo Bo Hotel.
Top right: Casa Calma.
Middle: Four Seasons
Hotel. Bottom: Rooney's
Boutique Hotel (2).

Casa Las Cañitas

Las Cañitas *Huergo 283, between Arévalo & Clay (011 4771 3878/www.casalascanitas.com). £££.*
This boutique hotel in Palermo's youthful sub-district offers great value in a superb location. The stylish and well-equipped rooms all have queen-size beds, air-conditioning and Wi-Fi. Just as appealing are the shared spaces, which include a wine bar (open 24 hours), a terrace and garden, and a business centre. In-house services include yoga and tango classes, massages, baby-sitting and a 'spa day', which includes cleansing, teas, a tantric massage and yoga.

La Cayetana Historic House

Monserrat *México 1330, between San José & Santiago del Estero (011 4383 2230/www.lacayetanahotel.com.ar). ££.*
Vintage meets ultra-modern: classic La Cayetana now has LCD TVs in every room. This thoughtfully restored 1820s home is hidden away on a back street behind a plain wooden door, and a buzz-to-enter policy only adds to the sense of sanctuary. Beyond the ivy-clad courtyard and its 200 year old *higuera* – fig tree – are 11 charming suites, whose decor is inspired by the early 19th-century post-colonial era. Lovely design touches include high, bare brick ceilings, original mosaic flooring and restored period furniture. Each suite has its own individual quirks – a spiral iron staircase in one; a clawfoot bathtub in another. Owners Estela Fitere and Silvina Tarrio named the hotel in honour of the house's original owner, Doña Cayetana Casanova.

The Cocker

San Telmo *Avenida Juan de Garay 458, between Defensa & Bolívar (011 4362 8451/www.thecocker.com). ££. No credit cards.*
Set in a grand and beautiful old house, this excellent-value San Telmo hotel has, since its opening in 2006, been blazing a trail as one of the most original and finest boutique establishments in the neighbourhood. The restored interior comes complete with a grand piano and a series of leafy roof gardens and terraces with entwined jasmine and soft breezes. Among the extras helping the Cocker to stand out are a daily afternoon *picada* – a selection of cold meats and cheeses, accompanied by wine and served on the terrace – plus a new yoga space. The name, in case you were wondering, was inspired by the former owners' cocker spaniel.

Craft Hip Hotel

Palermo Viejo *Nicaragua 4583, between Armenia & Malabia (011 4833 0060/www.crafthotel.com). £££.*
Hip, indeed. Craft is a cool, all-white art space and hotel. The works of contemporary artists such as feminist photographer Fabiana Barreda are featured, and a similarly creative sensibility has been applied to ten rooms with themes like Song (featuring a mini record player – vinyl LPs are available in the lobby) and Park (which has great views over the plaza below). The rooms are on the small side, but the innovative interior design uses the space wisely. And once you've had your fill of looking at works of art, you can discuss them over an afternoon cocktail on the sun-splashed roof.

Esplendor de Buenos Aires

Microcentro *San Martín 780, between Avenida Córdoba & Viamonte (011 5217 5710/www.esplendor buenosaires.com). ££.*
The original lodgings on these premises was the Hotel Phoenix, which opened in the early 1900s and was a first stop for many a hopeful immigrant. A few years ago, the hotel became the Esplendor de Buenos Aires, rising like a phoenix from the flames as the old Phoenix receded into the past. Monumental five-metre-high ceilings and huge doors give the place an otherworldly feel, with every century-old window and door carefully restored to its former glory.

Faena Hotel + Universe

Puerto Madero *Martha Salotti 445, Dique 2, Madero Este (011 4010 9000/www.faenahoteland universe.com). ££££.*
Designed by Philippe Starck, this opulent, camp lodging is built inside the shell of a red-brick former grain silo – part of the blooming Puerto Madero development, and one of the area's focal points both visually and conceptually. Intended to be more than just a hotel, as the 'Universe' part of its name might suggest, the Faena also includes a spa, outdoor pool, slick cabaret theatre and a spectacular restaurant, El Bistro, where the dramatically decadent decor and ostentatiously modern tasting menu is about as far from the average bistro as you could imagine.

Five Cool Rooms

Palermo Viejo *Honduras 4742, between Armenia & Malabia (011 5235 5555/www.fivebuenosaires.com). £££.*
As soon as it opened, this place quickly became one of the star players in the Palermo boutique hotel scene. It has all the credentials: minimalist, bare, pine flooring; a Zen-like gravel and bamboo shoots decorative scheme; a cool rooftop terrace; a sauna; and a massage parlour – all of which help to make this a popular Palermo base for trendy thirtysomethings. In addition to three large rooms, each with its own balcony and jacuzzi, there's also a pair of suites, one of which has a private decking area for peace and quiet in glorious, deeply comfortable solitude.

Four Seasons Hotel

Recoleta *Posadas 1086, at Cerrito (011 4321 1200/ www.fourseasons.com). ££££.*
Everyone from Madonna to Fidel Castro has stayed here at one point or another, but whether or not the illustrious/infamous guest list means anything to you, you'll still be treated like a VIP here. This 13-floor masterpiece, with marble walls, voluminous rooms and a handsome art collection lining the walls of the lobby and corridors, is a winning combination of modern amenities and old-fashioned hospitality. Behind the tower is a luxurious seven-suite mansion that features 24-hour butler service and is like a miniature French château with a rather Roman-looking swimming pool.

The Glu Hotel

Palermo Viejo *Godoy Cruz 1733, between Honduras & Gorriti (011 4831 4646/www.thegluhotel.com). £££.*

SYNERGIE

Malabia 1568 – Palermo Soho
Buenos Aires – Argentina
Tel 4832-0979
info@synergiehotel.com.ar
www.synergiehotel.com.ar

BLUE SOHO
Palermo lifestyle + Hotel

El Salvador 4735 - Palermo Soho
Tel: +54 (11) 4831-9147 / Fax: 4833-3034
www.hotelbluesoho.com
contacto@hotelbluesoho.com

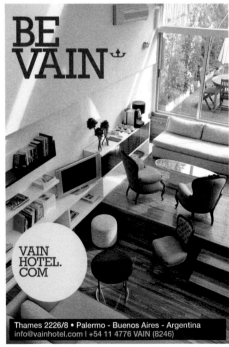

BE
VAIN

VAIN HOTEL. COM

Thames 2226/8 • Palermo - Buenos Aires - Argentina
info@vainhotel.com I +54 11 4776 VAIN (8246)

TAILOR MADE
HOTELS

WWW.TAILORMADEHOTELS.COM

Glu was built as a hotel from the ground up, so instead of cramming the odds and ends of every end-of-line designer sale into rooms the size of walk-in wardrobes, here the smallest room measures around 35sq m, and is decorated in irreproachably minimalist style. Immaculate rosewood furnishings, buff leather sofas, quality velvet chairs and spotless linen bedclothes are all pleasing to the eye and to the touch. There's also a rooftop jacuzzi, and a spa downstairs with a sauna.

Hollywood Suites & Lofts

Palermo Viejo *Nicaragua 5490, at Humboldt (011 5276 6100/www.hollywoodsuitesba.com.ar). £££.*
Hotel rooms in Palermo are notoriously cramped, but Hollywood Suites' high-rise building means sprawling quarters in a hopping neighbourhood can be yours at last. This upscale apart-hotel's 20 floors feature a range of large bi-level lofts with concrete floors, leather furniture, blackout curtains, fully equipped kitchens and balconies overlooking the Rio de la Plata. The public spaces, including a yoga studio and rooftop pool with glassed-in terrace, are modern and inviting. The ambience is cool and discreet, with a businesslike mood that's nicely warmed up by details such as home-made apple strudel on the breakfast tray, delivered to your door at the hour of your choosing.

Home Hotel Buenos Aires

Palermo Viejo *Honduras 5860, between Carranza & Ravignani (011 4778 1008/www.homebuenosaires.com). £££.*
It's not, truth be told, very homey at Home – unless, that is, your house looks out on to an exquisite garden complete with an azure pool; sits on a quiet street in one of the nicest parts of your city; and has a restaurant that serves popular weekend brunches, attracting the effortlessly hip and beautiful. Each of the rooms at this boutique hotel has its own distinctive look and supremely stylish decor (note the vintage French wallpaper). The lovely breakfast, included in the room rate, is presented like a tray studded with jewels: a thimble of juice here; a shot of yoghurt there; bread, cheese and jam; an elegant morsel of chocolate ganache and plenty of good coffee.

Jardin Escondido

Palermo Viejo *Gorriti 4746, between Armenia & Malabia (no phone/www.coppolajardinescondido.com). ££££.*
The *Godfather* trilogy may have kept you up at night, but at Francis Ford Coppola's Palermo pad you are guaranteed rest and relaxation. This inconspicuous property comprises two independent sections built around the *jardin escondido* (hidden garden) that inspired the hotel's name, which can be rented in their entirety or individually. An intimate atmosphere makes this urban retreat ideal for couples. Besides a small, single-bed studio, all but one of the six bedrooms – tastefully decorated and named after various members of the Coppola family – are fitted with double beds. Fancy staying in? The concierge, Martin, can arrange for an *asador* to come and fire up the parrilla, or you can order in a takeaway and watch one of the 150 DVDs in Coppola's collection.

Krista Hotel Boutique

Palermo Viejo *Bonpland 1665, between Gorriti & Honduras (011 4771 4697/www.kristahotel.com.ar). £££.*
Give an Argentinian a turn-of-the-century house, a prime location in Palermo and the financial means to turn it around, and the chances are that he or she will open a boutique hotel. Cue Krista. While this particular hotel might not reach the giddy heights of other similar boutiques in the *barrio* in terms of cutting-edge design, it offers down-to-earth service at a reasonable price. The bedrooms are large and comfortable and, although eight of the ten rooms are on the ground floor, indoor patios ensure there is plenty of natural light. A new massage salon and a mini spa add to the hotel's appeal.

Legado Mítico

Palermo Viejo *Gurruchaga 1848, between Costa Rica & Nicaragua (011 4833 1300/www.legadomitico.com). ££££.*
Theme hotels rarely work outside Las Vegas; only on the Strip does it really matter whether your bellhop is dressed as a Roman centurion or Sammy Davis Jr. So kudos to the designers of Legado Mítico, who have created a themed boutique hotel that doesn't sacrifice comfort and style to gimmickry. Each of the premises' 11 surprisingly spacious rooms is devoted to an emblematic figure from Argentinian history, including liberator José de San Martin, tango genius Carlos Gardel, author Jorge Luis Borges and, it hardly needs saying, former first lady Eva Perón. Each room is decorated and equipped according to its theme, with books, photographs and posters that not only look good but are genuinely illuminating. Mod cons, meanwhile, include large-screen TVs and a fast Wi-Fi connection.

Livian Guest House

Palermo Viejo *Palestina 1184, between Avenida Córdoba & Cabrera (011 4862 8841/www.livian guesthouse.com.ar). ££.*
Run by a former *telenovela* star and national-level gymnast, this family home-turned-guesthouse is furnished with a mix of vintage hand-me-downs and the couple's own intriguing collectables. The century-old house has six guest rooms, some with a small, private balcony and all having use of the lengthy garden out back. Amenities and services include Wi-Fi, mobile phone hire, yoga classes, personal trainers and even personal shoppers. The owners encourage a social environment, with a communal dining table, summertime *asados* and the occasional art exhibition. The house is situated on the outer limits of Palermo, so you'll be a bit out of the action – but this adds to the homey, non-touristy vibe.

Mansion Vitraux

San Telmo *Carlos Calvo 369, between Defensa & Balcarce (011 4300 6886/www.mansionvitraux.com). £££.*
Cutting-edge design details and luxurious soft furnishings are combined with antique finds under the beautiful stained-glass ceiling that inspired this San Telmo property's name. The 12 rooms of this sophisticated

Clockwise from top right:
Livian Guest House (2);
Home Hotel (3).

hotel range from Zen-like havens of minimalism to a glamorous black-walled den of decadence, fitted with a projector. Wine tasting sessions are held in the wine cellar, where gourmet cuisine is also served. You can work off the results of your gastronomic indulgence in the cardio gym or the heated terrace pool, which is equipped with a countercurrent swimming system. There's also a small dipping pool in the industrial-chic basement. The walls are a little on the thin side, but the sink-in beds should ensure a good night's sleep. The hotel's biggest selling point, however, is its location in the heart of San Telmo, just off Plaza Dorrego.

Moreno 376

San Telmo *Moreno 376, between Balcarce & Defensa (011 6091 2000/www.morenobuenosaires.com). £££.*
A truly stunning art deco exterior forms the shell of this seven-floor boutique hotel, with an interior design that runs very much along starkly modern, minimalist lines. There are, however, a few touches left over from the roaring 1920s, such as original stained-glass windows and wrought-iron lifts. Breakfast can be taken on the airy terrace, which is also used for *asados* (barbecues) in summer and is home to an open-air jacuzzi. The rooms themselves are sizeable, and the best have original artwork, whirlpool baths and either a balcony or views of the dome of the San Francisco church next door. Completing the scene are a bar, a 130-seat tango theatre and a new restaurant specialising in molecular cuisine, headed by a chef who learned his trade in Spain's illustrious El Bulli.

Nuss

El Salvador *4916, between Borges & Thames (011 4833 6222/www.nusshotel.com). £££.*
This former convent is located just steps away from Palermo Viejo's lively and popular Plaza Serrano, with its shops, bars and restaurants, meaning that your stay here will most likely be more about hedonism than asceticism. But if you are determined to remain cloistered away for a weekend of uninterrupted rest and relaxation, Nuss's comfortable, contemporary rooms, which are infused with an understated old-school sophistication, are ideal. A small gym and sauna are complemented by an attractive rooftop terrace, where you can soak in the sunshine or take a dip in the pool – though the latter is more ornamental than Olympic-sized.

Own Hotel

Palermo Viejo *Cabrera 5556, between Humboldt & Fitz Roy (011 4772 8100/www.ownhotels.com). £££.*
The paint has barely dried on this place, but already Own is looking like one of the city's hottest new boutique hotels. The spacious rooms are decorated in a timeless, contemporary style, kitted out with 500-thread count Egyptian cotton sheets, and range in size from a generous 35sq m to a rather impressive 55sq m. In an attempt to take the hotel's lounge area a step beyond the ordinary hotel bar, Own has created a stylish and welcoming New York-style cocktail lounge. A rooftop jacuzzi and parrilla area are in the pipeline too.

Posada Palermo

Palermo *Salguero 1655, between Soler & Paraguay (011 4826 8792/www.posadapalermo.com.ar). ££. No credit cards.*
After a visit to this B&B, you won't be surprised to learn that it's owned and managed by an architect. The tasteful Italian-influenced design scheme preserves the aura of the building's former life as a lodging for Italian immigrants in the early 20th century. The seven bedrooms are beautifully appointed, with bold colours, carefully-chosen paintings and ensuite bathrooms. Wind down in the patio or garden, or relax in the cosy living room, where three purring cats set the pace along with fellow housemate Pichincha, the dog. This is a solid choice for those seeking an intimate retreat in the heart of Palermo.

> "Guests at Rooney's Boutique Hotel have access to a lounge bar, café and tango patio, where free lessons are held nightly."

Rooney's Boutique Hotel

Tribunales *Sarmiento 1775, at Callao (011 5252 5060/www.rooneysboutiquehotel.com). ££.*
This lovely boutique hotel, a stone's throw from the Obelisco, has a literary past: the building was once the residence of the writer and poet Leopoldo Lugones. Today, its 14 rooms and suites still contain original wood floors, gilded mirrors, high ceilings and pretty chandeliers. Designer Paula Piatti reworked the original style with a palette of cream and soft green to create a calm downtown haven in a neighbourhood filled with theatres and *milongas*. Guests have access to a lounge bar, café and tango patio, where free lessons are held nightly.

Soho All Suites

Palermo Viejo *Honduras 4762, between Malabia & Armenia (011 4832 3000/www.sohoallsuites.com). £££.*
Each of the 21 roomy suites in this stylish, unpretentious boutique hotel is well-lit, equipped with a flatscreen TV, CD player, microwave and breakfast bar, and has a cream and beige colour scheme that's more soothing than striking. The 'superior' suites, which can sleep up to four people, have balconies facing the street. The penthouse has its own terrace, while the communal rooftop area has a set of sun loungers and a jacuzzi.

Tailor Made Hotel

Las Cañitas *Arce 385, between Chenaut & Arévalo (011 4774 9620/www.tailormadehotels.com.ar). £££.*
This may be one of the best-equipped hotels in Buenos Aires. There's an Apple Mac in every room, a high-

Krista
hotel boutique

Bonpland 1665 - (+5411) 4771-4697
www.kristahotel.com.ar

HOTELES
CON ENCANTO DE
BUÉNOS AIRES
BUENOS AIRES CHARMING HOTELS
www.buenosaireschanninghotels.com

Casa
Las Cañitas
Hotel Boutique

HUERGO 283 (C1426BQC), LAS CAÑITAS
CIUDAD AUTÓNOMA DE BUENOS AIRES, REPÚBLICA ARGENTINA
P. (+54 11) 4771-3878 / 4773-6523 - F. (+54 11) 4776-4300
INFO@CASALASCANITAS.COM - WWW.CASALASCANITAS.COM

La Cayetana
HISTORIC HOUSE · 1820

méxico 1330 - capital federal
buenos aires, argentina - tel: (5411) 4383 2230
info@lacayetanahotel.com.ar
www.lacayetanahotel.com.ar

POSADA
PALERMO
BED & BREAKFAST

HOTELES
CON ENCANTO DE
BUÉNOS AIRES
BUENOS AIRES CHARMING HOTELS

www.posadapalermo.com
info@posadapalermo.com

definition TV, an iPod dock and an IP phone for free international calls. Best of all, there are none of the charges for basic services with which so many hotels manage to leave a bad taste in the mouth. There are no US$6 peanuts here, and laundry is free. It's an approach that contrasts nicely with the slight irony that pretty much everything else in your room is for sale: the furniture, blankets, sheets, towels, pillows, photographs, books and wine.

Ulises Recoleta Suites

Recoleta *Ayacucho 2016, between Avenida Alvear & Posadas (011 4804 4571/www.ulisesrecoleta.com.ar). £££.*
If you came to Buenos Aires on a mission to shop until you drop, then it would be hard to think of a more conveniently located boutique hotel in which to store your newly bought acquisitions. Ask for a room facing the street so you can overlook the high-end designer stores (and their clientele) and plan your own retail immersion. All of the elegant and comfortable rooms are equipped with kitchenettes and, for an additional charge, Wi-Fi. Duplexes are split between two levels, and the penthouse suite features a large and lustrous living room topped off with a skylight.

Vain

Palermo Viejo *Thames 2226/8, between Charcas & Paraguay (011 4776 8246/www.vainuniverse.com). £££.*
The friendly folk at Vain believe there's nothing narcissistic about pampering yourself once in a while. When you check in to this 15-room boutique hotel, you're offered a complimentary drink as well as a 30-minute massage; if this isn't enough to de-stress, the 'senior' rooms are all equipped with hydromassage tubs. Since you're indulging in deadly sins, add a little gluttony to the list and make sure you don't miss the delicious, varied breakfast.

Vitrum Hotel

Palermo Viejo *Gorriti 5641, at Fitz Roy (011 4776 5030/www.vitrumhotel.com). £££.*
Instantly recognisable from the colourful patchwork tiles on its façade, this 16-room hotel offers up to the minute technology mixed with avant-garde art. Outfitted with lollipop-like floor lamps and psychedelic wallpaper, the rooms and suites come complete with espresso machines, L'Occitane bath goodies and flatscreen TVs. Public spaces include an art gallery, a spa and a suitably trendy restaurant and cocktail bar.

Factfile

When to go

Spring and autumn – October to December and April to June, respectively – are ideal times to visit Buenos Aires. The weather is gorgeous and there is a lot going on. The proximity to the Río de la Plata and sea-level location make the city humid, so the heat in summer (January to March) and the chill in winter (July to September) are felt more acutely. At any time of year, be prepared for rain; heavy storms or a day or so of solid downpour can create occasional sightseeing obstacles.

Getting there

All international flights arrive at and depart from Ezeiza (Aeropuerto Ministro Pistarini, 011 5480 6111, www.aa2000.com.ar), which is approximately 45 minutes by taxi from the city centre. For city centre destinations, go to the taxi desk in the arrivals hall and pre-pay a set fare of AR$80 to AR$100. Manuel Tienda León (011 4314 3636, www.tiendaleon.com) operates shuttle buses between the airport – there are stands in the arrivals hall and outside the terminals – and its downtown office (Avenida Eduardo Madero, Retiro). From the airport, there is 24-hour service, with buses every half hour; services to the airport run every half hour from 4am to 10.30pm. The fares are AR$38 one way and AR$69 return. Aeroparque Internacional Jorge Newberry (011 5480 3000, www.aa2000.com.ar) is Buenos Aires' downtown airport, serving domestic destinations and Uruguay.

Getting around

City buses (*colectivos*) cover the entire capital, run frequently and offer 24-hour service for either AR$1.10 or AR$1.25. The Subte – the small but reliable underground network – is a fast alternative that runs from 5am to 10.45pm (8am to 10pm on Sundays) for AR$1.10 per trip.

Taxis run on meters, with an initial fare of AR$3.80, plus AR$0.30 for every 200 metres or one minute of waiting time. Radio taxis and *remises*, which look like other private cars and do not run on meters, can be called in advance. Pidalo (011 4956 1200) and Radio Taxi Premium (011 4374 6666) are two reputable radio taxi companies, while Remises Blue (011 4777 8888) and Remises Recoleta VIP (011 4804 6655) offer *remise* service.

Tourist information

Microcentro Avenida Roque Sáenz Peña & Florida (no phone). Open 9am-6pm Mon-Fri; 10am-3pm Sat.
Recoleta Avenida Quintana & Ortiz (no phone). Open 10am-8pm daily. The tourist board website is www.bue.gov.ar.

Internet

Throughout central BA, you'll rarely be more than a block or two from a high-speed internet café or internet-equipped *locutorio* (call centre). You'll also be able to log on for free in most hotels as well as in many cafés and bars; look for the Wi-Fi signs.

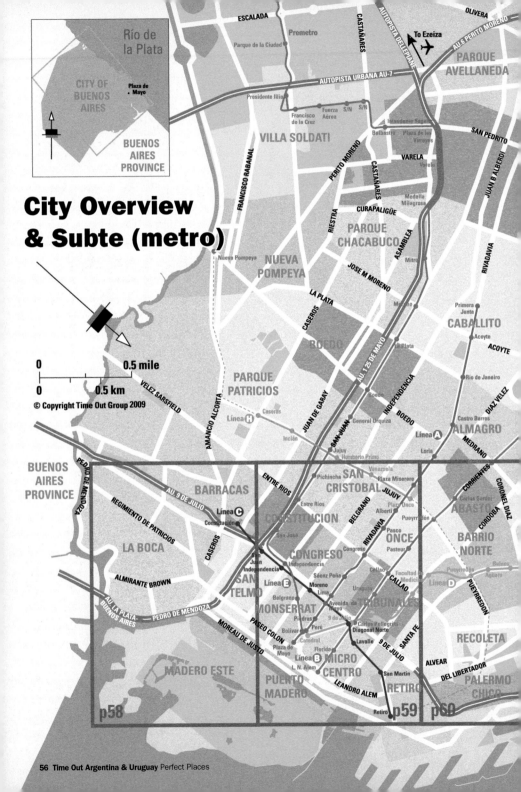

City Overview & Subte (metro)

Río de la Plata

CITY OF BUENOS AIRES

Plaza de Mayo

BUENOS AIRES PROVINCE

0   0.5 mile
0   0.5 km
© Copyright Time Out Group 2009

ESCALADA
Premetro
OLIVERA
CASTAÑARES
AUTOPISTA DELLEPIANE
To Ezeiza
AU 9 PERITO MORENO
Parque de la Ciudad
PARQUE AVELLANEDA
AUTOPISTA URBANA AU-7
Presidente Illia
Francisco de la Cruz
Fuerza Aérea
S/N   S/N
Intendente Saguier
PERITO MORENO
SAN PEDRO
VILLA SOLDATI
Balbastro
Plaza de los Virreyes
JUAN B ALBERDI
VARELA
Varela
CASTAÑARES
Medalla Milagrosa
RIESTRA
CURAPALIGÜE
PARQUE CHACABUCO
ASAMBLEA
Mitre
RIVADAVIA
JOSE M MORENO
Moreno
Primera Junta
CABALLITO
Nueva Pompeya
NUEVA POMPEYA
LA PLATA
La Plata
Acoyte
ACOYTE
CASEROS
Río de Janeiro
DIAZ VELEZ
BOEDO
AU 1 25 DE MAYO
Boedo
INDEPENDENCIA
Castro Barros
ALMAGRO
BOEDO
MEDRANO
PARQUE PATRICIOS
VELEZ SARSFIELD
AMANCIO ALCORTA
Caseros
Línea H
JUAN DE GARAY
SAN JUAN
General Urquiza
Línea A
Loría
Inclán
Jujuy
Humberto Primo
BUENOS AIRES PROVINCE
PEDRO DE MENDOZA
REGIMIENTO DE PATRICIOS
AU 9 DE JULIO
BARRACAS
Línea C
Constitución
ENTRE RIOS
Pichincha
SAN CRISTOBAL
Venezuela
Plaza Miserere
JUJUY
Carlos Gardel
CORRIENTES
CORONEL DIAZ
ABASTO
CORDOBA
CONSTITUCION
Entre Ríos
Alberti
Plaza Once
Pueyrredón
CASEROS
BELGRANO
RIVADAVIA
ONCE
BARRIO NORTE
LA BOCA
San José
Pasco
Congreso
Pasteur
Pueyrredón
Bulnes
Agüero
ALMIRANTE BROWN
CONGRESO
Facultad de Medicina
Línea D
PUEYRREDON
San Juan
Independencia
Independencia
Saénz Peña
Callao
CALLAO
SAN TELMO
Línea E
Moreno
Uruguay
PEDRO DE MENDOZA
AU LA PLATA-BUENOS AIRES
Belgrano
Lima
Avenida de Mayo
TRIBUNALES
RECOLETA
MONSERRAT
Bolívar
9 de Julio
Carlos Pellegrini
SANTA FE
PASEO COLON
Perú
Diagonal Norte
9 DE JULIO
ALVEAR
MOREAU DE JUSTO
Catedral
Lavalle
DEL LIBERTADOR
PALERMO CHICO
Plaza de Mayo
Florida
Línea B
MICRO CENTRO
MADERO ESTE
L. N. Alem
San Martin
PUERTO MADERO
LEANDRO ALEM
RETIRO
Retiro
p58
p59
p60

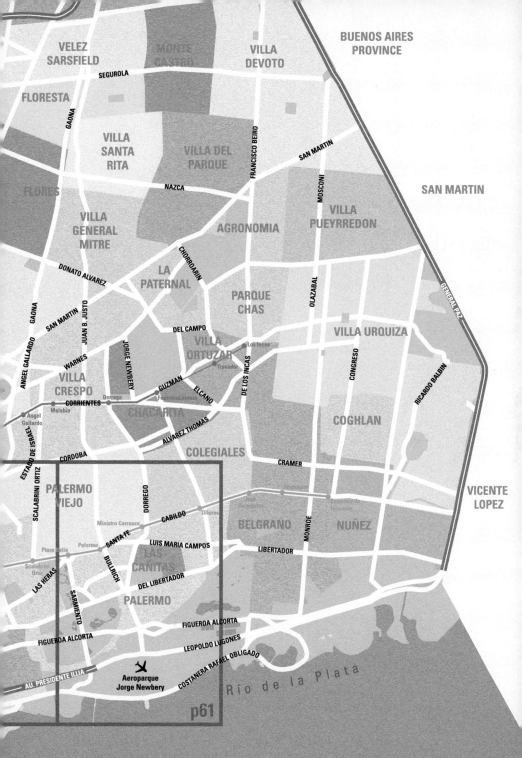

A   B   C   D

7

BARRACAS

Hospital Borda
Parque España
Hospital Rawson
Hospital Británico

AVENIDA MONTES DE OCA

AUTOPISTA 9 DE JULIO

Plaza Colombia

CONSTITUCIÓN

AVENIDA SUÁREZ

AVENIDA PATRICIOS

8

Plaza Almirante Brown

Plaza Matheu

AVENIDA MONTES DE OCA

AVENIDA CASEROS

Plaza de la Constitución

Fundación Proa

Museo de Cera

AVENIDA MARTÍN GARCÍA

RIACHUELO

Museo Benito Quinquela Martín & Teatro de la Ribera

Museo de la Pasión Boquense

La Bombonera

LA BOCA

Museo Histórico Nacional

Centro Cultural Torquato Tasso

Puente Trasbordador

Casa Amarilla

Parque Lezama

Ortodoxa Rusa

DON PEDRO DE MENDOZA

9

← to Avellaneda & Quilmes
Puente Nicolás Avellaneda

AVENIDA ALMIRANTE BROWN

AVENIDA BRASIL

AVENIDA JUAN DE GARAY

AVENIDA SAN JUAN

Museo del Cine
Museo de Arte Moderno
Museo Penitenciario

Plaza Dorrego

Torre Fantasma

Nuestra Sra de Belén

Plaza Solís

SAN TELMO

Dinamarquesa

AVENIDA PASEO COLÓN

Grupo de Teatro Catalinas Sur

Plaza Islas Malvinas

10

Autopista to La Plata & Mar del Plata

AUTOPISTA LA PLATA-BUENOS AIRES

Facultad de Ingeniería

DÁRSENA SUR

Casino

DIQUE 1

AVENIDA INGENIERO HUERGO

AVENIDA ALICIA MOREAU DE JUSTO

BENITO CORREA

DIQUE 2

COSTANERA SUR

AVENIDA ESPAÑA

11

Museo de Calcos

MADERO ESTE

AVENIDA COSTANERA ACHÁVAL RODRÍGUEZ

Cervecería Munich

0   300 yds
0   300 m
© Copyright Time Out Group 2009

12

Parque Natural y Reserva Ecológica Costanera Sur

Clockwise from top left: Teatro
Solís; Palacio Salvo on Plaza
Independencia; La Rambla;
mural in Ciudad Vieja.

Montevideo
Uruguay

A capital city with a laid-back vibe.

Ask a Montevidean what the best thing is about their city, and more often than not they'll look nonplussed, while fumbling helpfully for the words to describe Uruguay's unassuming capital. 'Tranquilo', they'll manage – and it is. There's a relaxed, thoughtful air about the place that's exemplified on La Rambla, a long waterside promenade surrounding the city, where, especially around sunset, locals come to cycle and stroll, to sit on the sea wall, to chat with friends and to gaze out to sea. Strictly speaking, these are the banks of the Río de la Plata, but Montevideans tend to call this vast body of water *el mar* (the sea).

Architecturally eclectic, Montevideo combines the crumbling remains of the old town's genteel zenith with a profusion of scowling, late 20th-century monoblocks and the local speciality: low-rise poured concrete houses with smooth sides that glitter in the sun. It's not everyone's idea of beautiful, but it is fascinating and it all adds to the impression of a city forgotten by time. Aside from the tall, harp-shaped headquarters of the national telephone company, there's little that sets the city obviously in the present.

A natural deep-water harbour, Montevideo owes its foundation in 1724 to a Spanish expedition sent from Buenos Aires to dislodge encroaching Portuguese settlements on what is now the Uruguayan coast. The city soon became the predominant port on the estuary and was granted a monopoly on the slave trade. Africans were trafficked through Montevideo to Argentina, Chile and Peru until 1810 – and it's to those slaves and their descendants that the city owes its passionate, secret rhythm. This isn't tango's languid slouch, though the city does its best to make itself synonymous with the genre: it's powerful, frantic *candombe* that beats at Montevideo's heart, giving life to its diffident façade and adding a fascinating layer to a city best savoured slowly.

Explore

With around 1.4 million residents, Montevideo accounts for a third of the population of Uruguay – though you'd never guess it to walk the streets, which rarely feel like those of a busy metropolis, even in the **Centro** and **Cordón** districts in the heart of the city. **Punta Carretas**, **Pocitos** and **Carrasco** are more interesting for eating out, but most of the sights are in the **Ciudad Vieja** (old town).

CIUDAD VIEJA

Seven blocks wide by 13 blocks long, the old town is a mix of grand government and banking institutions and run-down colonial housing – it looks like Havana in places, and even stood in for it in the filming of *Miami Vice*, the movie. The contrast makes the area relatively busy during the day (the best time to visit) and insalubrious at night and weekends, when the office crowd has gone. Pedestrianised calle Sarandí bisects the peninsula neatly from east to west, with the Rambla (promenade) to the south and the busy port on the northern shore.

Museo de Arte Precolombino & Indígena

25 de Mayo 279 (02 916 9360/www.mapi.org.uy). Open Apr-Sept 12.30-5.30pm Mon-Fri; 11am-4.30pm Sat. Oct-Mar 1-6.30pm Mon-Sat. Admission free.

Set in a fine old building still undergoing restoration, this modest museum consists of two main collections of indigenous and pre-Columbian artefacts, plus two large exhibition spaces given over to temporary shows. Don't miss the black laurel-wood canoe under the sweeping staircase, unearthed in Uruguay in 1941 and dating from some time between 1628 and 1810.

Museo de Artes Decorativas Palacio Taranco

25 de Mayo 376 (02 915 1101). Open 12.30-6pm Mon-Sat; 2-6pm Sun. Admission free.

The gloriously rococo interior of the Palacio Taranco, a sumptuous period house in the heart of the old town, harks back to a time when the area's crumbling mansions were at the height of their beauty. The house, which can be visited separately from the decorative arts museum located in its basement, is spectacularly lavish, with lashings of gilt and fine cornicing. There's little in the way of explanation of its contents or history, which lends weight to the impression that the mansion's wealthy 19th-century residents have merely stepped out for a moment. Downstairs, in the dingy decorative arts museum, there is an unexpectedly good collection of ancient Persian, Greek and Roman pottery.

Museo Gurvich

Ituzaingó 1377 (02 915 7826/www.museogurvich.org). Open 10am-6pm Mon-Fri, 11am-3pm Sat. Admission UR$30; free Tue.

Set on Plaza Matriz alongside the metropolitan cathedral, this small museum is dedicated to the works of José

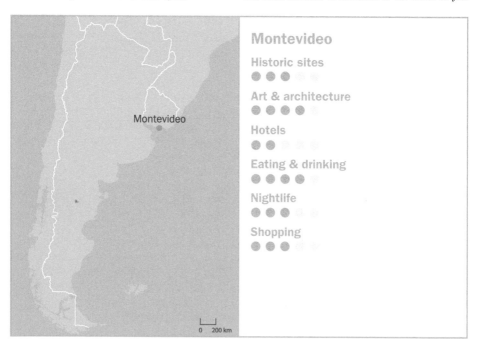

Montevideo

Montevideo

Historic sites
● ● ●

Art & architecture
● ● ● ●

Hotels
● ●

Eating & drinking
● ● ● ●

Nightlife
● ● ●

Shopping
● ● ●

0   200 km

Plaza Matriz, Ciudad Vieja.

Gurvich, a sometime disciple of Joaquin Torres Garcia. It's fascinating to see how Gurvich's style developed from his early canvases – which had a challenging and experimental style, like those of his mentor – into richer and more colourful paintings. A still-life painting on the museum's ground floor, *Dead Nature*, epitomises the way in which Gurvich's technically accomplished realism evolved away from his Constructivist starting point, while preserving its best aspects.

Museo Torres García

Sarandí 683 (02 916 2363/www.torresgarcia.org.uy). Open 9.30am-7.30pm Mon-Fri, 10am-6pm Sat. Admission free; suggested donation UR$50-$100.
You don't have to like the blocky, geometric canvases for which Uruguay's most celebrated artist, Joaquin Torres Garcia, found fame as one of the architects of the Constructivist movement; and you might wonder at some of the sketches and elementary shapes that pass for art in this centrally located museum. Nonetheless, there's much to admire in Torres Garcia's committed approach and his fierce engagement with the problem of visual representation, in which he renounced artistic realism as a sort of trickery, preferring instead to render the world using symbols and intuition.

PUNTA CARRETAS & POCITOS

Edged by the long Rambla, which runs right around Montevideo's shoreline, Punta Carretas forms a substantial peninsula jutting out into the water, east of the old town.

The centre of the promontory is dominated by the Sheraton Hotel and the Punta Carretas shopping mall. The latter was, until 1986, a prison, from which both 1930s anarchists and 1970s Tupamaru leftist guerrillas managed to make escapes. A final, violent prison mutiny in 1986 sounded the death knell for the jail, which closed a few months later, only to be transformed in 1994 into the city's nicest shopping centre.

The building's changing fortunes have helped to gentrify the neighbourhood, and these days Punta Carretas and Pocitos are both popular areas for eating out, with buzzing bar scenes and attractive beaches.

CARRASCO

This sedate, upmarket neighbourhood, some 14 kilometres east of the old town, started out as a breezy beach retreat for the smart set.

It has since become an exclusive residential *barrio* for that same crowd, with a clutch of bilingual private schools to prove it. The fine old Hotel Casino Carrasco was the hub of the zone in the 1920s and '30s, when Montevideo's glamourous heyday was in full swing. A long series of false starts and dashed expectations have left the lovely art-deco building in a sad state of disrepair, but it will surely get the renovation it deserves some day, and its vibrancy will be restored.

FURTHER AFIELD

BOUZA BODEGA BOUTIQUE

Already producing some of Uruguay's finest wines, despite its relatively recent 2001 beginnings, the Bouza Bodega Boutique is set in open countryside, just ten minutes from Montevideo (Camino de la Redención 7658, 02 323 7491, www.bodegabouza.com). To get there, take a taxi (around UR$250 each way) or catch a direct bus towards Progreso from the Río Branco bus terminal and get off at Camino de la Redención, where you can ask to be picked up.

Your visit should begin with a guided tour (11am and 4pm, every day except Wednesday), which starts in the experimental garden; here, the bodega's five vine varieties can be examined at close quarters. The tour continues with the vineyard and the bodega itself, where each step of the wine-making process is explained before a wine tasting rounds things off.

You can extend your visit by staying for lunch in the elegant restaurant. It's not cheap but it is exquisite, with a menu featuring the bodega's own Hampshire Down lamb, fresh local fish and excellent desserts.

Take home a bottle of tannat, a French variety that has become the Uruguayan grape par excellence: the Tannat A8, named for the particular plot on the vineyard on which its grapes were raised, is an outstanding wine, at UR$780. The bodega is open 9am-7pm every day except Wednesday, and reservations are essential. Tours cost UR$200, or UR$430 if they include a tasting session.

Eat

Like Buenos Aires, Montevideo is a place where both Italian influences and meat-worship reign supreme; the latter can be seen and enjoyed to wonderful effect at the Mercado del Puerto (Piedras & Pérez Castellano).

There's a wide range of fish and seafood, and no shortage of local specialties, from *pamplona* (stuffed chicken breast) to the almighty *chivito* (steak sandwich). The food here also has a marked Spanish influence.

There are some very good restaurants in the city, but you don't have to spend a fortune in order to eat well. If eating well also means dining in atmospheric surroundings, then keep your eyes peeled for one of Montevideo's classic corner bars or *boliches*, where elderly waiters are still shuffling paths into turn-of-the-century floor tiles and the menus have barely changed since the 1930s. If you spot a good one, dive straight in.

Clockwise from top left: Estrecho; Bouza Bodega Boutique (2); Mercado del Puerto.

Ubicado en Carrasco, el barrio más distinguido y exclusivo de Montevideo, Café Misterio es el restaurant y bar más elegante, vanguardista y moderno de la capital.
En verano abrimos Namm, un exótico y exclusivo restó en José Ignacio (Punta del Este)

café misterio

CHIVAS
LIVE WITH CHIVALRY

Ⓐ NAMM

Costa Rica esq Rivera, Montevideo
+5982 6018765

Ruta 10 km. 185, José Ignacio
0486 2526 (+5984862526)

Avancemos juntos

REPRESENTANTE EXCLUSIVO
Avancemos con confianza.

Rondeau y Valparaíso | Tel.: 924 0918 | Montevideo, Uruguay.
e-mail: info@ayaxonline.com y Red Nacional de Concesionarios.
www.ayaxonline.com

Bar Roldós

Ciudad Vieja *Mercado del Puerto, Local 9 (02 915 1520). Open 9am-6pm Mon-Sat; 9am-4pm Sun. £. Traditional.*

In business since 1886, Bar Roldós is a favourite stop for Montevideans on Saturdays, when the market throngs with locals. In this compact city, it seems everybody knows everyone else, so a spell at this classic bar in the company of a native guarantees you a steady stream of friendly introductions. The must-order drink here is a *medio y medio* (half and half): one part sweet sparkling wine to one part dry white. The lightly fizzy aperitif is best enjoyed with one of Bar Roldós' famous crustless sandwiches. Roquefort and walnut, or seafood, are good choices for those merely taking the edge off their appetites before a feast at one of the nearby grills. Alternatively, stay put and order a selection, including the more robust sandwich *olímpico*. Keep the *medio y medio* flowing, but be warned: it causes a wicked hangover.

> "Note the grand light fixture under the stairs at Bar Tasende – a statue of Venus, whose torch is switched off to signal closing time."

Bar Tasende

Ciudad Vieja *Ciudadela 1300 (02 900 2970). Open 10am-1am Mon-Sat. £. Italian/Traditional.*

The service at this dusty downtown jewel of a pizzeria steers a deft course between surly and politely unimpressed – and that takes practice. But these waiters were serving politicians from the nearby former Palacio de Gobierno when most of us were still in babygros, and their style is as no-nonsense as the excellent pizza, the very good range of beers, the passable coffee and the splendidly downbeat decor. Looking much as it did when it opened in 1931, Tasende's charms might not be instantly obvious; but once you're settled in and have attracted some service, you can start to appreciate the low-key style of the place: the worn but decorative ceramic floor tiles; the splendid high ceiling and the soaring columns; the light bulbs hanging insouciantly bare; and the grand light fixture under the stairs – a statue of Venus, whose torch is switched off to signal closing time.

Café Bacacay

Ciudad Vieja *Bacacay 1306 (02 916 6074/ www.bacacay.com.uy). Open 9am-2am Mon-Sat. ££. International.*

Just across the road from the Teatro Solis, Montevideo's grandest theatre, Café Bacacay has welcomed stars of ballet and opera as well as lowly musicians, technicians and stage-door johnnies through its doors since its 1844 inception.

Much admired by Montevideans, it underwent a sleek renovation in 1995 that kept its shell and its spirit intact, fusing an elliptical ceiling in concrete and metal with warm-toned wooden chairs in the retro-futuristic way the city does so well. The menu is similarly, and successfully, ambitious – go for a pre-theatre carpaccio of salmon and a glass of champagne, or come back later for the *lomo especial* – steak with ginger, peppers and sun-dried tomatoes.

Café Bar Tabaré

Punta Carretas *J Zorilla de San Martín 152 (02 712 3242/www.bartabare.com). Open from 8pm Mon-Sat. £££. International.*

Once a lowly *almacén* (neighbourhood shop) and bar, Bar Tabaré has gone significantly upmarket since its 1919 start-up, when sacks of pasta, barrels of olives and bottles of rum were its main attractions. Much of the original shop, including the marble bar, is preserved on one side of this gorgeous restaurant, with the other side functioning as a lighter, airier dining space. Down in the basement, you can, for a cover charge, enjoy a pocket-sized show with your dinner. An extensive menu offers excellent Italian-influenced pasta dishes, along with salads, steak and fish. Starters have an interesting bias to the raw; *jamón crudo*, carpaccio of beef, sushi and ceviche are among the options.

Café Misterio

Carrasco *Costa Rica & Avenida Rivera (02 601 8765/ www.cafemisterio.com.uy). Open noon-3.30pm, 8pm-12.30am Mon-Fri; 8pm-2pm Sat. £££. International.*

Worth the trip out to upmarket Carrasco, Café Misterio is a hot contender for the title of Montevideo's best restaurant. In its candlelit, bistro-style interior, well-heeled locals meet over excellent sushi or order from a deceptively simple menu that showcases the best of Uruguayan produce. The fig salad with *jamón crudo*, goat's cheese and rocket is given an interesting kick via a dressing that uses acidic *jus vert*, made from tiny, immature grapes. Meanwhile, the *tiradito*, a Peruvian dish of marinated raw fish, is served with a deliciously spicy, plummy ginger sauce. Ask about the specials, which reflect owner Juan Pablo Clerici's passion for seasonal produce – they might include fresh autumn mushrooms or locally fished *merluza negra* (Chilean sea bass). An impressive wine list includes an exceptional house special: the rich and chocolatey Cabernet Franc Café Misterio, created at Juanicó bodega.

Estrecho

Ciudad Vieja *Sarandí 460 (02 915 6107). Open noon-4pm Mon-Fri. ££. International.*

The hands-down best choice for a chic, simple lunch in central Montevideo, Estrecho is a long, narrow tunnel of a restaurant, whose unique shape and location have been put to inventive use by its Franco-Uruguayan proprietors. Set on the pedestrianised calle Sarandí, the restaurant has no tables, just a bar that stretches the entire length of the cheerful, duck-egg blue interior. A studious corps of young chefs and waiting staff patrol the long, open kitchen before you, cooking and serving the contents of an ever-changing menu that might include salad with seared steak slices, spicy home-made fish cakes and even a variation on a British steak pie.

El Palenque

Ciudad Vieja *Pérez Castellano 1579, Mercado del Puerto (02 917 0190/www.elpalenque.com.uy). Open noon-midnight Mon-Sat. £££. Parrilla.*

A visit to the Mercado del Puerto on a Saturday is more than a recommended element for a successful stay in Montevideo – it's compulsory. El Palenque is just one of dozens of restaurants in this wonderful old market, most of which amount to little more than polished bars facing a visceral, multicoloured tableau of meat, chicken, fish, sausages and red peppers, all sighing and hissing on the grill. You can do yourself proud at any of these joints, with sunshine slanting through the iron-and-glass roof on to a scene that hasn't changed in decades. If you fancy rubbing shoulders with politicos and diplomats, or feel like taking lunch up a notch and enjoying it at an outdoor table, then El Palenque is the place to go. Try the *picanha* (a tall, Brazilian-style cut of rump beef) or the grilled *abadejo* (haddock). If you're here in May or June, don't miss the seasonal house special of grilled swordfish.

La Pasiva

Ciudad Vieja *Sarandi 600 (02 915 7988). Open 8am-midnight Mon-Sat. £. Traditional.*

If you're lucky enough to make friends with some Uruguayans – not difficult, since they're an exceptionally hospitable bunch – then the chances are someone will eventually insist that you try a *pancho* (hotdog) at La Pasiva. It's a Montevideo classic, so heed their advice and head along to the Plaza Matriz branch, which, at 44 years of age, is the oldest in town since the original closed down. Admire the polished wood panelling, the gilt cornicing and the stunning sea-green ceiling, then ignore your new friends' advice and remember that a *pancho* is a hotdog, wherever you eat it, and the local obsession with simple frankfurters served in ordinary buns may leave you feeling distinctly underwhelmed. Go for the Uruguayan lunch of champions instead: the *chivito canadiense*, a triumph of sandwich engineering that loads thin steak with ham, cheese, bacon, egg, peppers and olives on a bed of lettuce and tomato.

La Perdiz

Punta Carretas *Guipúzcoa 350 (02 711 8963). Open noon-3.30pm, 8pm-midnight daily. £££. Parrilla/International.*

A busy restaurant just across the road from the Sheraton Hotel in Punta Carretas, La Perdiz is wildly popular with its middle- to upper-class regulars, who keep coming back for its friendly atmosphere, Basque-style cuisine and excellent grill (the fish is particularly good). The wait for a table can be fairly lengthy, but once you're settled in amid the cheerful clamour, it'll seem worth it. A huge Famous Grouse sign across the front of the premises is the mark of the restaurant's special relationship with the Scottish whisky, which stems from their shared name – *perdiz* meaning grouse. Upstairs, there is a decent-sized terrace, enclosed against the elements.

El Viejo y el Mar

Punta Carretas *Rambla Mahatma Gandhi 400 (02 710 5704). Open noon-2am. ££. Traditional.*

Decked out in cheerful red- and white-painted furniture, with nautical nods to the Hemingway novella that gives it its name, El Viejo y el Mar (The Old Man and the Sea) occupies a lovely spot on the Punta Carretas seafront. Head out to the waterfront garden if it's sunny, to an open-air table or one of the pretty gazebos around the shady rubber tree. Watch the yachts pass by while tucking in to *fritada de mariscos* (fried seafood) or *suprema de pollo* (chicken breast) with *puré de calabaza* (butternut squash purée). You won't necessarily be writing home about the food and the service can be patchy, but on a spring or summer's day this is a glorious place to dine. In the main room, the maritime theme calls for Spanish rice with mussels, or a tasty *cazuela* (casserole) of tuna, calamares, potatoes and chickpeas.

Shop

Shopping in Montevideo is mainly divided between a scattering of malls and markets, the long Avenida 18 de Julio, and the Ciudad Vieja. In the Ciudad Vieja, a plucky set of small designer shops has started to appear amid the crafts and arts outlets, helping the area along in its slow, much-needed process of sprucing up.

Ana Livni

Ciudad Vieja *25 de Mayo 280 (02 916 5076/ www.analivni.com). Open 11am-6pm Mon-Fri; 11am-4pm Sat.*

A pioneer in the Ciudad Vieja, on a stretch of 25 de Mayo where a number of design-oriented businesses have since set up shop, Ana Livni specialises in inventive yet highly wearable garments in wool and cotton. Expect smooth-felted merino wool in muted shades, decorated with hand-painted motifs, and soft, web-like moiré weaves in vivid, kingfisher colours.

Esencia Uruguay

Ciudad Vieja *Sarandi 359 (02 915 4472/ www.esenciauruguay.com). Open 9.30am-7.30pm Mon-Fri; 10am-4pm Sat.*

With a fine line in boutique Uruguayan wines, this is a great place at which to pick up a bottle of tannat. Go for the Cuna de Piedra from Los Cerros de San Juan, one of the oldest bodegas in Uruguay, or the more robust Bodega Pisano Tannat Reserva. You can taste the local version of port here, *licor de tannat*, and there's a selection of handmade sweets, sold in boxes or loose by weight. Don't miss the *natillas*, a chewy, delicious, white fudge.

Feria Tristán Narvaja

Cordón *Avenida 18 de Julio y Tristán Narvaja (no phone). Open 7am-3pm daily.*

This magnificent flea market is a Sunday-morning must. Block after block is lined with neat tables of jumble-sale goodness (books, bicycles, long-obsolete gadgets, naked dolls and front-room ornaments). The lunch spots are back on calle Tristán Narvaja – head for La Tortuguita for a

Clockwise from top left: Feria Tristán Narvaja (2); Belmont House.

chivito (Tristán Narvaja 1597) or the popular Verde for a tasty vegetarian lunch (Tristán Narvaja 1679).

Librería Puro Verso
Ciudad Vieja *Sarandí 675 (02 915 2589/www.libreria puroverso.com). Open 9am-8pm Mon-Wed; 9am-11pm Thur-Sat.*
Not far from the Museo Torres García, this splendid bookshop only opened in July 2008, having been an optician's shop from 1900 to 1990, but looks like it might have been here forever. A grand sweeping staircase and a splendid stained-glass window dominate the enormous, book-lined space. Upstairs is a very decent selection of novels in English, which you can peruse in the café.

Magma
Punta Carretas *Punta Carretas Shopping, Local 321 (02 711 1830/www.espaciomagma.com.uy). Open 10am-10pm daily.*
Featuring clothes by some of Uruguay and Argentina's best young designers, Magma offers a hip selection of wares, including work by Ana Livni (*see p70*) and Jazmin Chebar. It's not especially cheap, but it's worth a browse if fashion is your thing.

Manos del Uruguay
Punta Carretas *Punta Carretas Shopping, Local 252 (02 710 6108/www.manos.com.uy). Open 10am-10pm daily.*
With various branches, including one on downtown calle Sarandí, Manos del Uruguay is a non-profit organisation that sources and sells handicrafts by some 350 craftspeople from across Uruguay. The exceptionally chic and well-made pieces include elegant woollen textiles, baked clay cups, horn- and bone-handled knives, and beautifully soft leather gloves and purses.

> # "Locals warm their drums at fires, before moving through the streets to one of the most powerful rhythms on the continent."

Mercado de los Artesanos
Centro *Plaza Cagancha 1365 (02 901 0887/www. mercadodelosartesanos.com.uy). Open 10am-8pm Mon-Sat.*
This indoor crafts market, just off Avenida 18 de Julio, is an excellent place to pick up gifts. It showcases the work of dozens of small-scale *artesanos* (craftspeople). There are pieces in ceramic, leather and silver – and don't miss Daniel Guridi's carved ornaments in rock-hard, highly polished bone.

Arts

With a fairly low-key arts scene, Montevideo is nevertheless blessed with enough interesting museums and galleries to give your stay a dash of cultural seasoning. But beware: if you leave without having heard even a rumble of the drums at the heart of *candombe*, the uniquely Uruguayan music form, then you've missed something very special indeed.

You can catch the vanilla version of a *candombe* on Saturdays and Sundays at the Mercado del Puerto (12am-7pm), where roving drum troupes, complete with dancing carnival queens, ply the food stalls. Or take to the streets on a Sunday evening and hear the music on its home turf in almost any of the city's working-class southern *barrios*, such as Palermo, where locals gather from around 7pm to warm their drums at fires, before moving through the streets to one of the most powerful rhythms on the continent. Walk alongside the motley procession, or step in behind the drummers and feel your ribcage vibrate to the African beat. Note that this is not a spectacle for the unwary or the wide-eyed, and obvious tourists may not always be welcome. Watch your possessions and keep your wits about you.

Centro Cultural de España
Ciudad Vieja *Rincón 629 (02 915 2250/ www.cce.org.uy). Open 11.30am-8pm Mon-Fri; 11.30am-6pm Sat.*
Lucky Montevidean residents have this excellent cultural centre at their disposal. It has an innovative media library and facilities for listening, watching and even making films. But the CCE is also worth a look for visitors. There are two main exhibition spaces and a literary café, where a wall of magazine covers conceals some neat stacks of back issues to leaf through over coffee and cake.

Marte UpMarket
Ciudad Vieja *Colón 1468 (02 916 6451/ www.marteupmarket.blogspot.com). Open 2-6pm Mon-Fri; 11am-3pm Sat.*
Probably the city's edgiest, most energetic art gallery, Marte is run by an enthusiastic pair of young artists, Mercedes Bustelo and Gustavo Tabares, who keep the exhibitions of contemporary art fresh and frequently changing. The artists also work and give classes on the premises.

La Pasionaria
Ciudad Vieja *Reconquista 587 (02 915 6852/ www.lapasionaria.com.uy). Open 10am-7pm Mon-Fri; noon-6pm Sat.*
With a single art exhibition space in the main upstairs room, plus a clothes boutique, a bookshop and a café called El Beso, this lovely old house has become something of an arts hub in Montevideo. It's centrally located, too, not far from Plaza Independencia.

It takes two to tango

Despite being renowned for the world's most elegant dance, Argentina and Uruguay have been engaged in a rather more clumsy version of the tango across the Río de la Plata, and one that involves a lot of toe stepping and angry accusations. The dispute rages over where the dance originated. Contrary to the common belief that it's an Argentinian creation, Uruguay has long claimed that the fancy footwork first appeared on its side of the river.

In a move that could potentially end this rivalry, in 2008 Argentina and Uruguay put in a joint bid to Unesco to obtain World Heritage status for the dance. If the bid is successful, museums will be built in both country's capitals, along with a new institute to teach the dance. One of the principal motivations behind the move is to catalogue the thousand of existing tango recordings, and to distinguish the many modern and exported forms from the genre's original and distinctive form.

The most widely accepted view of tango's genesis is that it was born in the late 19th-century slums of Buenos Aires and popularised by wealthy young Argentinians, who were attracted to the sensual new dance form. However, Uruguay claims it can trace forms of tango back to Montevideo's own tenements. Furthermore, the most well-known and recognisable tango tune, 'La Cumparsita', was composed by Gerardo Matos Rodríguez, an unambiguous Uruguayan. The small nation

is so proud of the melody that the government went so far as to declare it the national hymn in 1997. Uruguayan feathers were understandably ruffled when Argentina commandeered the tune as its team's marching theme for the 2000 Olympic Games, the counterclaim being that the lyrics were penned by an Argentinian.

Perhaps the biggest bone of contention, though, is tango's greatest hero, Carlos Gardel, who is claimed by both countries. Although Gardel spent most of his life in Argentina, there has long been a question mark over whether he was born there. The man himself was more than a little reticent on his early years, famously responding to a question about his birth by saying he was born in Buenos Aires at the age of two and a half. It is thought that he didn't wish to expose the fact that he was born to a single mother. After his death in a plane crash over Colombia, Gardel's recovered passport was found to state his birthplace as being a small town in Uruguay. A further twist came when documentary evidence suggested he was actually born in Toulouse, France, and the Uruguayan birthplace may have been a clever ruse to escape military service in France.

Despite its dubious origins, tango continues to grow in popularity across these two countries and abroad. And if the Unesco bid is successful, we may even see two of its most reluctant dance partners produce a sudden *cambio de frente* and begin dancing in step.

Teatro Solís

Ciudad Vieja *Buenos Aires 652 (02 1950 3323/ www.teatrosolis.org.uy). Tours 4pm Tue, Thur; 11am, noon, 4pm Wed, Fri, Sun; 11am, noon, 1pm, 4pm Sat. Tour price UR$20 (UR$40 in English).*

One of the continent's finest old theatres, the Teatro Solís opened in 1896, and has seen greats like Caruso, Toscanini and Sarah Bernhardt grace its stage – as well as, more recently, Gilberto Gil, the Brazilian superstar musician-turned-politician. The theatre itself is a vision of plush red velvet and glowing gilt, with five tiers of vertical stalls and a magnificent painted ceiling rosette, suspended over an elegant, enormous chandelier.

Nightlife

Bar Fun Fun

Ciudad Vieja *Ciudadela 1229, Mercado Central (02 915 8005/www.barfunfun.com). Open from 8pm Tue-Sat.*

Incongruously located in an ugly 1980s block behind the Teatro Solis, this old workhorse of a bar has been up and running since 1895, changing location in tune with the patchy fortunes of the Mercado Central behind it. Musicians play here from Wednesday to Saturday, and tango has been the bar's main claim to fame ever since it had the profound honour of receiving maestro Carlos Gardel (*see p73* **It takes two to tango**), who sang here once in 1933. Things don't really get going until around 11pm.

> ## "Tranquilo Bar was once a neighbourhood hangout for Galician immigrants, who would dance the *paso doble* on the pavement outside."

El Pony Pisador

Ciudad Vieja *Bartolomé Mitre 1324/26 (02 916 2982/ www.elponypisador.com.uy). Open from 5pm Mon-Fri; from 8pm Sat, Sun.*

One of the best-known bars in the old town, the lively El Pony Pisador, named after the Prancing Pony pub in *Lord of the Rings*, is a safe bet most nights of the week. There are salsa bands and the like on weekends, and dancing and drinking way into the small hours.

La Ronda

Ciudad Vieja *Ciudadela 1184 (02 908 8191). Open noon-3am Mon-Sat; from 7pm Sun.*

Finding your way to La Ronda is a pivotal moment in a trip to Montevideo, since from that point on you have a reliable

place to go any night of the week and, indeed, during the day. This tiny joint is almost always quietly buzzing with locals and visitors enjoying the breeze out front, the dimly-lit bar inside and the better-than-average bar food. This is where the cool kids and the indie kids come, especially when there are rock musicians in town. Owner Felipe also runs Cheesecake Records next door, and the music at La Ronda, played on a record player, can include anything from alternative favourites like Johnny Cash, Belle & Sebastian and Sonic Youth to hip-as-they-come new tunes.

Tranquilo Bar

Pocitos *21 de Setiembre 3000 (02 711 2127/ www.tranquilobar.com). Open from 9.30am daily. No credit cards.*

This bar is a favourite among young Montevideans, especially from Thursday to Saturday, offering a decent bar menu and a good selection of beer. It was once a neighbourhood hangout for Galician immigrants, who would do the *paso doble* (an Old World dance based on the drama of a bullfight) on the pavement outside. Little is left of Tranquilo Bar's olden days, and there are no longer tables in the compact interior, so service is restricted to the outside terrace and the tables that spill on to the street.

Stay

Belmont House

Carrasco *Avenida Rivera 6512 (02 600 0430/ www.belmonthouse.com.uy). £££.*

Proudly displayed in Belmont House's reception is a letter from former Uruguayan president Julio María Sanguinetti, in which he quotes his French counterpart, Jacques Chirac, as calling this 'the best hotel in the world'. It's hard to know quite what to make of such hyperbole, but Chirac was certainly right in his praise for the hotel's deft balance of excellent service with a sense of being comfortably *chez vous*. Located in the laid-back beach suburb of Carrasco, it's a reliable classic, and has hosted many of the city's VIP visitors, including both Hillary Clinton and Fidel Castro. The hotel's style, however, is less South American capital city than British country mansion inside, with heavy draped curtains, high-backed armchairs, sweeping staircases and an old-school afternoon tea in the Victoria Salon.

Cala di Volpe

Punta Carretas *Rambla Mahatma Gandhi & Parva Domus (02 710 2000/www.hotelcaladivolpe.com.uy). ££.*

Set on a corner with an excellent view along the Rambla towards Carrasco, this Punta Carretas hotel is a very good option outside the Ciudad Vieja, if a little larger and more impersonal than the kind of boutique hotel on which it models itself. The corner suites are something special, with a 180° view of the water and a clutch of bonus extras, including plasma TVs and workstations with computers in each room (internet charged at an hourly rate; Wi-Fi free). An upstairs terrace with a small pool and access to a fitness room and sauna add to the appeal, as does a generous breakfast served in the light-filled lobby restaurant.

Ermitage Hotel

Pocitos *Juan Benito Blanco 783 (02 710 4021/ www.ermitagemontevideo.com). ££.*

A quiet little trooper of a hotel, set on an attractive waterfront square, the Ermitage has nothing of the boutique or bijoux about it. Nonetheless, it has been a good-value, respectable place to stay since its opening in 1945. Although it is still a little chintzy and staid, a 2002 renovation has brought it up to scratch in terms of amenities, and its peaceful Pocitos location is ideal for a simple excursion across the square to the beach, or to the area's excellent range of cafés, bars and restaurants.

NH Columbia

Ciudad Vieja *Rambla Gran Bretaña 473 (02 916 0001/www.nh-hotels.com). ££.*

Set just below the old town, the NH Columbia has the advantage of being right on the Rambla, where all it takes is a stroll over the road to the waterfront to join the laid-back natives at their leisure. The bright and sunny restaurant comes into its own at breakfast, when an enormous, shining river view is spread out before you. Insist on a superior, front-facing room – they're larger and better all round, and the views from the back rooms leave something to be desired. A squared-off, modern-looking building, the hotel seems a little out of place in the slightly run-down, seedy area that surrounds it, but its location is spot-on for old-town sightseeing.

Plaza Fuerte

Ciudad Vieja *Bartolomé Mitre 1361 (02 915 6651/ www.plazafuerte.com). ££.*

The high ceilings and Spanish-style tiled floors of Plaza Fuerte's atrium are just as they were when it started in 1903 as a quietly genteel hotel. The hotel's changing fortunes, mirroring the area's, have improved in the interim, with a renovation that has brought its rooms up to scratch in a contemporary style that blends well with the classical architecture. Some of the rooms have mezzanine floors with an upstairs sleeping area, but with their full-height ceilings, the airy corner rooms are by far the nicest option.

Radisson

Centro *Plaza Independencia 759 (02 902 0111/ www.radisson.com/montevideouy). £££.*

If you plan to spend most of your time in and around the Centro and the Ciudad Vieja, this location can't be bettered. The Radisson's lofty tower rooms afford views across the city, and most of the major sights are well within walking distance. A half-Olympic-sized indoor swimming pool is another standout feature, as are the regular tango and jazz shows held in the downstairs bar. The guest rooms are spacious and very comfortable – but best of all is the Arcadia restaurant on the 25th floor, where breakfast is served, and from which the views over Montevideo are truly spectacular.

Factfile

When to go

Between October and June is the nicest time to visit the city in terms of weather, although January and February can get uncomfortably hot.

Carnival season (between February and March) is a great time to see Montevideo at its exhuberant best, full of colour, music, theatre and dance.

If you visit in August, don't miss the 24 August 'Noche de la Nostalgia', a wildly popular festival, when bars and nightclubs vie to play the best old, gold classics, and what seems like the entire city turns out to hear them.

Getting there

The international airport is at Carrasco, some 20 kilometres from the city centre. If you're already close by in Buenos Aires, it's far nicer to take a ferry across the immense Río de la Plata.

Buquebus (02 916 8801, www.buquebus.com) is the main ferry company linking the two cities, but Colonia Express (02 400 3939, www.coloniaexpress.com) is often more economical, especially if you buy tickets well in advance.

Travelling by bus via Colonia to Montevideo as part of an all-inclusive ticket is cheaper still,

and gives you the chance to catch a glimpse of the countryside in between. You'll arrive at the Tres Cruces bus terminal (02 409 7399), a short taxi ride from Ciudad Vieja.

Getting around

Within Montevideo, local buses cost UR$15 per journey. Taxi fares are higher at night-time and on weekends and holidays, so don't be surprised when the driver takes out a laminated table and looks up the price corresponding to the number on the meter.

Tourist information

Montevideo Municipal Tourist Office Avenida 18 de Julio 1360 (02 950 1830). Open 11am-6pm Mon-Fri; 10am-6pm Sat, Sun.

Uruguay-wide tourist offices can be found at Avenida Libertador 1409 (02 409 7399), open 8am-10pm daily, and at the Tres Cruces bus terminal and the airport.

Internet

ANTEL Telecentro Convención Avenida 18 de Julio 891 (02 908 8738). Open 8am-11pm Mon-Sat, 9.30am-10pm Sun. Many hotels offer Wi-Fi, and you can find internet cafés across the city.

Central Montevideo

Puerto de Montevideo

Zona Portuaria

AGUADA

CENTRO

CIUDAD VIEJA

BARRIO SUR

Dique
Maúa

RÍO DE LA PLATA

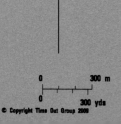

0   300 m
0   300 yds

© Copyright Time Out Group 2009

Top: Río Paraná.
Middle: Monumento
de la Bandera. Bottom:
Puente Rosario-Victoria.

Rosario
Argentina

An up-and-coming city on the banks of the Río Paraná.

To define Rosario as a mini Buenos Aires is to overlook its biggest asset. Unlike the capital, which shuns its waterways and faces squarely inland, Rosario embraces its riverside location. Alongside the tea-coloured Río Paraná, you'll find riverfront bars and boardwalks, residents lining up their kayaks and boats, and restaurants in which fish are a menu centrepiece, not just a hasty afterthought once all parts of a cow have been exhausted.

This port city has been through tough times since its industrial heyday in the 20th century. Now it's fighting back and reconnecting with its roots through a host of exciting regeneration projects: a silo has gained a new lease of life as a modern art museum; a train depot has turned into a shopping arcade; and an old water tower is now a stylish tango club.

As Rosario's fortunes have ebbed and flowed, one factor has been constant: local pride. Rosarinos argue that it's their town, not Córdoba, that is Argentina's second city. Much-lauded claims to fame include the city being the birthplace of both Che Guevara and the nation's flag. This latter fact will be unlikely to slip your mind: not only does a giant, 70-metre memorial dominate the skyline, but the city's status as the 'cradle of the flag' is plastered everywhere, from newspaper mastheads to car number plates.

Rosario also prides itself on having a thriving arts scene, a lively nightlife and, allegedly, the country's most beautiful women. Yet the star of the show remains the Río Paraná. Its riverside beaches may be packed in summer, but you don't have to head far into the inlets of the Delta to find peace; just do as the locals do and jump into a kayak. With these natural assets, a creative population and a proud history, Rosario's future has never looked brighter.

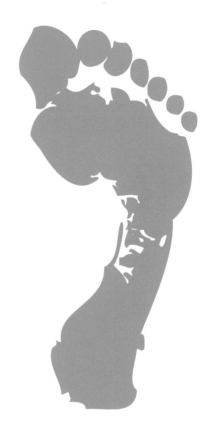

Whatever your carbon footprint, we can reduce it

For over a decade we've been leading the way in carbon offsetting and carbon management.

In that time we've purchased carbon credits from over 200 projects spread across 6 continents. We work with over 300 major commercial clients and thousands of small and medium sized businesses, which rely upon our market-leading quality assurance programme, our experience and absolute commitment to deliver the right solution for each client.

Why not give us a call?

T: London (020) 7833 6000

www.CarbonNeutral.com

Explore

The city spreads back from the river's edge, and an easy-to-navigate grid system means it's not hard to find your way around. The **Costanera** (riverside) helps with orientation; it stretches up as far as a striking suspension bridge, which links the city to the Entre Ríos town of Victoria, a favourite weekend spot for Rosarinos.

EL CENTRO

Downtown Rosario is generally defined as the triangle between Boulevard Oroño, Avenida Pellegrini and the river. The city's main square is Plaza 25 de Mayo, which is surrounded by, or in close proximity to, many of the city's most important buildings and monuments. These landmarks include the belle époque Palacio del Correo (post office), the Palacio de los Leones (named after the stone lions that guard the entrance) and, to the south, the Catedral de Rosario, with its mishmash of architectural styles and Italianate marble altar.

To the south and west of Plaza 25 de Mayo are the city's two pedestrianised shopping streets, San Martín and Córdoba. The sections of calle Córdoba just before it reaches Boulevard Oroño are known as the Paseo del Siglo, and contain some of the city's most precious architectural heritage.

Just east of Plaza 25 de Mayo, and a hair's breadth from the river, stands the indomitable Monumento de la Bandera (Santa Fe 581), a 70-metre tower glorifying the national flag, which was raised for the very first time on the opposite bank in 1812 by independence hero Manuel Belgrano. This is the world's only monument to a flag, a fact that may not have you rushing to visit; nonetheless, the views from the top across the Río Paraná and its islands make it worth a stop.

Ernesto 'Che' Guevara's first home can be found at Entre Ríos 480. As historic sights go, it's not Rosario's most impressive offering: the house isn't open to the public, and its effect on shaping Che's revolutionary ideas was no doubt limited as he only lived here until he was a few months old.

Che pilgrims can find a far better photo opportunity at Plaza del Cooperación (Mitre and Tucumán), where there's a striking black and white mural of the great man sporting his characteristic beret, or by heading across town to the four-ton bronze statue standing proud at calle Buenos Aires and Boulevard 27 de Febrero. The latter monument – inaugurated on 14 June 2008, a date that would have been El Che's 80th birthday – is made of donated household objects sent from across the world, including house keys belonging to Argentinians who fled the 1970s military dictatorship.

Rosario

Historic sites
● ● ●

Art & architecture
● ● ● ●

Hotels
● ● ●

Eating & drinking
● ● ●

Nightlife
● ● ●

Shopping
● ● ●

0   200 km

LA COSTANERA

The Costanera (riverside) is the city's biggest draw, and stretches some 20 kilometres. At its southern end is Parque Urquiza, where you'll find the city's planetarium (Montevideo & Avenida de la Libertad, 0341 480 2533). A little further north along the riverfront is the Estación Fluvial (Belgrano & Rioja), the start and finish point for boat rides on the Río Paraná. The city's main sightseeing boat is *Barco Ciudad de Rosario*, which offers two-hour trips up to Puente Rosario-Victoria and back on Saturdays, Sundays and holidays (0341 449 8688, www.barcocr1.com).

Lined with restaurants, cafés and the occasional market, Parque de España is a stretch of parkland and riverfront promenade that was funded by the Spanish government to mark the 500th anniversary of the discovery of South America. Tunnels extending back from the waterfront that were once a hotbed for smuggling have been reincarnated as exhibition space for artists, while La Isla de Los Inventos (Corrientes & Wheelright, 0341 449 6510) is a similarly admirable initiative, offering interactive art, technology and science exhibits for children. (It's open Tuesday to Sunday, but reservations are needed on weekdays.) Just below the promenade, a string of public barbecues are rented out by locals for low-cost gatherings with friends and family. The smell of sizzling steak wafting up to the boardwalk means this is not a place to stroll with an empty stomach.

> "Once a seedy den of mafia activity and prostitution, Pichincha is now the city's hippest *barrio*."

A 15-minute walk further north along the river, the iconic, pastel-painted silos of the Macro museum (*see p86*) stand proud. But riverside regeneration isn't stopping here: next in line is the Puerto Norte area, tipped to be the equivalent of the upmarket Puerto Madero docklands in Buenos Aires. Due to open in 2011, the Ciudad Ribera complex will see an old sugar factory transformed into towering apartment blocks.

The northernmost attraction on Rosario's waterfront, beyond the Rosario Central football stadium and just before the suspension bridge, is Florida beach, which in summer has a lively atmosphere fuelled by the surrounding beach bars and boat clubs. If you don't fancy laying your beach towel a few centimetres from the next person, opt for a trip to the tranquil Delta islands.

Sebastián Clérico offers kayaking trips for all abilities (0341 15 571 3812 mobile, www.bikerosario.com.ar). A former member of the Argentinian canoe team, Sebastián is well travelled, multilingual and fully clued up on his city's past and present. He also offers cycling tours of the city and hires bikes for independent use from his downtown office at Zeballos 327.

PARQUE DE LA INDEPENDENCIA

Parque de la Independencia sits 20 blocks to the west of the riverfront. Dating back to 1902, it was designed by Charles Thays, the celebrated French landscaper responsible for most of the major parks in Buenos Aires. Some of the city's biggest museums can be found here, including the Museo Municipal de Bellas Artes Juan B Castagnino (0341 480 2542, closed Tue) and Museo Histórico Provincial (0341 472 1457, closed Mon). The park is also home to Newell's Old Boys football club (Rosario Central's arch rivals) and the excellent Jardín de Los Niños adventure playground, which is open to schools only during the week, unless you call 0341 480 2421 to make an appointment.

PICHINCHA

Once a seedy den of mafia activity and prostitution, Pichincha is now the city's hippest *barrio*. The city's Secretaría de Cultura has made its home here in the old Rosario Norte train station (Avenida Aristóbulo del Valle 2736), and the area's antique shops and markets have led to comparisons with Buenos Aires' San Telmo district. Travellers who prefer aimless wandering to ticking off sights should make a beeline here for café culture and street theatre by day, and bar- and restaurant-hopping by night.

Eat

You won't be stuck for eating options along the riverfront; Parque de España is a good place to wander with an appetite and no set plans. The best inland options are the streets of Pichincha or Avenida Pellegrini. The latter is where you'll find Rosario's best-loved ice-cream parlour, Yomo (Pellegrini 1910), which serves gravity-defying mountains of flavours, including tiramisu and *sopa inglesa* (an Argentinian take on trifle).

El Cairo

Centro *Santa Fé 1102, & Sarmiento (0341 449 0714/ www.barelcairo.com). Open 7am-1am Mon-Thur; 7am-3am Fri, Sat; 9am-1am Sun. ££. Café.*
El Cairo's status as Rosario's most famous café was fuelled by the loyal patronage of one of the city's most cherished sons, cartoonist and comic Roberto Fontanarrosa. Since the 1940s, the café has been renowned as a haunt for intellectual

Macro.

Clockwise from top left: Verde Que Te Quiero Verde (2); Pobla del Mercat (2).

and cultural *sobre mesa* (table chat). Fontanarrosa died in 2007, but his regular spot, which he liked to call '*la mesa de los galanes*' (the table of handsome men), remains a shrine to the good times; you'll find it just opposite the bar, covered in photographs. Having survived financial meltdown and a serious fire, El Cairo now has shiny new premises and is more popular than ever. With giant windows looking out on to the street and seating for up to 250 customers, the people-watching opportunities here are endless.

Chinchibira

Pichincha *Santiago 101 (0341 439 8720). Open from 8am Mon-Sat; from 7pm Sun. ££. No credit cards. Café.*
This cute corner café is named after an old Argentinian cola drink known for its distinctive bottle with a glass marble in the neck. (Look out for the one in a display cabinet next to the bar.) The owners have clearly been visiting the area's famed antiques shops, stocking up on quirky decorations such as ancient typewriters and soda siphons. The attractive listed building has extra seating outside, shaded by trees. It's an ideal location for a low-key morning coffee or a leisurely afternoon beer, or as a first stop on a night out.

Comedor Balcarce

Centro *Balcarce & Brown (0341 425 6765). Open noon-3pm, 8.30pm-1am Mon-Sat. £. No credit cards. Traditional.*
You'd expect to give a wide berth to a place known locally as El Vomito, but Comedor Balcarce earned its famous nickname for rather more favourable reasons: Rosarinos say the food here is so good and so affordable that you could eat until you make yourself sick. It's not an accolade that all restaurants would aspire to, but Comedor Balcarce is as no-frills as they come – and all the better for it. This much-loved haunt provides soda siphons to dilute your wine, fizzy drinks in family-sized glass bottles and aged waiters to serve all the Argentinian classics, including predictably huge hunks of meat. Comedor Balcarce is a local institution, with multi-generational appeal and the best comfort food in town.

Don Ferro

Costanera *Arturo Illia 1690 (0341 421 1927). Open noon-4pm, 8pm-1.30am daily. £££. Parrilla.*
Don Ferro is yet another stylish restoration project, this time housed in what was once the city's riverside train station. Grilled meat and river fish are house specialities, and despite the vast dining area with a terrace along the former station platform, you can still expect to queue for a table at the weekend. It remains a place to be seen, and the huge arched windows facing out on to Parque de España will ensure your presence doesn't go unnoticed.

Escauriza Parrilla

Costanera *Bajada Escauriza & Paseo Ribereño (0341 454 1777/www.escaurizaparrilla.com.ar). Open noon-4pm, 8pm-1am daily. £££. Seafood.*
In case you forget the focus on fish at this beachside restaurant, the ceiling has been strung with not-so-subtle nets. Escauriza won't win prizes for its interior decor, but neither is it trying to. There are bigger fish to fry here, including surubí, pacú and boga. And when it's this good

and this fresh, why mess around with pretentious dressings? Lemon and a dash of every Argentinian's favourite spicy sauce, *chimichurri*, will do the job just fine.

La Estancia

Centro *Pellegrini 1501 (0341 440 7373/www.parrilla laestancia.com.ar). Open noon-3.30pm, 8pm-1am daily. £££. Parrilla.*
Rosario's most famous parrilla has been turning over steaks on Avenida Pellegrini for more than 25 years. Some Rosarinos will tell you this is more the real deal than its touristy *porteño* counterparts; it's certainly got a down-to-earth atmosphere, even if does attract the occasional celebrity, such as locally born football hero Lionel Messi. The huge, pack-'em-in dining room is not for an intimate tête-à-tête, but it's a great place to sit among crowds of locals to share in the reverence for all things *carne*. For those not in the mood for meat, the alternatives include all the usual suspects (stuffed pasta, salads), plus – and here's the part where it really can lord one over on its BA counterparts – a notable selection of fresh fish.

Flora

Costanera *Presidente Roca & el Río (0341 426 7887). Open 7.30am-midnight daily. ££. No credit cards. Modern.*
The name of this fishtank-shaped place remains a mystery; you won't find flowers inside, just giant bamboo in oversized vases. Still, the location in Parque de España makes it a great place to enjoy some river views. Sit inside the glass-encased dining room, or opt for a table out on the extensive patio. With tables set with chunky tumblers rather than wine glasses, it's best for a quick bite rather than a slap-up dinner. Try a Carlitos – a famed local sandwich named after tango legend Carlos Gardel, featuring a less-than-legendary ingredients list: cheese, ham and ketchup.

Metropolitan Grand Bar

Centro *Córdoba 1680 (0341 447 4598/www. metropolitanbar.com.ar). Open from 8am Mon-Sat. ££. Modern.*
The big screen behind a long counter says 'sports bar'; the menu (aubergine caviar, 12-year-old balsamic vinegar) is straight out of a gastropub; the white tablecloths and sharp edges would look perfectly at home in a minimalist restaurant. The Metropolitan's boundary blurring makes it a good option when your plans fall out of sync with your travel companion's. You have a coffee, they quaff a cocktail; you eat a sit-down meal, they order a bar snack. Anything goes, and no one will feel left out. There's also an imaginative range of salads for vegetarians craving respite from the standard Argentinian *ensalada mixta* of lettuce, tomato and onion.

Peña Bajada España

Costanera *España & el Río (0341 449 6801). Open noon-4pm, 9pm-3am Mon-Sat; noon-4pm Sun. ££. No credit cards. Seafood.*
Parque de España is lined with fancy restaurants and glass-walled gyms, whose patrons can show off their toned physiques. It's all change, however, if you take a rickety lift below the boardwalk to this down-to-earth restaurant in an old fishermen's club. At night, pull up one of the plastic chairs, get stuck into the 'catch of the day' that typically

serves two, and watch the Rio Paraná slowly fade to black between the foliage of palm trees and weeping willows.

Pobla del Mercat

Centro *Salta 1424 (0341 447 1240/www.pobla delmercat.com). Open 10.30am-3pm, from 7.30pm Mon-Fri; from 7.30pm Sat. £££. Modern.*

'Your tastes don't change, they evolve', reads the menu tagline here – and sure enough, Pobla del Mercat marks an evolution in Rosario's restaurant scene. This is the place to leave the city's student population behind and join a mature crowd of food-lovers as they relish the work of the city's most creative young chef – and renowned perfectionist – Luciano Nanni. Expect to find tapas with a dash of molecular foam; a delicate amuse-bouche served between courses; and an intriguing range of home-made ice-creams (try the *dulce de leche* with cognac). Wine is not taken lightly here (literally – you could kill a person with one blow from the hefty menu); each bottle is listed with a take-away price in case you want to leave with a souvenir, and there's a downstairs cellar to browse between courses. If you're in a group of four or more, call ahead to book one of the back-room tables, where you'll feel like you're at a private dinner party among the velvet drapes, as opposed to being with the masses in the stylish but slightly sterile main room.

Verde Que Te Quiero Verde

Centro *Córdoba 1358, Palace Garden, 1st floor (0341 530 4419/www.verdequetequiero.com). Open 8am-9pm Mon-Sat. ££. Vegetarian.*

In most places, shopping arcades mean only one thing on the menu: greasy fast food. The pocket-sized Palace Garden mall breaks all the rules by offering one of the most virtuous eateries in town. Main courses, which include quinoa risottos and Thai-inspired stir-fry dishes, can be hit and miss on the flavour front, but you can't go wrong with the plentiful Saturday brunch buffet (11am-3pm), which sees a central table loaded with inventive salads, tarts, cakes and home-made jams. Vegetarians should also try Sana Sana (Alvear 14 bis, 0341 438 2036, www.sana-sana.com.ar).

Shop

Shopping in Rosario is a fairly metropolitan affair, but siesta rules still apply: many shops shut in early afternoon and reopen around 5pm. The city has two big malls: Portal Rosario (Nansen 255, www.portalshopping.com.ar) and the more attractive Alto Rosario (Junin 501, www.alto-rosario.com.ar), which occupies a converted train depot. Don't miss Pichincha's excellent antiques market, known as La Huella (the footprint). It's located along Avenida Rivadavia between Ovidio Lagos and Rodríguez and held on Sundays and holidays from 10am until 8pm.

Dionysos

Centro *Rioja 1598 (0341 445 2355/www.dionysos. com.ar). Open 10am-7.30pm Mon-Sat.*

This irreverent, all-in-one shop has made its home in a palatial white building and sells funky local goods for both the body and the home, as well as housing an art space. The shop stocks a number of domestic clothing labels, such as streetwear king A Y Not Dead, the whimsical neon designs of Juana de Arco and the edgy tailored menswear of BA-based clothing store Bolivia. Also on the racks are international brands such as Converse and Diesel.

Mercado de Diseño

Centro *Córdoba 2073 (0341 425 4769/www.mercado dedisenio.com). Open 10am-8pm Mon-Sat.*

An epicentre of creativity, the Mercado de Diseño has caught the attention of most shoppers in Rosario, and some in Buenos Aires, for its unflagging dedication to hawking imaginative clothes, objects and accessories by independent designers. Invited virtuosos from around the country collaborate to dress up the storefront and decorate the walls, encouraging an atmosphere of all-out artistry. The shop has a lovely courtyard and bar, which open up for the occasional soirée.

Arts

All Rosario is a stage – or so it seems. From cafés to bookshops, everywhere appears to have an area, or small corner, set aside for performances. The city also has a great theatre scene, the best venues being El Círculo (Laprida 1223, 0341 424 5349, www.teatro-elcirculo. com.ar) and Teatro Astengo (Mitre 754, 0341 448 1150, www.fundacionastengo.org.ar). Rosario is known for its discerning audiences; many shows touring the nation make this city their first stop, in the belief that if a show can succeed here, it can succeed anywhere. The city also has a thriving visual arts scene. Keep an eye out for works by local artists reproduced on the sides of buildings around town.

La Casa del Tango

Costanera *Arturo Illia 1701 & España (0341 449 4666/www.lacasadeltangorosario.com). Open 11.30am-4pm, from 8.30pm Tue-Sun.*

In Rosario, tango has yet to experience the full renaissance that it has had in Buenos Aires, yet it is making a quiet comeback that looks set to accelerate now that La Casa del Tango is heading the scene. Converted from an old water storage unit, the *casa* cuts a rather grand figure in Parque de España, and offers a slick show from Wednesday to Saturday. There's also a café and a parrilla that serves a mean *bife de chorizo*, with chips as sharp as a gaucho's knife.

Macro

Costanera *Oroño & el Río (0341 489 4981/www. macromuseo.org.ar). Open 2-8pm Mon, Tue, Thur-Sun. Admission AR$4; AR$2 reductions.*

Macro (Museo de Arte Contemporáneo de Rosario) is 21st-century Rosario encapsulated – and in a vibrant package of green, violet, blue and magenta. The boldly repainted silo

Clockwise from top: Parque de la Independencia; central Rosario; Pichincha.

was opened to the public in 2004 as a modern annex to the city's fine arts museum. The best way to approach its thought-provoking collection is to head up to the top floor in the lift and then work your way down. You never know quite what to expect here: serious documentary photography on one level gives way to abstract installations, such as live canaries in a cage, on the next. Families with some knowledge of Spanish should visit on Saturday, when children from five to ten years old get to role-play as detectives on a series of challenges around the gallery; it's an open event with no set hours, but children must be accompanied by an adult.

Nightlife

Rosario is famed for its nightlife – known as *la movida* (the scene). But be warned, this is not a seven-night-a-week city. If you want to party, you need to time your visit for a weekend. As in the rest of the country, clubs don't get started until the early hours. Good places for warm-up drinks are Davis (*see below*), Chinchibira (*see p85*) and Metropolitan Bar (*see p86*).

Café de la Musica
Centro *Santa Fe 2018 (0341 449 2617/www.cafedela musica.com). Open 7.30am-8.30pm Mon-Thur; 7.30am-2am Fri, Sat. ££.*
This sweet 1920s townhouse with a patio courtyard makes for a sophisticated yet laid-back night out. The decor is an elegant blend of dark wood and black and white tiles, with ivy creeping up the outside walls. Evenings bring performances of jazz, bossa nova and tango, accompanied by a menu of home-made pasta, *picadas* and some sinful desserts. The café is handily located just off Plaza San Martín.

> **"The Savoy's makeover into the grand-by-name, grand-by-nature Esplendor Savoy Rosario has finally given the city some accommodation worth talking about."**

Davis
Costanera *Avenida La Costa Brigadier Estanislao López 2550, & Oroño (0341 435 7142). Open 9am-midnight Mon-Fri; 8am-midnight Sat, Sun.*
Davis was the company that owned the silo that became the city's iconic Macro museum (*see p86*), and this modern, glass-fronted bar now sits at the museum's foot. By day it's a relaxed place to pull up a seat under a parasol; by night a hip crowd of barflies gather under the blue neon lighting. At any time of day or night, don't forget your designer sunglasses.

MDM (Madame)
Pichincha *Brown 3126 (0341 15 620 5739 mobile/ www.mdmdisco.com). Open 1-5.30am Fri, Sat. Admission AR$20-$25.*
This huge brick building's days as a working brewery may be over, but it's still managing to churn out the drinks in its reincarnation as South America's biggest club, with 19 bars, seven dance floors and four levels. Glitter balls, thumping music and sweaty crowds make it a love-it-or-hate-it venue. MDM, often referred to locally as simply Madame, also prides itself on top-notch security and an over-25s policy.

Stay

Rosario's hotel scene has long been all about serviceable mid-range establishments, with a handful of slightly faded four-star numbers, but this situation could be about to change. The old Savoy's makeover into the grand-by-name, grand-by-nature Esplendor Savoy Rosario has finally given the city some accommodation worth talking about, as will another renovation project that will soon transform an old silo in Puerto Norte into a glass-topped boutique hotel as part of the Ciudad Ribera project.

Esplendor Savoy Rosario
Centro *San Lorenzo 1022 (0341 448 0074/ www.esplendorsavoyrosario.com). ££.*
Following a stunning restoration programme, the Savoy is back – and just in time for its centenary in 2010. The developers have managed to retain the hotel's sense of history, while giving it a cutting-edge look that elevates it a notch above every other hotel in town. Grand, sweeping staircases and wide, tiled corridors lead off into spacious suites. Some of the smaller rooms have rather poky bathrooms, but this can be attributed to the makeover having stayed true to the building's design. At the time of writing, a huge street-side bar and restaurant were being dusted off, while a gym, spa and pool were under construction in the hotel's basement.

Garden Hotel
Pichincha *Callao 45 (0341 437 0025/ www.hotelgardensa.com). £.*
The best asset here is – as you might have guessed – the garden, which offers plenty of space to pull out a sun lounger, and has a good-sized pool. Inside the hotel, floral bedspreads continue the garden theme, as does the plant-filled atrium in the lobby and, more tenuously, the spa's grass-coloured flooring, possibly last seen on a pool table. The reception is slightly old-fashioned, but the rooms are decent, the four-bed ones being good options for small groups or families.

Esplendor Savoy Rosario.

Hotel Boulevard

Pichincha *San Lorenzo 2194 (0341 447 5795/ www.hotelboulevard.com.ar). £.*
One of Rosario's very few B&Bs is housed in a beautiful 1920s mansion, just off palm-lined Boulevard Oroño. The matrimonial room is the one to book; it has its own private bathroom and high wooden shutters that swing out to offer romantic views across the grand boulevard below. The other seven rooms share a bathroom, though there are plans to make them en suite. The decor is plain but classic.

"With no sign outside, Lungomare Trieste feels even more like one of Rosario's best-kept secrets."

Lungomare Trieste

Pichincha *Tucumán 2687 (0341 439 8887/ www.lungomarebb.com). £.*
Run by the eager-to-help Oliver, with his mother Monica and sister Alejandra, this cheerful townhouse is Rosario's best home-from-home experience. Lungomare Trieste was the name of the street where Monica's mother lived in southern Italy, and the European heritage doesn't stop there: the house itself is Catalan in style, with original tiles to prove it. The five bedrooms are painted in vibrant colours and come with private bathrooms. Upstairs is a small roof terrace with a *pileta* (plunge pool). The location is ideal for exploring Pichincha, and having no sign outside makes this B&B feel even more like one of Rosario's best-kept secrets.

Río Grande

Centro *Dorrego 1261 (0341 424 1144/ www.riograndeapart.com.ar). ££.*
This small apart-hotel's plain exterior belies its surprisingly modern interiors. Sporting the classic red, white and black uniform of an aspiring boutique hotel, the 15 apartments have king-size beds, flatscreen TVs and kitchenettes; those containing two small double beds are good for families. The location makes it a handy base for sightseeing.

Ros Tower

Centro *Mitre 299 (0341 529 9000/ www.rostower.com.ar). £££.*
Encased in a sturdy high-rise and possessing an equally sturdy reputation, this grand hotel and convention centre opened in 2006, amid much fanfare, as the city's first five-star accommodation. It's an accolade the hotel still wears proudly, with guests greeted by doormen in top hats and tails, and whirled ceremoniously through the lobby's revolving doors. The decor is far from imaginative, but the Ros Tower doesn't aim to surprise, it aims to deliver. Service is ever-courteous and rooms have all the hallmarks of classic luxury: widescreen TVs, sink-in pillows and marble bathrooms. There's also a small rooftop pool and jacuzzi.

Factfile

When to go

Rosario is considered as having a pampean climate, meaning the seasons aren't well defined. It's generally hot between November and March, and cold between June and August. Tourism (mainly domestic) focuses on weekends or holiday periods. Be sure to visit at the weekend if you want to party, and in low season if you want some space on Florida beach.

Getting there

Rosario is located 300 kilometres north-west of Buenos Aires. The trip between the cities takes four hours 30 minutes by bus. Rosario's bus station, Mariano Moreno, is located ten minutes from the city centre, at Cafferata 702 (0341 437 3030, www.terminalrosario.com.ar). The airport, which is served by Aerolíneas Argentinas (www.aerolineas.com.ar), is 13 kilometres from the centre. Trains run from Buenos Aires' Retiro station and take six hours 30 minutes (Trenes de Buenos Aires, 0800 3333 822, www.tbanet. com.ar; Ferrocentral, 0800 1221 8736, www. ferrocentralsa.com.ar).

Getting around

With a relatively compact city centre, most of Rosario's sites can be seen on foot, with an occasional taxi hop to the northern beaches. There is also a good bus system, but be warned that on football days public transport is overrun with rowdy fans and is best avoided.

Tourist information

Ente Turístico Rosario Avenida Belgrano & Buenos Aires (0341 480 2230, www.rosario turismo.com). Open 9am-7pm daily.
There is also an information point, with the same opening hours, at Mariano Moreno bus terminal.

Internet

Wi-Fi is available in most modern hotels, as well as many of the city's restaurants and cafés. Public Wi-Fi is available in the city centre (Monumento de la Bandera, Plaza 25 de Mayo & Avenida Córdoba).
There's an internet café at Urquiza & Moreno, open 8am-11pm daily.

Central Rosario

ISLA DEL ESPINILLO

RÍO PARANÁ

Alto Rosario Shopping
Museo Ferroviaria
AV. CENTRAL ARGENTINO
Parque Scalabrini Ortiz
AV. MONGSFELD

AVENIDA E. LÓPEZ
AV. CASEROS
AV. FRANCIA

Parque Sunchales
Estación Rosario Norte
Museo de Arte Contemporáneo
AV. DEL VALLE

Parque Rodríguez
Parque de las Colectividades

AVENIDA WHEELWRIGHT

La Isla de los Inventos

AV. DEL HUERTO

Parque de España

PICHINCHA
DR. LUIS AGOTE
Estación Terminal de Omnibus
Hospital Provincial del Centenario
Parque Pres. Juan D. Perón
Facultad de Ciencias Médicas

SALTA
CATAMARCA
SANTA FE
CÓRDOBA

Iglesia María Auxiliadora

CATAMARCA
Plaza Zabala Zabala
Tribunales Federales
Edificio de Aduana
Parque Nacional de la Bandera

Museo de Ciencias Naturales Dr. Angel Gallardo
Plaza Cívica
Biblioteca Argentina Juan Álvarez
Facultad de Derecho
Plaza San Martín
Plaza Pringles
Bolsa de Comercio

Palacio Fuentes
Museo Municipal de Arte Decorativo
Palacio Municipal
Plaza 25 de Mayo
Monumento Nacional a la Bandera
Catedral de Rosario

CENTRO II
PASEO DEL SIGLO
MENDOZA
Facultad de Ciencias Económicas

CENTRO

Plaza Montenegro
Plaza Sarmiento
Centro Cultural Bernardino Rivadavia
Estación Belgrano
Parque Belgrano

AV. DE LA LIBERTAD
AVENIDA BELGRANO

Museo Municipal de Bellas Artes Juan B. Castagnino

Universidad Tecnológica Nacional

Plaza Bélgica
Parque Urquiza
Anfiteatro Municipal Humberto de Nito
Complejo Astronómico Municipal

Cementerio El Salvador
Plaza de la Lealtad
Jardín Francés
Club A. Newell's Old Boys
Museo Histórico Provincial
Jardín de los Niños
Club Gimnasia y Esgrima de Rosario
Plaza del Foro Dr. V. Sarsfield
Plaza Int. Lamas
AVENIDA PELLEGRINI

AV. INT. MORCILLO
AV. LO VALVO

Hipódromo
PARQUE INDEPENDENCIA
Club A. Provincial
Rosedal
Museo de la Ciudad
Jardín Botánico

AVENIDA PELLEGRINI
Plaza López
Instituto Politécnico

ABASTO
REPÚBLICA DE LA SEXTA

Plaza Libertad

BOULEVARD 27 DE FEBRERO
Plazoleta Tte. Aviador A. Vázquez

Estación Central Córdoba

Centro Universitario Rosario

JORGE CURA
Hospital de Niños Victor J. Vilela
ESPAÑA Y HOSPITALES
Hospital de Emergencias Dr. Clemente Alvarez
Parque Yrigoyen
Plaza Biblioteca C. Vigil

Club Atlético Provincial

SAN MARTÍN

300 m
300 yds

© Copyright Time Out Group 2009

Rural Escapes

Clockwise from bottom left: La Sirena (2); wind generators at La Vigna, Colonia Valdense.

El campo

Uruguay

Pure countryside, with little tourism and lots of potential.

The farthest reaches of tiny Uruguay are just a few hours from Buenos Aires, through lush pine and eucalyptus forests, storybook hills and vast savannahs. The country's interior is little visited by outsiders, making these oft overlooked lands unrivalled territory for a holiday of easy exploring.

With most of the nation's people clinging to the coast, only around a million souls populate the entire interior of Uruguay, meaning bona fide gaucho culture is alive and well. Most estancias are first and foremost working ranches, so guests can be fairly certain that the daily cattle round-up is not staged simply for their viewing pleasure.

The inhabitants of the Uruguayan *campo* (countryside), though living well back from the Atlantic, still gravitate to the shores, but this time to those that stretch alongside the Río Uruguay and Río Negro, in an area known as El Litoral. Here, work and play are divided between the sprawling riverside farmlands and the slow-moving rivulets that wind through the region. Meanwhile, recent times have seen an upswing to the country's little-known, century-old wine culture, which is centred in the Canelones area, just north of Montevideo. Even further inland, Treinta y Tres offers idyllic scenery for hiking and horse riding.

However, the incomparable advantage of a visit to the Uruguayan campo is the delightfully unexplored feel of the place. The little tourism that does exist here is generated by national visitors, plus a handful of in-the-know Brazilians and Argentinians. Bank on a crowd-free holiday among plenty of friendly locals. Bring your riding boots, outdoor clothes and a spirit of adventure; leave the mobile and laptop at home.

Explore

Touring the interior of Uruguay makes for a glorious road trip. Distances are easily manageable and the *campo* can be dipped into as a short inland diversion from one of the country's more established destinations – such as Montevideo (*see pp62-77*) and Colonia del Sacramento (*see pp138-47*) – which lie along its rim. Lovely estancias can be found, but with plenty of space in between.

CANELONES

Situated just north of Montevideo, the softly undulating hills surrounding **Canelones** are home to the bulk of Uruguay's wineries, many of which have been in the owners' families for generations. Here, away from the massive continental shadow cast by the Andean wine giants, Uruguay has a sneaky trick up its sleeve in the form of tannat, the country's signature grape variety, which is gradually gaining popularity.

Tours to bodegas in this close-knit area can be arranged through the well-organised Los Caminos del Vino (099 149662, www.uruguaywinetours. com). The following wineries offer tastings, with advance notice, and some also have restaurants. If you are setting off from Montevideo, you can start your wine tour at the paramount Bouza Bodega Boutique (*see p66*).

Castillo Viejo

Las Piedras, 25km NE of Montevideo *Ruta 68, km 24 (02 368 9606/www.castilloviejo.com). Open by appointment 8am-noon, 2-6pm Mon-Fri. Tours by appointment. Tour price UR$345.*
Castillo Viejo's tannat has caught the attention of oenophiles around the world, and is one of Uruguay's best-sellers. In operation since 1927, the winery is one of the country's bigger set-ups, producing over a million litres of wine per year. Upscale tastings are held in the restored brick cellar.

Filgueira

Cuchilla Verde, 65km NE of Montevideo *Ruta 81, km 7, Riberas del Río Santa Lucia (033 46438/www. bodegafilgueira.com). Open 9am-3pm Mon-Wed, Fri. Tours Mon-Sat by appointment. Tour price UR$300.*
This pretty, family-run vineyard was established by a Galician in the early 20th century near the banks of the Río Santa Lucia. Though tannat is the bodega's pride and joy, the sauvignon gris is also recommended, and can be combined with a hearty meal or cheese platter. Reservations for meals, private tastings, and the guided tour (which includes a wine tasting) are requested, with 48 hours' notice; walk-ins will be met with a flurry of confusion. Otherwise, turn up during opening hours for a simple tour with no extras.

Juanicó

38km NE of Montevideo *Ruta 5, km 38.2 (033 59725/094 847482/www.juanico.com). Open 9am-6pm daily. Tours 10am, 1pm, 3pm Mon-Sat; 9am, noon, 2pm Sun. Tour price UR$400-$1,200.*

El campo

Historic sites
● ● ○ ○ ○

Art & architecture
● ○ ○ ○ ○

Hotels
● ● ● ○ ○

Eating & drinking
● ● ● ○ ○

Scenery
● ● ● ● ○

Outdoor activities
● ● ● ● ○

Río Negro.

Tannat is the main player at 180-year-old Juanicó, where oak barrels age the rich wines in a stone cellar built by the family patriarch in 1830. The rest of the establishment is far from old-fashioned, however, featuring state of the art technologies gathered on the proprietor's travels around Argentina, Chile, the US and Australia. Winery tours include a stroll through the vineyards and a closer look at the ultra-modern production system, and are followed by a tasting session. Reservations are recommended, and essential if you choose to take the tour that includes lunch at an extra cost.

Pizzorno Family Estates
Canelón Chico, 23km N of Montevideo *Ruta 32, km 23 (02 368 9601/www.pizzornowines.com). Open 7.30am-6pm Mon-Fri; 7.30am-noon Sat. Tours by appointment. Tour price UR$232.*
The century-old Pizzorno winery carries on the original boutique practices of harvesting, bottling and corking its blends by hand. Proprietor Carlos Pizzorno began adapting Uruguay's premium varietals of pinot noir, sauvignon blanc and tannat into more palatable blends in the 1980s. Today, his fusions are beginning to make small inroads into the international market. Reservations – for tours or for lunch – are essential.

Viñedo de los Vientos
Atlántida, 45km NE of Montevideo *Ruta 11, km 162 (037 21622/099 372723/www.vinedodelos vientos.com). Open 9am-5pm daily. Tours by appointment. Tour prices UR$232-$579.*
Bodega kingpin and unconventional oenologist Pablo Fallabrino takes a sustainable approach to harvesting grapes and uses unorthodox tactics to produce the wide range of blends at his family's 75-year-old operation. Most of Viñedo de los Vientos's boutique vintages are marketed in the US, including the unique unfiltered ripasso de tannat and the grappa-fortified alcyone. With 24 hours' notice, basic tastings and gourmet food and wine pairings can be enjoyed in the restaurant, the Winery Kitchen.

EL LITORAL
The sleepy river towns of western Uruguay are whistle-stops along the mighty Río Uruguay, which is known as the 'river of the painted birds' in the Guaraní language. The river runs alongside the western border of the country before emptying out into the Río de la Plata estuary in the south, with Río Negro jutting in from the east. The Río Uruguay dominates activity in this region, known as **El Litoral**, which is dappled with little islands. In the 19th century, Carlos IV of Spain believed this water had healing powers and used to ship barrels of it back to Europe.

In more recent times, the zone has been rattled by a conflict between Uruguay and Argentina over the operation of a paper mill that has caused Argentinian protesters to block the bridge linking Gualeguaychú in Argentina to Fray Bentos in Uruguay. This was previously one of the principal access routes between the two countries, and El Litoral, which relies heavily on holidaying Argentinians, has been suffering a drop in tourist numbers as a result.

With its lovely riverside promenade and quiet, tree-lined, cobblestone streets, **Mercedes** is one of El Litoral's prettiest towns. The neoclassical Catedral de Nuestra Señora de las Mercedes on the main plaza, Plaza Independencia, was constructed between 1788 and 1867, although its stately twin towers were an early-20th century afterthought. It is widely regarded as one of Uruguay's most impressive cathedrals.

Some 30 kilometres west of Mercedes is the town of **Fray Bentos**, best known for an obsolete slaughterhouse that attracted hordes of immigrant workers in the 1940s and now functions as a quirky museum.

From Mercedes, you can also take a side trip to pretty **Villa Soriano**, 32 kilometres south-west, at the junction of the Río Uruguay and the Río Negro. Uruguay's first European settlement, Villa Soriano was founded in 1624, which gives it 50 years on its popular younger brother, Colonia del Sacramento. Tourist information can be found at www.villasoriano.net, through which guided tours can also be arranged.

Further inland, Easter week gets rowdy at the massive annual beer festival in Paysandú (www.paysandu.com/semana), and Tacuarembó hosts a huge annual gaucho festival in November (*see p386* **Festivals & Events**).

Museo de la Revolución Industrial
Fray Bentos *Avenida Dr Andrés Montaño, no number, Barrio Anglo (056 23690/056 22918). Open 9am-6.30pm daily. Tours Jan-Mar 10am, 6pm daily; July-Sept 10am, 3pm daily; Apr-June, Oct-Dec 10am daily. Admission UR$20, UR$30 with tour.*
Situated on the lower level of the imposing, abandoned waterfront factory that housed the Liebig Extract of Meat Company is this engrossing museum that tracks the production of the world-famous Oxo beef cube. It shut its doors for good in 1979, though in its heyday the factory was the biggest industrial powerhouse in Uruguay, exporting meat products to all reaches of the globe.

TREINTA Y TRES
This placid section of eastern Uruguay, in the province of **Treinta y Tres** (with its eponymous capital), is thinly populated and devoted mainly to cultivating pine forests and rearing cattle. The natural beauty of the hills remains practically untouched, making for wonderful outdoor excursions and scenic drives.

Quebrada de los Cuervos, 24 kilometres west of Treinta y Tres, provides one of the more spectacular encounters with the eastern Uruguayan ecosystem. Spread out over 360 hectares, this gap in the Sierras de Yerbal has a dramatic matrix of creeks and streams, which wind through jagged hills and cliffs to create an ideal landscape for low-impact climbing, hiking

Ruta 26, between
Paysandú & Tacuarembó.

Clockwise from bottom left: Estancia Paz (4). Fortín de San Miguel (2).

or just wandering around the well-maintained trails to take in the area's rich native flora and fauna. Birdwatching is also excellent here. Check out www.turismo33.com.uy for more information.

OUTDOOR ACTIVITIES

Explore Uruguay's largely untainted ecosystem by tracking regional migratory birds through palm groves, subtropical estuaries and rugged mountains with Guyrapyta Birdwatching (094 427409, www.birdwatching-guyrapyta.com), which runs one- to 15-day tours.

Other ecotours can be arranged through Canelones-based Aqva Terra (0376 1276, www.aqvaterra.com), which specialises in bespoke trips catering to various interests. Horse riding excursions that head into the interior are available through Hidden Trails (+1 888 987 2457 US, www.hiddentrails.com) and the Spain-based Safari Riding (+34 934 069849, www.safaririding.com).

"Expect finger-licking regional cuisine, the way it would have been had grandma been raised in Uruguay."

Eat

Steak and spuds reign this side of the Río de la Plata, just as they do across the way in Argentina. Upmarket cuisine is best left to the hotels and wineries; many country estancias will serve delicious home-made meals of local cuisine to non-guests who give notice (ideally 48 hours). Expect finger-licking regional cuisine, the way it would have been had grandma been raised in Uruguay. Bodegas with recommended restaurants include Filgueira (see p96) and Viñedo de los Vientos (see p98).

El Tannat

Mal Abrigo, 90km SE of Colonia del Sacramento *Ruta 23, km 125 (034 03118/www.fincapiedra.com). Open noon-3pm, 8-11pm Sat; noon-3pm Sun. ££££. Parrilla.*
Organic, home-grown eats are the chief speciality of this restaurant at the Estancia Finca Piedra, located a 90-minute drive east of Colonia del Sacramento. Typical fare includes the treasured mixed-meat parrilla, prepared painstakingly over an open-pit grill in the wooden-beamed dining salon. Accompany your meal with a hearty tannat, aged on site.

The estancia can also arrange a *dia de campo* (day in the country), which for UR$1,160 includes wine tasting, horse riding and lunch. Accommodation is also available on the estancia, with 13 rooms offered.

Stay

Estancia Paz

30km N of Treinta y Tres *Ruta 8, km 316 (099 878313/0450 2977/www.estanciapaz.com). ££.*
The warm and welcoming Panizza family receives guests at this gorgeous estancia with an open-door policy that extends from the pool and the horses right down to the refrigerator. Following stints in Miami and Barcelona, brothers Martin and Rafael returned to their homeland and began restoring the colonial house with hopes of attracting friends to visit their peaceful little corner of the Uruguayan countryside; the idea of opening the property to visitors as a business was an afterthought. Five ample suites are tastefully furnished with a mix of auction finds and stunning leather-and-wood pieces made on site; for extra space, ask for the farm-facing master loft.

La Estiria

Flores, 80km E of Mercedes *Ruta 3, km 209.3 (099 607789/0360 4136/www.laestiria.com). ££.*
A working ranch that offers guest lodgings in a lovingly restored foreman's house, La Estiria is an ideal option for those heading into the heart of Uruguay's countryside. Couples will want to claim one of the two spacious double suites. Guests are invited to while away their days traipsing through the surrounding forests on horse back, exploring the nearby territory in a 4x4, or giving a hand around the farm. Tasty meals are accompanied by flavourful regional wines in the country-chic dining room – unless, of course, the outdoor parrilla is fired up for a massive afternoon *asado*.

La Sirena

15km E of Mercedes *Ruta 14 (099 102130/ 053 02271/www.lasirena.com.uy). ££.*
Trade in Egyptian cotton sheets and poolside lazing for fresh air and wholesome hinterland fun at this colonial estate along the sandy shores of the Rio Negro. It's a working cattle and wheat farm, as well as a country retreat that's ideal for horse riding and river outings. The beautiful, 200-year-old *hacienda* was reopened to guests a decade ago by the delightful Rodney and Lucia Bruce, who rescued the decaying property from a gang of feuding brothers and painstakingly restored the broken tiles, wooden mantels and wrought ironwork. The rooms are rustically furnished, with antique wardrobes and lovely wood-inlaid floors.

San Pedro de Timote

142km NE of Montevideo *Ruta 7, km 142 (0310 808688/www.sanpedrodetimote.com). £££.*
With its throng of horses, inviting pools, tennis courts and colonial chapel, San Pedro de Timote is a vision of rural bliss. This well-run country hotel, built in 1854, is now

recognised as a national historical monument, and has been carefully looked after during its long and illustrious existence. Gargantuan in Uruguayan estancia terms, it has 40 rooms, each with a wood stove and private bathroom.

"A combination of innate creativity and sheer hardwork has given La Vigna new life as an 'art and *agro*' hideaway."

La Vigna
Colonia Valdense, 120km W of Montevideo *Ruta 51, km 120 (0558 9234/www.lavigna.com.uy). ££.*
Tucked away in the sleepy countryside midway between Colonia del Sacramento and Montevideo, this 19th-century bodega was little more than a shell when Argentinian couple Lucila and Agustín first fell in love with it. A combination of innate creativity and sheer hard work has

given it new life as an 'art and *agro*' hideaway, notable for its rustic charm and phenomenal attention to detail. On-site facilities include an art workshop, an Outback-style swimming pool and an intimate restaurant with inventive set menus. All the food is home-made and organic, including the increasingly renowned cheese made with milk from the establishment's own sheep. Choose to enjoy your after-dinner drinks in front of the roaring open fire or sip them outside, in a hammock-like bed suspended under a canopy of trees.

FURTHER AFIELD

Fortín de San Miguel
Chuy, 140km E of Treinta y Tres *Ruta 19, Paraje 18 de Julio (0474 6607/www.elfortin.com). £.*
Just below the Brazilian border at Chuy, this hotel is a little slice of living history. It is located alongside Fuerte San Miguel, an early 18th-century Spanish fort that has been declared a national monument, and surrounded by palm-dotted subtropical pampas that are ideal for horse riding. Though the restaurant is hardly gourmet, it redeems itself with an inviting continental breakfast. A stay here can be tacked on to a trip to the coast; Punta del Diablo (*see pp278-39*) is just 70km south.

Factfile

When to go
The interior of Uruguay is quiet and calm throughout the year, and is lovely – albeit steamy – in summer (January to March), when the masses make a beeline for the coastal beach resorts. November and March are ideal, as they are temperate, low-season months. Crackling fires can make the relatively mild winter season of June to August rather atmospheric.

Getting there
Many visitors to Uruguay fly directly into Montevideo or get transport from Buenos Aires via Buquebus (www.buquebus.com) or Colonia Express (www.coloniaexpress.com) ferries, both of which serve the ports in Colonia and Montevideo. Driving from Argentina to Uruguay is also an option, via the Colón-Paysandú bridge.

Getting around
Uruguay has excellent bus services, with most routes starting or ending up in Montevideo. Heading laterally across Uruguay may pose a few problems time-wise, as there are limited direct services. Timetables can be accessed through the website of Montevideo's Tres Cruces terminal (www.trescruces.com.uy).
Hiring a car is the better option. The paved main roads are in tip-top condition, although side roads tend to be gravel or dirt. Note that some

water crossings that look possible on a map may be passable by ferries only, meaning that you have to cross before those manning the ferries finish for the evening. Multicar (02 902 2555, www.redmulticar.com) offers great rates and service, as does Thrifty (0800 8278, www.thrifty.com.uy).
Lares (02 901 9120, 099 592009, www.lares.com.uy) and Cecilia Regules Viajes (02 916 3011, 02 916 3012, www.ceciliaregules viajes.com) both handle rural estancia tourism, and can arrange visits.

Tourist information
Tourist offices are not common outside of the country's main hubs. Information can be found on www.turismo.gub.uy and www.visit-uruguay.com.

Internet
Some estancias in the Uruguayan *campo* have internet and even Wi-Fi, but it is best not to rely on it. Internet cafes can be found in most reasonably sized towns.
In Mercedes, El Byte (Colón 390, 053 27700) is open Mar-Nov 10am-10pm Mon-Sat; Dec-Feb 9am-1pm, 5pm-midnight Mon-Sat. The best approach, however, is to check your emails in larger places, such as Montevideo and Colonia del Sacramento, and then make the most of switching off.

La Vigna.

San Antonio
de Areco.

San Antonio de Areco & Around

Argentina

Estancias, gauchos and the dizzying expanse of the pampas.

To drive out of Buenos Aires is to swap the most European of cities for the most American of landscapes. Welcome to the pampas, Argentina's vast, flat heartland; an area which is as rich in heritage as its geography is austere. Small towns such as San Antonio de Areco and Luján, both just a short trip from the capital, allow the traveller a vantage point on the *campo* (countryside) and its people. Pre-dating the towns, and deeper still inside this tamed wilderness, are the large estancias founded by the 19th-century cattle barons who ruthlessly forced Argentina's transformation from post-colonial backwater to economic powerhouse. Many of these aristocratic country mansions are now open as luxury bolt-holes for tourists.

As influential as Argentina's rural oligarchy was (and still is), it is hardly the stuff of song, poetry or legend. That role belongs to the gaucho. Living partly on horseback, partly around the campfire – and wholly on their wits – these *criollo* cowboys were, from their berets to their boots, the antithesis of European urbanity. Their legacy is everything that is most 'Argentinian' about the pampas: the handcrafted silverware, the folkloric music, the traditional dress and customs. This legacy is ongoing; unlike the cowboy of the American West, the gaucho has survived into the modern age with many traditions intact. Don't imagine that those men in espadrilles and *bombachas* (billowing trousers) striding around San Antonio de Areco are hired by the tourist board.

Delving into gaucho lore is one reason to visit the pampas but, increasingly, it's far from the only one. Estancia owners are incorporating (mostly tasteful) modern amenities into their ancestral estates; once-deserted railway towns are filling up again with day-trippers on shopping and dining jaunts; and world-class polo schools are drawing in everyone from profesionals to curious beginners. But if your only reason for visiting the pampas is to stretch out under a prodigious blue sky and forget about malls, roads and airports for a few precious moments, that's reason enough.

Explore

The pampas (the word means 'plains' in the Quechua language) are grasslands; fertile plains that cover over 700,000 square kilometres, stretching from the Atlantic Ocean to the Andes mountains. The size of this region dwarfs that of most European countries but, conveniently for the tourist, many of its most interesting visitor attractions are located just north-west of Buenos Aires. A one-hour journey from the city puts you in the middle of cattle country, where grassy plains, interrupted by small towns and estancias, stretch to the horizon in all directions.

SAN ANTONIO DE ARECO

Nicknamed the 'cradle of tradition' and immortalised in Ricardo Güiraldes's 1926 novel *Don Segundo Sombra*, **San Antonio de Areco** is just over 100 kilometres from Buenos Aires. It's an easy day trip, but the town and its surroundings warrant at least an overnight stay. Sitting on the banks of the Río Areco, San Antonio de Areco is a gaucho hub where residents can be seen sporting berets (*boinas*) and billowing trousers with chaps (*bombachas*), and where folkloric music is often performed in the plaza. Shops sell local artisans' work, including silver and leather, chocolate, and sheepskin apparel.

Historic buildings and art galleries surround the main square, Plaza Arellano de Ruiz, where the sound of dirt bikes blends with the engine noise of vintage Citroens and the squawks of migrating parakeets overhead. From the plaza, it's a short walk down calle Alsina to the Museo de Molina Campos, where some of the key works of Argentina's most famous visual chronicler of gaucho life are on display (*see p108*).

A right on Lavalle takes you towards La Olla de Cobre chocolate factory (Matheu 433, 02326 453105, www.laolladecobre.com.ar) – famous for its *alfajores* (biscuits filled with *dulce de leche*) and hot chocolate – with small boutiques to admire along the way. Lo de Arnaldi (Arellano 45, 02326 456641, www.lodearnaldi.com.ar) is a favourite for high-quality crafts and leather. Silversmith Juan Manuel Pereyra's shop (corner of Alsina & Zerboni, 02326 454843, www.areco plateria.com.ar) is a find for personalised silver belt buckles and jewellery.

If sleepy San Antonio de Areco has a high season, it's in November, when a buzz of rural activity leads up to the spirited gaucho festivities of the annual Día de la Tradición, celebrated on 10 November. Exhibitions of the traditional *gato* (cat) dance and performances by folkloric bands are coupled with feats of country skills and horsemanship, in a busy programme spread across two weeks. The celebrations culminate in the Día de la Tradición itself, with a procession

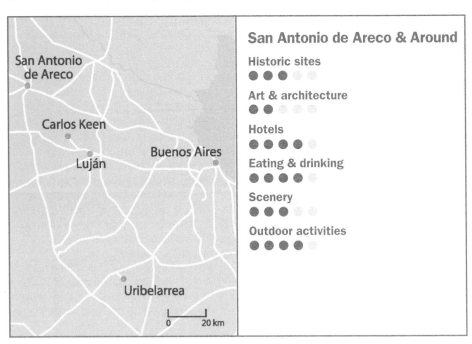

San Antonio de Areco & Around

Historic sites
● ● ● ○ ○

Art & architecture
● ● ○ ○ ○

Hotels
● ● ● ● ○

Eating & drinking
● ● ● ● ○

Scenery
● ● ● ○ ○

Outdoor activities
● ● ● ● ○

San Antonio de Areco

Carlos Keen

Luján

Buenos Aires

Uribelarrea

0   20 km

Clockwise from top left: abandoned petrol station on Ruta 11; La Candelaria; San Antonio de Areco (3); Chascomús.

of gauchos clad in full regalia, riding horses adorned with silver and gold.

The best way to experience San Antonio de Areco is to combine a trip to the town with a visit to one of the historic estancias located nearby. A *día de campo* is a half- or full-day visit to an estancia, and typically includes a grilled steak lunch, a horse ride and a show. A weekend stay offers more of the same, and allows more time for horseback riding, lounging by the pool, birdwatching and long country walks. El Ombú (*see p114*) offers a tasteful *día de campo*, and Inside the Pampas (011 4807 3450, www.inside thepampas.com), based just west of San Antonio de Areco, offers a twist on the standard package by giving visitors the chance to experience everything from herding and riding in traditional attire to attending a rodeo.

Museo Molina Campos de Areco
Moreno 279 (02326 456425/www.museomcdeareco. org). Open June-Aug 10am-6pm Fri-Sun. Sept-May 10am-8pm Fri-Sun. Admission AR$20; AR$10 reductions; free under-12s. No credit cards.
Even newcomers to Argentina might recognise the rubicund country figures in Florencio Molina Campos' iconic cartoons and paintings. The illustrator painted country scenes with a satirical and often grotesque edge. An artistic consultant to Disney studios, his illustrations usually poked fun at life on the ranch. This museum comprises three exhibition rooms; the admission fee includes a complimentary coffee and *medialuna* (croissant), served in the museum café.

Museo Taller Draghi
Lavalle 387 (02326 454219). Open 10am-1pm, 3.30-7.30pm Mon-Fri; 10am-1pm, 3-8pm Sat; 10am-1.30pm Sun. Guided tours 11am, noon, 4pm, 5pm, 6pm. Admission AR$5. No credit cards.
The work of world-renowned silversmiths Juan José Draghi and sons is displayed in all its burnished glory at this immensely popular workshop and museum (try to get there early to avoid the large tour groups). Jewellery such as brooches and hair clips, as well as scenic belt buckles, daggers and ornamental *mate* gourds, are among the gaucho items that have been transformed into valuable collectors' objects by these master craftsmen.

Parque Criollo y Museo Gauchesco Ricardo Güiraldes
Camino Güiraldes (02326 455839). Open 11am-5pm Mon, Wed-Sun. Admission AR$4; AR$1.50 reductions; free under-12s. No credit cards.
Güiraldes's novel *Don Segundo Sombra* is second only to José Hernández's *Martín Fierro* in the canon of Argentinian gaucho literature. This museum, which opened in 1938, pays homage to the writer, exhibiting early editions of *Don Segundo Sombra*, photos of the real-life characters from the book, and random curiosities such as an old and regal safety deposit box and a bed that once belonged to General Rosas (an Argentinian leader in the 19th century).

LUJÁN

Every October, a pilgrimage of almost one million Argentinians converges on the small city of **Luján**, some 70 kilometres north-west of Buenos Aires. The central Basílica de Nuestra Señora de Luján is a monumental neo-Gothic edifice, which was designed by French architect Ulderico Courtois and built in stages between 1889 and 1937.

The basilica's 100-metre twin spires can be seen for miles around, and the structure dominates the south side of the city's main square, Plaza Belgrano. Around it are dozens of *santerías*, or religious memento stores. If you're in the market for some holy water, a plastic Jesus or a Virgin Mary fridge magnet, step right up.

"Alongside the Río Luján, an old-fashioned boardwalk with amusement-park rides evokes a downsized Coney Island."

Of greater cultural interest is the Enrique Udaondo museum complex (02323 420245), which runs along the west side of the square on Lezica and Torrezouri. Its exhibition spaces are housed inside several contiguous colonial-era buildings, including the town's Cabildo (government house), which dates from 1872 and was used as a prison for British soldiers captured during the botched 'English Invasions' of 1806, and the Casa del Virrey (viceroy's residence), which has lovely gardens. The Museo de Transportes (exhibiting vintage cars and trains) complete the complex.

Behind the museums is the Río Luján. Along the riverfront, an old-fashioned boardwalk with amusement-park rides evokes a downsized Coney Island. There are paddle boats to rent, and children will enjoy riding the mini-train. Picnic tables and parrilla grills line the riverfront – it's a popular spot for family barbecues and languorous *mate*-drinking sessions.

Outside of Luján proper is a community called Open Door (*see p110* **Saddle up**), one of the foremost polo locations in the world. **Carlos Keen**, 15 kilometres north of Luján and easily accessible by bus or taxi, is a former railway town that has recently reinvented itself as a gourmet getaway for food-loving locals. Life in Carlos Keen once revolved around the central train station, but the focus has now shifted to the high-quality restaurants that have

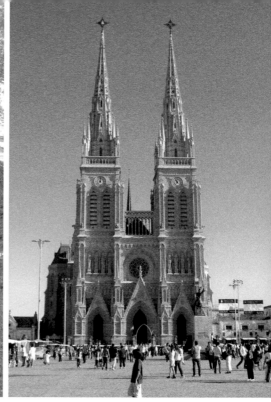

Clockwise from top left: Carlos Keen; Basílica de Nuestra Señora de Luján; a santería, Luján; Luján's amusement park.

sprung up in all corners of town. The picks of an impressive bunch are Angelus and La Casona (*see below*), which are packed with diners at weekends, in striking contrast to the deserted streets outside.

Wherever you pull up a seat, you're likely to find yourself next to Argentinians rather than fellow tourists, so be sure to adopt the national approach to social lunches by keeping them long and leisurely. Carlos Keen is certainly worth a detour, or a trip in its own right, but service is very much in tune with the tiny village's plodding pace of life.

Basílica de Nuestra Señora de Luján

San Martín 51 (02323 420058/www.basilicadelujan. org.ar). Open 10am-5pm Mon-Fri; 10am-6pm Sat, Sun. Admission AR$3. Guided tours by appointment, with 24hrs notice. Tours AR$50 for groups of 1-5; AR$5 per person for groups of 10 or more. No credit cards.

In 1630, Antonio Farías Sáa, a rich landowner, was travelling by oxen-pulled cart from Brazil to his home province of Santiago del Estero. His cargo included two icons of the Virgin Mary, which were to be the centrepieces of a new chapel on Sáa's estate. The cart, however, got stuck in some mud close to the Río Luján and despite the best efforts of man and beast, wouldn't budge. Only when one of the Virgins was removed from the cart, so the story goes, could the party continue its journey. Locals regarded this as a miracle, and built a makeshift chapel to house the Virgin. The chapel was rebuilt, enlarged, restored and replaced over the centuries until 1889, when work on the current neo-Gothic basilica began. Recent restoration of the exterior shows off the structure in all its glory, while inside, marble and chandeliers contrast with a surround-sound public address system and a pipe organ the size of a small apartment. Most pilgrims, however, come to see the original Virgin, Sáa's unwilling passenger, on display down in the crypt.

URIBELARREA

Much of the 1996 film *Evita*, starring Madonna, as well as Francis Ford Coppola's recent black and white flick *Tetro*, were filmed around the late 19th-century town of Uribelarrea (population: 900) located around 85 kilometres south-west of Buenos Aires. Small wonder it's popular with film directors – the impressively preserved, traditional country houses and tree-lined dirt roads of this railway town might have been built to a set designer's specifications.

Uribe, as locals call it, is the perfect setting for a bike ride back in time, pedalling around the town square and stopping to peek inside the neo-Gothic Iglesia Nuestra Señora de Luján. El Palenque, also on the main plaza, is a *pulpería* (rural general store and bar) and parrilla, which dates back to 1890. Like Carlos Keen, Uribelarrea's raison d'être was the railway line, and when the trains stopped in the 1970s the town's economy was drastically affected.

Eat

Angelus

Carlos Keen *San Carlos, no number, next to the church (02323 495077/www.angelusrestaurant.com.ar). Open noon-4pm daily. ₤₤₤. No credit cards. Parrilla/Traditional.*

Angelus is the oldest restaurant in Carlos Keen (it opened in 1998) and also the best. Though very much a country restaurant, its stylish interior and immaculately laid tables wouldn't look out of place in Buenos Aires' Palermo. But this is not a themed restaurant – the proof being right outside the window, where peaceful countryside is laid out in front of you. The menu – cold cuts, grilled beef cuts and offal, stuffed pastas and sticky puddings – will seem like an old friend to anyone who's been in Argentina more than a couple of days. Angelus's style is to polish up the rough edges of country dining, so you leave feeling pampered.

"La Casona de Carlos Keen's pumpkin ravioli with cracked black pepper and artisanal honey is outstanding."

La Casona de Carlos Keen

Carlos Keen *Quintana & Mitre (02323 495006). Open noon-3pm Sat, Sun. ₤₤. No credit cards. Parrilla/Traditional.*

There's a lively atmosphere inside this attractive, ivy-covered colonial building. Come weekends, families and groups of friends settle around the distressed-wood tables for a set lunch that is as Argentinian as they come. Start with an empanada to keep the wolf from the door, then progress on to a huge platter of meat that will make you wonder if you've driven the wolf away forevermore. Vegetarians feeling like they took a wrong turn when leaving the capital will be comforted by the range of home-made pasta; the pumpkin ravioli with cracked black pepper and artisanal honey is outstanding.

L'Eau Vive

Luján *2km SE of town centre, Constitución 2112 (02323 421774). Open noon-2pm, 8.30-10pm Tue-Sat; noon-2pm Sun. ₤₤. International/Traditional.*

Carmelite missionaries serve dauphinoise potatoes and crêpes suzettes to an after-church public at this well-known French restaurant. Some 16 nuns from Asia, Africa and the Andes wait on tables in their respective traditional dress.

La Esquina de Merti

San Antonio de Areco *Arellano 149 (02326 456705/www.esquinademerti.com.ar). Open 9am-midnight daily. Restaurant noon-3.30pm, 8.30pm-midnight daily. ₤₤. Traditional.*

Saddle up

Watching a polo match at the national stadium in Buenos Aires involves champagne and fashionistas, celebrity rubbernecking and after-parties. Actually learning to play this ancient sport, on the other hand, is less ritzy. Thanks to the proliferation of high-quality polo schools and instructors, the sound of thundering hooves and a stick hitting a ball can be found all over the 'polo belt' around Luján and nearby Lobos. And, unlike in some countries, playing polo in Argentina does not have to be expensive.

To become a proficient *polista* you need good hand-eye coordination, which you either have or you don't, and horsemanship, which can be learned. Polo instructor and player Diego Avendaño says that anyone in good physical condition can easily learn how to play, and then advance to enter tournaments.

There are a number of polo clinics to help beginners improve their game in a relatively short period of time. El Rincón (*see p114*) is a good alternative to the large estancia model, with a playing field next to the three-bedroom house and stables, and good instructors. El Antojo (*see p113*) also offers an intimate setting for learning, as well as excellent home-cooking to replenish lost energy. Villa María (*see p115*) has one of the premier polo schools in the country, with organised practices and matches on the historic grounds. El Metejón (*see p115*) offers weekly matches in a luxury setting, while the lovely El Rocío (*see p115*) also offers classes. La Candelaria (*see p114*) gives out-of-the-saddle workshops to improve your understanding of the game.

Most schools will throw you straight into the action. The first lesson involves donning the gear, mounting the horse and heading out to the field to hit the ball around. New skills involve holding the reins with your left hand to guide the horse and learning how to hold the stick properly in your right (no lefty options). Uniting stick and ball occupies your thoughts for the next hour or so, as working on the swing takes precedence. Learning how to control the horse with your legs, getting behind the swing and working out the timing involved are enough to keep you busy for the next few lessons. A sore right forearm should be the only casualty, as riding is kept to a slow pace while you focus on the ball.

The best way to improve your game is by playing with superior players – and the four Novillo Astrada brothers, aka the first family of polo, are the best. La Aguada (011 5168 8817, www.laaguadapolo.com), in Open Door, is their home and Argentina's premier polo retreat. An extended stay at the clinic affords guests the opportunity to play with the family in afternoon practices, following morning lessons with top instructors. After all, champagne lifestyles and the *campo* need not be mutually exclusive.

Top: El Rocio. Middle: La Horqueta. Bottom left: Estancia Candelaria. Bottom right: Dos Talas.

Argentinian comfort food of cold cuts, *picada* platters and pasta are on the menu at this spacious, recently renovated bar-restaurant, but coffee and company seem to be the main attraction for customers. The location – right on the town square – is particularly convenient, and the high ceilings and wooden tables make an interesting backdrop for musical performances.

Macedonia
Uribelarrea *Castro & de Crotto (02226 493159). Open noon-4pm Fri-Sun. ££. No credit cards. Traditional.*
The best food in town is on offer at this highly popular neighbourhood joint. Pumpkin- and mozzarella-filled ravioli, grilled steak and delicious home-made flan are just a few of the options that keep the crowds coming back for more. The building itself dates back to the 19th century, the restaurant to 1920. Here, bikes are left unlocked, and customers cheerily hail passing strangers. And the only thing more impressive than the wine list is the mammoth ice-cream sundae, with *dulce de leche* and whiskey sauce.

"La Uribeña is a country-kitsch dream, with everything from vintage bicycles to household appliances hanging on the walls."

El Palenque
Uribelarrea *Plaza Centenario, Belgrano & Nuestra Señora de Luján (02226 493158). Open 10am-midnight daily. £. No credit cards. Parrilla/Traditional.*
Bridles, animal skins and rifles line the walls of this authentic *pulpería*, which serves some of the finest steak in town. There's always a wait at lunchtime but, in the meantime, you can pick up something from behind the counter, where a makeshift convenience store sells shoe insoles, razors, crisps and other essential items for the cowboy on the move. Farm tools hang from the walls, next to old photographs, and one gets the feeling that this eatery is its own time capsule – a worn and faded memorial of days gone by.

La Uribeña
Uribelarrea *9 de Julio 516 (no phone). Opening hours vary. £. No credit cards. Traditional.*
This restored bar from the 1900s is also a micro-brewery serving a house pilsner and stout on tap or in bottles. It's a country-kitsch dream, with everything from vintage bicycles to records and household appliances hanging on the walls. Regional dishes such as *locro* (beef stew), pastas and *picadas* help keep patrons thirsty while they take in the view from the vintage bar.

Zarza
San Antonio de Areco *San Martin 361 (02326 453948). Open 8pm-midnight Mon, Wed-Fri; noon-3pm, 8pm-midnight Sat; noon-3pm Sun. £. Modern/Seafood.*
This modern, light-filled restaurant, just off the main square, has delicious crab ravioli with baby prawns and saffron sauce, and an appealing range of desserts that includes frozen strawberry soufflé with chocolate sauce. Brick walls and red-tile floors share the space with tree branches that double as pillars.

Stay

El Antojo
15km E of Luján *Ruta 34, Cuartel 4 (011 15 4186 8914 mobile/www.elantojopolo.com). £££.*
This cottage in the heart of polo country is the perfect place for students of the game to recover from saddle soreness. Nico Belaustegui and his family provide personal attention in a friendly environment just down the road from polo hub Open Door. The three-bedroom house, painted a cheerful blue and white, maintains its original stone floors and beamed ceilings and is furnished with vintage country items. It makes a charming backdrop for the business at hand – polo. Mornings are spent practising horsemanship and learning to manoeuvre the stick and ball – all guided by patient, bilingual Nico – while afternoons involve practice sessions with other guests and locals.

La Bamba
12km NE of San Antonio de Areco *Ruta 31, km 7.5 (02326 456293/www.la-bamba.com.ar). ££££.*
One of Argentina's most storied estancias, La Bamba offers an authentic window into the region's past. The 1830s main house, painted blood red, was the backdrop for the legendary Argentinian film *Camila*, and Carlos Gardel was a regular guest here. Newly remodelled, the elegant ranch is set amid expansive grounds that beg to be explored at dusk, before the aromatic smoke of an impending barbecue lures you back to the supper table. The rooms are furnished with antiques, family keepsakes and four-poster beds. The main building contains 11 doubles and suites, while two separate annexes offer greater space and privacy for families and small groups.

La Figura
Uribelarrea *Valeria V de Crotto & Camino Panello, RN 205, km 82 (011 4343 4644/www.estanciala figura.com.ar). ££.*
This grand, colonial hacienda doesn't skimp on the amenities: it has a themed golf course and four swimming pools. At the main house, a sunken Spanish fountain with intricate 19th-century Andalucian tiles faces an immense outdoor grill in front of the watchtower. Guests breakfast in the copper and wrought-iron nook, with the sun pouring through a wall of windows. The view takes in the old wagons and carriages on the mounds outside; beyond are lagoons, gazebos and wide-open fields surrounded by a forest of thin, scruffy trees.

El Ombú

15km NE of San Antonio de Areco *Ruta 31, Cuartel 6 (02326 492080/www.estanciaelombu.com). £££.*
Set behind vine-covered walls at the end of a tree-lined lane, this working estancia doubles as a country lodging. The rooms are simple but classy, with high ceilings, antique armoires and pot-belly stoves. Traditional, robust food is served in a dining room under wooden harness chandeliers, or outside during the gaucho show that involves a dancing horse and youthful gaucho trainer. Segundo Ramírez was the real-life inspiration for the main character in *Don Segundo Sombra*, the book that immortalised much of his life, and his son Oscar has worked at El Ombú much of his life. Like his father before him, Oscar worked as a herder and cattle breeder, and now leads visitors on horse rides and sings folkloric songs at lunch out in the garden. An organic vegetable garden was being added at the time of writing.

Patio de Moreno

San Antonio de Areco *Moreno 251 (02326 455197/ www.patiodemoreno.com). £££.*
Aimed squarely at the previously neglected gauchos-with-iPhones market, Patio de Moreno is a modern boutique hotel inside a lovely whitewashed colonial building in the centre of San Antonio de Areco. The nine rooms, which either look out on to the street or the covered central patio garden, are large, spare and chic, forgoing rustic atmospherics in favour of Wi-Fi, flatscreen TVs and shiny bathrooms. There's also a small heated pool, a wine bar and a comfy library. Activities such as horse riding and golf can be arranged with the helpful, English-speaking reception staff.

El Rincón

12km from Luján *(011 15 5228 9453 mobile/ www.elrincondelpolo.com). ££££.*
Sipping mint juleps on a wide veranda, with an old well to one side and polo fields to the other, you can easily lose track of time in this charming 1930s country house, located in the Open Door polo hub. Three bedrooms with wrought-iron bed frames and massive antique armoires complement the family photos on the walls.

FURTHER AFIELD

Many of the pampas' best escapes are out in the middle of nowhere. The following list picks some of the finest accommodation options in the Argentinian *campo* that are easily accessible from Buenos Aires. Most estancias will arrange transportation from the capital.

Bella Vista Guerrero

200km SE of Buenos Aires *Castelli, Ruta 2, km 168 (02245 4811234/www.estanciabellavista.com.ar). £££.*
One of Argentina's oldest and best-known estancias, Bella Vista, a German-style mansion with a tower and turrets, offers far more than the good views suggested by its name (though there are plenty of those too). Horse riding through the dense forest is invigorating, while studious hours in the museum will enable you to connect with the estate's history. There is a spa, swimming pool and games room,

but the best thing about Bella Vista is the accommodation. Sleek, modern bathrooms, reclining chairs on the sun-soaked balconies and amazing beds are the details to be appreciated at this classy rural lodging.

La Candelaria Estancia & Polo Club

Lobos, 115km SW of Buenos Aires *RN 205, km 114.5 (02227 424404/www.estanciacandelaria.com). £££.*
The most regal and perhaps the most incongruous of Argentinian estancias is this French-style chateau, set in 250 glorious hectares of landscaped park and forest. Among the treasures amassed beneath the castle's high ceilings are Murano crystal chandeliers, silk-panelled walls, tapestries, stained-glass windows and a creaky oak staircase. Substituting comfort for elegance, the colonial servants' quarters offer converted family suites with fireplaces, while the old mill house contains a private guest apartment. Rates are significantly cheaper for midweek stays, though you'll miss the gaucho shows, which are held on Saturdays only.

"The oak-scented library at Dos Talas is perfect for a glass of Argentinian wine before supper, or a cup of Earl Grey at high tea."

Dos Talas

Dolores, 220km SE of Buneos Aires *Ruta 2, km 204 (02245 443020/www.dostalas.com.ar). £££.*
A legendary artists' retreat from the 1920s to the 1940s, this small estancia remains a family home. Elena Sansinena de Elizalde was a feminist who fought for Argentinian women's suffrage, and when she wasn't curating avant-garde art exhibitions in BA, she was hosting famous artists and intellectuals at Dos Talas. Guests stay in the belle époque main house; there is also an original colonial structure, a chapel with notable art and stained glass imported from Europe in the 1920s and, deeper into the estate, a secluded, romantic cottage popular with honeymooners. All rooms are furnished with Depression-era antiques. The living room and entrance hall are white and canary yellow, set up like an English parlour and drawing room. The oak-scented library is perfect for a glass of Argentinian wine before supper, or a cup of Earl Grey at high tea. The estancia's crown jewel is its Carlos Thays-designed English garden.

Estancia La Fe

Chascomús, 140km S of Buenos Aires *28.5km from Ruta 2 on Ruta 20 to Magdalena (02241 15 442222 mobile/www.estancialafe.com.ar). ££.*

This sprawling 200-hectare ranch, set along the Rio Samborombón, is a no-frills country escape. It's reached via a long stretch of dirt road bordered on both sides by golden pastures. Owner Marcela Tuccio has made her home amid a forest of acacias, conifers, eucalyptuses and looming poplars. The first sign of seclusion is the diminishing mobile-phone reception: there's no Wi-Fi, car horns or city sounds, just the incessant chirping of birds, whose giant nests can be seen in the tree tops. The five guest rooms are spacious and furnished with restored antiques, while a dressing room separates each bedroom from a large, modern bathroom. Activities include horse riding, trekking and fishing in the river, although the prime attraction is the peace and quiet of the pampas, and the flavours of home cooking.

La Horqueta
Chascomús, 135km S of Buenos Aires *3.5km from Ruta 2 on Ruta 20 to Ranchos (011 4777 0150/ www.lahorqueta.com). ££.*
At La Horqueta, children play football, fathers and sons swing croquet mallets and couples sit in the shade of giant oaks. The land has been in the Pieri family for over a century. Fishing and boating excursions can be made at nearby Lago Chascomús, while the expansive estancia grounds can be explored on horseback or by bicycle. The rooms in the original 1928 Tudor-style chalet, as well as the adjacent house, come with lovely antique furnishings and modern bathrooms.

El Metejón Polo Resort
70km SW of Buenos Aires *Siempreviva & Almirante Brown (02226 432260/www.elmetejon polosuites.com.ar). ££.*
It's easy to become enamoured with the game at this serious polo resort. Overlooking the immaculately groomed main field, the guest rooms come in various hues of white, while

the furnishings are a blend of modern chic and rustic antique. Chef Mercedes bakes her own bread, salads come straight from the garden, and guests can help themselves to drinks from the open bar.

El Rocío
San Miguel del Monte, 100km SW of Buenos Aires *Ruta 3, km 102.5 (011 4815 3101/www.estancia elrocio.com). ££££.*
French-born Patrice sketched out the plans for his dream ranch when he was just 12 years old. Following a career in global finance, he and his fashionista wife have realised his fantasy with this superlative estancia. The main house contains five luxuriously appointed rooms, including a two-level suite in the loft, and there's an adjoining cottage for families. During the day, guests can enjoy the usual run of estancia activities – horse riding, polo lessons, walks across the pampas and *asados* with guitar playing and folk dancing – as well as trips to the Laguna de las Perdices birdwatching sanctuary, where more than 200 species have been spotted.

Villa María
50km SW of Buenos Aires *Ruta 205, km 47.5, near Cañuelas in Máximo Paz (011 6091 2064/ www.estanciavillamaria.com). £££.*
The setting of Villa María is pure storybook: impossibly tall palm trees surround an artificial lake, and cattle and horses graze in fields just beyond manicured trails flanked with stone benches and fountains. Topped by turrets and towers, the Tudor-style mansion is filled with 1920s furniture; a former chapel, with its striking stained glass and stone arches, has been refitted as a bar. Guests can take tea on the veranda, with its natural ceiling of vines and lake view. The rooms are elegant, four-poster-bed affairs, with spacious antique bathrooms; room service is summoned via walkie-talkie.

Factfile

When to go
The climate in the pampas is mild and dry throughout the year. Some estancias close from May to September; many hike up their rates during high season, from December through February.

Getting there & around
Estancias arrange transfers for guests travelling from Buenos Aires as a matter of course. If you plan to visit more than one estancia, or would like to explore the towns as well, renting a car is advisable.

Buses and *combis* (minibuses) also travel between Buenos Aires and the pampas. Condor Estrella (011 4313 1700, www.condorestrella. com.ar) and Rápido Argentino (0800 333 1970, www.rapido-argentino.com) run services from

Retiro station in Buenos Aires to various towns in the province, including San Antonio de Areco. The number 57 bus from Plaza Italia travels to and from Luján.

Tourist information
Luján San Martín de la Basílica 1, edificio La Cúpula (02323 427082). Open 9am-5pm Mon-Fri; 10am-6pm Sat, Sun.
San Antonio de Areco Zerboni & Arellano (02326 453165, www.pagosdeareco.com.ar). Open 8am-7pm Mon-Fri; 8am-8pm Sat, Sun.

Internet
In San Antonio de Areco, Planeta Virtual (Alsina 158, 02326 455555) is open daily from 8am to midnight. Some restaurants and cafés have Wi-Fi.

Top left: El Colibri.
Top right & middle: La
Constancia. Bottom:
La Cumbre.

Las Sierras de Córdoba

Argentina

Hills made for relaxation and adventure.

They may not compare to the Andean cordillera in strict terms of height, but ask a *porteño* what he thinks about the sierras of Córdoba, and you'll find they loom large in the Argentinian imagination. Conveniently close to the province's capital city of Córdoba, these hills and valleys have called out to urban dwellers for generations.

Visitors come here to have *asados* at the cabañas that dot the roadsides in the Valle de Punilla, or to ride horses through tall tufts of pampa grass in the Sierra Chica. The more adventurous might climb Cerro Champaquí, the province's tallest peak, while those looking to relax simply marvel at the majestic Sierra Grande from the Valle de Traslasierra below.

A break in the sierras seems to appeal to everyone, from powerful politicians to blissed-out hippies. Although visitors tend to congregate at the same handful of places, these hotspots are easy enough to avoid, and nowhere better than at one of Córdoba's estancias. Hidden throughout the hills, behind nondescript fences and at the ends of nameless rock-strewn roads, wonderful Cordobés hospitality and delicious food await, in as relaxing an environment as you'll find anywhere.

What you won't find are many foreign tourists. But if you've drunk the *mate* and danced the tango, well, why not relax like an Argentinian too?

La Posta
MOUNTAIN RESORT - CORDOBA

Mountain Bike
Trekking - Cabalgatas
Gastronomía Regional

+54 (03544) 472532
+54 (011) 43140230
laposta@qenti.com
www.qenti.com

PROMOTING A PRINCIPLED RESPONSE TO TERRORISM
PROTECTING THE RIGHTS OF WOMEN DEFENDING THE
SCOPE OF HUMAN RIGHTS PROTECTION PROTECTING
CIVILIANS IN WARTIME SHAPING FOREIGN POLICY
ADVANCING THE INTERNATIONAL JUSTICE SYSTEM
BANNING INDISCRIMINATE WEAPONS OF WAR
LINKING BUSINESS PRACTICES AND HUMAN RIGHTS
RESPONDING FIRST TO HUMAN RIGHTS EMERGENCIES
PROMOTING A PRINCIPLED RESPONSE TO TERRORISM
PROTECTING THE RIGHTS OF WOMEN DEFENDING THE
SCOPE OF HUMAN RIGHTS PROTECTION PROTECTING
CIVILIANS IN WARTIME SHAPING FOREIGN POLICY

HUMAN RIGHTS WATCH
AS LONG AS THERE IS OPPRESSION
TYRANNY HAS A WITNESS
ADVANCING THE INTERNATIONAL JUSTICE SYSTEM
BANNING INDISCRIMINATE WEAPONS OF WAR
LINKING BUSINESS PRACTICES AND HUMAN RIGHTS
RESPONDING FIRST TO HUMAN RIGHTS EMERGENCIES
REPORTING FROM CLOSED SOCIETIES PROMOTING A
PRINCIPLED RESPONSE TO TERRORISM PROTECTING THE
RIGHTS OF WOMEN LINKING BUSINESS PRACTICES AND
HUMAN RIGHTS PROMOTING A PRINCIPLED RESPONSE TO
TERRORISM PROTECTING THE RIGHTS OF WOMEN DEFENDING
THE SCOPE OF HUMAN RIGHTS PROTECTION
RESPONDING FIRST TO HUMAN RIGHTS
EMERGENCIES PROMOTING A PRINCIPLED
RESPONSE TO TERRORISM **WWW.HRW.ORG**

HUMAN
RIGHTS
WATCH

El Puerto
Sierras de Córdoba

El Puerto - San Esteban,
Córdoba Province
(+5411) 4815.0946
(+54911) 4440.5188
info@elpuertoalegre.com
www.elpuertoalegre.com

Explore

VALLE DE PUNILLA & LA SIERRA CHICA

Just west of the capital, Córdoba, at the southernmost tip of the **Valle de Punilla**, lies the biggest and brashest resort town in all the sierras, Villa Carlos Paz. Skip it. Instead, head north into the valley, at least to La Falda, where the most famous attraction, the Edén Hotel (Avenida Edén 1400, 03548 426643, www. hoteledenlafalda.com), actually predates the city itself. Built by a German entrepreneur in the late 19th century so the world's elite could enjoy endless summers, the hotel went into decline and was eventually left derelict. It is now open only for tours (in Spanish) that offer a unique insight into Argentina's perception of its own history.

The Edén – a beautiful, if slightly depressing ruin – is actually in better shape than the railroad on which the hotel's fashionable guests once arrived. Today, the infrequent rail service ends at Cosquín, about 30 kilometres south of La Falda. The trains once went even further north to **La Cumbre** (the summit), so-named because it was the highest point on the railroad. Some of the English railway engineers were so taken with La Cumbre that they decided to stay; their influence can be seen in the city's numerous Tudor-style buildings, including the clubhouse of the English-founded golf club.

These days, the area is popular with artists and writers. Residents include the writer Manuel Mujica Láinez, whose house and garden in nearby Cruz Chica is open for visits (03548 15 630043 mobile, www.fundacionmujicalainez.org), and the painter-diplomat Miguel Ocampo, who recently built a luxurious white-box gallery behind his La Cumbre house in which to display his work (José Hernández 630, 03548 457036).

Selling ceramics, metalwork, knitted garments and other handicrafts, the shops on the Camino de los Artesanos – which is near Villa Giardino, eight kilometres from La Cumbre on RN 38 – have become somewhat more conventional since the artisans first started settling here in the 1970s. If the sign on the locked door here says *toque timbre* (ring the bell), embrace your inner Alice and ring. The *camino* (walkway) is an intriguing place, where following the sign that says *vivero* (plant nursery) will take you to a 100-year-old house covered in dried flowers. Here, you can buy home-made liqueurs, jams and loose teas, all made from home-grown garden produce. Trespass politely.

If La Cumbre is an established getaway town for the wealthy, the towns further north present a kind of counterpoint. San Marcos Sierras is a magnet for alternative lifestyles, and **Capilla del Monte** is, strangely enough, best known for

Las Sierras de Córdoba

Historic sites
● ● ● ● ◉

Art & architecture
● ● ● ◉ ◉

Hotels
● ● ● ● ◉

Eating & drinking
● ● ● ◉ ◉

Scenery
● ● ● ● ◉

Outdoor activities
● ● ● ● ◉

Valle de Punilla & La Sierra Chica

Capilla del Monte • Santa Catalina • La Cumbre • Jesús María • Córdoba • Mina Clavero • Alta Gracia • *La Sierra Grande & Valle de Traslasierra* • ★ Cerro Champaquí

0   20 km

La Constancia.

the nearby peak, Cerro Uritorco, which has been the location of many UFO sightings. Since 1998, the Centro de Informes Ovni (Juan Cabús 397, 03548 482485, www.ciouritorco.org) has been telling people the truth about our intergalactic visitors.

In the **Sierra Chica**, 15 kilometres north-east of Capilla del Monte, lurk Los Terrones: hulking masses of sand that have been shaped by erosion into unusual shapes (www.losterrones.com). Further along Ruta 17 are the Grutas de Ongamira, caves that were once home to the native Comechingones. In a brutal 1620 battle against the Spanish colonising army, the Comechingones, finding themselves trapped, climbed up the mountain and threw themselves to their deaths. There's little to see here – everything of archeoological interest was taken to the museum in La Plata in the mid 20th century – but the view from the site of the mass suicide is breathtaking, albeit with a macabre resonance.

From there, the road continues on towards **Santa Catalina** and, eventually, to the town of **Jesús María**. Though we know only a little about the region's first inhabitants, Córdoba as we know it today was shaped by the Jesuits, who arrived in the region in 1599. Over the next 150 years, using the labour of enslaved Africans and natives, the Jesuits built a central college in the city of Córdoba and five estancias to support it. The estancias in Jesús María and Colonia Caroya have nice exhibits, but Santa Catalina is particularly worth a visit. In 2000, UNESCO declared all six Jesuit constructions World Heritage Sites.

Estancia Santa Catalina

Santa Catalina, 20km NW of Jesús María *(03525 421600/www.santacatalina.info). Open Apr-June, Sept 10am-1pm, 2-6pm Tue-Sun. Oct-Dec, Mar 10am-1pm, 3-7pm Tue-Sun. Admission AR$3.*
The largest and best-preserved of the Jesuit estancias around the province, Santa Catalina is also the only one in private hands. Bought by Don Francisco Antonio Diaz in 1773 after the expulsion of the Jesuit order from the Spanish colonies, it is still owned by his descendants. Private ownership has its downsides – none of the rooms on the cloisters are open to the public – but informative tours (in Spanish only) given by members of the Diaz family than make up for the lack of an on-site museum. Visitors should note that the cloisters and church are closed during Easter and on public holidays.

LA SIERRA GRANDE & VALLE DE TRASLASIERRA

Crossing the **Sierra Grande** via the sinuous Nueva Ruta de las Altas Cumbres is, on a sunny day, a very pleasant drive. On a foggy night, the complete darkness on the uninhabited Pampa de Achala can be terrifying. This route passes the Fundación Condór (0351 464 6537,

ramallotr@arnet.com.ar), which has an informative photographic exhibit about its efforts to protect the endangered Andean condor. Just 40 years ago, there were only nine condors in the area; thanks to the foundation, today more than 300 can be seen flying over the sierras. In the nearby Parque Nacional Quebrada del Condorito (www.quebradacondorito.com.ar), you may even be able to watch them feed and bathe.

This 'high-peaks route' is the only way to reach the **Valle de Traslasierra** (literal translation: 'valley beyond the sierra'), and the sweeping views as you descend make it worth the trip. Valle de Traslasierra's biggest city, **Mina Clavero**, is either filled with tourists or with shuttered hotels, depending on the season. It is famous for two things: deep-black ceramics and the rally car driver Jorge Raúl Recalde, aka 'El Cóndor de Traslasierra', who was born here. Follow the street named after Recalde – the only Argentinian to win the Rally Argentina, along this very road in 1988 – and you will arrive at the Camino de Los Artesanos, where a number of workshops selling pots, bowls and other pieces can be found.

Beyond Mina Clavero, the towns strung along Ruta 14 become progressively smaller. San Javier and Yacanto sit at the base of **Cerro Champaquí**, and are both peaceful places in which to spend some time.

Rocsen Museo Polifacético

Nono, 10km S of Mina Clavero, *Alto de la Quinta (03544 498218/www.museorocsen.org). Open 9am-sunset daily.*
This museum is packed with over 30,000 different items. Its eclectic collection includes a few horse-drawn carriages, walls of glass-encased bugs and butterflies, a lamp post from Mendoza, at least 15 different vacuum cleaners, musical instruments from around the globe, various cash registers and adding machines, and even a collection of 555 miniature liquor bottles. The museum, which aims to present 'the whole of man for all mankind', has not closed a day since it opened in 1969. Founder and director Juan Santiago Bouchon, now 81, still guides visitors around, explaining his ever-growing collection and his humanist-pacifist philosophy in both Spanish and French. Not to be missed.

ALTA GRACIA

Situated 36 kilometres south of Córdoba city and 36 kilometres from Villa Carlos Paz is **Alta Gracia**. The Jesuit estancia (Avenida Padre Domingo Viera 41, 03547 421303) from which this sleepy little town of 45,000 grew is elegant enough to warrant a visit, but the real attraction in Alta Gracia is the childhood home of Ernesto 'Che' Guevara.

On the advice of a doctor, the Guevara family moved to these hills so that their asthmatic first-born son could breathe the crisp, clean air. It was from here that the future revolutionary set out in

1952 on his now-famous journey across Latin America, so memorably described by Guevara himself in *Diarios de Motocicleta* (*The Motorcycle Diaries*). The Guevara family home is now the site of the small Museo del 'Che' Guevara (Avellaneda 501, 03547 428579, admission AR$5), where Che's story is told through various photographs, reproduced documents and replicas of significant items, including a twin of the celebrated motorcycle. Look out for the display of pictures and mementos from Fidel Castro and Hugo Chavez's joint visit in 2006.

OUTDOOR ACTIVITIES

Some 11 kilometres from La Cumbre, you'll find the hilltop of Cuchi Corral. In addition to offering a gorgeous view of the Río Pintos below, it is also home to a world-renowned paragliding site (03548 494017, 03548 15 636592 mobile), whose staff can get you flying with a licenced pilot in just a few minutes. They'll pick you up from the bus station in La Cumbre, or you can hire a bike in town (Rent-a-bike, Carraffa 301, 03548 15 637451 mobile) and ride to Cuchi Corral, a journey that follows the route of a popular annual mountain-bike race.

Jorge González, the elder statesman of *turismo alternativo* (alternative tourism) in Valle de Punilla, has written a book outlining more than 50 hiking trails for visitors to follow. He's been working as a mountain guide and rock-climbing instructor for more than 30 years, and you can still take a walk with the man (03548 492271, georgmallo@yahoo.com). Over in Valle de Traslasierra, experienced guide Roberto López leads day treks through the surrounding areas. López also offers a night-time ascent of Cerro Champaquí (03544 15 616181 mobile, ril_andar@hotmail.com).

There is also a charming young English-speaking couple living in La Cumbre, whose company, Sendas Travel, will help to plan every part of your sierras trip, with a special focus on the outdoors (03548 15 532177 mobile, www.sendastravel.com).

Eat

La Casona del Toboso
La Cumbre *Belgrano 349 (03548 451436). Open 12.30-3pm, 9-11pm daily. ££. Parrilla/Traditional.*
During the summer, tables spill out of La Cumbre's oldest parrilla on to the veranda and into the garden. This place has been owned by the same family for three generations, and the speciality is *chivito a la parrilla* (grilled goat). Many of the other recipes were brought over by the restaurant's founders, who came from Villafaleto in Italy. Herbivores should look for the spinach and roquefort filled crêpes.

El Faro
Jesús María *Juan Bautista Alberdi 245 (03525 466258). Open noon-3pm, 8.30pm-1am Tue-Sat; noon-3pm Sun. ££. Parrilla.*
The reputation of this parrilla, widely agreed to be the best in the province of Córdoba, is fully deserved. Many residents of the provincial capital drive the 60km north to eat the beef here – despite the fact that the nephew of El Faro's owner has since opened up a branch with an identical menu in Córdoba city.

"Many residents of the provincial capital drive the 60km north to eat the beef at El Faro."

Kasbah
La Cumbre *Sarmiento 6 (0348 15 401926 mobile). Open 8.30pm-12.30am Mon-Fri; 12.30-3.30pm, 8.30pm-12.30am Sat, Sun. ££. No credit cards. International.*
To assemble Kasbah's eclectic menu, chef Fabian Onori travelled the world for six years. Dishes from Thailand, India, China and Mexico take the lead at this vegetarian-friendly restaurant. The menu includes Italian favourites and enough meat to keep the locals happy, but on the whole, Kasbah is a welcome departure in this land of parrillas. This isn't one of those places that gives you an empanada and calls it a spring roll: the samosas taste just right, and the home-made tomato chutney that comes with them is divine.

Macadam
Colonia Caroya, 4km S of Jesús María *Avenida San Martín 3210 (03525 469777/www. macadam.com.ar). Open from 6pm Mon, Wed-Fri; from noon Sat, Sun. ££. No credit cards. Traditional.*
In a renovated house on the main avenue of Colonia Caroya, the Uanino family has been serving traditional Friulian food from north-eastern Italy since 2003. A large 1955 photograph of the clan hangs on one wall, and the knitted seat-cushions on the chairs add to the homey feel. Menu items are written in Friulian, and the most popular dish is the fondue-like *bagna cauda*, a cream, garlic and anchovy sauce that comes with an array of pasta, chicken and vegetables for dipping.

The Owl Beer House
La Cumbre *Belgrano 437 (03548 452314/ www.theowlbeerhouse.com.ar). Open Dec-Mar from 8pm daily. Apr-Nov from 8pm Thur-Sun. £. No credit cards. Modern.*
Often referred to locally as 'El Buho' (the owl), this pub makes its own beer, including an Indian pale ale (called *cerveza roja*) that has just the right bitterness. Order the sampler of El Buho's four house brews, then choose from over 50 varieties of pizza on the menu.

The finest horses in gaucho country

Almost everywhere you go in Córdoba, someone is hawking a ride on the back of a horse. But in two opposite corners of the sierras, two breeders are sending travellers out on the backs of animals of a decidedly different class, making for thrilling equestrian adventures.

Estancia Los Potreros (011 6091 2692, www.estancialospotreros.com) is a 2,400-hectare cattle ranch in the Sierra Chica that has been in the same Anglo-Argentinian family for four generations. Its dual heritage has made it the sort of place where you stir your tea with a delicate silver spoon, then unsheath a gaucho knife for your *asado* dinner.

Los Potreros is known for producing a unique breed of horse, the Paso Peruano (pictured). Most horses have four natural gaits, a bit like the different gears of a car: walk, trot, canter and gallop. Only a few breeds in the world have a fifth gear, and the Paso Peruano is one of them. Its fast-walking gait is quick, efficient, and very comfortable. One guest at Los Potreros likened her ride to 'flying British Airways, first class'.

Guests at Los Poteros typically ride four to six hours a day, almost always returning to the estancia for meals and, at the end of the day, a hot shower and a comfy bed. They can also participate in some of the daily tasks, such as bringing in the mares and foals for the night, and try traditional gaucho games like *la corrida de sortija*, which involves a fast-moving horse, a tiny stick and a small hanging ring for a target.

Over in the Valle de Traslasierra, **Haras Ampascachi** (0351 422 1257, www.haras ampascachi.com)is another reputable operator that specialises in rides on Paso Peruanos. Located at the base of the Sierra Grande, it offers a six-day trip to the Jesuit Estancia of La Candelaria and a nine-day journey across the Pampa de Achala.

Meanwhile, guests who don't fancy camping have the option of a riding week that starts and ends each day at the company's elegant base, a 19th-century Spanish colonial mansion. After all, if you wouldn't camp out after a first-class flight, why should you after a ride on a first-class steed?

Top: Kasbah (3).
Below: El Colibri (3).

El Pial

Mina Clavero *Boulevard de Ingreso & General Paz. Open high season noon-3pm, 9pm-midnight daily. Low season noon-3pm, 9pm-midnight Wed-Sun. ££. Parrilla/Traditional.*

Only about 100m from the Valle de Traslasierra end of the Ruta de las Altas Cumbres, this roadside restaurant serves simple Argentinian fare that should help travellers find their footing after completing the dizzying route. In the winter months, El Pial's tasty *humita en chala* (cornmeal wrapped in a corn husk) and *locro* (a hearty meat stew) should warm you up nicely.

Refugio Uritorco

Capilla del Monte *Diagonal Buenos Aires 161 (03548 481485/refugiouritorco@yahoo.com.ar). Open Jan-Feb, July 6pm-midnight daily. Mar-Jun, Aug-Dec 6pm-midnight Mon, Thur-Sun. ££. No credit cards. Modern.*

This storefront on Capilla del Monte's main drag used to be an ice-cream parlour, but you'd never know it. Rough-hewn wooden booths and walls of split logs and stone give the interior an alpine feel. A long list of beers and fondues complements the decor. Be patient; even the *sandwiches de miga* are made to order. Pizza is also on the menu, but more unexpected items such as houmous and a vegetarian *picada* remind you that you're in Capilla del Monte.

Sabía Que Venías y Preparé un Pastel

Capilla del Monte *Pueyrredón 681 (03548 482699). Open high season 9am-1pm, 5-9pm daily. Low season 9am-1pm, 4.30-8pm Tue-Sun. £. Café.*

The owners may not know you're coming, but they've baked cakes, strudels, streusels and pies just in case. They used to work as pastry chefs at some of Buenos Aires's swankiest hotels, and you can taste their expertise in the cupcakes and mousses. To accompany the sweet stuff, skip the coffee and create an original herbal infusion from the different leaves and flowers on offer.

"A stay at El Colibri is punctuated by all sorts of surprises, such as wine tasting in its candlelit bodega."

Stay

A word about estancias: many are quite isolated, so people stay for at least a few days and hardly leave during that time, except perhaps on horseback. Most of the estancias listed offer rooms on a full-board basis, and staff will happily arrange day trips around the area for guests.

El Castillo de Mandl

La Cumbre *San Josemaría Escrivá 73 (03548 452001/ www.elcastillodemandl.com). ££.*

Set high in the hills overlooking La Cumbre, this lodging started off as a medieval-looking pile, complete with a crenellated roofline and pointed turrets. But when Austrian arms manufacturer Fritz Mandl bought 'the castle' in 1940, he gave it a complete overhaul. The interior decor has changed little since then, and some rooms have Gothic-style beds left over from the house's first owner. The views from the house – and from the pool behind it – are magnificent. Avoid the newly created guest rooms on the top floor, which are less elegant than the others.

El Colibri

Santa Catalina *Camino a Santa Catalina, km 7 (03525 465888/www.estanciaelcolibri.com). ££££.*

An exquisite chateau with just nine rooms and suites, this estancia embraces you in an air of dreamlike luxury. A stay at El Colibri is punctuated by all sorts of wonderful surprises, such as the evening of wine tasting in its candlelit bodega. The estancia is perfect for a honeymoon, but families are also welcome. Children can work at different farm activities – cutting salad greens from the garden for lunch, say, or collecting eggs from the chicken coops before breakfast – while the spa, swimming pool and peaceful surroundings keep adults happy. Horseback riding is available, and one of El Colibri's French owners is a polo player, so the estancia's two pristine fields and 70 sprightly polo ponies are at your disposal. Lessons are available for beginners; for experienced players, games can usually be arranged.

La Constancia

San Javier, 65km S of Mina Clavero *Quebrada del Tigre (03544 482826/011 4372 7160/www.la constancia.net). £££.*

The first structure on this site was built from adobe brick in 1895, nestled by an *arroyo* (creek) at the foot of Cerro Champaquí, and the estancia developed piecemeal around it. The name comes from the perseverance that was needed to complete the construction, the same quality required of anyone attempting the seven kilometre rocky drive up to the entrance (4x4s are recommended). The nine rooms have a welcoming, lived-in feel and are furnished in a rustic style. Hikes and horseback rides to the top of Cerro Champaquí are highlights.

Dos Lunas

60km NE of Jesús María *Todos los Santos, Ischillín, RP 17 (03525 442847/www.doslunas.com.ar). ££££.*

Horse riding is the activity of choice at Dos Lunas, and the estancia's 2,250 mountainous hectares present ample and diverse terrain for every ride. Excursions bring guests back to the lodge in time for lunch and dinner, with a menu designed by television chef Dolly Irigoyen; even afternoon tea (served with fresh scones) is worth galloping back for. The wine list is excellent too. The 100-year-old ranch house has eight rooms and suites, keeping the atmosphere intimate, and the attentive hosts make guests feel like part of the family.

Estancia la Paz

14km NW of Jesús María *RP 66, km 14 (03525 492073/www.estancialapaz.com). ££££.*
Once the rural retreat of Argentinian president Julio Argentino Roca, Estancia la Paz is now an opulent 20-room hotel. The history of its former owner lends an irony to the name: la Paz means 'the peace', but Roca led the massacre of innumerable indigenous Patagonians during his 1879 'Campaign of the Desert'. Still, the grounds are indeed peaceful, particularly when strolling around the 70-hectare park. Estancia La Paz has all the usual luxuries – spa, tennis court, swimming pool – as well as two polo fields and a few horses. Day visits are also available.

"El Puerto Alegre's Moorish arcade dates back over 200 years."

Posada del Camino Real

10km NW of Santa Catalina *(0351 15 552 5215 mobile/www.posadacaminoreal.com.ar). ££.*
This recently built posada lies just off the dirt road that runs through Santa Catalina. Clustered around a swimming pool are ten modestly sized rooms, distributed between a few tile-roofed cabins. Rates include breakfast; for lunch and dinner, guests can order à la carte from a typical Argentinian menu or choose a fixed 'gourmet' menu that changes every week. Non-guests may also dine at the posada; calling ahead is recommended.

La Posta Mountain Resort

45km E of Mina Clavero, Pampa de Achala *Ruta 34, km 101 (03544 472531/www.qenti.com). £££.*
Like an old ski resort that only locals know about, La Posta is rough around the edges. A former military post, the lodging is anchored into the rugged terrain of the Sierra Grande. Specialising in adventure sports, La Posta offers rappelling and rock climbing, mountain biking, trekking and, of course, horse riding. It's a child-friendly place that soon fills up during school holidays; for the rest of the year, the stark surrounding landscape of the Pampa de Achala lends itself to quiet relaxation.

El Puerto Alegre

5km NW of La Cumbre *Ruta 38, km 74.5 (03548 494007/www.elpuertoalegre.com). £££.*
Tucked into the Sierra Chica, El Puerto Alegre is a five-suite hotel whose Moorish arcade dates back more than 200 years. The main attractions are horses and peaceful hills. Spa treatments and gourmet meals keep guests satisfied on-site. For adrenaline junkies, there are paragliding and 4x4 adventure excursions.

Factfile

When to go

Popular parts of the sierras fill up during high season, which is from December to March, as well as during the school holidays in July, Easter and on long weekends year-round. During the rest of the year, look for bargains on accommodation and expect to find fewer restaurants open.

There are hot days in summer (January to March) and cold ones in winter (July to September), but, overall, the weather in the sierras is temperate year-round. Rain in the summer months is typically minimal.

Getting there

Frequent daily flights from Buenos Aires to Córdoba's international airport are offered by Aerolíneas Argentinas (www.aerolineas.com.ar) and LAN (www.lan.com). Córdoba's Terminal de Omnibus (Boulevard Juan D Perón 380, 0351 428 4141) is well served by national intercity buses. The bus journey from Buenos Aires to Córdoba city takes ten hours.

Getting around

Minibuses leave frequently from both the Terminal de Omnibus and the Terminal de Minibus (Avenida Illia 155) in Córdoba city, and serve even the smallest towns in the sierras. Once out in the hinterlands, however, travelling between towns separated by only 30 kilometres of dirt road will either require two 70-kilometre minibus rides (all routes go to and from the capital), or taking a *remise* (car and driver). If you're planning on travelling around a lot, hiring a car in Córdoba city is your best bet. A number of companies, such as Hertz, have offices both at the airport (0351 475 0581) and in the city centre (Avenida Coon 835, 0351 475 0581, www.mille trentacar.com.ar). Out in the hills, driving is easy and pleasurable, if sometimes bumpy.

Córdoba Nativo Viajes (0351 424 5341, www.cordobanativoviajes.com.ar) organises day-trips from Córdoba capital, as well as car-and-driver hire.

Tourist information

Córdoba City Tourist Information Cabildo de la Ciudad, Independencia 50 (0351 434 1200, www.cordobaturismo.gov.ar). Open 8am-8pm daily

Internet

Most hotels and estancias have Wi-Fi, no matter how remote their locations, and *locutorios* with internet access are easy to find in every town.

Top: Estancia La Paz.
Bottom: La Constancia (3).

Clockwise from top:
Amaicha del Valle (3);
Ruinas de Quilmes;
Tafí del Valle.

Tafí del Valle

Argentina

An oasis town full of history and artisans.

Between the humid plains of Tucumán to the south and the dry valley of Cafayate to the north, you'll find Tafí del Valle, a high-altitude oasis of rolling grasslands. The town's name stems from the ancient Quechua word meaning 'welcome to the splendour of the valley', which seems perfectly suited to a place with a delightful climate, an abundance of locally grown produce and striking views from its valley depths and mountain top.

The changing of seasons here heralds dramatic transformations. Summer brings hues of luscious green, while winter leads to a patchwork of golden brown and, very occasionally, a gleaming mantle of snow.

The town was once the summer escape for the wealthy Tucumán elite, who took advantage of its crisp air and spectacular vistas to ride horses from the numerous old estancias that mark the early Jesuit settlements. Horse riding is still as popular as ever, and the town has developed a thriving scene of artisanal crafts, drawing on its indigenous roots as much as its colonial ones.

Tafí del Valle retains little history in its architecture, but, with horses as likely to be spotted in the streets as cars, it has a wonderfully slow and relaxing pace that will leave you feeling fully refreshed.

Explore

Tafí del Valle centres around two main streets, Avenida Presidente Perón and Avenida Gobernador Critto, where you'll find food, phones, internet and all the other comforts for your stay. The town all but shuts down during the siesta, and business hours tend to be more of a guideline than a rule.

Finding your way around is as easy and pleasant as the weather and the people, and all parts of the town are accessible on foot. Beyond that, you can take taxis, rent a bike or hire a guide to show you the way by horse or 4x4.

South of the centre, a small bridge crosses the meeting of the Tafí, Churqui and Banda rivers, and beyond the town's stone and dirt roadways lies a gorgeous expanse of nature. Highlights include the Los Alisos waterfall; La Ciénaga, archeological ruins accessible only on horseback or on foot; and Cerro El Pelao, the only mountain popping up from the centre of the valley, which offers beautiful views and endless opportunities for trekking. It is advisable to hire a guide to show you around: try La Cumbre or Estancia Las Carreras (for both, *see p135*). Tafí del Valle is also well situated for day trips to Amaicha del Valle (57 kilometres north), a community dedicated to conserving the culture of the indigenous Diaguita people.

Dique La Angostura can be seen from just about any part of Tafí del Valle. Like most man-made lakes, it will not blow you away with its beauty; however, it is a lovely addition to a day spent driving around Cerro El Pelao. In the warmer months, you can rent a boat, fish, windsurf and kitesurf on its waters.

Some 60 kilometres north of Tafí del Valle on RN 40, Las Ruinas de Quilmes (the Quilmes ruins) is Argentina's largest pre-Columbian archaeological site, and has a beautiful hilltop location that stands in stark contrast to the tragic history of its Diaguita inhabitants. Having successfully fought off Incan control, they were finally defeated by the Spanish, who punished them for their resistance by forcibly relocating them 1,500 kilometres away, near Buenos Aires. Many perished en route; the rest were wiped out by sickness and interbreeding. This episode resulted in the name of the present city of Quilmes in Buenos Aires province and, perhaps the final insult, Argentina's national beer.

You can easily spend a morning or afternoon hiking among the ruined structures, some now partially restored. The AR$10 entrance fee includes a Spanish-only guided tour, but the ruins are easy enough to navigate on your own. If you are heading to Tafí del Valle from Salta province, it makes sense to stop en route, as these Tucumán-province ruins are nearer to Cafayate (*see p350*).

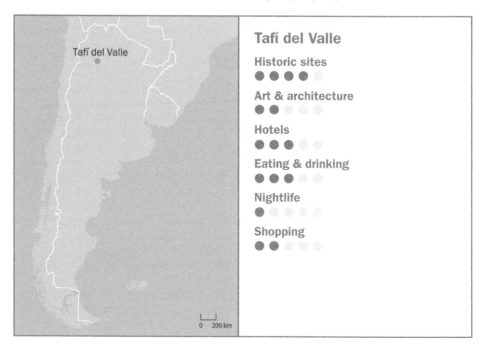

Tafí del Valle

Tafí del Valle

Historic sites
● ● ● ● ○

Art & architecture
● ● ○ ○ ○

Hotels
● ● ● ○ ○

Eating & drinking
● ● ● ○ ○

Nightlife
● ○ ○ ○ ○

Shopping
● ● ○ ○ ○

0   200 km

Clockwise from top: Tafí del Valle; Amaicha del Valle (2).

Museo Jesuítico La Banda

La Banda no number, Avenida José Frias Silva,
500m past the bridge, on the left (no phone). Open
9am-6pm daily.
This house and museum reflects the full range of Tafí del
Valle's history. Originally part of the Jesuit settlement, it was
taken over by the Frias Silva household, a wealthy Tucumán
family, after the Jesuits were expelled from the area in the
1760s. Today, it displays archaeological pottery finds,
ecclesiastical art and antiques that belonged to the Frias
Silva family. The grounds are peaceful, if a bit run-down.
Opening times are not set in stone.

"In Parque Menhires stands an impressive collection of statues, created in 300 BC."

Parque Provincial los Menhires

El Mollar, 10km S of Tafí del Valle *Ruta 307.*
Admission ARS3.
The town of El Mollar sits just south of Dique La Angostura
and is home to Parque Menhires. Here stands an impressive
collection of ancient menhir statues, which were created in
around 300 BC and are thought to have been used in fertility
rituals. Once dotted throughout the valley, they were moved
to El Mollar to protect them from vandalism. One is shaped
like a pregnant woman, another like a llama. Some have
patterns of faces, and most are, well, just plain phallic. This
is a short stop, and best added to a day tour of the valley.

Eat

Los Alisos Restaurante

12km N of Tafí del Valle *RP 325, km 13, Estancia*
las Carreras (03867 421473/03867 421800/www.
estancialascarreras.com.ar). Open Jan-Easter 8am-
midnight daily. Apr-Dec 8am-3pm, 8pm-midnight
daily. ££. Modern.
Los Alisos offers the most sophisticated dining in town. Sit
in the comfortable wooden interior to enjoy a meal of freshly
caught trout or llama ragoût. Depending on the season,
expect to find strawberries, broad beans and potatoes grown
in the estancia's private garden. Dinner is by reservation
only, so call ahead. In the daytime, a less elaborate on-site
restaurant serves wine and traditional foods (*see p135*).

Don Pepito

Avenida Presidente Perón 193 (03867 421764/
www.donpepitodetafi.com.ar). Open noon-3.30pm,
8-11.30pm daily. £. No credit cards. Parrilla.
Don Pepito is your usual Argentinian parrilla, and
everything here is executed perfectly. You may find yourself
tempted by the *cabrito* (young goat) roasting over burning

wood in the front window, but dorado fish, grilled on an
open flame, is the main draw. The wine list is the most
extensive in town, and you can choose half or full bottles
from regional vineyards. Eat inside in the spacious dining
room or outside at the pavement tables.

Flor Sauco

Avenida Gobernador Critto, Paseo Artesenal Los
Cuartos (0381 15 548 3483 mobile). Open 9am-1pm,
3.30-8.30pm daily. £. Café.
Flor Sauco may well convince you to give up regular meals
in favour of its wonderful cakes and pies. Choose from
flavours that include home-made ricotta, raspberry and
custard, walnut, apple, and a deep, rich chocolate. This tea-
house opens in the morning for breakfast and in the
afternoon for *merienda* (afternoon tea). You'll also find jams
and *dulce de leche* from the Campo del Molino organic farm
available for purchase here. The carrot and lemon jam is
particularly good.

Lunahuana Restaurant

Avenida Gobernador Critto 540 (03867 421330). Open
noon-2.30pm, 8-11.30pm daily. ££. Traditional.
This restaurant, connected with the Lunahuana hotel (*see*
p135), is a pleasant place for a meal or snack. High ceilings
complement comfortable wooden tables, where you sit
looking out at a view of Estancia Los Cuartos across the
street. Lunahuana serves regional cuisine, including *quesillo*
(a moist goat's or sheep's cheese) empanadas with slightly
spicy peppers, and excellent *humitas*. The menu also
includes classic main dishes, such as trout in almond sauce.

Shop

The first thing visitors should do on arrival in Tafí
del Valle is ask for a copy of the *Ruta de Artesano*
guide. Any hotel or shop should be able to provide
one – or try the tourist information centre. The
guide contains a map of Tafí del Valle and
surrounding areas, with a list of just about every
local artisan. Follow the route to discover the pre-
Columbian-inspired products of the Rodocrosita
metal workshop, or La Quebradita's *alfajores* (a
type of biscuit). A slight detour off the paved road
leads to Los Suris, a workshop whose ceramics
are made from *arcilla*, a soft red clay from the
mountain. The majority of stops on the route
are in town, or along Rutas 307 and 325.

Arte AlterNativo

Avenida Presidente Perón, Galeria Popey, Local 8
(03867 421876/www.artealternativo.com). Open
10am-1pm, 4-8pm daily.
Beautiful, bright colours – greens, blues, reds and oranges
– line the shelves of Arte AlterNativo, all naturally created
from the flowers and plants of the valley. Choose from
sweaters, ponchos, tablecloths, hats and gloves, all of which
have been hand-woven by members of this ten-year-old
collective of Tafí del Valle families.

The queen of the empanadas

Every September, Argentina's self-proclaimed 'Capital de la Empanada' – the town of Famaillá, in Tucumán – hosts the Fiesta Nacional de la Empanada, a high-octane celebration of one of the country's most beloved foods.

It's a fiesta that doesn't dress up for tourists, drawing an average of 30,000 to 40,000 food-lovers a day and culminating in the crowning of an empanada queen. In contrast to other Argentinian festivals, where sovereigns are chosen for their beauty, here the queen is elected solely on the basis of her empanada-making prowess. This contest is all about cooking, not curves.

To enter, contestants must be natives of Famaillá, and sponsored by someone from the municipality. They then have to cook before a panel of judges, whose identities remain secret until the challenge commences. Their quest is to create the perfect clay-oven-baked, Tucumán-style empanada: stuffed with *carne cortada a cuchillo* (diced meat), green and white onion, and hard-boiled egg; seasoned with cumin, paprika and chilli pepper; and surrounded by a delicate *masa* (pastry), just thick enough to hold in the juice.

Many regard the Tucumán version of the empanada as the finest in Argentina, although every region in the country has its own riff on this portable delicacy.

Originating with the Arabs, spreading to Spain with the Moorish conquest, and travelling to the Americas along with Spanish colonisers, the empanada developed a myriad of incarnations across Argentina. Today, fillings and cooking methods still differ from province to province,

each variation being a mixture of tradition and readily available ingredients.

In the north-western province of Salta, empanadas are filled with potato along with beef and onions, and chilli sauce is served on the side. Thanks to an influx of Middle Eastern immigrants, empanadas from Córdoba often have raisins and a dusting of sugar. Lamb is the most popular filling in the empanadas of the Patagonian provinces (including Neuquén, Santa Cruz and Tierra del Fuego), while seafood is common in coastal areas. In Buenos Aires, the preferred empanada is similar to that of Tucumán but with a wider range of fillings, including mozzarella, tomato and basil or roquefort, celery and walnuts.

According to judge and former empanada queen Elena Britos, the task of handling the pastry, seasoning the filling and cooking an empanada to perfection is not for amateurs. One does not become a great *empanadera*, much less an empanada queen, overnight. And although there is no cash prize, many women vie for the title year after year.

The Fiesta Nacional de la Empanada usually takes place during the first or second weekend of September, although the Municipality of Famaillá doesn't fix the dates until two to three months prior. Check online at www.famailla. gov.ar to confirm the dates. The festivities begin at around 10pm on Friday night and continue through to Sunday night; the empanada queen competition starts between 11am and noon on Sunday. A bus from Tafí del Valle to Famaillá takes around two hours (0800 444 9275, www.transporteaconquija.com.ar).

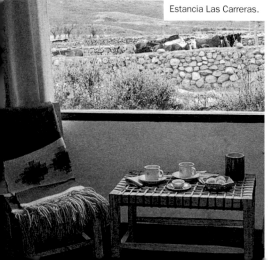

Estancia Las Carreras.

Dulce Art de Tafi Bombones & Chocolates

Avenida Presidente Perón, Galería Popey, Local 10 (no phone). Open 9am-2pm, 5.30-9pm Thur-Sun.

Dulce Art's *bombones* are smooth and creamy, not too sweet, and perfectly accented by fillings such as almond, peach, plum and, of course, *dulce de leche*. They're made in a workshop in the owner's home and brought to this clean, bright store on Tafi del Valle's main street.

Kkechuwa Cervecería

Avenida Presidente Perón, Galería Los Arcos, Local 1 (no phone). Open 10am-7pm daily.

Sharing a space with a *kiosco* where you can make phone calls and buy gum, Kkechuwa is easy to miss. To find it, look for the decrepit sign advertising artisanal beer outside. Walk to the back of the *kiosco*, and you'll find a a rough wooden bar and a couple of stools. Here, you can buy a refreshing home-brewed beer in one of six flavours, including a lemony red *rubia* (lager), a stout and a Belgian trappist recipe. Buy some bottles to take away, or enjoy them on the spot, served in a frosty mug.

Stay

Estancia Las Carreras

RP 325, km 13 (03867 421473/03867 421800/ www.estancialascarreras.com.ar). ££.

Located about 20km from town, Las Carreras isn't exactly easy to reach at night – but once you arrive, you won't want to leave. This impeccably restored estancia has everything you could want for a restful holiday. Walk the spacious grounds by day, or hire guides directly from the estancia to explore the surrounding areas. The hotel's two restaurants provide some of the best food in the area (*see p132*). Breakfasts include wonderful manchego cheese, made in the estancia's *quesería*.

Estancia Los Cuartos

Avenida Gobernador Critto, no number, 150m from Tafi del Valle bus terminal (0381 15 587 4230 mobile/ www.estancialoscuartos.com). £. No credit cards.

Llamas roam the great expanse of lawn leading to the main gate of Estancia Los Cuartos. Inside the ranch you enter a stately old library and then the dining room, where guests can eat lunch or dinner (*see p132*). The sleeping quarters were built significantly later, and are sparser – and not quite as striking – as the other areas of the house. A two-room *quesería* provides cheese for breakfast and offers daily morning tours. You can buy the cheese (as well as textiles, chocolates and other goods) in the Paseo Artesanal, in front of the property on the main road.

Estancia Las Tacanas

Avenida Presidente Perón 372 (03867 421821/ www.estancialastacanas.com). ££. No credit cards.

This 17th-century Jesuit estancia turned bed and breakfast maintains an air of antique authenticity with its adobe walls and leather-string roof construction. Here, you can spend the night in the four-poster bed of Nicolas Valerio Laguna, three-time governor of Tucumán province. Las Tacanas is centrally located and well positioned for visiting the town, but its surrounding gardens – filled with long curly leafed molle bushes and purple geraniums, and with a view of the distant dam – leave you feeling as if you're staying deep in the countryside.

Lunahuana Hostería

Avenida Gobernador Critto 540 (03867 421330/ www.hosterialunahuana.com). ££.

Lunahuana may be larger than the other accommodation offerings in town, but it's still got character. The rooms combine modern design with antique furniture, and there's a communal sitting room with a large open fire, and a traditional restaurant (*see p132*). The *hosteria* also offers duplexes with room for up five people. On-site amenities include a tennis court.

Factfile

When to go

Visit any time of year, depending on your weather preference. In summer (January to March), it's hot during the daytime and refreshingly cool at night. Winter (from July to September) is sunny, although significantly colder.

Getting there & around

Aconquija is currently the only bus company serving the town. It's a two hour 30 minute ride from San Miguel de Tucumán, the central bus hub of the area.

To reach Tafi del Valle from Salta, the fastest way is to first take a bus (four hours 30 minutes) to Tucumán. You can also take the four-hour scenic route to Cafayate, where you catch a connecting bus for another four-hour ride ending in Tafi del Valle. Bike rentals are available from Fernández Vidrios (Avenida Calchaquí 427, 03867 15 494453 mobile). Tours are available through La Cumbre (Avenida Presidente Perón 120, 03867 421768, www.lacumbretafidelvalle.com).

Tourist information

Tafi de Valle Tourist Information office corner of Peatonal Los Faroles & Avenida Gobernador Critto 311 (no phone).

Internet

Computer access, including internet and printing services, is available at Galería Los Arcos, on Avenida Presidente Perón.

Rivers & Wetlands

Colonia.

Colonia
& Carmelo

Uruguay

Cobbled streets, retro style and river beaches.

This is what it looks like when time stands still – or refuses to break a sweat. Colonia del Sacramento, Uruguay's oldest town, may lack the cachet of Argentina's capital across the Río de la Plata, but it has more than its fair share of charm. Inside the historic quarter, a UNESCO World Heritage Site, the only thoroughly modern sight is the people walking the ragged cobblestone streets. What you won't find are chain restaurants, pumping nightlife or cinema multiplexes, but this doesn't rule out excellent dining options, as well as plenty to see inside the pocket-sized walled city and on the expanse of riverside beaches beyond.

Colonia was claimed by Portugal in 1680 and served as a home to the governor of Río de Janeiro. Today, the influence of both Portugal and Spain – who traded rulership throughout the town's formative years – is evident in its intriguing blend of colonial architecture.

Just under 70 kilometres away, Carmelo is another snapshot from days gone by – and one that's far less established on the international tourist's itinerary. Horses, Model T Ford automobiles, wide open spaces and dirt roads set the retro tone, while pristine beaches and a tiny wine country keep visitors busy enough, without losing touch with the laid-back pace of local life.

Whether you're looking for a relaxing day trip or long-weekend destination, these quaint towns on the shores of the Río de la Plata offer a memorable escape.

Explore

COLONIA DEL SACRAMENTO

Colonia del Sacramento juts out into the Río de la Plata on a narrow peninsula that is just a few blocks wide. The town's historic centre is compact, and perfect for a leisurely stroll or an easy bike ride along the cobblestone streets. Whether you pedal or ramble, the action is in the direction of Plaza Mayor and the adjacent Plaza del Gobernador. Avenida General Flores runs through the middle of the old town and is lined with souvenir stores and restaurants.

On exiting the ferry terminal, head down Manuel Lobo, a small street on the left, to get to the tourist information office at no.224. It's about a ten-minute walk; or you can rent a bicycle on the way. Just beyond here is El Portón del Campo, the historic quarter's imposing entrance. Built in 1745, the old fort has a drawbridge and trench, where an intimidating moat once flowed.

Inside the walled town's confines lies Plaza Mayor, a tranquil square lined with colonial houses. Some of these buildings are open to the public as small museums, detailing various periods in the town's history; in total, seven such museums are scattered across town. You can buy an all-inclusive pass for UR$50 from the Museo Municipal (Calle del Comercio 77), Museo

Portugués (Enrique de la Peña 180) or Museo Español (corner of de San José & España). The museums open from 11.15am to 4.45pm, with each one closing on a different day of the week. (Check with tourist information for a complete list.)

Tucked off Plaza Mayor, on the side nearest the water, lies Calle de los Suspiros (street of sighs), which has become Colonia's most famous street on account of the distinctive rough cobblestones, laid by Portuguese colonisers. At the other end of the plaza is the town's lighthouse, which you can climb for excellent views over the river and peninsula.

The historic centre's other main square is Plaza del Gobernador, which is centred around the remains of the house and gardens of the governor of Río de Janeiro, who founded Colonia del Sacramento in the name of Portugal in 1680. On one of the plaza's sides is the Basílica Matriz del Santísimo Sacramento, the church where the governor's household worshipped. The church has withstood fires and wars; it was expanded in 1808 and underwent major restoration in 1957.

Closer to the water, Bastión del Carmen (Rivadavia 223) dates from 1880 and could easily be mistaken for another fort. It's actually a former soap and glue factory, with crumbling brick walls and a garden chimney once used for curing meat. Inside, a glass floor looks down on to tunnels that were used as escape routes when

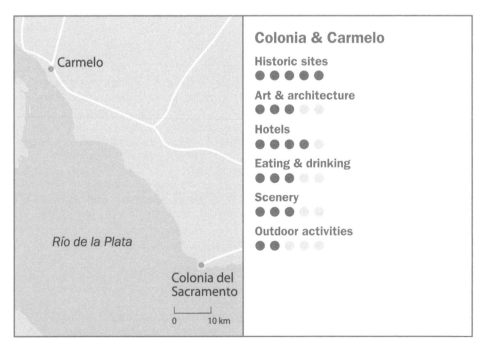

Carmelo

Río de la Plata

Colonia del Sacramento

|_____|
0   10 km

Colonia & Carmelo

Historic sites
● ● ● ● ●

Art & architecture
● ● ● ◌ ◌

Hotels
● ● ● ● ◌

Eating & drinking
● ● ● ◌ ◌

Scenery
● ● ● ◌ ◌

Outdoor activities
● ● ◌ ◌ ◌

Clockwise from top: Carmelo (2); Colonia (2).

the town was attacked. Today, the building has a much more peaceful existence as a theatre and cultural centre.

Near the Bastión del Carmen is the family-friendly Acuario (Virrey Cevallos 236, www.acuario.com.uy, open 2-6pm Mon, Wed-Sun, admission UR$30), said to be South America's only river aquarium. Glass tunnels enable visitors to stroll among the colourful fishes.

"Outside of high season is an ideal time to visit Colonia's river beaches, as you're likely to have them all to yourself."

On the outskirts of the old town, at the intersection of Intendente Suárez and Dr Daniel Fosalba, the town's market sells local items such as *mate* gourds, yarn vests and jewellery. Further along Dr Daniel Fosalba, heading away from the historic town, you'll meet Rambla Costanera, a coastal road lined with a series of beaches. The best way to explore them is by scooter, stopping when you find a quiet spot. Midweek, outside of high season (December-March) is an ideal time, as you're likely to have the sands all to yourself. The low-key beaches are perfect for a leisurely stroll, or to watch the sunset.

A ten-minute drive north along the coast is Plaza de Toros Real de San Carlos, a large Moorish-style construction that was built for boisterous bullfights and is in desperate need of repair. The only bullring in South America, it is currently off-limits due to crumbling walls and missing stairs. There is constant talk of restoration projects, but as yet nothing has been confirmed. In the meantime, you can view the imposing structure from the outside, and visit the hippodrome next door.

CARMELO

Carmelo also dates back to colonial times – but barely; the bulk of what you see pays homage to the close of the 19th century. In the town centre the buildings are mostly single-storey, giving the town what many visitors refer to as an 'Old West' feel. On the storefronts, decorated in faded, colourful paint, you can still make out old advertisements for fishing gear and groceries.

The entrance to the town is a source of local pride. The red swing bridge, built in 1912, is the only one of its kind in South America. A key is placed in the lock at the bridge's centre; once it's turned, the bridge swings apart to allow tall ships to pass. Locals say whoever crosses the bridge always returns. The bridge connects the town to the campsite and beach, Playa Seré – home to a yacht club, and the setting for numerous watersports.

Carmelo is situated on the 34th parallel, the Southern Hemisphere's wine belt, and the surrounding area is said to have a climate comparable to France's Bordeaux region. Local wine production is improving all the time, and you can test it for yourself by heading out of town on Ruta 97 to the Irurtia vineyards for a winery tour. Also along this highway is the Estancia y Capilla Narbona (nine kilometres from Carmelo). Narbona's chapel (open 10am-6pm Mon, Wed-Sun) was built between 1732 and 1738.

Heading a bit further away from Carmelo proper, 13 kilometres along Ruta 21 on the way to Punta Gorda, is the Calera de las Huérfanas. These ruins are all that remains of a Jesuit estancia built in 1741, at one time owned by the family of General San Martín, South America's liberation hero.

The nearby lake was once a stone quarry that provided the source material for building projects in Buenos Aires. Since flooding, it has been used by Argentinian and Uruguayan scuba diving schools, which practise deep-water dives amid sunken machinery. Diving school options include Buenos Aires Buceo (Avenida del Libertador 7500, 011 4702 2502, www.bab.com.ar) and Montevideo Diving School (02 600 2463, www.montevideodiving.com).

Further down the hilly dirt road is Punta Gorda, where Darwin stopped to study some of the local species in 1833 and undoubtedly enjoyed the fine view. On the hillside stands the distinctive Parador Hotel, a 1950s construction made of glass and cubes that was designed to make visitors feel as if they were by the ocean rather than the river. This is the start of the Río de la Plata, and the end of the Río Uruguay; both rivers converge with the Río Paraná and the Río Sauce here, giving the area its name, meaning 'fat point'.

Irurtia Winery

Ruta 97, km 2,300 (054 22323/www.irurtia.com.uy). Open 8am-noon, 1.30-5.30pm daily. Tours by reservation only.

The largest vineyard in Uruguay lies just outside Carmelo, next to the estuary of the Río de la Plata, where the Río Uruguay meets the Río Paraná. The winery began production in 1913, and today uses precision methods and machinery to turn out more than 25 different varieties, including tannat, pinot noir, riesling, chardonnay, malbec and viognier. The star of the cellar is gewürztraminer – the result of botrytis, a mould that attacks the vines every few years, altering its flavour in the most delightful way. On visits to the winery's atmospheric cellar, you can sample pairings of popular Irurtia varietals with local cheeses, below arched brick ceilings and stained glass.

Clockwise from centre left: Narbona (3); Posada Plaza Mayor (2); Casa de los Limoneros.

Isla Martín García

Estación Fluvial de Carmelo. Departures Sept-May 10.30am Sat, Sun.

Technically, Island Martín García is in Argentina, but it is actually closer to Uruguay's shores (only 50 minutes by boat). From its discovery in 1516 until the close of the 20th century, politics and its prisoners have determined the fate of this small island. It has been a jail and a naval base, before finding itself a popular day-trip destination. Transport, lunch, and a guided tour cost around UR$700; enquire at Cacciola Viajes (www.cacciolaviajes.com), in the port next to the swing bridge. You can also arrange trips from Tigre in Argentina (*see p166*).

Eat

The proximity of these tiny towns to Buenos Aires is reflected in their restaurant scenes. As visitors find their way here in increasing numbers, local eateries are branching out, with exciting results. A few Argentinians have hopped the pond and opened restaurants here, while local spots serve their own version of classic comfort food, including pastas and steak. And unlike Buenos Aires, both towns – especially Colonia – take full advantage of their riverside location and specialise in fresh fish and seafood.

If you don't plan to stay in a luxury hotel, you can still get a taste of one: the best hotel restaurants in the area are at the Four Seasons Resort and the Estancia Tierra Santa, both in Carmelo (*see p146*).

"Bodega y Granja Narbona is everything you could want in a country restaurant, with more style than you've ever found down a rural back road."

Bodega y Granja Narbona

Carmelo Ruta 21, km 267 (054 04778/www.fincay granjanarbona.com). Open 9am-midnight daily. £££. Italian.

This 1909 farmhouse on the road to Punta Gorda is reason enough to go to Carmelo. Bodega y Granja Narbona is everything you could want in a country restaurant, with more style than you've ever found down a rural back road. Signature cheeses, olive oil, preserves, wine and cognac are all crafted on the premises. Everything from organic

vegetables to home-made pasta can be found in this traditional Italian kitchen, and the soothingly-lit restaurant is decorated with antique collectables. Start off with a colourful garden salad and crisp viognier, and follow it with mushroom gnocchi or bolognese paired with a rich tannat roble. Don't forget to ask for the grand tour of the farmhouse's nooks and crannies, including the cold storage full of ageing cheeses, the vintage car garage and the showroom suites upstairs. Reservations for lunch are strongly advised.

El Drugstore

Colonia del Sacramento Vasconcellos 179, & Portugal (052 25241). Open noon-midnight daily. ££. No credit cards. International.

With pop-culture decor that would put Andy Warhol's Factory to shame, the brightly coloured, polka-dot interior of El Drugstore is almost as busy as its menu. Music sessions, an open kitchen and vintage cars add plenty of atmosphere, but the main allure is the vast array of dishes, which includes everything from a dense portion of *chivito* (Uruguayan steak sandwich) to home-rolled sushi, or even a bowl of fresh borscht. Choose from a pitcher of sangria or a bottle of local tannat to accompany whatever jumps off the menu. The best seat in the house is the table inside the converted Model T Ford, parked outside.

La Florida

Colonia del Sacramento Florida 215 (094 293036). Open noon-3.30pm, 8.30pm-midnight Mon, Tue, Thur-Sun. ££££. No credit cards. Modern/Seafood.

Set by the Portón de Campo entrance to the walled city, this low-ceilinged, candlelit restaurant is said to be Colonia's finest. Chef Carlos Bidanchon puts his own creative spin on national dishes like *morcilla* (blood sausage), and sticks to continental inspiration for fish and steak sauces. Home-made pâté or organic greens show up as starters, and seafood is a staple. Note that the opening hours aren't fixed, and reservations are mandatory.

Gibellini

Colonia del Sacramento Rivadavia 249, & Ituzaingó (052 29161). Open 11am-3.30pm, 6pm-midnight daily. £££. No credit cards. Italian.

Jazz records, family heirlooms and photos from the historic Teatro Colón in Buenos Aires coat the walls of this charming corner restaurant in the heart of the old city. The sounds of a tinkling piano and sultry tangos waft out of the door along with the tempting aromas of Italian and Spanish dishes, cooked up in a jazzy improvisational style by the chef and owner, Alejandro Gibellini.

Lentas Maravillas

Colonia del Sacramento Santa Rita 61 (052 20636). Open 11am-8pm Mon, Wed-Sun. ££. No credit cards. Café.

Whether you take tea on the lawn in the sunshine or enjoy a proper English breakfast in the library, the newest addition to Colonia's dining scene will have you agreeing with its ethos that slowing down is a virtue. Ginger-honey iced tea, cherry sangria or a frozen iced coffee accompany

Four Seasons Resort.

cucumber and goat's cheese toast or eggs and bacon out in the garden, cooled by the river breeze. The seating is designed for one or many, making this place a refuge for the solo traveller. Reading material is on hand, and there is no pressure to order, settle your bill, or do anything but enjoy the *lenta maravilla* ('slow miracle') of simply being here. Note that the restaurant closes one day a week, typically Tuesday but sometimes Wednesday.

Puerto Tranquilo
Colonia del Sacramento *Playa Álamo, Rambla de las Americas (052 23475/www.puertotranquilo.com). Open high season 24hrs daily. Low season 10am-7.30pm daily. £. Traditional.*
Just outside of town, on the way to the bullring, you'll find a rustic park and beach where tall grasses line the river shore. Puerto Tranquilo restaurant and bar sits on the cliff above, serving fried calamari, fresh fish, hamburgers and blended drinks. Concerts on the terrace make for a festive stop-over along the coast.

Viejo Barrio
Colonia del Sacramento *Vasconcellos 169 (052 25399). Open noon-3pm, 8pm-midnight Mon, Thur-Sun; noon-3pm Tue. ££. No credit cards. Italian/Traditional.*
To describe this atmospheric eaterie as child friendly would be an understatement. Known for its great service, good pasta and Uruguayan comfort food, Viejo Barrio is also home to Tatan the waiter clown, who tells jokes, does tricks and frequently exits the front of the restaurant singing. He works with a slew of props, mostly oversized felt hats stockpiled against the far wall of the restaurant. Fortunately, he also serves tasty dishes in generous portions, keeping the parents just as happy as the kids.

Stay

Barcelona
Colonia del Sacramento *De Portugal 191, Plaza del Gobernador (052 25241/www.colonia-alojamiento. com.ar). ££.*
Dating from 1850, this two-bedroom apartment sleeps five comfortably. It's located above the Barcelona vintage gallery and gift shop on Plaza del Gobernador, facing El Drugstore (*see p144*). Barcelona is a proper home from home, with a living room and a terrace with a view over the plaza. Outside, the tree-lined, cobblestone streets are filled with antique cars, and wool and silver shops.

La Casa de Los Limoneros
9km N of Colonia del Sacramento *Real de Vera, 700m from Rio de la Plata (052 31028/www.lacasa deloslimoneros). £££.*
In the late 1800s, high-class *porteños* would avoid Colonia proper – then a seedy sailors' hangout – and head to a more sophisticated enclave just under 10km to the north. Although the area's past attractions (the casino, hippodrome and bullring) have fallen into disrepair, Casa de los Limoneros is

flying a new flag in luxury in the sleepy, out-of-town countryside. Set amid the lemon groves, this romantic, ivy-covered (and gay-friendly) property looks out over reed-lined ponds and sprawling grounds, which include an outdoor pool. Rooms have high, beamed ceilings, polished wooden floors and wrought-iron bedsteads. Many also have giant shutters that open out on to the veranda, and spooky doors that were salvaged from an old Montevideo prison.

Don Antonio Posada
Colonia del Sacramento *Ituzaingó 232 (052 25344/ www.posadadonantonio.com). ££.*
Three levels of clean white rooms surround an outdoor gravel courtyard, occupied by a small swimming pool and clay-tile fountain. A buffet breakfast is included in the rates of this mid-sized hotel, located in the heart of the old town. The modern Spanish decor is in keeping with amenities such as Wi-Fi, a hydromassage bath and a solarium. Guests can enjoy the sun in the quiet courtyard, or lounge with a book under the white canvas umbrellas.

"Uruguay goes exotic at the Four Seasons Resort, with velvet sofas from Bali and a massive, wood-carved entrance."

Estancia Tierra Santa
Carmelo *Costa de las Vacas (054 02331/ www.estanciatierrasanta.com). £££. No credit cards.*
Located at the top of a long, dusty road, Tierra Santa is very much a country retreat. Treat yourself to a champagne picnic and enjoy the view of grazing cows and green fields, or breakfast on home-baked scones and honey. Farm-raised lamb or beef, grilled on the parrilla, are accompanied by home-grown organic vegetables. The magic here is in the details, including attentive service and a seasonal menu designed by the owners. The colonial-era building has been carefully restored to showcase its courtyards, tiled fountain and original well.

Four Seasons Resort
Carmelo *Ruta 21, km 262 (054 29000/ www.fourseasons.com). ££££.*
Uruguay goes exotic at this South-east Asian-themed resort, set in a pine forest along the riverbank. Silk and velvet settees from Bali and a massive, wood-carved entrance with an elephant motif seem out of context upon arrival, but prove oddly in tune with the river-beach backdrop. The ultra-luxurious complex consists of private bungalows lined up beyond a feng-shui spa, along with an elegant outdoor pool and a shady gazebo. In a nice twist, the bungalows each have their own outdoor shower, propped against the vine-covered wall of a private garden. There's an excellent on-site restaurant, which is open to non-guests.

Hotel Playa Seré

Carmelo *Tabaré 2671 (054 26202/*
www.hotelplayasere.com). ££. No credit cards.
With their clay-tile floors, colourful indigenous tapestries
and wood sculptures, the rooms at this Spanish-owned hotel
exude a welcoming warmth, and are anything but generic.
Even the hotel lobby is more like a living room, with its
grand fireplace and wood-beamed ceilings. The beds , kitted
out with high-thread-count sheets and fluffy down
comforters, are supremely comfortable – expecially after a
long day of watersports at the beach.

Posada de Campo Gondwana

10km N of Colonia del Sacramento *Casilla Correo
39439 (052 02155/www.posada-gondwana.com). £££.*
Horses, hammocks and an organic winery set the tone at
this Swiss-run ranch in Colonia's backcountry. Part
boutique hotel, part lodge, Gondwana comprises a series
of one-storey structures, with sunny porches overlooking
the gardens and fields beyond. Each room has a fireplace,
ceiling fan, bath and panoramic view. Personal touches,
such as a bedtime chocolate on your pillow and vintage
guitars scattered around the common areas of the estancia,
give it a homely feel, while cold cuts and muesli in the
breakfast buffet add a distinctly Swiss accent. Guests can
grill their own *asado* out by the saltwater swimming pool

after a game of tennis or golf, or take off on horseback
along the sands of the nearby river beach.

Posada del Virrey

Colonia del Sacramento *De España 217
(052 22223/www.posadadelvirrey.com). £££.*
With its marble chequerboard floor and lovely green tiling
along the walls, the Virrey mansion is a colonial treasure.
The town's history is reflected in its construction: Spanish
exposed brick in the lobby, Portuguese stone in the dining
room. Embroidered lace covers the beds, and the rooms
have high ceilings and time-warp treasures such as red-
leather lounge chairs and stately, claw-foot bathtubs. Head
up the communal roof terrace to catch the sunset.

Posada Plaza Mayor

Colonia del Sacramento *Calle del Comercio 111
(052 23193/www.posadaplazamayor.com). ££.*
A Portuguese ranch built in 1700 got a second lease of life
when it was transformed into a Spanish manor and, once
again, when it became this hotel. Located on the town's main
square, the posada comes with all the comforts of modern
boutique accommodation, as well as traditional decor: wood
rafters, iron gates, brass door-knockers and green shutters.
The beautiful courtyard garden, with a fountain at its
centre, is a highlight.

Factfile

When to go

Colonia and Carmelo are great towns to visit
year- round, though in summer (January to March),
reservations may be harder to come by. Winter
(July to September) can feel colder than across
the water in Buenos Aires. Spring (October to
December) and autumn (April to June) are good
times to enjoy deserted beaches.

Getting there

From Buenos Aires, Buquebus (Avenida Antártida
Argentina 821, 011 4316 6500, www.buquebus.
com) and Colonia Express (Avenida Pedro de
Mendoza 330, 011 4317 4100, www.colonia
express.com.ar) both offer daily ferry services
to Colonia. Buquebus's rapid service takes one
hour, and the slow ferry takes three hours, with
boats leaving every one to two hours. Colonia
Express is usually cheaper.

For travel to Carmelo, Cacciola Viajes (Lavalle
520, 011 4749 0329, www.cacciolaviajes.com)
has a two-hour service from Tigre (*see p166*).

From Montevideo, Colonia is a two hour 30
minute drive along Ruta 1. Carmelo is one hour
by car from Colonia, along Ruta 21.

Getting around

In Colonia, the centre of town is small and
distances are walkable, but the beaches are

farther out, so it's a good idea to have some
sort of transportation to get around.

For car hire in Colonia, try Europcar (Avenida
Artigas 152, 052 28454, www.europcar.com.uy)
or Thrifty Car (Avenida General Flores 172, 052
22939, www.thriftycar.com.uy). Thrifty also offers
golf-cart rentals; both require credit or debit card
authorisation. Moto Rent Colonia (Virrey Cevallos
223, 052 22266, www.motorent.com.uy) has
scooters, bicycles, golf carts and dune buggies.

In Carmelo, Walking Tour (099 520898) offers
tours of downtown as well as English tours of
Irurtia Winery.

Tourist information

Colonia del Sacramento 224 Manuel Lobo (052
28506/052 26141). Open 9am-6pm daily.
Carmelo 19 de Abril 246, Casa de la Cultura (054
23840/054 22001). Open 9am-6pm Mon-Fri;
10am-6pm Sat; 11am-6pm Sun.

Internet

In Colonia, the Thrifty Car (*see above*) office
has a computer with a high-speed connection.
Otherwise, many of the town's restaurants and
hotels have Wi-Fi.

In Carmelo, New Generation Cyber Games
(Uruguay 373) is open 9am-2am daily, and Compu
Service (19 de Abril) is open 8am-midnight daily.

Clockwise from top left: local wildlife (3); Rincón del Socorro.

Esteros del Iberá

Argentina

A watery wonderland brimming with biodiversity.

You'll find peace in Esteros del Iberá, but not quiet. Man-made noises are rare in this vast, largely unpopulated reserve – the occasional growl of a jeep taking passengers on a night safari, perhaps, or a snatch of *chamamé* folk music on a local FM station. Instead, the air is filled with a rich and raucous polyphony of squawks, burps, splashes, howls and bizarre whirring noises, the concerted effort of more than 350 types of bird, plus dozens of rare and exotic species of mammal, reptile and amphibian. Dawn's chorus gives way to noon's concerto, then dusk's oratorio; sometimes it seems like only the anacondas are keeping their counsel.

The pit in which this natural orchestra plays is the second-largest wetland in the world, after Brazil's Pantanal, and covers 14 per cent of Corrientes province. Once part of the main stream of the Río Paraná, Esteros del Iberá is now a subtly shifting – and steam-iron flat – terrain of lakes, marshes, savannah and floating islands. The reserve lacks asphalt roads, chain hotels, fast-food restaurants, cable television access and reliable mobile-phone coverage. And those are just five of its virtues.

Before it was given protected status in 1983, Esteros del Iberá was home to trappers who lived a hand-to-mouth existence spear-fishing for piranha and trading capybara and caiman hides. Many of these erstwhile hunters have been retrained as park rangers, while the giant rodents and mini-alligators they once stalked now roam and bask with impunity. Guaraní is still widely spoken in these parts, and is most obvious in the name given to the marshlands by its original inhabitants: 'Iberá', or 'glittering waters'. Late in the day, when the setting sun has gilded the water hyacinths and rushes in syrupy light, and the pale moon has cast its ghostly hue on the primordial waterland, you'll understand precisely what they were driving at.

Explore

MERCEDES

If you're coming to Esteros del Iberá by road (and unless you charter a small plane, it's the only way), you will come via **Mercedes**, a medium-sized town (population 35,000) that is the closest transport hub to the reserve. If you have some time to kill before your connection, take a stroll around this atmospheric town, which has a slice of South Americana on every corner. School-uniformed teens kick up dust on their mopeds, attracting the censorious gaze of men in full gaucho regalia. (Note the wide-brimmed sombreros, much larger than those worn by pampas gauchos, and the coloured neck-handkerchiefs, which denote the political bias of the wearer.) The main thoroughfare, Avenida San Martín, leads from the bus station to the town square, where people gather at dusk to pass around a *mate* and tap their feet to *chamamé* folk music or Colombian *cumbia*. You'll meet no one at siesta time, unless it's a stray dog or another confused tourist.

Mercedes is famous nationwide for being the birthplace of Antonio 'Gauchito' Gil, a 19th-century farm worker turned outlaw who diverted capital from the rich to the poor in the approved fashion. His sanctuary is located six kilometres from town on Ruta 123. Pilgrims (up to 200,000 in recent years) flock here on 8 January, the anniversary of Gil's death.

COLONIA CARLOS PELLEGRINI

A quiet hamlet with a permanent population of around 500, **Colonia Carlos Pellegrini** is the focal point for tourism in Esteros del Iberá. Located 110 kilometres north-east of Mercedes on the banks of Laguna Iberá (one of the few sizable stretches of open water in the area), it can be accessed only via RP 40, a *ripio* (dirt road).

There are no formal street addresses in Carlos Pellegrini, but as the village is little more than a dusty square surrounded by lodges and posadas, and as everyone here knows everyone else, you won't get lost. The two most important public buildings are the Tourist Information Office, where you can pick up maps and find out about excursions, and the Interpretation Centre, which is on the opposite side of the Laguna Iberá and can be reached via a Bailey bridge. The centre is mostly staffed by former trappers who have been retrained as park rangers. It's worth visiting the centre soon after arriving in town, as it contains numerous resources – photographs, scale models and subtitled videos – that serve as a good introduction to the topology and biodiversity of the reserve. Several wildlife trails radiate out into the evergreen gallery forest from here, including a 'monkey path' which takes

Esteros del Iberá

Esteros del Iberá

Colonia Carlos Pellegrini

Mercedes

0   10 km

Esteros del Iberá

Historic sites
● ◉ ◉ ◉ ◉

Art & architecture
● ◉ ◉ ◉ ◉

Hotels
● ● ● ● ◉

Eating & drinking
● ● ● ● ◉

Scenery
● ● ● ● ◉

Outdoor activities
● ● ● ● ◉

Keeping it wild

If you're a hiker, a camper or simply a devotee of wilderness chic, your wardrobe probably contains at least one item connected to Douglas Tompkins, founder of the North Face and co-founder of Esprit, or his wife Kristin, former CEO of Patagonia Inc. But why stop there? If you're visiting Esteros del Iberá, you can shave off another degree of separation by staying at the Tompkins' ranch, Rincón del Socorro.

The estancia is one of several projects in Argentina and Chile owned and run by the couple, who turned in their corporate credentials in the early 1990s to focus on conservation. Both are fervent followers of the radical deep ecology movement and its eight-point, planet-saving programme. Put crudely, proponents of deep ecology believe that human beings are part of nature, and not above it. Those who believe otherwise are simply deluding themselves, and unless the human race wakes up and gets with the programme, it will continue sleepwalking to its own destruction.

This is perhaps a little heavy for those who still feel smug about separating their used wine bottles into 'green' and 'clear', but you don't have to sign up to the philosophy to appreciate how it works in practice. At Rincón del Socorro, full-time biologists are employed to monitor the impact that reintroducing extinct but native animals, such as the giant anteater, might have on the local ecosystem. Tompkins hopes

eventually to reintroduce the long-vanished native jaguar, a plan that has not endeared him to local livestock farmers.

It isn't the first time this eco-entrepreneur has faced controversy. His first major project in the region, Parque Pumalín, a Yosemite-sized nature reserve in Chile, drew the ire of the logging industry and Chilean nationalists, and bizarre accusations that Tompkins was a CIA insurgent or had plans to turn his reserve into a future Jewish homeland (Tompkins is not, in fact, Jewish).

The former clothing magnate has found the going easier in Argentina. In 2001, Tompkins bought Estancia Monte León in Santa Cruz province through his trust, Conservación Patagonica (www.patagonialandtrust.org). The land was immediately handed over to the Argentinian government to become the country's newest national park.

It remains to be seen whether the Tompkins' and their latest foundation, the Conservation Land Trust (www.theconservationlandtrust.org), can make the same impact in Esteros del Iberá, where the fragile ecology is threatened by hydroelectric projects and environmentally irresponsible farming. In the meantime, places like Rincón del Socorro are a useful standing reprimand to those who think 'eco-tourism' is little more than a gimmick dreamed up by the travel industry.

Clockwise from top: Rincon del Socorro; Posada de la Laguna (3).

walkers through habitat favoured by howler monkey families (you'll know them when you hear them). A much quieter spot is the village cemetery, where the tombstones are painted in colours that signify the political affiliation of the deceased – proof, if you needed any, that Argentinians take their politics very seriously.

But it's the living, not the dead, that draws people to Esteros del Iberá; and there is no shortage of life. A comprehensive list of the area's flora and fauna would take up an entire book, but even a short synopsis gives an idea of the region's incredible biodiversity. Among the mammals, the capybara – or *carpincho*, as it's known locally – is the most emblematic. This herbivorous rodent, the biggest in the world, rarely ventures far from the water's edge and can often be seen grazing or swimming in large family groups. Other mammals that can be seen – or, in some cases, heard – include the black howler monkey, the neotropical otter, the marsh deer, the pampas deer, the viscacha (a type of chinchilla) and, if you're lucky, the maned wolf.

Among the reptiles, the caiman tops the billing. There are two species of this mini-alligator in Esteros del Iberá: the broad-snouted caiman and the spectacled caiman. You will often see them motionless on the banks of the lake, or on a floating island, their mouths hanging agape to help regulate their body temperature. At night, the caimans feed on piranha, their long snouts floating on the waterline and their orange eyes lighting up in the darkness. Other reptiles you may (or may not) enjoy seeing in the marshlands include the false water cobra, the venomous wutu (a type of fer-de-lance) and the yellow anaconda, which, at up to three metres long, is the largest boa in Argentina.

"Arrive on 1 January with a plan to spot a different species of bird each day, and you won't complete your task until Christmas."

And then there are the birds, which are likely to bring out the inner twitcher in even the most hardened city-dweller. If you arrive in the marshlands on 1 January, with a plan to spot a different species of bird each day, you won't complete your task until around Christmas. The reserve is home to big birds such as greater rheas and storks, as well as small birds (kingfishers, cowbirds), brightly coloured birds

(vermillion flycatchers, parakeets), monochrome birds (hawks, buzzards, vultures), noisy birds (the southern screamer, the burrowing owl), silent birds (white-throated hummingbirds) and comic birds (several species of toucan and numerous woodpeckers). If you don't know your yellow-breasted crake from your southern lapwing, don't worry: most lodges and posadas provide guests with an illustrated bird checklist. If, on the other hand, you're a dedicated ornithologist, make advance arrangements with your accommodation for a specialised tour with a local expert.

Eat

The vast majority of mid- to upper-range lodgings in and around Esteros del Iberá offer full board: three meals a day, plus tea and snacks in the afternoon. For some, the phrase 'all-inclusive' may stir up thoughts of hermetically-sealed Caribbean resorts, but much of the home-cooked food found here puts that of most big-city Argentinian restaurants to shame. Ingredients are locally sourced, not because it's fashionable to do so, but because there are no major roads on which freight can be carried into the marshlands. In the case of Rincón del Socorro, whose kitchen turns out minor masterpieces of rustic cuisine, most of what ends up on the plate comes from the estancia's organic garden.

Vegetarians and people with special dietary needs are well catered for at most places, though it's best to give your hosts advance notice of any requirements. If you fancy popping out to a local restaurant, you'll come up against the fact that there are no local restaurants in the marshlands. Colonia Carlos Pellegrini has a general store and a couple of *comedores* – think upscale soup kitchen – of no fixed abode (just ask around).

Several regional specialities are worth noting, each of which can be traced back to Corrientes' pre-Columbian Guaraní culture. The most famous of these is *mate* (*see p329* **Tea time**), the green tea served and shared in gourds. Correntinos get through gallons of the stuff, and on a hot day, drink it chilled from jugs, a concoction known as *tereré*. In Corrientes, if there is *mate*, there will almost certainly be *chipá*, small loaves of bread made from manioc flour and topped with grated cheese. Other classic regional dishes include papaya jelly (often served with cheese), *quibebe* (puréed pumpkin mixed with milk and cheese) and fish such as dorado, pejerrey and surubí, netted in the Río Paraná and either baked or grilled on the barbecue. Most locals would laugh at the idea of eating caiman (*yacaré*), but several lodges call it a 'native dish' and serve it up anyway. It tastes like chicken.

If you need to grab a bite to eat in Mercedes en route to the marshlands, we recommend one of the following: the parrilla La Casa de Chirola (Pujol and Sarmiento), El Quincho (San Martín 1240, 03773 420314), whose varied menu includes pastas and vegetarian options, or Pizza Libre (Plaza 25 de Mayo).

Stay

If you need to stop for the night in Mercedes, try Casona Silvia Lacour Bed & Breakfast (Belgrano 520, 03773 421622, www.casonasilvialacour.com.ar) or Hotel El Sol (San Martín 519, 03773 420283). A reliable budget option in Colonia Carlos Pellegrini is Don Justino Hostel (03773 499415, www.iberatours.com.ar).

Unless otherwise stated, the rates quoted in these listings include full board (alcoholic drinks usually excluded) and guided excursions in the reserve. Transfers from Mercedes or Posadas are not generally included, though your lodging will happily make the necessary arrangements.

Hostería Ñande Retá
Colonia Carlos Pellegrini *(03773 499411/ www.nandereta.com). £££.*
Meaning 'our land' in Guaraní, Ñande Retá lives up to its name: the main house, a double-eaved structure that resembles an oriental pagoda crossed with a jungle lodge, and all the furniture is constructed entirely from local wood and stone. Set among pine, eucalyptus and mulberry trees, the property contains five double rooms, four triples and one apartment that sleeps five. Excursions include short boat trips, horse-rides, night safaris and longer day trips to estancias and more remote parts of the marshlands.

Irupé Lodge
Colonia Carlos Pellegrini *(03773 15 402193 mobile/www.irupelodge.com.ar). £££.*
Appropriately for a lodging named after a type of giant water lily, Irupé sits snugly on the banks of Laguna Iberá. The thatched huts that double as guest rooms have been raised on stilts, which serve both to improve the views and frustrate the snakes. A full range of day and night excursions are offered, including horseback rides and trips to local estancias. The tasty home-made meals can be taken on the veranda, weather permitting. Between them, the Swiss-Argentinian owners can get by in most European languages.

Posada Aguapé
Colonia Carlos Pellegrini *(03773 499412/ www.iberaesteros.com.ar). £££.*
Open since 1997, Aguapé is the oldest tourist lodge in Colonia Carlos Pellegrini and still one of the best. It consists of four buildings set in an attractive garden that slopes down to the lake's edge. The 12 simple but immaculate suites are complemented by a restaurant/bar, a living room, a swimming pool and a private pier jutting out towards the

floating islands that drift across the lake. Day-long guided treks are organised, taking guests by jeep to the Camba Trapa and Aguará marshes, 40km from the lodge. There, you'll get the chance to glimpse the shy marsh deer as well as aquatic birds such as the giant jabiru stork and the roseate spoonbill. Good home-made regional food is dished up four times a day.

Posada de la Laguna
Colonia Carlos Pellegrini *(03773 499413/ www.posadadelalaguna.com). ££££. No credit cards.*
The pick of the accommodation in Carlos Pellegrini, Posada de la Laguna is exactly what it says it is – a country lodge next to the lake. Set in a spacious private park, the property consists of two elegant, vine-covered buildings – one housing a comfortable living room and dining area, the other offering six airy guest rooms giving out on to a colonnaded veranda. Between motor launch and kayak excursions on the lake, guests can take a dip in the pool or bird-watch from a hammock on the veranda as woodpeckers, yellow flycatchers, southern screamer vultures and many other species flit and strut around the park. Owner Elsa Güiraldes is an excellent, hands-on host, determined that her guests get the most from their stay.

Posada Ypa Sapukai
Colonia Carlos Pellegrini *(03773 420155/ www.iberaturismo.com.ar). £££.*
A warm welcome awaits weary travellers at Ypa Sapukai, a family-run lodging built by Claudia and Pedro Noailles and their children. The secluded garden runs down to the lake and is dotted with lounge chairs and hammocks strung up on shady pergolas; there is also a well-maintained pool. Lake excursions (daytime and nocturnal) leave from the posada's private jetty. Other organised activities include guided horse-rides and walks in the town's back country. It's good value for money.

"Puerto Valle's 18th-century manor house has a howler monkey footpath, a private beach and an outdoor bar."

Puerto Valle
230km NE of Colonia Carlos Pellegrini, *RN 12, km 1282 (03786 425700/www.hotelpuertovalle.com). £££.*
This upscale complex is located at the northern tip of Esteros del Iberá, where the marshlands creep up to the banks of the Río Paraná. The property's main building, El Casco, is an adobe-walled manor house that dates back to the 18th century; it contains four guest rooms. The annexe, Casa Chica, is a two-floor duplex suite whose tall windows afford views of the river. The menu of excursions is long

and includes – with a surcharge – trips to the Iguazú Falls and the San Ignacio Miní Jesuit ruins, both in neighbouring Misiones province (*see pp322-29*). Most guests, however, will be happy to potter around the complex's own extensive amenities, which include a caiman nursery, a howler monkey footpath, a private beach and a lovely outdoor bar. If you've always wanted to say, 'Bring me some alligator croquettes, and make it snappy,' you'll appreciate the on-site restaurant's 'native menu'.

Rincón del Socorro
20km SW of Colonia Carlos Pellegrini *(03782 497172/03782 497073/www.rincondelsocorro.com).* *££££.*
Modestly describing itself as a 'small eco-tourist hotel', Rincón del Socorro is in fact a high-end estancia in the middle of Esteros del Iberá. It's perfect for travellers who don't see why milk and honey and wilderness can't be combined. Formerly a cattle ranch – several of the original adobe structures have been carefully restored – the property, which occupies 120sq km of savanna and shallow marsh, is owned by entrepreneur and ecologist Douglas Tompkins (*see p151* **Keeping it wild**). The six spacious guest rooms blend the kind of comforts you expect at these rates (Egyptian-cotton linen, for example) with a pastiche

frontier aesthetic (including stuffed alligators and sepia wildlife prints). Away from the main house, three cottages offer greater space and seclusion. The food is outstanding, with most ingredients sourced from all of 45m away, in the estancia's kitchen garden. Between meals, guests can explore the grounds in a jeep, on a horse or simply on foot; viscachas, armadillos, grey foxes, marsh deer and giant anteaters are among the species that thrive on the ranch. Night safaris are particularly memorable. (Daily transfers to and from the estancia are available on its private plane; Corrientes and Posadas airports are both served.)

San Alonso
Laguna Paraná, 83km NE of Mercedes *(03782 497172/03782 497073/www.rincondelsocorro.com).* *££££.*
Rincón del Socorro's sister ranch, San Alonso is located in the remote heart of Esteros del Iberá, and is not easy to reach. (Guests must either take a jeep-boat combination or charter the estancia's private plane.) Up to ten people can be accommodated in the main house, a model of comfortable rusticity that has five simple bedrooms and a spacious living/dining area with open fireplace. Most guests are here for the fly-fishing, with organised and bilingual excursions giving anglers the chance to land a 22lb dorado.

Factfile

When to go
Esteros del Iberá is a year-round destination, and most lodgings close only for the owners' annual holiday (check the website), if then. Corrientes has a subtropical climate, which means heavy rains and high temperatures are possible at any time. (Temperatures can drop quite steeply at night, so pack a fleece.) January and February can be particularly torrid, with temperatures often climbing above 40°C.

Getting there
Flechabus operates several daily bus services to Mercedes from BA's Retiro station (011 4000 5200, www.flechabus.com.ar). The best option is to take the overnight service, which leaves at 9pm and arrives in Mercedes just after 7am. The other option is to take the 90-minute flight from the capital to Posadas and then to proceed to Colonia Carlos Pellegrini by taxi or, for those with experience driving on dirt roads, by hire car.
   Getting from Mercedes to Colonia Carlos Pellegrini presents the biggest challenge. A taxi ride along the 110 kilometres of RP 40 will take approximately two hours and set you back around AR$400. El Rayo (office at the Mercedes bus station, 03773 420184) and Itatí II (03773 421342) both run bus services from Mercedes to Carlos Pellegrini, leaving at around 12.30pm. The journey takes at least three hours 30 minutes

and often longer, as the buses are poorly maintained and prone to breaking down.
   In theory, there is a return service from Carlos Pellegrini to Mercedes twice daily; in practice, you should always have a back-up option.

Getting around
Once in the wetlands, getting from A to B will involve either a jeep, a horse, a boat, a bike or your own two feet. All transport will be arranged by your lodging. Unfortunately, this destination cannot yet be recommended for travellers with physical disabilities.

Tourist information
Mercedes Tourist Office José M Gómez & Caá Guazú (03773 15 414384 mobile, www.mercedescorrientes.gov.ar). Open 7am-1pm, 3-7pm Mon-Fri; 9am-1pm, 2-8pm Sat; 2-8pm Sun. **Colonia Tourist Office** Carlos Pellegrini, main plaza (03773 15 401205 mobile). Open 8am-6pm Mon, Wed-Sun.

Internet
The best internet café in Mercedes is Hugo Peralta (San Martín 932, 03773 42900). Most lodgings provide Wi-Fi internet (often in the communal area only), but don't expect a fast connection. Mobile phone coverage is decidedly patchy.

Top: Río Uruguay (2). Bottom:
Parque Nacional El Palmar.

El Palmar de Colón

Argentina

Sprawling palm forests by a sleepy riverside town.

Parque Nacional El Palmar and its surrounding area seem caught in a time warp where little changes or even moves much, apart from the Río Uruguay, which ponderously pushes its massive bulk south to the Atlantic. In El Palmar's lush prehistoric landscape of tall Yatay palms, it's easy to imagine a brontosaurus lumbering by. On the park's waterfront, the crumbling remains of Jesuit settlements and old mining equipment create an air of nostalgia for the abandoned efforts of man to get a foothold on these backwater riverbanks.

In the sleepy riverside town of Colón, this languid atmosphere continues. Here, little streets run past leafy plazas and old townhouses before finishing up at the river, where locals sit and drink *mate* on the promenade wall. Recent years have seen the town occasionally stir from its slumber as foreigners join the throng of *porteños* who invade its beaches in summer and on long weekends.

Visitors come to explore the river, to visit Parque Nacional El Palmar, or just to let the laid-back ambience and warm sun work its soothing magic. A three-hour drive north of Buenos Aires, the area makes an ideal short excursion from the capital, or detour on a trip north to Iguazú Falls or the wetlands of Esteros del Iberá.

The original Swiss settlers who landed on these river shores found a natural paradise untouched by man. With much of that paradise still largely intact, it's a backwater worth staking a claim to – at least for a night or two.

Explore

Many of the sights advertised in and around **Colón**, such as regional museums, historic buildings and the numerous spa facilities, are aimed primarily at the Argentinian market. For foreign visitors passing through, the main attractions can be visited over two days or even crammed into one if time is pressing.

PARQUE NACIONAL EL PALMAR

Created in 1966 and situated 56 kilometres north of Colón, **Parque Nacional El Palmar** is open from 8am to 6pm daily (03447 493053, www.parquesnacionales.gov.ar, admission AR$30). Its palm forests, undergrowth and grasslands are home to a wealth of species, including the squirrel cuckoo, capybara (an enormous guinea pig-like rodent), vampire bat and pit viper. Don't get too excited, though, as many are nocturnal, difficult to spot or fervently avoid homo sapiens. Notable exceptions are the plains vizcachas, large rodents that beg for food from visitors in the campsite, and the huge tegu lizards, who sun themselves in the open spaces.

At the park entrance, visitors are provided with maps delineating the vehicle tracks that cross the 85 square kilometre area, and the walking paths that branch off from these. The first road off the main route winds up to La Glorieta, the highest point in the park and the best place from which to view the lush, undulating terrain. Watching the sunset over the palms from here is spectacular. Before reaching the hilltop, you can take a short detour to view some of the denser stands of Yatay palms. The park was originally created to protect these modest-looking palms, which were once the dominant tree species of the region and can live to a staggering 700 years old. Native peoples used to collect the fruit for food, but the arrival of Europeans saw the ancient trees cleared for grazing and ignominiously used as telegraph poles.

Regenerating the palms has proven to be difficult at times, but an initially tragic-seeming bush blaze in 1979 demonstrated that resistance to fire was one natural advantage. The palms emerged unscathed, while the dense undergrowth which smothered the young palms was burned away. The park wardens now run a controlled burning regimen.

Below La Glorieta is a one-kilometre path which leads into the depths of the gallery forest. The cool, shady interior makes it a good spot to take a breather beside the stream or the small set of rapids. Look out for golden-crested woodpeckers and jays hopping through the bushes.

Down on the riverfront lie the remains of a small 18th-century Jesuit community, where locally produced lime was used to tan leather for export. A few walls of the living quarters still remain.

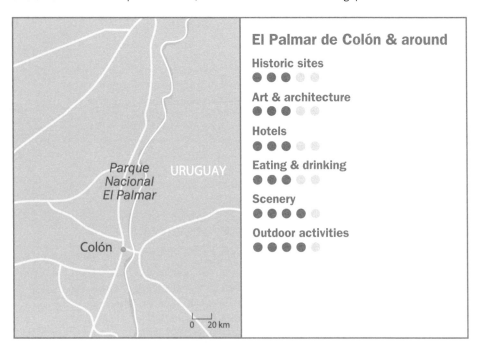

El Palmar de Colón & around

Historic sites
● ● ● ○ ○

Art & architecture
● ● ● ○ ○

Hotels
● ● ● ○ ○

Eating & drinking
● ● ● ● ○

Scenery
● ● ● ● ○

Outdoor activities
● ● ● ● ○

Parque Nacional El Palmar

URUGUAY

Colón

0   20 km

Parque Nacional El Palmar.

Following the continent-wide expulsion of the Jesuits, the area was developed as a lime works, which supplied much of the material for the growth of Buenos Aires. Active until the 20th century, it was redeveloped as a gravel works; loading wharves can be seen rusting at the river's edge. Swimming in the water on the clean and often deserted beach is highly recommended, but be careful of strong currents further out.

Set just back from the beach, a path leads to a colony of monk parakeets, who occupy huge communal nests of woven branches in the palm tops. Other trails lead to the grasslands at the edge of the forest and down to the lime works. It's worth stopping at the visitor centre to get an idea of the plant and animal life in the park. There is a restaurant and café here, as well as a campsite for those who don't want to leave. A business called Capybara organises bicycle tours from the campsite.

COLÓN

Colón was originally built as a port to serve the nearby town of San José, but its position on the river soon allowed it to overtake its progenitor. Floods of Swiss-French immigrants filled it with attractive buildings such as the old Estación Fluvial (now the tourist office) and the Teatro Centenario (12 de Abril, between Esteva Berga & Andrade), now a cultural centre. Four kilometres outside town on the road to San José, the incongruous-looking Dutch windmill had to be powered by mule, due to a lack of wind. If you're interested in local history, the tourist office produces a good information leaflet. The broad, sandy beach is a wonderful spot for a freshwater dip. It is bath-water warm in summer, and swimmable for at least eight months of the year. Beware of strong currents further out.

OUTDOOR ACTIVITIES

Colón's outdoor activities inevitably focus on the river. The town's most experienced adventure travel agency, Ita i Cora (San Martín 97, 03447 423360, www.itaicora.com), is owned by Charlie Adamson, a character who seems to have leaped straight off the pages of a Graham Greene novel. He offers overland tours in an enormous ex-army vehicle, and the boat trips (narrated in Charlie's impeccable English) are highly recommended. Sites visited include the huge, abandoned meat-packing plant of Pueblo Liebig, Río Uruguay's vast sandbanks, and abandoned quarries for semi-precious stone and fossil collecting.

For splashing about a little closer to the shore, plenty of businesses spring up during the summer months, renting canoes and pedal boats. If you're visiting out of season, head to Camping Piedras Coloradas (Juan José Paso & Avenida Costanera, 03447 423548), on the southern edge of town, where you can rent a range of nautical equipment year round, including boats, jet skis and windsurfing boards.

Eat

Colón's restaurant strip is the busy 12 de Abril; with a few exceptions, it consists of parrillas and pizzerias serving standard fare at reasonable prices. The more upmarket eateries are found around the harbour, away from the town centre.

La Bita
Colón *Gouchón 28 (03442 15 416988 mobile). Open high season noon-3.30pm, 8pm-midnight daily. Low season noon-3.30pm, 8pm-midnight Thur-Sun. ££. No credit cards. Seafood.*
A welcome addition to a waterside town with a distinct lack of fish restaurants, La Bita is a charming café-style set-up overlooking the water, from the depths of which local fishermen pull much of its menu. Aquatic dwellers from both the Río Uruguay and the southern coast are put to good use, served solo or with pasta. Try starting with a plate of crispy *rabas* (calamari), which is big enough to share, then move on to grilled surubí, a river fish served with roasted vegetables. Alternatively, opt for the ravioli stuffed with salmon and drenched in a creamy seafood sauce. Staff here are genuinely excited about the food, which is almost always a sure sign of excellence.

La Cantina
Colón *Alejo Peyret 79 (03447 423791). Open noon-2.30pm, 8pm-midnight Tue-Sun. £. No credit cards. Traditional.*
If the authentic Argentinian neighbourhood restaurant is what you're after, make your way to friendly La Cantina. Though it lacks the decorative and gourmet trappings of many of the newer eateries, it makes up for it with traditional quality and almost absurd quantities at a very affordable price. A juicy chicken supreme (breast fried in breadcrumbs) with chips, washed down with a bottle of torrontés, will leave both your stomach and bank account feeling as if they've negotiated a good deal. The informal atmosphere makes it a good place to take kids.

La Cosquilla del Ángel
Colón *Alejo Peyret 180 (03447 423711). Open noon-3pm, 8pm-midnight Mon, Wed-Sun. £££. International.*
La Cosquilla del Ángel (the Angel's Tickle) is intimate, warm and friendly. If the name doesn't tickle your fancy, the food surely will. Each dish has been given a cryptic name by owner Sergio in an effort to stimulate conversation among reticent diners. If you end up at a linguistic cul-de-sac, he will be happy to explain, for example, that 'Ombligo de Venus' is pumpkin-stuffed pasta. The menu offers imaginative and successful combinations, such as chicken in a sweet and sour beer sauce with carmelised onions. Team it with a delicious bottle of '4 Variedades' from local bodega Vulliez-Sermet (*see p161*).

Juanes

Colón *12 de Abril & Juan José Paso (03447 421942). Open 8am-1am Mon, Wed-Sun. £. Café.*
A sort of all-day, all-round corner café, Juanes is the perfect place to eat breakfast, have a sandwich, enjoy a light lunch or sip a cocktail in the evening. On the corner of Plaza San Martín, with outside seating overlooking the square, Colón's blue-chip café has a young and friendly staff as well as reliable food and drinks.

El Sótano de los Quesos

Colón *Chacabuco & Avenida Costanera (03447 427163). Open high season 7pm-1am daily. Low season 11am-8pm daily. ££. Traditional.*
'The Cheese Cellar' is an unusual type of place to find outside the capital or alternative hotspots such as El Bolsón (*see p182*). All of the beautifully displayed foodstuffs on sale in the brick cellar are locally produced, and the dairy produce comes from the organic milk of the restaurant's own herd. For those keen to know the difference between a *pategrás* and a provolone, the staff will happily show you around. At a garden table overlooking the river you can share an enormous board of meats, cheeses and bread, washed down nicely with a mug of ice-cold beer from a local microbrewery.

"Verde Gourmet is a surprise: a vegetarian restaurant in small-town Argentina that not only serves a fantastic range of flavours, but also garners the respect of local meat-eaters."

Verde Gourmet

Colón *Belgrano 75 (03447 15 424071 mobile/www. verdegourmet.com). Open 10.30am-3pm, 7.30-11pm Mon-Sat ££. Vegetarian.*
As many Argentinian restaurants seem to approach vegetarian food with barbecue blinkers on (throw on salt, pepper, oil, and all will be well), dining out as a herbivore can be disappointing. It's surprising, then, to find a vegetarian restaurant in small-town Argentina that not only serves a fantastic range of flavours, but also garners the respect of local meat-eaters. The restaurant cooks up crêpes with a filling of your choice, and is generally open to creating custom-made meals. Protein-high, soy-based dishes abound, and although booze is absent along with flesh, there's a great selection of teas and juices that will make you feel as if you've done both your body and the beasts some good.

El Viejo Almacén

Colón *Urquiza & Juan José Paso (03447 422216). Open noon-3pm, 8pm-midnight daily. ££. Parrilla.*
This is Colón's establishment restaurant – and being in Argentina, it is, of course, a parrilla. More than 40 years of service, a broad selection of meat, and a substantial, well-regarded wine cellar bring locals flocking to this large, rustic dining room on most nights. If you have assigned yourself the task of making a dent in the country's herd, you can continue to do so here with great gusto. If you don't fancy meat but want to stay local, the chef also knows how to treat freshly caught river fish.

Stay

Be sure to book early if you're visiting in January or February. Much of the accommodation is spread out around the town, so unless you have a car, find something central. Outside of the busy summer and Easter holidays, prices drop and you can almost always negotiate a bargain, especially if staying for more than one night.

La Aurora del Palmar

3km N of Parque Nacional El Palmar *RN 14, km 202 (03447 421549/www.auroradelpalmar.com.ar). ££.*
This is the only accommodation located close to the park. The owners of this estancia were inspired by its publicly owned neighbour to collaborate with Vida Silvestre, Argentina's largest nature conservation body, to protect the last privately owned areas of palm landscape that haven't been eaten up by agribusiness. La Aurora offers rustic but comfortable accommodation – try and snap up one of the old converted railway carriages, which are more quirky and attractive than the cottages. Excursions to see the national park can be arranged, and tours around the estancia by vehicle, as well as riding trips, are also offered. Leisurely plucking mandarins from the lush groves as you ride along is not be missed. A wholesome selection of pastas and meat is served in the restaurant, and watching the sun set behind the tall stands of palms from the veranda with an ice-cold beer in hand is the perfect end to a day.

Bodega Vulliez Sermet Cabañas

Colón *RP 135, km 8 (03447 15 645925 mobile/ www.bodegavulliezsermet.com.ar). £. No credit cards.*
Since 1997, when a law banning the production of wine outside the western provinces was repealed, the Vulliez family has been able to return to its ancestral activity, building this, the only vineyard in the region. The friendly owners rent three cabañas, spread across the spacious garden of the pretty bodega. Built in Swiss-French style, with green shutters and painted tiles on the ceiling, the accommodation includes use of the lovingly restored farmhouse where breakfast is served, as well as other meals on request. The award-winning wines are excellent, and if you are not planning a trip to Mendoza (*see pp200-215*), this is a great opportunity to boost your knowledge of the grape – how it is made and, of course, how it goes down.

Hostería Restaurant del Puerto
Colón *Alejo Peyret 158 (03447 422698/ www.hosteriadecolon.com.ar). £. No credit cards.*
Overflowing with old-world charm, this is Colón's only lodging where you feel like you could have just dragged your luggage up from a 19th-century paddle steamer. The 100-year-old building has been immaculately restored, maintaining an idiosyncratic layout that includes some corridor-shaped bedrooms. Quirky period rooms are decorated with antique furniture, and there's a heated pool to the rear. It's worth booking one of the 12 rooms in the original hostería, as the adjoining new construction, despite its use of recycled antique materials, does not match the atmosphere of the old building.

"Designated a national historical monument in 1974, the Palacio Santa Cándida has rooms fit for royalty."

Hotel Costarenas
Colón *Avenida Quirós & 12 de Abril (03447 425050/ www.costarenas.com.ar). £££.*
In this modern construction on the waterfront, rooms facing the river offer magnificent views on to the water and Uruguay beyond. The services are first-class, with an outdoor pool and terrace, and the best spa in town hidden beneath the building. Prices, however, seem to be firmly in line with Argentina's inflation rate, especially considering the modest size of a standard room. If you want to splurge on luxury with a view, book a suite and let the attentive staff see to your every need.

Hotel Plaza
Colón *Belgrano & 12 de Abril (03447 421043/ www.hotel-plaza.com.ar). £££.*
Looking like a moored cruise liner, this new hotel sits rather incongruously on the corner of leafy Plaza San Martín, which is otherwise surrounded by pretty townhouses. However, the interior is tastefully designed with an airy, minimalist layout, and a spacious garden with a pool and bar is at the rear. Rooms are spacious and comfortable, and those facing the plaza have beautiful views over the tree tops to the river. Beside the pool is an area offering basic spa facilities, including massage treatments.

Palacio Santa Cándida
Concepción del Uruguay, 35km from Colón
Eva Perón 114 (03442 422188/www.santacandida. com). ££.
Though this Italianate palace, which sits in almost 100 acres of elegant parkland near the town of Concepción, is some way from El Palmar and Colón, its 19th-century opulence makes the drive worthwhile. Commissioned in 1847 by General Justo José de Urquiza, Santa Cándida was built by Italian architect Pedro Fossatti and was named a national historical monument in 1974. The entire building, including the 11 rooms, is decorated in magnificent period furniture. Besides sleeping in a room fit for royalty, you can amuse yourself with kayaking, riding, fishing and, for those who really fancy themselves as landed gentry, small-game hunting. For those arriving by bus, pickups from Colón or Concepción del Uruguay can be arranged. At the time of writing, the hotel was undergoing renovation and was expected to re-open in late 2009.

Factfile

When to go
In January and February, the combination of the area's beaches with its proximity to the capital sees it overrun with weekend- and day-trippers. Spring (October to December) and autumn (March to May) offer plenty of sun and fewer tourists. As the region never receives substantial rainfall or cold, even winter can be a pleasant time to visit.

Getting there
The bus terminal is on the corner of Sourigues and Paysandú (03447 480146). Flechabus and Rápido San José (011 4000 5200, www. empresasanjose.com, www.flechabus.com.ar) jointly offer services from Buenos Aires almost every hour. Travellers can be dropped off in Colón or in Subajay, six kilometres from the park entrance. The journey from Buenos Aires takes five hours 30 minutes.

Getting around
The easiest way to get around is by car, typically hired in Buenos Aires. Alternatively, El Palmar can be visited by calling a local taxi service (Radio Taxi, 12 de Abril 322, 03447 421481). Travel agents LHL (03447 422222, www.lhlturismo. com.ar) can arrange tours with guides.

Tourist information
Colón Tourist Information Office corner of Avenida Costanera & Gouchón (03447 426040, www.colon.gov.ar). Open 6am-8pm Mon-Fri; 8am-8pm Sat, Sun.

Internet
Most hotels, particularly those in Colón, have reliable Wi-Fi. Alternatively, Cyber Colón (12 de Abril 289, Galería del Greco) offers broadband internet and is open daily until 11pm.

La Aurora del Palmar.

Tigre and the Delta del Paraná.

Tigre

Argentina

Charming Victorian town at the mouth of an idyllic river delta.

Most visitors to Tigre come directly from Buenos Aires, and at less than an hour north of the capital by train, the trip leaves little time for the mental transition from city chaos to hushed tranquillity. Tigre is a small, charming town with leafy Victorian neighbourhoods, a whistle-stop on the way into the magnificent Delta del Paraná. On its doorstep lies a sweeping, exotic labyrinth of verdant isles, narrow estuaries and secluded homes and lodgings, as well as the occasional plodding *almacén flotante* (floating general store).

Tigre and the Delta are an endearing mix of upmarket and ramshackle. Though experiencing a revival of sorts, Tigre had its heyday in the last quarter of the 19th century. After a yellow-fever epidemic, the European farmers and jaguar-hunters that had established the town in 1820 were joined by high-society *porteños*, aiming to get as far upstream as possible. They left almost as quickly as they came, in the early 1900s, when the seaside resort of Mar del Plata was established on the Atlantic coast. The stately English rowing clubs, elegant Victorian manors and river marinas that dot the shores today date from this brief *belle époque*.

In 2000, UNESCO named the upper Delta a part of the World Network of Biosphere Reserves to help protect the area's natural habitat, while encouraging sustainable use of natural resources by the zone's very few inhabitants. Several companies have developed guided tours to take the area's visitors into the lush, island-specked reserve, the outer limit of which lies only two hours from Tigre.

Explore

Tigre is situated 28 kilometres north of Buenos Aires and is the gateway to the delta of the mighty Río Paraná, the continent's second largest river after the Amazon. Tigre proper is a fairly standard suburban town, where middle-class houses have driveways and fenced-off gardens, but the massive Delta is far from typical. It's split into three parts and extends for nearly 20,000 square kilometres.

The lower Delta, surrounding Tigre, is the more populous area; the upper Delta is the largely unpopulated Biosphere Reserve, dotted with flooded islands, weeping willows, vibrant violet hyacinths, giant water lilies and the ubiquitous rufous-fronted thornbird, whose nests can be seen on low branches just above the river.

Several companies offer boat tours of the area, which includes the town of San Fernando, about ten minutes from Tigre. Barbacharters Nautical Tours & Fishing (011 4501 3175, 011 15 4403 2829 mobile, www.barbacharters.com.ar) runs a luxury cruiser that can be chartered for tailor-made excursions. Crucero de Solís (Marina Buen Puerto, San Fernando, 011 4501 3175, 011 15 4408 8434 mobile, www.crucerodesolis.com.ar) offers a variety of options, including day tours, romantic dinner cruises for two and overnight honeymoon trips.

Leading the way in the eco-tourism sector, DeltaSur (011 4553 8827, www.deltasur ecoturismo.com.ar) goes beyond simply letting you watch the Delta float past. Instead, tailor-made tours (in English) can cover anything from birdwatching and fishing to history.

If you'd prefer to take in the view from above, Patagonia Chopper Flight Tours (www.patagonia chopper.com.ar) organises 12- and 18-minute helicopter flights that circle the Delta's spectacular maze of canals, streams and rivers. Tickets can be purchased through Sturla in Estación Fluvial (Mitre 319, Local 10, 011 4731 1300, www.sturlaviajes.com.ar).

For a truly upscale experience, Marina Yachts Baires (Marina del Norte, Calle del Arca & Río Luján, San Fernando, 011 15 4025 0624 mobile, www.marinayachtsbaires.com) offers a sleek, fully equipped Segue 46 – skipper not included. The yacht can be rented for up to six people for a day, a dinner or a three-day cruise. With three cabins, two bathrooms, a kitchen, a bar, air-conditioning, heating and four LCD television screens, it's a floating luxury suite.

Isla Martín García

Estación Fluvial de Tigre, Mitre 305. 9am daily departures; 5.30pm daily departures from island.
Some 35km from the western shores of the Río de la Plata, this lush island – a tiny land-mass that is practically bumping into Carmelo, Uruguay – is officially a part of

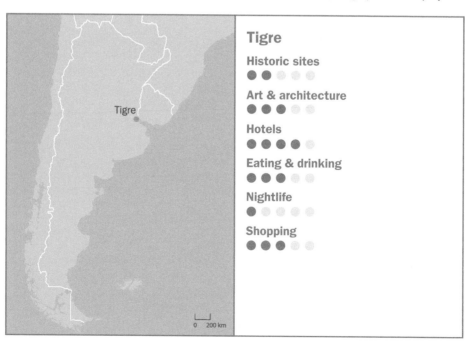

Tigre

Tigre

Historic sites
● ● ◦ ◦ ◦

Art & architecture
● ● ● ◦ ◦

Hotels
● ● ● ● ◦

Eating & drinking
● ● ● ● ◦

Nightlife
● ◦ ◦ ◦ ◦

Shopping
● ● ● ◦ ◦

0   200 km

Tigre.

the Republic of Argentina. It was discovered in 1516 by Juan Díaz de Solís – one of the many early explorers who incorrectly assumed he was in the ocean, rather than a massive river. Over the years, a number of political prisoners were incarcerated on the island, which also served as a naval base, and was home to Nicaraguan poet Rubén Darío. Its sandy beaches and scattered historical points of interest are worth investigating, though day trips are recommended rather than overnight stays. If you're not staying in Tigre proper, inquire at Cacciola about transportation from Buenos Aires to the port of departure (Lavalle 520, 011 4749 0329, 011 4731 1151, www.cacciola viajes.com). You can also arrange trips to the island from Carmelo, Uruguay (see p142).

Museo de Arte Tigre
Paseo Victorica 972 (011 4512 4528/www.mat.gov.ar). Open 9am-6.30pm Wed-Fri; noon-6.30pm Sat, Sun. Admission AR$5.
The fairly recent arrival of this art giant, which sits like a king on the edge of the Río Luján, is a big step up for otherwise sleepy Tigre. Located in a stunning 1913 estate that previously housed the Tigre Club, this collection of predominantly 19th- and 20th-century Argentinian art is a must-see. Recent visiting exhibitions have brought contemporary Panamanian art and select entries from Havana's X Biennial to the riverside.

"Come to Beixa Flor for lunch; stay for the private beach, expansive garden, and hip and arty clientele."

Museo del Mate
Lavalle 289 (011 4506 9594/www.elmuseodelmate.com). Open 11am-6pm Wed-Sun. Admission AR$8.
This little establishment puffs itself up with claims of being the only *mate* museum in the world. The robust collection of *mates*, *bombillas* and all of those other mysterious little *mate* gadgets that Argentinians lug around faithfully will be of interest to *mate* fanatics, *mate* novices and decorative-art enthusiasts alike. It certainly scores extra points for being the quirkiest spot in town.

Museo Histórico Sarmiento
Río Sarmiento & Arroyo Reyes, Delta (011 4728 0570). Open 10am-6pm Wed-Sun. Admission free.
The retirement homestead of former president Domingo Sarmiento is now a museum, enclosed in a bizarre, super-sized glass case to protect the 19th-century building from succumbing to the humid Delta air. It was named a National Historic Monument in the 1960s, and can be reached by *lancha colectivo* (water bus) from Estación Fluvial de Tigre.

Eat

Grabbing a casual bite to eat in Tigre is usually just that; most visitors prefer to load up their river cruisers with steaks and sausages for an *asado* on the Delta, rather than take time for long, leisurely restaurant meals. That said, there are a few choice options, most of them serving traditional Argentinian cuisine. Most hotels, especially isolated Delta lodgings, have dining services for guests, some of which are also open to non-residents.

Beixa Flor
Arroyo Abra Vieja 148, Delta (011 4728 2397/ www.beixaflor.com.ar). Open from noon daily (by reservations only). £££. No credit cards. International.
Come for lunch; stay the whole afternoon. This Delta restaurant offers home-made food, a private beach and an expansive wooded garden, attracting a hip and arty clientele. Service is swift and attentive, and decent, no-frills rooms are available should you decide to stay the night – or if you manage to miss the last *lancha* back to town. Call ahead to reserve a table.

La Cabaña: the Riverside
Paseo Victorica 708 (011 15 6497 2250 mobile). Open 4pm-2am daily. £. No credit cards. Café.
Aside from the super-sized ceramic teapot decorating the front lawn, there isn't much to distinguish this tiny tea-house from the other Victorian homes along Paseo Victorica. Don't expect Ritz-style high tea, but do settle back into a vintage magenta velvet booth for a herbal infusion. Located just blocks from the Museo de Arte Tigre, Villa Julia and Hotel Villa Victoria, La Cabaña is worth a peek if only for the novelty of the place.

El Gato Blanco
Río Capitán 80, Delta (011 4728 0390/www.gatoblanco. com). Open noon-5pm daily. £££. Traditional.
This gigantic Delta spot features plenty of indoor and outdoor seating, a tea room and a separate bar. Argentinian parrilla favourites such as steak and chorizo are served alongside freshly-caught river treats such as hake and sole. The riverside dining experience is most enjoyable during the clement days of spring and autumn.

Il Novo María del Luján
Paseo Victorica 611, & Vito Dumas (011 4731 9613/ www.ilnovomariadellujan.com). Open 8.30am-midnight daily. ££. Seafood/Traditional.
Situated along the Río Luján, opposite a crumbling Victorian mansion, this is the most noteworthy eaterie in town. Formerly a grand family estate, the luxurious riverside restaurant has an atmospheric interior, although the spacious patio is what draws the crowds. The upscale but inexpensive cuisine includes good-quality seafood and traditional Argentinian fare; give the home-made pastas a try, or, if you're with a group, share the seafood platter. The wine list is excellent.

Spas by the riverside

Tigre's slow-moving waters and velvety breezes inspire complete and utter relaxation. It's hardly surprising, then, that a handful of establishments offering luxurious pampering have popped up here. Like most good things on the Delta, the real gems tend to be tucked away deep in the labyrinth of waterways and lush, leafy foliage.

Set on its own island, **Rumbo 90° Delta Lodge & Spa** (see p172) offers a day-spa package that includes access to the recently revamped steam room, sauna, jacuzzi and pool, as well as an appealing set-menu lunch and afternoon tea. Massages and special treatments, although not included, shouldn't be missed. The 50-plus options offered in the slick poolside area run the gamut from post-sun skin care to lymphatic drainage, shiatzu and hot stone massage.

If you're looking for something particularly river-centric, give one of Rumbo 90°'s algae-therapy ministrations a try. The water weeds are said to help to stimulate the circulation, eliminate nasty toxins and restore a healthy sheen to the skin. An algae wrap leaves your outer layer feeling supple and your inner self thoroughly revitalised; a firming algae face mask is also offered.

A day of indulgence at Rumbo 90° can be combined with an excursion on the private cruise line Crucero de Solís (see p166). The yacht departs from the marina at San Fernando, with champagne and canapés served en route to the island. If you book through the cruise line, your spa day includes a 30-minute relaxation massage.

Over at the Eden that is **La Becasina Delta Lodge** (see p171), there may not be full spa services, but lodge guests (whether overnight or day visitors), can book in for blissfully relaxing massages on weekends. The lodge's jacuzzis and Delta-view dipping pool also help to ease any stress away.

Alternatively, skip over to the eco-spa at **Isla Escondida** (011 4728 3032, www.isla escondidadelta.com.ar, pictured). A classic Californian anti-stress massage feels that much better when it's administered on an outdoor table, surrounded by luxuriant river vegetation. Should your body call for something more specialised, try the hot stone treatment or some Peruvian turquoise-gem therapy. For the ultimate decadence, spend the night on the island. In the morning, breakfast is served in bed – and comes complete with a foot massage for two.

La Becasina Delta Lodge.

Shop

At the weekend, the Puerto de Frutos market (Sarmiento 160, www.puertodefrutos-arg.com.ar) is the place to be, fruit smoothie in hand, as the vendors set out a varied array of local and hand-made products. It's a lively maze of stalls, with high-quality, hand-crafted wooden furniture at dirt-cheap prices. The following listings cover some of the best finds. As is the custom here, store hours are subject to change without notice, especially since these particular 'stores' consist of little more than a counter and a thatched roof.

Artesanías Balbina
Puesto 59/60, Puerto de Frutos (011 15 5040 5935 mobile/www.artesaniasbalbina.com.ar). Open 11am-7pm Mon-Fri; 10am-8pm Sat, Sun.
Pick up some of the wooden cutting boards and serving platters, or the stackable carved bowls. They're all very typical country-style homewares that would be far pricier in the commercial districts of Buenos Aires, Bariloche or Salta, but can be scored for a song at this market stall.

"Tigre is ideal for a weekend getaway, but to truly escape, head to the islands of the Delta."

La Casa del Mimbre
Local 39 & 40, Calle las Casuarinas, Puerto de Frutos (011 4731 4436/www.lacasadelmimbre.com.ar). Open 10am-6pm daily.
Baskets aren't the most logical of souvenirs, especially when there is plane travel involved, but check out the huge selection of wicker baskets and furniture here anyway. The ridiculously low prices might persuade you to take one or two of them home.

JLS Pieles
Guareschi 16, Puerto de Frutos (011 15 6002 4225 mobile/www.cuerosypieles-arg.com.ar). Open 10am-6pm Thur-Sun.
Nothing says Argentina like hanging up an entire cow-hide on the wall, and Tigre has better quality and prices than the outlets in Buenos Aires. Look, too, for the intricate patchwork rugs. JLS also has a variety of leather coats and jackets that can be fitted to size.

Nativa Artesanías
Local 41 & 42, Calle las Casuarinas, Puerto de Frutos (011 4749 4668/www.nativa-artesanias.com.ar). Open 9.30am-6pm daily.
This is the place to stock up on that sweet temptation, *dulce de leche*, before heading home. Taste before you choose at this stall, and try the *dulce de leche* liqueur, an ideal coffee-spiker. When you've hit your sugar high, rummage through the woven textiles, rugs, blankets and hammocks.

Quebracho Chatard
Sarmiento 260 (011 4749 0011/www.quebrachochatard.com.ar). Open 10am-6pm daily.
Quebracho Chatard is best known for its custom-made pieces, such as doors, gates and decks, made from local wood. The showroom is jammed full of beautifully carved furniture – benches, chairs, stools and low coffee tables, among other items, most of which preserve the organic shape of the tree trunk for a delightfully earthy feel. Smaller, more transportable pieces include chopping boards, clocks and wine racks.

Stay

Tigre has a small handful of places to stay that are ideal for a weekend getaway, but to truly escape, head out to the lush, sequestered islands of the Delta. Reservations are absolutely essential – particularly for places that can only be reached by chartered boat. High and low season rates often vary quite considerably, with prices dropping between May and October. As Tigre is a popular weekend getaway, the same goes for midweek stays.
Mabel Gilardoni Propiedades (Arenales 1273, San Fernando, 011 4745 6549, www.mabelgilardoni.com.ar) has impressive furnished short-term rentals (from one week up to one year), both in Tigre and on the Delta.

La Becasina Delta Lodge
Arroyo Las Cañas, Delta (011 4328 2387/www.labecasina.com). ££££. No credit cards.
Occupying a secluded Delta island, 90 minutes from Tigre's port, this impeccably designed boutique resort toes the line between rustic and chic with remarkable finesse. The 15 bungalows, each with a private deck, have been crafted entirely from lumber reaped from the island. Guests can indulge in the spa facilities or try typical Delta activities such as birdwatching, fishing, hiking and canoeing, as well as testing their athletic skills with wakeboarding, waterskiing or windsurfing. Evenings can be spent lingering over a poolside cocktail, followed by a gourmet dinner, before winding down with a dip in the jacuzzi or a quiet stroll around the grounds. Transfers from Tigre can be arranged at least one day in advance, but are not included in the rates.

Hotel Villa Victoria
Liniers 566 (011 4731 2281/011 15 601 61296 mobile/www.hotelvillavictoria.com). ££.
The latest project from Argentinian/Swedish owners Alicia and Bjorn, this charming, petite hotel is a recent arrival in Tigre. Each of the five suites in this immaculately restored estate opens out on to a scenic pool-view patio and features

eclectic art and tasteful furnishings. Breakfast is served on the wide, sunny veranda, which overlooks the lovely flower garden and clay tennis court. Ask for the Victoria Suite, whose atmospheric fireplace and massive bathroom raise it a notch above the other rooms.

"Guests at Rumbo 90° can wander the tropical, wooded paths and walkways alongside curious peacocks."

Rumbo 90° Delta Lodge & Spa
Canal del Este & Rio de la Plata, Delta (011 15 5843 9454 mobile/www.rumbo90.com.ar). ££££.
As the sprawling, sunbed-lined riverside deck of Rumbo 90° hoves into view along the Canal del Este, it's clear that this is an ambitious, upmarket affair. The stately lodge accommodates a maximum of 12 guests in six suites, all with private verandas; try to nab the front-facing deluxe suite for a gorgeous river view, and an enticing curtained jacuzzi. Guests can wander the tropical, wooded paths and walkways alongside curious peacocks, or opt for a canoe excursion on the secluded side canal. The day spa (*see p169* **Spas by the riverside**) offers facials, body wraps and massages. Non-residents can also book in for treatments, catching a special boat service that leaves the Estación Fluvial de Tigre at 10.30am, returning at 6pm – also the transfer times for overnight hotel guests.

Villa Julia
Paseo Victorica 800 (011 4749 0242/ www.villajuliaresort.com.ar). ££.
Set on the banks of the Rio Luján, in a mansion built in 1906, this extraordinary boutique hotel has six distinctive rooms. Ask for the Villa Julia Suite for the best terrace view of the waterway. The hotel's interior has been thoughtfully restored, preserving period detailing such as the original art-deco tile work in the bathrooms. The restaurant is open all day and you can take afternoon tea in the salon, with the grand piano tinkling in the background. The gardens, riverview terrace and heated pool are added attractions.

Factfile

When to go
March and November are the months with the most pleasant temperatures, and the best times to avoid summer crowds and snag off-season prices. Tigre is in full bloom (and more than a little overcrowded) in Argentina's sticky late-spring and summer months of December to February, when *porteños* head for the cool waterways. June to August can get downright cold.

Note that midweek prices in Tigre are generally lower than Friday to Sunday rates; by staying in the week, you'll also avoid the weekend swarm of city folk.

Getting there
Take city bus number 60 from Plaza Constitución in Buenos Aires for a 90-minute ride through the city to downtown Tigre. Another option is to take the Mitre line train from Retiro; trains leave every 15 minutes from 5am to midnight Monday to Saturday, and from 6am to 11.30pm on Sundays and bank holidays. A more scenic rail option is the Tren de la Costa, a coastal light railway that picks up passengers in the town of Olivos and travels through the upscale riverside suburbs north of Buenos Aires, terminating in Tigre.

Cacciola (Lavalle 520, 011 4749 0329, 011 4731 2003, www.cacciolaviajes.com) offers transport between Tigre and Uruguay, with daily departures from Montevideo (six hours) and Carmelo (two hours 30 minutes).

Líneas Delta (011 4731 1236, 011 4749 0537, www.lineasdelta.com.ar) operates ferries to Tigre from Colonia and from Nueva Palmira.

Getting around
Boats are the preferred method of transport in Tigre. *Lanchas colectivos* (public river buses) provide access to the Delta from the boat terminal (Estación Fluvial de Tigre, Mitre 305). Otherwise, one- to three-hour river excursions can be booked at Sturla (Mitre 319, 4731 1300) or Cacciola (*see left*).

Though the town proper is small enough to be covered on foot, taxis and *remises* (a hired driver and car) are available in Tigre. Try La Costa (Tacuarí 47, 011 4731 3020, 011 4731 5544) or ask hotel or restaurant staff to call one for you.

Tourist information
Ente Municipal de Turismo Estación Fluvial de Tigre, Mitre 305 (011 4512 4400, www.tigre. gov.ar). Open 9am-5pm daily. The office is staffed by very helpful, bilingual tourism guides.

Internet
Several basic internet cafés have opened up in Tigre, dotted around the train station. Be on the lookout for the 'Locutorio' and 'Internet' signs. Many cafés and restaurants, as well as the more high-end hotels in Tigre and on the Delta, have Wi-Fi.

Rumbo 90° Delta Lodge & Spa.

Mountains & Lakes

Clockwise from top left: Bariloche; Lago Nahuel Huapi; Parque Nacional los Arrayanes; Lago Perito Moreno, Bariloche; El Bolsón (2).

Bariloche, El Bolsón & Villa La Angostura

Argentina

Patagonia's stunning lake district.

The massive national parkland surrounding the towns of San Carlos de Bariloche, Villa La Angostura and El Bolsón is an Andean stage displaying natural drama in its rawest form. Standing thousands of metres over the plains, rock faces obscure even the higher summits of ice-capped volcanoes; turbid rivers carry glacial spring water to vast turquoise lakes in the valleys below; shores are stitched with forests that shelter some of the rarest trees on the planet, the arrayanes.

Each town in this region offers a different kind of travel experience. Bariloche is not only the gateway to Argentina's first national park, Parque Nacional Nahuel Huapi, and the serpentine Ruta de los Siete Lagos (Seven Lakes route), which has become world-famous, but it is also one of Argentina's top tourist centres, with an advanced infrastructure that supports year-round activities. Villa La Angostura is a smaller version of Bariloche, with equally high levels of dining and accommodation. El Bolsón is the laid-back member of this mountainous triumvirate, and still reflects the influence of the hippie squatters who first dreamed of creating an ecological haven here in the 1970s.

There are few requirements that can't be satisfied between these three Patagonian towns. Collectively, they present a split personality: equal parts national park and pampering. Both sides are well worth getting to know.

Estancia
Peuma Hue
Carre Lauquen

Hideout>

The Place of your Dreams

**Ruta 40, Cabecera Sur Lago Gutiérrez
Bariloche, Patagonia, Argentina.
(54-9-2944) 501030 / www.peuma-hue.com**

Take Time Out to broaden your horizons at...
www.oxfam.org.uk

Oxfam

THE BEST BOUTIQUE HOTELS
HOTELS & EMOTIONS

Meet the First Quality Club that represents unique & truly authentic Boutique Hotels in Argentina.

DISCOVER THE BOUTIQUE ROUTES AT
WWW.THEBBH.COM

Explore

BARILOCHE

Bariloche is situated on the south-eastern shore of **Lago Nahuel Huapi**, close to 800 metres above sea level. It is 123 kilometres north of **El Bolsón** via RN 258, and 83 kilometres south-east of **Villa La Angostura**.

It is fair to say that the Bariloche experience is what you make of it. It has become fashionable in recent years to complain about the city's excessive development, but to decry the expansion of the town itself is to neglect a simpler and more enticing truth: the backcountry is still just down the road for those seeking it. Within a few hours of arriving in Bariloche, you can be heading out for a three-day trek, sleeping in bare-bones *refugios* (refuges) high up in the mountains along the way. And when you return, filthy and exhausted, you can reward yourself with a chocolate fondue or a nice bottle of Argentinian red. Why force a choice between simple pleasures and sophisticated luxuries when both are so readily available?

The best sights are on the roads leading out of town, but at least a short tour of the local architecture will introduce you to the work of the Bustillo brothers, the most important builders in the region. Two of their greatest hits are the Centro Cívico (at the end of Bartolomé Mitre,

where it intersects with Urquiza) and the Intendencia de Parques Nacionales (National Park Headquarters, one block north at San Martín 24). Bartolomé Mitre is also the main tourist drag, and sampling the produce from one of its famed chocolate shops, such as Mamuschka (Bartolomé Mitre 216), is irresistible. If you plan on doing any day-trekking, you should stop at one of the local markets and pick up trail food of a particularly Patagonian nature, such as *jabalí* (wild boar) or *ciervo* (deer) jerky.

The main natural attractions of Bariloche date back to the time of Patagonian explorer Francisco Pascasio 'Perito' Moreno. In the early 20th century, he donated the land the state bequeathed to him for his exploratory zeal in claiming territory for Argentina, and this was used to create the **Parque Nacional Nahuel Huapi**. The park is dominated by Lago Nahuel Huapi, which meanders through multiple fjords and peninsulas across its vast, 560-square-kilometre surface.

In the middle of the lake is Isla Victoria, the largest island in Argentina and home to one of the most interesting lodgings in Bariloche (Hostería Isla Victoria, *see p188*). Most of the lake's boat tours leave from Puerto Pañuelo, 25km from Bariloche town centre, and go as far as Chile and Parque Nacional los Arrayanes in Villa La Angostura (though there is no reason to take a boat trip from Bariloche if you're travelling on to

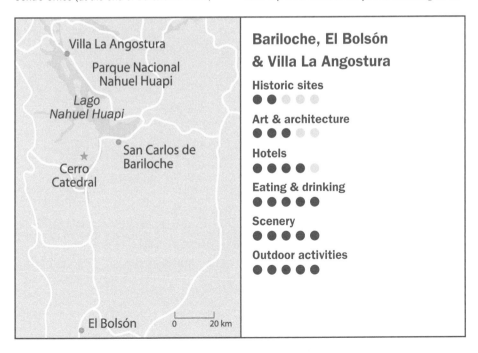

Villa La Angostura

Parque Nacional Nahuel Huapi

Lago Nahuel Huapi

Cerro Catedral ★

San Carlos de Bariloche

El Bolsón

0   20 km

Bariloche, El Bolsón & Villa La Angostura

Historic sites
● ● ○ ○ ○

Art & architecture
● ● ● ○ ○

Hotels
● ● ● ● ○

Eating & drinking
● ● ● ● ●

Scenery
● ● ● ● ●

Outdoor activities
● ● ● ● ●

Villa La Angostura by car or bus). For views of the lake and its environs, there is a cable car to the top of Cerro Otto (though the *cerro*, or hill, can be trekked on foot) and a chairlift to the summit of Cerro Campanario. There's a revolving tea-house at Cerro Otto's summit, and a restaurant at the top of Cerro Campanario.

For those looking for a road trip, there are two main circuits leaving from town, the Circuito Chico (short circuit), a 65-kilometre round trip that can also be done by local bus, and Circuito Grande (long circuit), a 250-kilometre round trip, which pass all the important sites and trails.

The shorter circuit starts out on Avenida Bustillo downtown and goes as far as the Llao Llao Peninsula, at kilometre 25, which shares its name with one of the most famous hotels in Argentina, Llao Llao (*see p190*). Even if you're not staying at the hotel, it's worth dropping in for a snack, or a hot chocolate, which at AR$20 gives you an idea of the pricing. Shutterbugs intent on clogging up their memory cards should also note that at kilometre 40 the circuit passes the Punto Panorámico viewing point, which offers spectacular vistas of Llao Llao and beyond.

The circuit then returns to town via the hamlet of Colonia Suiza, named after its original Swiss settlers. Just past the turn-off to Colonia Suiza is Meli-Hue (02944 448029), a lavender farm with a shop and tea room.

"A trek from *refugio* to *refugio* is about the best in-the-wilds, non-extreme adventure you can get in the lake district."

The best day-hike option just off the circuit is Cerro López. It's a four- to six-hour round trip, and the views are spectacular once you reach Refugio López, looking out over the lake and its many forested furrows. About halfway up the trail, the trekker is rewarded by the site of a beautiful, and still working, wooden cantina. Refugio López (02944 15 580321 mobile, www.cerrolopez bariloche.com.ar) is another two hours further on.

The Argentinian national park system has a well-run series of *refugios* in these peaks. Refugio López is a potential overnight stop on what can be a multi-day trek reaching still higher peaks and panoramas of the major volcanoes and glaciers leading into Chile. The *refugios* are spartan, with bunk beds and simple meals cooked by a warden, but if you can survive a few nights without a jacuzzi and four-star meal, completing a two- to three-day trek from *refugio* to *refugio* is about

the best in-the-wilds, non-extreme adventure you can pursue in the lake district. Club Andino, in town (*see p184*), can provide all the necessary information to plan properly. *Refugio* beds fill up during the summer (January to March), so if you are considering this option, reserve at the Club Andino office.

Another, more gruelling day trip takes you in search of the source of the Río Manso at Cerro Tronador, a once-petulant but now-extinct volcano. It's a 215-kilometre round-trip, and can be done either by car (though you will be driving for a long time through dust) or by bus. The access road also has restricted hours for traffic during high season: in the morning, traffic can only travel up the volcano, and cannot come back down until late in the afternoon. Club Andino runs a bus service from its downtown headquarters from January to March.

Driving south from Bariloche on RN 258, and following the shorelines of Lago Gutiérrez and Lago Mascardi, leads you to the gravel road to Cerro Tronador. The Cascada de los Alerces waterfall, considered by many the most beautiful of the falls in the area, is on a separate dirt road before crossing the Río Manso bridge. To reach Cerro Tronador, backtrack and cross the river bridge and you will arrive at Ventisquero Negro (Black Glacier), the eastern face of Tronador, only a short distance from the base of the volcano. Pampa Linda is the starting point for several long day-hikes reaching as high as 2,000 metres on Cerro Tronador, which has eight glaciers and countless cascades to admire.

Brazilians flock to Bariloche from June to September (hence the town's nickname, 'Brasiloche') for a rare glimpse of snow, but most visitors from Europe and the US tend to favour the summer season. Nevertheless, some serious investment in lifts and base services, and the inevitable re-creation of the Alps' après-ski scene, has made Bariloche's **Cerro Catedral** (www.catedralaltapatagonia.com), 20 kilometres south of downtown, the most developed ski resort in Argentina.

The views of Lago Nahuel Huapi and the Andes from the slopes don't hurt its appeal; even the bigger ski resorts in Chile and Mendoza can't equal Cerro Catedral's vistas. The growing off-piste options, starting right from Cerro Catedral's lift, are making the area increasingly popular with extreme skiers and snowboarders (*see p183* **Off the beaten slopes**).

VILLA LA ANGOSTURA

Situated on the north-western shore of Lago Nahuel Huapi, between *cerros* Bayo, Inacayal and Belvedere (which can be hiked for some excellent views), the town of **Villa La Angostura** had its beginnings when settler Primo Capraro built a sawmill here in 1917 (now the Correntoso

Lago Nahuel Huapi.

Lake & River Hotel, *see p188*). These days, the town prefers to protect its trees, and Villa La Angostura has become a holiday magnet for two primary reasons: its location at the start of an isthmus linking the mainland with the peninsula that features the Parque Nacional los Arrayanes, a once well-hidden grove of extremely rare and uniquely beautiful trees; and its position as the gateway to the Ruta de los Siete Lagos, which runs between it and San Martín de los Andes (*see pp216-25*).

"Walt Disney was said to have been inspired by the arrayanes trees of Parque Nacional Los Arrayanes when creating his imaginary forest for *Bambi*."

While the downtown area is little more than a three-block strip that goes by three different names – Avenida Arrayanes, Avenida de los Siete Lagos or RN 231 – Villa La Angostura's more secluded enclaves at various points along Lago Nahuel Huapi's shoreline make for supremely relaxing hideaways, notably Puerto Manzano. Villa La Angostura is also home to some of the most famous constructions of Alejandro Bustillo, including the Villa El Messidor residence, a French-influenced castle that sheltered the Argentinian president Isabel Perón at the time of the military coup of 1976.

A legend that Walt Disney was inspired by the arrayanes trees when creating his imaginary forest for *Bambi* still endures, but Parque Nacional los Arrayanes doesn't need the Mickey Mouse endorsement. Its bizarre trees, usually described as cinnamon in colour, make an impressive sight. The entrance to the park is found at Puerto Bahía La Mansa. From here, boats travel to the far point of the peninsula, where the greatest concentration of arrayanes is located. Sailing times vary, so call to confirm before planning your trip (Greenleaf Turismo, 02944 494405).

There is also a 25-kilometre round-trip walking trail to the same point. To get the best of both worlds, you can take the boat there and walk back. (Note that by doing it the other way round, you run the risk of not coinciding with a return boat.) Before setting out by boat or on foot, you also need to pay the park entrance fee in the office beside Bahía La Mansa's pier.

While much of the walking trail snakes through typical regional forest, the portion nearest Bahía La Mansa offers incredible views out across the lake; as you approach the arrayanes, you'll also pass a few secluded beaches.

If you prefer to see the world through a windscreen, try the Ruta de los Siete Lagos between Villa La Angostura and San Martín de los Andes, a short road trip of worldwide renown. The route covers 110 kilometres of RN 234 and can be completed in a few hours. The drive traverses both Nahuel Huapi and Lanín national parks, and passes by nine lakes, including the magnificent seven: *lagos* Lácar, Machónico, Falkner, Villarino, Escondido, Correntoso and Espejo. A must-stop on the route is the tiny fishing town of Villa Traful, 63 kilometres north of Villa La Angostura, involving a detour along RN 65. Five kilometres past the town is the lookout point Mirador del Traful, which provides vertiginous panoramas of the waters. There is also a boat trip available from the town to the Bosque Sumergido (submerged forest), part of a wooded mountain slope that slid into the lake 30 years ago. The sight of submerged trees popping their crowns through the surface of the turquoise water is both eerie and beautiful.

EL BOLSÓN

Surrounded by high snow-capped mountains and backed by the breathtaking Río Azul, **El Bolsón** lies in the province of Río Negro, just over the border from Chubut. The small town, which now has a permanent population of around 15,000, attracted an influx of hippies at the start of the 1970s and was declared a non-nuclear municipality in 1984. It's still known for its alternative lifestyles and for producing a lot of the country's fruit and hops. There are numerous organic farms, where locals make delicious jams and honeys, as well as fruit beers.

Hiking through the stunning peaks and forests around the town is a popular pastime here. Treks can be done independently, lasting a couple of hours, or in organised groups, lasting a couple of days. Located on a ridge high above town is the Mirador del Río Azul, which affords exquisite views of the sparkling blue river below and snowy mountains beyond. Further on up the trail is the Cabeza del Indio, a cliff-side rock formation that resembles a man's face in profile. This is a simple, half-day trek. Other attractions, which you can hike to or around, include a series of stunning waterfalls about ten kilometres north of the town and the spectacular Cajón del Azul, a very deep, narrow canyon a few kilometres further on.

Overshadowing the town to the east, like a great rock sentinel, is Cerro Piltriquitrón, at 2,260 metres. The base can be reached by taxi or a 13-kilometre hike from town. Further

Off the beaten slopes

For skiers who prefer a bit of danger added to the typical ski-chalet experience, the area around Bariloche's Cerro Catedral is ripe for daredevil action. The region still has some way to go until it competes with the world's truly terrifying off-piste ski haunts – and to the north, the area around Mendoza remains the centre for Argentinian heli-skiing – but bolder types won't be disappointed by the opportunities to venture away from the trails from the top of the Cerro Catedral lifts.

For skiers really looking to raise the lift bar and leave the resort experience behind, the best options are all-terrain vehicle trips or hiking with guides. The duration of these adventures can range from single-day runs near the Catedral resort on Cerro López and Cerro Challhuaco, to overnight stays in *refugio* (refuge) huts high up in the peaks. The most famous is Refugio Frey, which can be made into a two-day trip or serve as the first leg of a longer off-piste experience. Bariloche is also the gateway town for the only hut-to-hut skiing area in South America, allowing off-piste adventurers to travel for days among some spectacular mountain, volcano and glacier scenery.

If you make it into the rugged, less-travelled terrain of the backcountry on skis, the blinding white canvas will become a private ski resort.

The peak months for skiing are July and August, and the best snow typically falls at the end of this period and up to October. Late in the season, the region's signature volcanic summits, such as Cerro Tronador or Volcán Lanín, are where the most daring head, due to the higher elevations.

Bariloche's smaller, neighbouring ski resorts also offer a range of off-piste opportunities. At San Martín de los Andes' Chapelco resort (*see p220*), the backcountry can be easily accessed from the main ski area. Volcán Lanín, with its 3,776 metres of elevation, is the highest of the steep volcanoes in the region and has a classic long descent, just off the highway that connects San Martín de los Andes and Junín de los Andes with Pucón, Chile. Even Villa La Angostura's small Cerro Bayo ski area has some off-piste terrain, with the bonus of spectacular views across Lago Nahuel Huapi.

If you're an off-piste fanatic, you should also consider Las Leñas in Mendoza (*see p209*), which is said to have some of the best free-riding areas in the world. There are also ski resorts near Esquel (La Hoya; *see p197*) and Ushuaia (Cerro Martial and Cerro Castor; *see p370*).

Information about off-piste options, from novice introductions to disappearing for a week or ten days on the circuit of *cerros* (hills) and *refugios*, are detailed on the websites of three Bariloche-based adventure outfitters: Andes Cross (02944 633 581, www.andescross.com), All Mountain Ride (02944 520123, www.allmtn ride.com) and Meridies (02944 462675, www. meridies.com.ar).

on from here is the Bosque Tallado, where you'll find a bizarre series of sculptures carved out of tree trunks by Argentinian artists.

Back in town, one of the biggest attractions is the Feria Artesanal (Plaza Pagano), open Tuesday, Thursday and Saturday from 10am to 3pm. People come here to buy wood carvings, jewellery, leather products, and peculiar gnome and goblin figurines. Visit with an empty stomach, as the fair also has a variety of food stalls, selling chips, sandwiches and freshly-made waffles, loaded with raspberries, chocolate sauce and cream.

OUTDOOR ACTIVITIES

Fishing, white-water rafting, horse riding, trekking, mountain and volcano climbing, skiing, hunting, birdwatching, biking, rock climbing and kayaking are all available in the area. Most of the hotels reviewed in this chapter (*see pp187-90*) offer guided excursions, or will coordinate tours with a preferred outfitter.

Two sections of the Río Manso, south of Bariloche and cutting through picturesque valleys, offer the best rafting in the region. It can be a family day on the lower section, with lazy paddling and wildlife watching, or a real rafter's run on the *frontera* section by the Chilean border. A lake-district adventure operator for all seasons is Bariloche-based Meridies (02944 462675, www.meridies.com.ar). Aguas Blancas (02944 601024, www.aguasblancas.com.ar) focuses on rafting.

Activities in El Bolsón include mountain biking, which can be arranged via Grado 42 (02944 493124, www.grado42.com). There are also some fantastic horse riding treks in the area; contact Cabalgatas del Azul (02944 483590).

The English-speaking staff at Club Andino's main Bariloche office (02944 422266, www.club andino.com) have an encyclopedic knowledge of the area's trails.

Eat

Cassis
Bariloche *Ruta 82, Lago Gutiérrez, Peñón de Arelauquen (02944 476167/www.cassis.com.ar). Open 8pm-midnight Mon-Sat. ££££. No credit cards. International.*
Cassis is situated by a small lake off the main Bariloche circuit, but it wasn't always this way. Run by a husband-and-wife team, the restaurant started life in Esquel, moved to Germany, then relocated to downtown Bariloche. Its success necessitated a move to larger premises, and in 2006 Cassis moved to the grounds of the fancy Arelauquen Golf & Country Club. The couple's German and Austro-Hungarian heritage make for one of Bariloche's most

unique marriages of regional and modern European cuisine. Patagonian sheep strudel, Andean venison sautéed in pistachio butter and poached local trout were just some of the Europe-meets-Patagonia offerings on the most recent seasonal menu.

La Delfina
Villa La Angostura *Avenida Arrayanes 7014 (02944 475313). Open noon-3.30pm, 8.30-11.30pm Tue-Sun. £££. International.*
Unusually for this region, La Delfina has a pan-Asian menu. Tuesday nights are often devoted to sushi, while the main menu offers teriyaki lake trout, salmon ravioli with Thai spicing, and lobster served with tamarind sauce and basmati rice. Expect creative and thoughtful dishes from a chef who is constantly seeking, and finding, new inspiration. The restaurant is set in the grounds of the high-end Hosteria La Escondida, in the secluded lake enclave of Puerto Manzano.

"Días de Zapata is a colourful, family-run cantina, which brought its recipe book all the way to Bariloche from Mexico City."

Días de Zapata
Bariloche *Morales 362 (02944 423128/ www.diasdezapata.com.ar). Open noon-3pm, 7pm-12.30am daily. £££. International.*
Historic migrations over the Andes have nothing on this colourful family-run cantina, which brought its recipe book all the way to Bariloche from Mexico City. This is a great alternative for visitors looking to take a night off from vicariously hunting the Patagonian wildlife with their knife and fork. While fajitas might seem the obvious choice, the menu is loaded with more interesting options. The chicken *mole*, generally a love-it or hate-it taste, is a fitting dish for chocolate-centric Bariloche. The margaritas are poured with a generous hand, and early arrivals are rewarded with a two-for-one happy hour (7-9pm daily).

Jauja
El Bolsón *Avenida San Martín 2867 (02944 492448). Open 9am-midnight daily. ££. Modern.*
Stepping into this restaurant, which is set in a wooden chalet, feels like walking straight into Switzerland. Colourful glass lamps hang low over the tables, while friendly waiters serve the local delicacy of trout cooked in white wine, as well as a few good vegetarian dishes, such as breaded aubergine. In winter, you'll appreciate what are surely the tastiest hot chocolates in town, and summer is the perfect excuse to check out the attached ice-cream

Top: Nahuel Huapí
National Park. Middle:
Parque Nacional los
Arrayanes. Bottom:
Bariloche (2).

Bariloche.

parlour and chocolate shop. Flavours to try include chocolate filled with dark chocolate mousse, banana split or even *yerba mate*.

Naan

Bariloche *Campichuelo 568 (02944 421785). Open Dec-Easter, Aug, Sept 7.30-11pm daily. Easter-July, Oct, Nov 7.30-11pm Tue-Sun. £££. No credit cards. International.*

The couple behind Naan (he's the chef, while she runs the dining room) have scoured the globe, from Italy and France to the Middle East and Vietnam, in search of inspiration for the menu. They returned from their travels with fragrant lamb curries, coconut chicken and prawns, souvlaki and tofu creations, all of which give the local staples a run for their money.

Otto Tipp

El Bolsón *Islas Malvinas & Roca (02944 493700). Open 12.30-3.30pm, 8pm-2.30am. Tue-Sun. ££. Modern.*

This restaurant and brewery is located in a wood and glass building, surrounded by trees. Visitors can watch the beers being made, then put them to the test. They're made from locally grown fruits and hops, and flavours include raspberry, cherry and chocolate. Accompany your choice with regional trout dishes, pasta or pizza.

Patio Venzano

El Bolsón *Avenida Sarmiento & Pablo Hube (02944 15 633112 mobile). Open noon-4pm; 8pm-midnight Mon-Sat; noon-4pm Sun. ££. No credit cards. Modern.*

This small, family-run restaurant serves regional dishes in big portions. The trout-stuffed sorrentinos are especially good, as are the *dulce de leche* pancakes with ice-cream. In summer, there is outdoor seating in the private garden, as well as a large parrilla.

Tinto Bistro

Villa La Angostura *Nahuel Huapi 34 (02944 494924). Open June-Apr 8.30pm-midnight Mon-Sat. £££. Modern.*

Tinto Bistro is famed locally for being the restaurant owned by Princess Máxima of the Netherlands' younger brother, Martín Zorreguieta. Co-owner and chef Leanardo Andres prepares eclectic dishes with Asian and Mediterranean influences, as well as dressed-up regional fare. There is also an ample wine selection to accompany the fusion dishes. The restaurant offers the best gourmet experience in town, and has been such a success since opening in 2002 that a second branch has been created in the Panamericano hotel in Bariloche (San Martin 536/70).

Virtuoso y Tarquino

Bariloche *24 de Septiembre, at Saavedra, Plaza Belgrano (02944 434774/www.virtuosoytarquino. com.ar). Open noon-3pm, 8pm-midnight daily. £££. Parrilla.*

In a handsome building made of cypress wood, with a tree growing in the middle of the dining room and sprouting through a hole in the roof, Tarquino offers a straightforward

version of Argentinian parrilla, handled with the careful preparation but lack of fanfare that is true to the roots of the cuisine.

Zucchini

El Bolsón *Avenida San Martin 2518 (02944 498797). Open 11am-midnight Mon, Tue, Thur-Sun. ££. No credit cards. Traditional.*

This tiny wood-panelled restaurant on El Bolsón's main street has intimate booths with seats made from tree trunks and small tables decorated in spring colours. As the name would suggest, Zucchini serves some good vegetarian dishes, including breaded courgette with pumpkin mash, mixed vegetable chop suey and ravioli stuffed with ricotta and spinach. Service can be a little slow, but the food and atmosphere make up for it.

Stay

The biggest accommodation decision in the area comes in Bariloche, when deciding whether to lodge in town or outside on the picturesque RN 237 that runs along the edge of Lago Nahuel Huapi. Unlike other lake-district towns, Bariloche has a real urban buzz. So ask yourself which you'd prefer: a short walk to an Irish pub at 1am, or a view of the moon's reflection on the water from your lake-side patio.

Aldebarán

Bariloche *Península San Pedro, off Avenida Bustillo, km 20 (02944 448678/www.aldebaranpatagonia.com). ££££.*

This hotel provides a distinctive perspective on Lago Nahuel Huapi. Most travellers on Bariloche's *circuito chico* bear left around the km 20 mark and continue in the direction of the Llao Llao peninsula and its renowned resort. Aldebarán is off to the right, on the less-travelled Península San Pedro, approximately ten kilometres down an unpaved track. The unique views of the natural surroundings more than compensate for the over-the-top glass construction. The common areas are built around stone walls and cement floors that evoke European palaces of former ages, while the curved stone ceilings throughout are a refreshing contrast to the Alpine-chalet style so typical of the lake district. The excellent restaurant, Sirius, has Mediterranean leanings.

Las Balsas

Villa La Angostura *Bahía Las Balsas, no number, off RN 231 (02944 494308/www.lasbalsas.com). ££££.*

A high-end hotel without in-room televisions must really believe in its power to enthrall visitors, and Las Balsas has this self-confidence in spades. There are only 15 rooms, each of which has its own style; all have generously-proportioned windows, meaning channel surfing will seem a distant memory. Some of the rooms are relatively small, but nicely decorated in warm, muted tones. Las Balsas' restaurant is one of the more innovative establishments you will find in the lake district, serving everything from trout ceviche to Peking duck. But what really make the rooms here stand out are the views – best enjoyed lying in bed, or wallowing in a claw-foot tub.

Buena Vida Social Club
El Bolsón *Calle Los Nires, no number, Villa Tourismo (02944 491729/www.buenavidasocialclubpatagonia.com). ££. No credit cards.*
This B&B is just the place to feel at home in hippie El Bolsón. It is decorated in autumnal colours and features hand-made, chunky furniture and brightly coloured art by local artists. The rooms are calmer, decorated in soft creams, and have views overlooking the garden. The owners are artists from the US and Argentina, and a great source of local knowledge.

La Confluencia Lodge
El Bolsón *Ríos Encanto Blanco & Azul, Mallín Ahogado (02944 498375/www.laconfluencia.com). ££.*
Nestled among forests, rivers and mountains, this small, intimate wooden eco-lodge is the perfect place to connect with the natural world. The eco-friendly building was built using straw bales and dead or fallen wood to maximise energy efficiency and minimise harm to the environment. Electricity for lighting and appliances is produced on site using a small hydroelectric turbine, and there is a large organic garden in which herbs, fruits and vegetables are grown. The rooms are small and basic, but the emphasis is more on the communal areas, such as the large lounge with fireplace, the reading spaces and the outdoor deck overlooking the Río Azul. The lodge also has a spa, log-fired saunas and outdoor hot tubs, overlooked by the snow-covered mountains.

Correntoso Lake & River Hotel
Villa La Angostura *RN 231, km 66, along Río Correntoso (02944 15 619728 mobile/www.correntoso. com). £££.*
When settler Primo Capraro built a small wooden cabin on this site in 1917, he set in motion a century of successive hotel-building that has resulted in one of the region's signature lodgings. The hotel is located at the mouth of the Río Correntoso, where it enters the famed national park lake, a place once only accessible by boat or plane. Not every room has lake views, so be sure to ask when reserving. The library has a large and alluring collection of books devoted to the region's history, in which this hotel plays a part; other amenities include a luxurious hammam and spa, and a stunning infinity-edge pool.

Design Suites
Bariloche *Avenida Bustillo, km 2.5 (02944 457000/ www.designsuites.com). £££.*
With the Bariloche branch of the stylish Design Suites chain, modernism and minimalism have their say in a town where even luxury lodgings often rely too obviously on the rustic. The use of country-building motifs – lots of stone and wood – blends well with the sleek structure; this is the place for travellers who favour urban chic wherever they wander. The rooms are huge, and outfitted with trendy

Scandinavian touches. The property is close enough to the centre to be considered 'in town', but the on-site Monet restaurant warrants a night or two of staying in.

El Faro
Villa La Angostura *Avenida Siete Lagos 2345, RN 231, km 64 (02944 495485/www.elfaropatagonia.com). £££.*
'El faro' means lighthouse, and this striking property is shaped accordingly; part of the tower doubles as a lobby. As with all of the high-end lodgings around the lake, El Faro's rooms offer excellent views over the lake and the Andes. The suites are located in the lighthouse tower, one with a direct connection to the beach and the other with a private jacuzzi. All the rooms have a unique air (quite literally, as the interior wood is scented), along with Wi-Fi, satellite TV and stately marble bathrooms. With only 15 rooms in total, the hotel is pleasantly small-scale and tranquil, while also offering big-hotel spa services that include a sauna, gym, whirlpool spa and extensive treatments menu. When it comes to the spa, things can get dirty: there is a mud-bath room that complements the natural spring pool.

"If you want a retreat far from Bariloche's chocolate shop-lined streets, you cannot do better than the only hotel located on the country's largest island, Isla Victoria."

Hostería Isla Victoria
Isla Victoria, Parque Nacional Nahuel Huapi *(02944 448088/www.islavictoria.com). ££££.*
If you're looking for a remote retreat, far from Bariloche's chocolate shop-lined streets, you cannot do better than the only hotel located on the largest island in the country (it's 20km long and 4km across at its widest point). Only accessible by boat, from the co-managed Hotel Tunquelén (*see p190*), it is similar in its classic room design. In spite of only having 20 rooms it still offers all the big-hotel services: a bar, sauna and hydromassage, as well as a few unique flourishes, such as a library that doubles as a musical salon, and a wine cellar highlighting the best labels from Argentina's many bodegas. A relic of the powerful glaciers that shaped the region and left the island with some fine sandy beaches, Isla Victoria is a great place to explore, and explore some more, until the boat ferries you back to civilisation. It's designed as a peaceful getaway for grown-ups, and children under 12 are not allowed to stay here.

El Faro.

Hotel Tunquelén

Bariloche *Avenida Bustillo, km 24.5 (02944 448233/ www.tunquelen.com). £££.*
Situated on a forested slope of the Llao Llao peninsula, Tunquelén is no poor traveller's version of the famed Llao Llao hotel, but a classic in its own right. Rooms overlook either the forest or lake and have a simple design that, even if occasionally reminiscent of a 19th-century sanatorium, keeps the focus where it should be: out of the window. Balconies overlook the lake or the forest, and the 40-room hotel has a sterling range of services: a heated swimming pool, sauna, gym, massage room, bar, restaurant and library. Families will appreciate the tennis court, games room and club room for children.

Llao Llao

Bariloche *Avenida Bustillo km 25 (02944 448530/ www.llaollao.com.ar). ££££.*
If *The Shining* had been shot in Argentina, this is the secluded mountain resort where Jack Nicholson's character would have gone nuts. Built by the Argentinian government and famed architect Alejandro Bustillo in 1940, Llao Llao is one of the best-known hotels in the country. Its setting on a beautiful lake peninsula is as impressive as they come – and in a town like Bariloche, where gorgeous views are commonplace, that's really saying something. The dining areas have especially inviting views over the forested slopes and water. The main hall and interior design are reminiscent of the lodges of the United States' national parks. Your options range from economy rooms to positively palatial suites, or a sweet two-bedroom cabin overlooking the lake. Prices are steep, and when you first enter you may feel as if you are a visiting head of state or diplomat invited to a tsar's country palace. Once you spot the gift and jewellery shops, you'll know it's just a hotel – but a legendary one.

Peuma Hue

24km S of Bariloche *South shore of Lago Gutiérrez, RN 40, km 2014 (02944 501030/www.peuma-hue.com). ££££.*
Many hotels talk the talk of a high-class 'personal touch', but don't deliver anything more than 24-hour room service. Peuma Hue walks the walk – in hiking boots, snow shoes, on skis – placing the focus on the guest. The owners don't see themselves as lodge-keepers but creators of holidays, and take their mission very seriously. Eco-tourism is a major focus here, with hiking, biking and horseback riding on 500 acres of terrain that connects to the national park's system of trails. Guests can also try kayaking and sailing on the lake; Peuma Hue has two miles of private shoreline.

Factfile

When to go

If you're here for winter sports, the peak months are typically July and August, although the winter season can start as early as June and last until October, depending on snow conditions. The summer months (December and January) are great for hiking in the national parks. Summer is short, with freezing rain not uncommon in December.

Getting there

Bariloche is the tourist hub of the lake district, and there are regular flights to its airport, Aeropuerto Internacional Bariloche (02944 426162), from Buenos Aires. Most travellers fly from Buenos Aires' domestic airport, Jorge Newberry. Both Aerolineas Argentinas and LAN offer flights throughout the year. Buses run regularly from Buenos Aires, but it is a 22-hour trip. Buses run between all the other lake district towns and Bariloche's Terminal de Ómnibus (02944 432860), which is located on RN 237 around three kilometres from downtown.

Villa La Angostura's bus station is located at Avenidas Siete Lagos and Arrayanes. The journey to Bariloche takes just over an hour. There is no central bus station in El Bolsón. However, there are a number of different companies located around town that make regular trips to Bariloche (two hours) and other destinations. Companies include El Valle (Roca 357, 02944 455554), Grado 42 (Avenida Belgrano 406, 02944 493124) and Don Otto (Avenida Belgrano, between Perito Moreno & 25 de Mayo, 02944 493910).

Getting around

The lake district has plenty of car-hire companies, and a car is the best option for convenient travel between the towns. There is also a local bus service between all key destinations, though relying on public transport does not allow travellers the flexibility or time to properly enjoy the Ruta de los Siete Lagos.

Tourist information

Bariloche Centro Cívico (02944 429850, www.barilochepatagonia.info). Open 8am-9pm Mon-Fri; 9am-9pm Fri, Sat.
Villa La Angostura RN 231, locally known as Avenida Arrayanes or Siete Lagos (02944 494124, www.villalaangostura.gov.ar). Open 8am-8pm daily.
El Bolsón Avenida San Martín & Roca (02994 492604). Open 9am-9pm daily.

Internet

Bariloche has numerous internet cafés. In Villa La Angostura, you'll find several along the main drag of Avenida Arrayanes. In El Bolsón, there is an internet café on the corner of Avenida San Martín and Avenida Belgrano.

Aldebarán.

Top: road between
Esquel and Trevelin.
Middle & bottom left:
Parque Nacional los
Alerces. Bottom right:
La Trochita.

Esquel & Parque los Alerces

Argentina

Small-town Patagonia meets a forest of giants.

The tiny town of Esquel teeters on the brink of invisibility. You could easily pass right through it, while gazing up at the soaring, surrounding mountains. Yet as you meander down its dirt paths, all the rest of the world is rendered distant. A matrix of just 20 blocks, speckled with one- and two-storied buildings, it is the largest community for miles around.

Aside from getting away from it all, the main reason to come to Esquel is to explore the neighbouring Parque Nacional los Alerces. Here, towering *alerce* trees, or Patagonian cypresses, grow in chestnut-coloured thickets amid a series of emerald-green lakes. Beyond its shady canopies and calm waters sits the area's other famed attraction: a small steam engine known as La Trochita, or the Old Patagonian Express. It is a marker of times past, when pioneers searched for the edge of the earth and founded pockets of civilisation along the way. The train traverses two worlds, beginning in Esquel and travelling through three hours of panoramic beauty before reaching a Mapuche village.

Nearby is the old Welsh settlement of Trevelin; its culture is held intact by tea, scones and Celtic songs, all of which can be sampled at delicately decorated tea houses. Those looking for something more adventurous will find kayaking, hiking and fly-fishing during the hotter months, while in the winter the area brims with ski aficionados, anxious to conquer Cerro La Hoya.

Modest Esquel isn't going to shout from the mountain tops about its attractions. It is far from the glamour of other Patagonian tourist resorts – in fact, it's far from most things. Yet it is this combination of modesty and remoteness that makes Esquel and the surrounding area what they are: a rewarding stop for those armed with curiosity and a passion for the outdoors.

Explore

ESQUEL

To outsiders, **Esquel** may seem like a town still under construction, but the dirt roads and picturesque cottages support a simple way of life. Tourism is relatively new here, so local hospitality is genuine and welcoming. The shopping district is around Avenida 25 de Mayo and Avenida 9 de Julio, where you can stock up on outdoor clothes, locally made chocolate and keepsakes.

Centro Cultural de Esquel

Belgrano 330 (02945 451929/cultureesquel@esquel. gov.ar). Open 7.30am-12.30pm, 3-9pm Mon-Fri. Admission free.

The Centro Cultural de Esquel offers great rainy-day activities. The upper floor houses a gallery space for local and visiting artists, while classes are conducted on the lower floor. Since Esquel has no cinema, the centre's amphitheatre hosts film screenings and theatre productions. The workshops are predominately free and include lessons in the indigenous Mapuche language. The main attraction is the planetarium, which is part of an initiative to foster the study of astronomy. Considering how many millions of stars appear in clear view over Esquel nightly, a bit of background might lend some extra enjoyment to the late-night hours. The centre is currently without a website, so stop by, or email, for information on the latest scheduled events.

La Trochita

Roggero & Urquiza (02954 451403/www.latrochita. org.ar). Open 9am-2pm Mon-Fri; 9am-noon Sat. Admission AR$50; AR$20-AR$35 reductions. No credit cards.

La Trochita, or the Old Patagonian Express, offers a three-hour trip back in time. Some 6,000 people a year board it to ride through the sculpted Patagonian landscapes from Esquel to the Mapuche colony of Nahuel Pan. The steam train runs twice daily, and during the course of the trip, tour guides educate passengers on the history of the railroad in several languages. The tracks run past mountains, valleys and a dormant volcano before reaching Nahuel Pan, where there is a Mapuche cultural museum and market of indigenous crafts. Passengers have 40 minutes to explore the settlement before the return journey to Esquel. Plans to renovate the home station into a comprehensive railway museum are underway. On occasion, there are special night-time rides and private parties. Remember to check the website for schedule changes, and arrive early to bag the most comfortable seats.

PARQUE NACIONAL LOS ALERCES

With its majestic 4,000-year-old *alerce* trees and mesmerising emerald lakes, **Parque Nacional los Alerces** is well worth a visit or two (02945 471015, infoalerces@apn.gov.ar). The park is situated 50 kilometres outside Esquel, on Ruta 71. Upon entering, the information building on the left is the place to gather resources and trail maps. You'll also

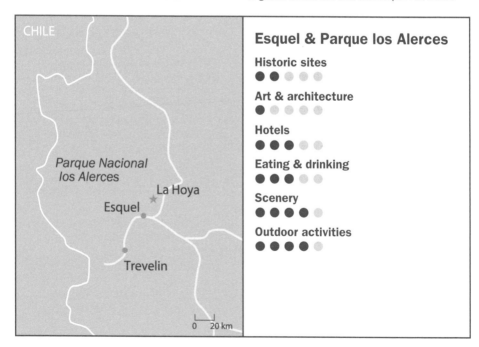

Esquel & Parque los Alerces

Historic sites
● ● ◉ ◉ ◉

Art & architecture
● ● ◉ ◉ ◉

Hotels
● ● ● ◉ ◉

Eating & drinking
● ● ● ◉ ◉

Scenery
● ● ● ● ◉

Outdoor activities
● ● ● ● ◉

Top: La Trochita.
Bottom: Don Chiquino.

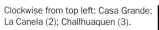

Clockwise from top left: Casa Grande; La Canela (2); Challhuaquen (3).

find extensive information about the various hikes and their level of difficulty. If you plan to trek overnight, you must sign in and leave some form of identification. If you're looking for a leisurely drive, Ruta 71 passes through the entire park and offers plenty of stunning views.

During the summer (January to March), visitors can swim in the immense (and immensely beautiful) Lago Futalaufquen at Puerto Limonao. The name Futalaufquen means 'big lake' in Mapuche, and it doesn't disappoint. There are several campsites within the park.

Numerous varieties of ibis and other native birds delight birdwatchers and novice nature spectators. However, you'll be hard pushed to spot the park's most elusive inhabitants: the puma and the world's smallest deer, the pudú.

For many visitors, the draw of los Alerces is the fly-fishing. If you choose not to go with a guide, you can purchase fishing permits at most service stations in Esquel. All fishing is catch and release, so be sure to have your camera ready to capture the moment. The Servicentro Abrojal (25 de Mayo & Alvear) sells supplies and permits.

LA HOYA

Located about 12 kilometres outside of Esquel, **Cerro La Hoya** offers an abundance of winter activities, including Alpine skiing, snowboarding, snowtubing, and even a freestyle area for the extreme-sports enthusiast. La Hoya is known for being a family resort, and childcare is offered for under-fives; those searching for challenging pistes may find it constricting.

For information on prices, classes and transportation schedules, consult the office in the centre of Esquel (Almeghino 1199, 02945 453018, www.skilahoya.com), which is open from 7am to 9pm daily. Most hotels in the area will have buses or vans to drive you to the top of the mountain.

The ski season runs from June to October, but the ten different chairlifts to the summit are open all year round. From the top, you have over 60 hectares of trails to choose from. Simple *confiterías* speckle the mountainside for hot chocolate stop-offs and snacks.

TREVELIN

Approximately 25 kilometres from Esquel sits **Trevelin**, a Celtic colony that's a long, long way from Wales. Settled by the Welsh in the mid 19th century in order to preserve their customs and language, the town currently has a population of about 9,000; some estimate that nearly 80 per cent of the inhabitants still speak the Welsh language, or at least have some knowledge of it. In Welsh, 'tre' means town and 'velin' means mill, translating to 'town of the mill'; the first flour mill in the region was built here.

"If you're lucky, you may happen upon a festival, where Welsh music and culture are paraded through the streets."

Twenty minutes along Ruta 259 will take you to the village centre. Visitors can learn about Welsh Patagonian history at the Museo Regional Trevelin, as well as taste some of the inherited customs at traditional tea shops. If you're lucky, you may happen upon a festival, where Welsh music and culture is paraded through the streets.

Museo Regional Trevelin
Molino Viejo 488 (no phone). Open July-Sept 11am-6pm daily. Jan-Mar 9am-9pm daily. Admission AR$4.
Three blocks away from the central square stands the town's namesake mill – now an educational museum. It has four rooms filled with historical artefacts, such as farm machinery, antique clothing and phonographs. Each exhibit has a description in Spanish, English and Welsh. The majority of the items were donated by the community.

OUTDOOR ACTIVITIES

Many people hire guides to traverse the mountainous region, but there are a few hikes you can do on your own. The two most popular are to Laguna de la Zeta and La Cruz. The former is a five-kilometre walk that takes you to a secluded sector of the forest, and a beautiful view over the water. Head north-east on Avenida Fontana, then follow the markers. Another popular hike is to La Cruz, a wooden crucifix that towers above the town. Begin by heading south-west on 25 de Mayo, then continue climbing upwards to the cross.

For more daring visitors, there is white-water rafting, paintballing, biking, week-long camping trips and horse riding. Check to see if your hotel has special rates for day trips. Companies include Limits Adventure (Avenida Alvear 1069, 02945 455811, www.limitsadventure.com.ar) and Esquel Patagonia Aventura (Avenida Fontana 482, 02945 457015, www.grupoepa.com). Be sure to clarify if meals are included in the prices.

Eat

You're likely to eat lunch on trails and mountain tops, and many restaurants in Esquel only open for dinner, at around 8pm. The restaurant at Cumbres Blancas hotel (*see p199*) is open to non-guests.

Casa Grande

Esquel *Roca 441 (02945 15 469712 mobile/ casagrandeesq@yahoo.com.ar). Open noon-2.30pm, 8.30pm-midnight daily. ££. No credit cards. Traditional.*
With its wooden floors, golden walls and oak details, Casa Grande seems to have been hewn from the wilderness. The well-spaced tables and intimate setting mean it's easy to linger, and the dishes are designed to be savoured. Each meal is preceded by a selection of pâtés, while the home-made pastas, crêpes and tender salmon steak are house favourites. Owner Carlos often chats with the clientele, and may even try and convince you that the paintings on the walls are real Van Goghs.

"With its teapots and home-made jams, Nain Maggie was inspired by the owner's Welsh grandmother."

Don Chiquino

Esquel *Avenida Ameghino 1649 (0295 450035/ saynopelado@hotmail.com). Open noon-3pm, 8pm-midnight daily. ££. Italian.*
Charismatic owner Tito explains the philosophy of his restaurant as 'a place where children feel like adults and adults play like children.' The walls of this Italian trattoria are lined with an eclectic display of hay, shrubbery, licence plates, business cards and napkins with messages. The playful ambiance is further emphasised by the folk tale in the menu that tells of a magical volcano emitting the very first pasta. Fairy tales aside, you'll be more than satisfied with the home-made pasta and gnocchi; don't miss the plump ravioli, stuffed with ricotta, pine mushrooms and ground nuts. This place may be ostentatious, but the personal touches make it worth a trip.

La Luna

Esquel *Avenida Fontana 656 (02945 453800/ www.lalunarestobar.com.ar). Open noon-4am Mon, Wed-Sun. £. No credit cards. Traditional.*
The rustic ambience inside this local watering hole is similar to most other Patagonian restaurants, but this place has evidence of past revelry carved into each table, in the form of phone numbers and poems. The restaurant-bar offers lights snacks and hearty beer, and a DJ spins dance music at around midnight. During the summer months (January to March), you can sit outside on the patio.

Mirasoles

Esquel *Pellegrini 643 (02945 456390). Open 9pm-midnight Tue-Sat. ££. No credit cards. Modern.*
Mirasoles has the area's most adventurous menu. It serves an assortment of healthy options, including soya burgers, brochettes of smoked trout, and home-made nut bread. The restaurant specialises in trout and offers several varieties – one doused in vodka, another served with oranges and almonds. The signature sauces and dishes are rotated depending on the season and the whim of the chef, and there are over 30 local and international wines to choose from. It's one of the only local restaurants to offer a delivery service, although if you order in, you'll miss out on the interesting art exhibited on the exposed-brick walls.

Nain Maggie

Trevelin *Perito Moreno 179 (02945 480232). Open high season 10am-12.30pm, 3.30-8.30pm daily. Low season 10am-12.30pm, 3.30-8.30pm Mon, Wed-Sun. ££. Café.*
This, the original Trevelin tea room, was inspired by the owner's grandmother Maggie (*nain* means grandmother in Welsh). Teapots, home-made jams and wind chimes set the scene, while Celtic music plays softly in the background. Choose between a selection of several organic and freshly mixed teas, accompanied by a platter of sandwiches, scones, muffins and home-made rolls. The on-site shop specialises in Celtic crafts.

Stay

La Canela

1km S of Esquel *Villa Ayelén, Los Notros & Los Radales (02945 453890/www.canelaesquel.com). £££. No credit cards.*
There are only five rooms for rent in this amiable bed and breakfast, so be sure to book early. People love coming back to visit Veronica and Jorge, whose reservations book can fill up more than three months in advance. The couple share their rich Patagonian heritage with guests via Jorge's photographs and Veronica's oil paintings. Jorge has written several books on Patagonia, as has Veronica's father. The rooms are furnished not just with antiques but with some good books as well. Each has a country-style interior, with curtains and exposed wooden beams that reflect the rustic feel of this quiet swathe of land.

Challhuaquen

25km from Trevelin *Ruta 259, km 59 (02945 15 507882 mobile/www.challhuaquen.com). ££££.*
This five-star hotel is located on a 30-hectare plot deep within the valley of Trevelin. Down a long dirt road, past scattered farms and gorgeous scenery, it has no address, only a name and km number. The Challhuaquen, which means 'fishing place' in Mapuche, can accomodate a maximum of 12 people, allowing the staff to provide personal service. Gustavo, the gourmet chef, lives on site year round with his wife, who is the hotel's housekeeper, and their young son. The walls are painted with vibrant yellows, oranges and greens, mirroring the colourful vistas outside the windows. The oak-floored rooms are generously proportioned, and each has its own pristine bathroom. Other amenities include four boats, a jacuzzi with a river view, and a central salon and bar where the chef presents the day's meals.

Cumbres Blancas

Esquel *Avenida Ameghino 1683 (02945 455100/ www.cumbresblancas.com.ar). ££.*

Despite being one of the larger hotels in the area, with 20 large rooms, Cumbres Blancas doesn't compromise when it comes to service. There are a number of different living arrangements, from single rooms to a private suite, all decorated in pastel tones. The main entrance leads to the lounge, where a fireplace adds a homely touch. Weather permitting, there's an outdoor mini-putting green; inside, guests are welcome to unwind in the sauna or play a game of table football. In the restaurant, you can order platters of smoked Patagonian deer, cheese, salmon and trout, presented on a wooden paddle that stretches the width of the table. The attentive staff will help you to find your way up mountains and into forests; when you've finished exploring, Cumbres Blancos is the perfect place to sit by the fire and recuperate for the following day.

Ibai Ko Mendi

Esquel *Rivadavia 2965 (02945 451503/ www.ibaikomendi.com.ar). £££.*

Even more impressive than the eight private, petite log cabins at Ibai Ko Mendi is its aquamarine wading pool. Half of it resides in the central building, heated to a perfect 22°C, while the other half is out in the open air. The spa area includes two saunas and a massage room, while the dining area doubles as a screening room for the films available for loan. Upstairs in the main building, the guestrooms feature pastel, floral decor, Wi-Fi internet and

individual fireplaces. Outside, the cosy cabañas are equipped with jacuzzis, kitchens and multiple balconies. Set by a river on the edge of the city, the complex makes a fine base for exploring the area.

"There are two saunas and two vast jacuzzis at Plaza Esquel – and an assistant on call to bring drinks."

Plaza Esquel

Esquel *Avenida Ameghino 713 (2945 457002/ www.patagoniaandesgroup.com.ar). ££.*

With a glass chessboard and silver couches in the lobby, this centrally-located hotel is touted by its owners as the town's most modern option. The 16 rooms and five full-service apartments all share a similar sleekness, but most guests come here for the spa; if you're not staying at the hotel, a visit costs AR$40 for two hours. There are two enormous jacuzzis and two saunas (one dry, the other humid and fragranced with eucalyptus). There is an assistant on call to bring drinks, and massages on request, making it a hard task to leave.

Factfile

When to go

The action centres on the slopes of La Hoya in the winter (July to September): during the summer (January to March), the focus shifts to Parque Nacional Los Alerces. From May to August, temperatures stay close to zero, and May and June have the most precipitation. The summer season is known for drastic changes between night and day temperatures (the average high is 19°C; the average low 6°C), and it's important to carry water to combat the dryness of the region.

The peak tourist seasons are from October to April and July to September; outside this period, hotels and restaurants take a break and tend to open only for special occasions.

Getting there & around

If you are travelling to Esquel by car, take RN 40 from the north and south, and Ruta 25 if you're coming from Trelew to the east. The bus terminal is located at Avenida Alvear 1871 (02945 451584), and companies such as Andesmar (02945 450143, www.andesmar. com.ar), Vía Bariloche (02945 454676) and Tramat (02945 453037, www.tramat.com.ar)

run regular services. Buses for Trevelin leave from the terminal every hour. Once in Esquel, you can hire a car from El Condor at Avenida Alvear 1871 (02945 15 410259 mobile).

The airport is 30 kilometres east of town. Aerolíneas Argentinas and Austral offer flights here, and share a joint office at Avenida Fontana 408 (02945 453614, 02945 453413). The office is generally open 9am-1pm, 3.30-7.30pm Mon-Fri; 9am-1pm Sat.

Tourist information

Esquel Avenida Alvear & Sarmiento (02945 451927, www.esquel.gov.ar). Open Jan, Feb 7am-11pm daily. Mar-Dec 8am-9pm daily. **Trevelin** Plaza Coronel Fontana, Rotonda 28 de Julio, no number (02945 480120, www.trevelin. org). Open Apr-Oct 8am-7pm daily. Nov-Mar 8am-10pm daily.

Internet

Cyber Club (Avenida Alvear 961) is open 10am-midnight Mon-Fri; noon-midnight Sat; 4pm-midnight Sun. Most hotels here have internet – often a Wi-Fi service.

Top: the Andes. Middle: Puente del Inca train station. Bottom left: Puente del Inca. Bottom right: fly-fishing.

Mendoza

Argentina

A land of mountains and wine.

The subtle flavours of the malbecs and syrahs develop in the mouth almost before you touch down in this relaxed, verdant city, set on the edge of a desert and cradled by the powerful Andes. Wine is big business both here and in the valleys all around, as people push forward innovative *vino* culture with an entrepreneurial spirit that is endemically Argentinian. The province ranks, alongside San Juan, as the country's primary wine-producing region – hence the local phrase 'to be between Mendoza and San Juan', signifying you've had a few too many.

It rarely rains in Mendoza, a city of some 800,500 inhabitants that sits gracefully on a plateau in the shadow of the awe-inspiring mountains. After suffering a severe earthquake in 1861, it was rebuilt intelligently, incorporating innovative urban design, large squares and wide, tree-lined streets. The abundant greenery is made possible by the network of water channels that branch off in all directions and generate the feeling of a calm oasis. They're fed by melted snow from the Andes through a series of brilliantly engineered aqueducts, developed first by the indigenous Huarpes, and then taken on by the Spanish.

But this attractive town and its surrounding region aren't just for wine-lovers. The mountains and valleys are awash with opportunities for nature- and adventure-lovers to enjoy their ultimate holiday pursuit, whether it be climbing to the top of Cerro Aconcagua, the continent's highest peak; ambling on horseback through the peaceful valleys; or rafting in the rushing waters of the Río Mendoza.

Parque San Martín.

Explore

MENDOZA CITY

Standing in the central square of Plaza Independencia, the two things that immediately strike visitors to **Mendoza** are the surrounding nature and the city's well thought out urban plan. The Andes rise up behind it, beckoning adventure-lovers; closer still lies the man-made oasis of Parque San Martín.

Plaza Independencia, commemorating the independence of Mendoza from the Spanish nearly 200 years ago, is located in the banking district. Elegantly adorned with fountains and pergolas, it marks the city centre and the focal point for cultural activity. In the middle of the square stands a bronze equestrian statue of General San Martín, El Libertador. Four further plazas – San Martín, Chile, Italia and España – are located symmetrically, two blocks away from each corner of Plaza Independencia.

Parque San Martín, designed by acclaimed 19th-century landscape architect Carlos Thays, extends over 350 hectares, with almost 18 kilometres of well-worn pathways and 300 species of carefully tended plants and trees. Within its boundaries you'll find a zoo, the football stadium built for the 1978 World Cup and the Universidad Nacional de Cuyo. A panoramic view of the city can be enjoyed from the top of Cerro de la Gloria. Local inhabitants put this beautiful hill to good use, and its slopes are dotted with dog-walkers, joggers and couples out for a stroll. The amphitheatre in the middle of the park is the location for the Fiesta de la Vendimia, Mendoza's annual harvest festival, held on the first weekend in March. A tourist office near the park's main entrance provides information on park activities, including cycling, boating and hang-gliding. If you stay in the park's campsite, you can hear the lions in the nearby zoo roaring at night; sitting in your tent, you could swear you're in Africa.

Built in 1897, the park doesn't just function as a place to relax and get back to nature. Its real purpose is to improve the quality of the air in Mendoza. The park acts as a huge humidifier, a necessity in such a dry city. When you enter the main gates, turn left to see the elaborate fountain, rose garden and lakeside restaurants. Tour buses leave every half hour from the tourist information office, ferrying people to Cerro de la Gloria.

Mendoza city was founded by the Spanish in 1561. Before that 'discovery', the area was inhabited by three peaceful indigenous peoples: the Incas, the Puelches and the Huarpes. You can catch glimpses of their cultures in the decorative details of local handicrafts, or find references them in the new wineries and wine labels, which use ancient Indian vocabulary such as Ruca Malen and Antucura.

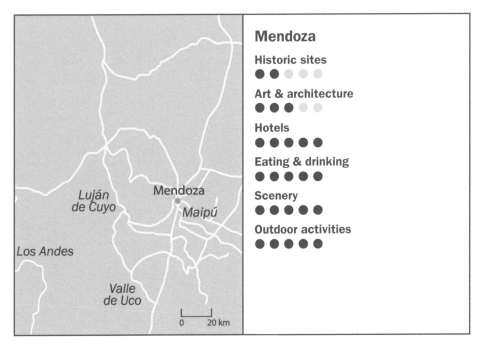

Mendoza

Historic sites
● ● ○ ○ ○

Art & architecture
● ● ● ○ ○

Hotels
● ● ● ● ●

Eating & drinking
● ● ● ● ●

Scenery
● ● ● ● ●

Outdoor activities
● ● ● ● ●

The main thoroughfare between Argentina and neighbouring Chile runs through Mendoza city and up into the Andes. Throughout history, the route has made its mark on the Argentinian psyche, playing a crucial role in the country's struggle for freedom. In 1813, Argentinian general José de San Martín, who fought for South America's independence from its colonial overlords, famously holed up in Mendoza city with his army, going on to liberate neighbouring Chile and Peru from the Spaniards.

Wine is, undoubtedly, the major draw of this fascinating landscape, with the majority of the bodegas – as wineries are known – in the **Luján de Cuyo**, **Maipú** and **Valle de Uco** areas, all of which are short drives or bicycle rides out of town. Argentinian wine has hit the world stage, and over the last 20 years the focus for the region has been to produce wines of international standing, with many bodegas upgrading their equipment, launching new labels and hiring eminent oenologists. The wineries offer a fine day out, and sometimes top-notch food as well. Several have art galleries attached, and many are architectural masterpieces in themselves. A glut of agencies – check out www.troutandwine.com and www.mendozawinetours.com – offers tours. Alternatively, you can go it alone, but remember that the majority of wineries require reservations for visits, and most are closed on Sunday.

"Luján de Cuyo has the best variety of wineries, incredible views of the mountains and relative proximity to the city."

Mercado Central
Patricias Mendocinas & Las Heras. Open 9am-1.30pm, 4.30-9pm daily.
A lively Latin experience, Mendoza's working market is host to a range of stalls selling good-quality fresh produce and handicrafts. Drink a quick *cortado* coffee at one of the stand-up *puestos* and watch the locals go about their business. This is a good place to snack on empanadas and pizzas, or to sniff out the ingredients for a picnic.

Museo del Área Fundacional
Videla Castillo, between Beltrán & Alberdi (0261 449 5184). Open 8am-8pm Tue-Sat; 3-8pm Sun. Admission AR$5.
Located in the heart of Mendoza's restored colonial quarter, this museum of civic history has an underground chamber containing archaeological remains of Mendoza's Cabildo (town hall), largely destroyed by an earthquake on 20 March

1861. The museum explores the city's history, taking visitors on a journey from the time of indigenous peoples, through Spanish colonisation and on to independence.

Museo Municipal de Arte Moderno
Underground, Plaza Independencia, between Rividavia & Mitre (0261 425 7279). Open 9am-8pm daily. Admission AR$5.
Tucked neatly underground in Plaza Independencia, this museum has a permanent collection of art from Mendoza, with works dating from 1930 to the present day, including paintings, ceramics, drawings and sculptures. It is also a venue for free cultural events, including concerts and theatre, so it's worth stopping in for the weekly programme.

Ruinas de San Francisco
Necochea 201 (0261 425 6927). Open 9am-6pm Mon-Fri.
The statue of the Virgin housed here was a miraculous survivor of the earthquake that destroyed the city in 1861. These ruins are part of the original city centre, now preserved as the Área Fundacional. The church was built in 1731 as a residence for the Compañía de Jesús (Jesuits) and was given to the Franciscan order in 1798, after the Jesuits had been expelled from the Americas in 1767 by order of the Spanish crown.

LUJÁN DE CUYO

Luján de Cuyo is Mendoza's finest region for wine tours, thanks to its wide variety of bodegas, incredible views of the mountains and relative proximity to the city. The first of Luján de Cuyo's wineries are 20 minutes from the city, and the furthest 40 minutes away, along the RN 7 to Chile. Call ahead to confirm tour times and reserve places – although poor public transport and limited opening hours mean it's often easier to use a wine tour company. Unless otherwise stated in the listings, tours are free.

Achaval Ferrer
Cobos 2601 (0261 488 1131/www.achaval-ferrer.com). Open 9am-4pm Mon-Fri; 9-11.30am Sat; 9.30am-1pm Sun. Tours (in English & Spanish) 9.30am, 11am & 12.30pm Mon-Sat; noon Sun. Tour price AR$38.
Not content with producing some of the finest wines in Argentina, Achaval Ferrer offers one of the most interesting wine tours in Mendoza. The barrel tasting includes a unique sampling of each varietal that makes up its top label, Altamira, followed by the impressive blend itself. The guides are passionate about their subject, and not afraid to divulge some of the bodega's wine-making secrets. The cost of the tour is deducted from any purchases made.

Alta Vista
Alzaga 3972, Chacras de Coria (0261 496 4684/www. altavistawines.com). Open May-Sept 9am-6pm Mon-Sat; Oct-Apr 9am-6pm daily. Tours (in English & Spanish) 9.30am, 11.30am, 3pm daily. Tour price AR$10.
Alta Vista combines the best of modern and traditional approaches in its winemaking and design. The 100-year-old winery is set in beautiful gardens and vineyards, 20

Top: Achaval Ferrer.
Bottom: Altavista (2).

minutes south of the city. Its owners have invested in the latest technology and this shines through in the wines, from the distinctive torrontés to the mouth-watering, single vineyard malbecs. Once again, the tour price is refunded if you invest in some wine at the end.

Bodega Ruca Malén
RN 7, km 1059, Agrelo (0261 562 8357/www.bodega rucamalen.com). Open 9am-5pm Mon-Sat; noon-5pm Sun. Tours (in English & Spanish) 10am, 11am, 3pm & 4pm Mon-Fri; 10am & 11am Sat.
The hugely popular lunches served at this welcoming winery see chef Lucas Bustos creating truly memorable food and wine pairings. Another plus is the generous habit of keeping guests' glasses full with ample tastings of the range, including the top wine, Kinien. Stellar views of the Andes add to the appeal. Although tours of the bodega are free, it's essential to book a place in advance.

Carmelo Patti
San Martín 2614 (0261 498 1379). Open 11am-1pm, 3-5pm Mon-Sat. Tours 11am & 3pm Mon-Sat.
One of Argentina's most famous boutique winemakers, Patti is an affable character with plenty of stories and insight into the industry. The winery itself is nothing but a shed, and its owner truly puts the garage into *garagista* winemaking. His cabernet sauvignon is one of Argentina's finest, and if you're lucky, you'll get to taste from the barrel. Call ahead for reservations and to make sure that a translator is available, as the great man speaks no English.

Lagarde
Avenida San Martín 1745 (0261 498 0011/www.la garde.com.ar). Open 9.30am-4pm Mon-Sat. Tours (in English & Spanish) every 30mins 9.30am-2pm Mon-Fri; 9.30am-12.30pm Sat. Tour price AR$15.
Founded in 1897, this long-established winery currently holds stocks of the oldest white wine in South America – a 1942 semillon. Another of its more unusual offerings is a sparkling wine, produced in limited quantities each year using traditional methods. Aesthetically, the winery is a pleasing series of courtyards with mud ovens, clay urns and one space artistically adorned with empty birdcages; the surrounding vines are almost 100 years old and are tilled by a mule called Pinocchio. Enthusiastic guides do a sterling job of showing how Argentinian wine has evolved over the past century.

MAIPÚ
Maipú is the closest wine district to the city, and has really upped its game in recent years. This is the best area in which to take an economical wine tour, ideally by bicycle. Many wineries here have street locations with little or no vineyards – but the further south you go, the prettier the landscape becomes, with the city opening up into olive groves and vineyards. Take buses 171, 172 or 173 from La Rioja street in the city centre and alight on Urquiza. You'll find several establishments with bikes to rent; try Mr Hugo (0261 497 4067, www.lavidyelvino.com.ar).

Bodega La Rural
Montecaseros 2625 (0261 497 2013/www.bodegala rural.com.ar). Open 9am-5pm Mon-Fri; 9am-3pm Sat. Tours (in English & Spanish) every hr from 9am-5pm.
What makes La Rural stand out from other local bodegas is its engaging museum. Reminders of winemaking history, showing how the industry has progressed from cow-hide wine presses to the high-tech process of today, lie scattered throughout the winery and its grounds. Giant oak tanks stand in large, cavernous halls, while side rooms hold Victorian pumps and bottle corkers. The tours are free, but by reservation only; when it comes to the wine tasting, it's worth spending a little extra to try the decent varietals.

Carinae Viñedos & Bodega
Videla Aranda 2899 (0261 524 1629/0261 15 554 5422 mobile/www.carinaevinos.com). Open 10am-6pm daily. Tours (in English, Spanish & French) 10am-5.30pm daily. Tour prices AR$15-$40.
In addition to its liquid assets, this charming little winery has delightful owners – Frenchman Philippe and his wife Brigitte. Tours of the old-style building and facilities, which are surrounded by vineyards and olive trees, are followed by enjoyable tasting sessions. Philippe has really embraced the delights of the region, and combines his love of winemaking with stargazing, to provide an interesting tour with astronomical references.

"With stunning views of the mountains, Valle de Uco is the new frontier in Mendoza wines."

VALLE DE UCO
A high-altitude valley with stunning views of the mountains, Valle de Uco is the new frontier in Mendoza wines. Most of the wineries here are new concept wineries, foreign-owned and with imposing architecture. The vineyards are often newly planted, although some areas, such as La Consulta, have 100-year-old vines and are producing incredible wines. The closest wineries are a 90-minute drive from the city.

Andeluna Cellars
RP 89, between km 11 & 12 (02622 423226/www. andeluna.com). Open 10am-5pm daily. Tours (in English & Spanish) 10am, 11.30am, 2pm & 4pm. Tour prices AR$15-$36.
This bodega's romantic name was inspired by the view of the moon over the Andes. For such a modern installation, the tasting room has an inviting, old-world feel, and there is a cooler system that allows for wine tastings by the glass. Spectacular lunches are available by prior reservation (minimum six people); the quality is high, and the service supremely attentive.

Boutique bodegas

Tasting your way through Mendoza's wineries can be an all-consuming experience, whether you are doing it by car, the popular bicycle option or, at Familia Zuccardi, by hot-air balloon (*see p220*). One aspect of the wine boom that can't be missed is the small-scale artisan, or boutique, bodegas. But where do you start? Take heed of the experts: **Nigel Tollerman**, who runs Buenos Aires-based 0800-Vino.com and is sommelier to Francis Ford Coppola at Jardín Escondido (*see p51*); **Charlie O'Malley**, who is editor of Mendoza-based magazine, *Wine Republic* and runs a tour company called Trout & Wine; **Alejandro Iglesias**, sommelier of Private Cellars Argentina; and **Heather Willens**, a wine broker, sommelier and head of www.hwvinos.com.

What's the best artisanal bodega to visit in Mendoza, and why?

Nigel: My favourite small-production, traditional winery has to be Carmelo Patti in Luján de Cuyo (*see p206*). It's named after the owner, who makes some of the best cabernet sauvignon in Argentina in a wonderful, aged style.
Charlie: For me, it's Carinae (*see left*), because the friendly French owners show you around personally, with tastings conducted in the family home. The owner's obsession with stargazing gives the experience a quirky twist.
Heather: I'd also vote for Carmelo Patti, because the man himself leads all the visits and is one of the most passionate wine-makers in Mendoza. He doesn't speak English, but his enthusiasm needs no translation.
Alejandro: Bodega Antucura (*see p213*) is a delightfully luxurious place in the Valle de Uco, with rich wines and a lovely boutique hotel.

What's the best 'boutique' wine to spot on a local menu?

Nigel: Try the wines of Vina el Cerno, a tiny artisanal winery in Maipú (0261 496 4929, www.elcerno.com.ar). It makes excellent old-world style wines, including merlot and syrah, as well as cabernet sauvignon and malbec.
Charlie: Your average restaurant in Mendoza often has a disappointing wine list. Go to the top hotels and restaurants for the best selections. Look out for Carmelo Patti cabernet franc, Clos de Chacras malbec, Sottano Judas blend, Pulenta Estate sauvignon blanc and Enrique Foster malbec.
Heather: Familia Marguery malbec; the bodega puts its heart and soul into each bottle (0261 423 7559, www.marguerywines.com).

Alejandro: The two brothers that run Durigutti Winemakers (0261 498 3115, www.durigutti. com) are using different local vineyards to bring out the best of the terroir and the malbec grape. The best one is Durigutti Reserva malbec 2006; good quality, and a great price at just AR$80.

And the best one to take away?

Nigel: Carmelo Patti 2003 cabernet sauvignon (or he may now be serving the no-doubt excellent 2004). Heaven!
Charlie: Try the sangiovese from Benvenuto de la Serna in Valle de Uco (0261 420 0782, www.benvenutodelaserna.com). It's a rare grape here and makes for a good story: the winery is run by cousins of Che Guevara.
Heather: Don Juan Reserva is an excellent blend of malbec, syrah, bonarda and merlot.
Alejandro: Ángel Mendoza and sons produce an intriguing wine by the name of Pura Sangre (pure blood) from Domaine St Diego in Maipú (0261 439 5557). This label is very difficult to find in BA, and is a fantastic blend of cabernet sauvignon and malbec.

PuLp TRAVEL

MENDOZA . ARGENTINA

Personalized wine tours
Daily group departures - Countryside hotels

Phone (54-9-261) 5433292 - Nextel 54*640*3977
www.pulptravel.com - info@pulptravel.com

A PREMIUM WINE TOUR

Enjoy a spectacular day in the heart of Mendoza wine country

Small private groups
Special tastings
Lunch in winery

Free bottle of wine with this magazine

TROUT & WINE

Galeria San Marcos, Sarmiento 133, Mendoza - Tel 0261 4255613 Cell 155 413892
ask@troutandwine.com - www.troutandwine.com
OPERADOR RESPONSABLE: CONSTELACION TOUR S.R.L. DNT LEG 3779-RES.789/83

Discover the city from your back pocket

Essential for your weekend break, 25 top cities available.

POCKET SIZED *from £6.99 / $11.95*

Amsterdam · London 2010 · New York 2010

TIME OUT GUIDES
WRITTEN BY
LOCAL EXPERTS
visit timeout.com/shop

Time Out Guides

Bodegas Salentein

*Los Arboles, RP 89, no number (02622 429500/www.
bodegasalentein.com). Open 10am-6pm daily. Tours (in
English) 11am, 1pm, 3pm daily; (in Spanish) 10am,
noon, 2pm & 4pm daily. Tour price AR$15.*
This grand, Dutch-owned complex feels like Mendoza's own
temple to wine and showcases some of the area's sleekest
architecture. The sprawling site also contains an excellent
modern art gallery and a stylish posada. You don't need to
reserve to visit the gallery and visitors' centre, but it's best
to call ahead for the winery tour. The only downside is that
the slickness of the operation can make the experience feel
slightly impersonal.

O Fournier

*Los Indios, no number (02622 451088/www.ofournier.
com). Open 9am-6pm daily. Tours (in English, Spanish
& Italian) 9.30am-4.30pm daily. Tour price AR$35-$175.*
Architecturally, with its nods to space-age fantasy, this is
one of the most innovative wineries in the world. Set in a
secluded part of Valle de Uco, the winery is well worth the
two-hour trip, thanks to its excellent, well-crafted wines. Big
plans are underway for a five-star hotel on the site, but there
is already a small posada for those who cannot wait. O
Fournier also provides excellent lunches in the modern
visitor centre; cookery classes, concentrating on local
cuisine, are also available. Tour costs vary depending on
whether you take part in various tasting options.

THE ANDES

Mendoza's stunning landscape provides
excellent opportunities to get down and dirty
with the great outdoors (see below). The most
popular excursion into the Andes is a tour that,
along with the chance to travel down the RN 7
(the road to Chile), typically takes in the Parque
Provincial Aconcagua and the Puente del Inca
(Inca bridge), a geological phenomenon where the
river has bored through the mountain, creating a
natural stone bridge. The coppery-gold colour of
the rocks comes from minerals in the water.

Rising up into the clouds to 6,962 metres,
Cerro Aconcagua (180 kilometres from Mendoza
city) is the highest mountain in the Americas. The
awe-inspiring summit is a must-do for serious
mountain climbers from all over the world, who
spend between 13 and 15 days ascending its
rugged terrain. Climbers need to purchase a
permit from the Aconcagua park authority in
Mendoza. Many of the tour agencies in the city
will be able to offer mountain trips of varying
degrees of difficulty. A less challenging option
is a trek to the Plaza de Mulas base camp.

OUTDOOR ACTIVITIES

Andes & Fire (www.andesfire.com.ar, 0261 15
333 8530 mobile), a Mendoza-based agency,
offers guides for everything from river rafting
to trekking and horse riding. There are rafting
activities an hour outside of Mendoza city, upriver

from the Potrerillos dam, through Argentina Rafting
(0261 429 6325, www.argentinarafting.com).

For horse riding, try Cordón del Plata (0261 423
7423, www.cordondelplata.com) or Toso Boehler
(0261 15 454 9004 mobile, www.tosoboehler.
com.ar). Paragliding is also becoming a popular
activity. Mendoza Parapente (0261 426 8424,
www.mendozaparapente.com.ar) will let you take
to the skies from Cerro Arco, 20 minutes from
Mendoza city centre.

Located 450 kilometres away from the city of
Mendoza, Las Leñas is the key ski destination of
the region, drawing the crowds with its off-piste
skiing, high-end accommodation and top-notch
gastronomy. Contact Argentina Ski Tours (0261
630 0026, www.argentinaskitours.com).

Eat

1884

Mendoza *Belgrano 1188, & Godoy Cruz (0261 424
2698). Open 8.30pm-midnight Mon-Wed, Sun; 8.30pm-
1am Thur-Sat. £££. International.*
Celebrity chef Francis Mallman's restaurant is located
inside the atmospheric, Romanesque Bodega Escorihuela.
Mallman put Argentinian haute cuisine on the map with
dishes such as kid or salted chicken baked in mud ovens,
and there's an impressive 36-page wine list. The whole place
has an upbeat, energetic atmosphere; come to savour the
flavours, or combine your meal with a tour of the bodega
and art gallery.

Anna Bistro

Mendoza *Avenida Juan B Justo 161 (0261 425 1818).
Open noon-3pm, 8pm-late Tue-Sun. ££. International.*
A hip lounge-restaurant run by two French proprietors,
Cyril and Jerome, Anna Bistro is relatively new on the
Mendocino dining scene. Comfortable sofas are conducive
to a tranquil dining experience, overlooking a lovely garden.
The menu is elaborate, though simpler dishes include *chivito*
(kid goat) and a robust *ojo de bife* (ribeye steak). It's a perfect
spot for a sinful late afternoon cocktail; as the evening wears
on, the atmosphere is buzzing.

Azafrán

Mendoza *Avenida Sarmiento 765 (0261 429 4200/
www.bve.com.ar). Open noon-midnight daily. £££.
International/Modern.*
With its attractive antique furniture, chequered floors and
bouquets of dried flowers, this classic Argentinian
restaurant is always busy, and reservations are
recommended. The eclectic menu draws on good-quality
produce from all over Argentina: Patagonian deer and lamb,
Tierra del Fuego crab, and beef from the Argentinian
pampas. The restaurant's name means saffron in Spanish,
and the chefs are adept at flavouring dishes in an interesting
way using different herbs and spices. Set aside a little time
to peruse the 500-bottle wine menu, which includes wines
from over 80 different bodegas.

Bistro M

Mendoza *Chile 1124 (0261 441 1234/www. mendoza.park.hyatt.com). Open 6.30-11am, 8.30pm-midnight daily. £££. Modern.*

If you want to pamper yourself, the restaurant at the Park Hyatt has a sumptuous menu and mannered surrounds. Perfectly executed dishes such as marinated goat with chilli and garlic sauce, or grilled salmon with fennel and asparagus risotto, are prepared in the busy open kitchen, then delivered to diners by exquisitely polite, attentive staff. The restaurant has large windows looking out over Plaza Independencia, and an appealing outdoor terrace. When it comes to choosing a wine, the sommelier will guide you through a dizzying array of regional offerings, stored in a two-storey gallery by the spiral staircase.

La Bourgogne

Luján de Cuyo *Roque Sáenz Peña 3531 (0261 498 9400/www.carlospulentawines.com). Open noon-3pm, 8pm-midnight Tue-Sat. £££. International.*

With its modern design and Incan flourishes, La Bourgogne promises to become as famous as its sister eaterie in Buenos Aires's Alvear Palace Hotel. The food is inventive and beautifully presented, and represents some of the finest dining in the wine country, with dishes such as veal ribs in malbec or Andean trout with dijon mustard in sauvignon blanc. Ask for a table on one of the balconies and enjoy your meal with a superb view across the vineyards of the restaurant's host winery. There is a two-room posada for those who want to stay.

Casa del Visitante

Maipú *RP 33, km 7.5 (0261 441 0000/www.familia zuccardi.com). Open 9am-5pm Mon-Sat; 10am-3.30pm Sun. ££. Traditional.*

Head to the Casa del Visitante, set within the grounds of the Familia Zuccardi winery, for a sophisticated country lunch. The fresh, flavourful food is typical Argentinian fare and includes meat or cheese empanadas baked in clay ovens, grilled meats and locally produced vegetables. There's even an olive-oil tasting on the menu. Large windows open on to the surrounding vineyards. Eating a perfectly cooked steak on a sunny afternoon, with a Vistalba malbec in hand, you get the sense that all is right with the world. For an extra treat, book one of Familia Zuccardi's hot-air balloon rides over the vineyards; note that you need to book this at least 48 hours ahead.

Francesco Barbera Ristorante

Mendoza *Chile 1268 (0261 425 3912/www. francescoristorante.com.ar). Open 7.30pm-1am daily. ££. Traditional.*

This elegant, Italian-style eaterie is located near the centre of Mendoza city. It serves good meat dishes, pastas, desserts – including a wonderfully rich tiramisu – and over 1,000 bottles of fine wines, the latter courtesy of a knowledgeable sommelier. The garden offers a romantic setting for dinner on a balmy evening, or a leisurely lunch session. Try the sole with orange sauce or the malbec-marinated lamb, then round off proceedings with limoncello cheesecake served with grapefruit ice-cream.

La Marchigiana

Mendoza *Patricias Mendocinas 1550 (0261 423 0751/www.marchigiana.com.ar). Open noon-3pm, 8pm-midnight daily. ££. Italian.*

Founded 50 years ago by 'Nonna' Fernanda and still owned by an Italian family, this classic restaurant has stayed true to the culinary ways of the old country. The menu features a wide range of tempting options, including suckling pig, lemon-roasted chicken, grilled trout in almond sauce and all manner of pastas and gnocchi. Tiramisu, lemon pie and chocolate bombón headline the extensive dessert menu. Service is polite and professional (the restaurant also serves as a waiters' school), and illustrious former customers include Brad Pitt.

Las Negras

Mendoza *Pasteur 177 (0261 424 0008). Open 8.30pm-1am Mon-Sat. ££. International.*

It's worth venturing into the unassuming Mendocino suburb of Godoy Cruz to dine at this sleek, modern restaurant. The menu features inventive, modestly-priced global combinations such as red tuna with sesame seeds or tandoori duck, while the comprehensive wine list is gleaned from Mendoza's best bodegas. Low tables and glimmering candles add to the cosmopolitan flavour of the whole experience.

La Sal

Mendoza *Belgrano 1069 (0261 420 4322/ www.lasalrestaurante.com). Open noon-3pm, 8.30pm-midnight Mon-Sat. ££. International.*

The seasonal dishes here flit between the experimental and the traditional, and are served with live music and a hip, arty atmosphere that's enjoyed by locals as much as tourists. La Sal offers a stylish take on the Argentinian staples of wine (among the restaurants in the area, it has one of the most extensive wine lists), meats and salads. It marries contemporary decor and traditional Mendocino charm with elegantly presented and well-flavoured food; the staff are welcoming, too.

Stay

Bohemia Hotel Boutique

Mendoza *Granaderos 954 (0261 423 0575/ www.bohemiahotelboutique.com). ££.*

This contemporary design hotel is a delightfully intimate affair, with eight charming rooms set over two floors. The decor is Italianate, with plenty of wrought iron and polished marble; outside is a relaxing garden with a swimming pool. Decorated in a muted palette with the odd flash of colour, the guest rooms are a vision of understated good taste, and have good-sized bathrooms. Staff are disarmingly friendly, and happy to offer advice on where to head for the best spa treatments, or to hook you up with a good tour guide. The hotel is located on a quiet street that's just a five-minute walk from the lively Calle Aristides, with its plethora of bars. The tranquil Parque San Martin is also nearby.

Azafrán.

Clockwise from top:
Cavas Wine Lodge (2);
Club Tapiz (3).

Casa Antucura

Valle de Uco *Vista Flores, Tunuyán (0261 524 8686/ 15 154 1432 mobile/www.casaantucura.com). ££££.*
Overlooking vineyards set against the dramatic backdrop of the Andes, the Casa Antucura is a modern take on the traditional country lodge. An eclectic collection of sculptures, murals and paintings lends it a distinctly arty feel, and there's a grand two-level library and lounge in which to relax. The spacious rooms have wooden floors and inspiring views of the mountains; each has a different decor and visual character, striking a balance between minimalist chic and homely comfort. The hotel also has a large outdoor swimming pool, a jacuzzi, a small cinema and, naturally, a wine cellar.

"Cavas Wine Lodge's private cabañas each have their own roof deck, plunge pool and alfresco shower."

Cavas Wine Lodge

Luján de Cuyo *Costaflores, Alto Agrelo M 5507 (0261 410 6927/www.cavaswinelodge.com). ££££.*
A 20-minute drive from central Mendoza brings you to this serene country house, with a spectacular view of the Andes. Cecilia Díaz Chuit, Cavas's owner, worked for high-end international hotel chains before launching her own elegant enterprise. Her husband, Martín Rigal, is the wine expert. There are 14 hectares of bonarda vines to set you dreaming, and an underground *cava* (cellar) stacked with dozens of notable Argentinian labels to top you up. If you can't get enough of the grape, try a *vino*-therapy bath or grape-seed exfoliation in the spa. (Guests receive a complimentary massage.) All in all, this is an indulgent base from which to explore the Mendoza region and all it has to offer in terms of winery tours, hiking, rafting and horse riding. The private cabañas each have their own roof deck, private plunge pool and alfresco shower. After dining on South American specialties in the restaurant, sit by the fire and savour a glass of wine while looking out over the vineyards and snow-capped mountains.

Club Tapiz

Luján de Cuyo *Russell 5517, Ruta 60, km 2.5 (0261 496 3433/www.tapiz.com). £££.*
This intimate seven-room period hotel, set among the grapevines in the heart of Luján de Cuyo, is an easy 20-minute drive from Mendoza city centre. Club Tapiz's premises date from 1890, and the charming fin de siècle details are matched with attractive minimalist updates, such as a contemporary water fountain, stylish decking and vast picture windows. The rooms, accessed from a central courtyard, are comfortable and well-equipped. The hotel combines relaxing surroundings with sumptuous dining

in its restaurant, and also has a luxurious spa. A delightful, lovingly-tended garden and a swimming pool add to the atmosphere of laid-back elegance. The website can be temperamental, but you can also make reservations through www.newage-hotels.com.

Estancia Ancón

Mendoza *RP 89 km 21 (02622 420 0037/ www.estanciancon.com). ££££.*
This sizeable estancia is owned by the Bombal family, pioneers of the Argentinian wine industry. The property comprises vineyards, a modern winery, and that other Argentinian classic, a cattle ranch. Overtones of the family's aristocratic lineage are evident in the library, music room and six stately guest rooms, while attentive staff ensure that everything runs like clockwork. In the grounds, you can explore the simple charms of the cherry orchards and vegetable gardens, which provide the home-grown ingredients for supper – served with a glass or two of the estancia's fine wine.

Finca Adalgisa

Luján de Cuyo *Pueyrredón 2222 (0261 496 0713/ www.fincaadalgisa.com.ar). £££.*
Secluded and peaceful, this elegant hotel is located 20 minutes from Mendoza's city centre and within walking distance of Chacras de Coria, a small, thriving community with a couple of restaurants. An early 20th-century manor house and vineyard estate in the heart of the premier wine-growing region of Argentina, this place was converted into the first boutique hotel, *finca* (country estate) and winery in the Mendoza region in 2001. It has 11 simply designed guest rooms; the suite, with a king-size bed, sitting room, fireplace and kitchenette, is a wonderfully relaxing retreat. Outside, there are verdant gardens and a pleasant swimming pool; the winery is a short walk away. Note that the hotel is closed during the winter season, between June and September.

Hotel Aconcagua

Mendoza *San Lorenzo 545 (0261 520 0500/www. hotelaconcagua.com). ££.*
Recently refurbished, this upmarket city-centre hotel was originally built for the World Cup's 1978 arrival in Mendoza. The Aconcagua, named after the region's spectacular mountain, has a huge lobby with floor-to-ceiling windows, opening on to a perfectly manicured lawn. Innovative in its time, the hotel employs indigenous-style decorative touches to pleasing effect. A beautiful garden, outdoor swimming pool, spa, sauna and relaxation room add to the appeal; check the website for last minute reductions to room rates.

Huentala Hotel Boutique

Mendoza *Primitivo de la Reta 1007 (0261 420 0766/ www.huentala.com). ££.*
Built in a colonial style in 1976, this property was remodelled as a boutique hotel in 2004. It's a comfortable, centrally located option with modern, well-appointed rooms, friendly staff and its own bistro and cocktail bar. Grape massages are available in the beauty salon, and

there's a wine cellar and bar in the basement, where carefully-controlled temperature and humidity levels enhance the tasting experience.

Mendoza Park Hyatt
Mendoza *Chile 1124 (0261 441 1234/ www.mendoza.park.hyatt.com). £££.*
Set in a prime position on the Plaza Independencia, the Park Hyatt is the most luxurious hotel in town, exuding the opulence and self-assurance of Argentina's early 20th-century golden age. The restored Spanish colonial façade and grand lobby hint at the elegance of the landscaped courtyard, which is lined with palm trees and fountains. Inside, the hotel is a gleaming expanse of soaring granite columns, marble floors and sleek contemporary furnishings. Housed in a modern extension, the 186 elegant rooms are a good size, with equally spacious – and spotlessly clean – marble-clad bathrooms. Facilities include a spa, a gym, an outdoor pool and several on-site eateries.

Termas Cacheuta
Luján de Cuyo *RP 82, km 39 (02624 490139/ www.termascacheuta.com). ££. No credit cards.*
Termas Cacheuta occupies the site of a once-luxurious thermal complex that was built during Argentina's early 20th-century heyday, then destroyed by a flood in the 1930s. The modern hotel is a simple wooden structure, with basic but comfortable rooms; far more of a draw are its open-air thermal pools, overlooking Rio Mendoza and the precordillera mountains. Surrounded by flowers and cacti, the stone-built pools vary in temperature and are wonderfully relaxing. Enjoy an underground sauna, then smear yourself in warm medicinal mud. Afterwards, dry off in the sunshine beside the fast-flowing river, and admire the views over the mountains beyond.

"The verandas at Valle de Uco Lodge look out on to fruit orchards and rose gardens, cooled by mountain streams."

Valle de Uco Lodge
Valle de Uco *Taberna, no number, Colonia Las Rosas, Tunuyán (0261 496 1888/www.postalesdelplata.com). £££.*
Expect charming simplicity rather than boutique design at this rural retreat, centrally located in Valle de Uco and a ten-minute drive west of the provincial town of Tunuyán. The spacious rooms have verandas that look out on to fruit orchards and rose gardens, cooled by streams of clear mountain water. The lodge has nine suites, and there's also a private farmhouse that sleeps four to six people.

Villaggio Hotel Boutique
Mendoza *25 de Mayo 1010 (0261 524 5200/ www.hotelvillaggio.com.ar). ££.*
The Italian-influenced Villaggio is a spacious, chic boutique hotel. Behind a restrained façade, its lounge areas and guest rooms are stripped down and effortlessly stylish. The 26 rooms feature elegant furniture and modern art, and are equipped with flatscreen TVs and free Wi-Fi. The spa and sauna on the roof are a delight after a day of trekking, and the city centre address means that there are great restaurants and bars just a short stroll away.

Factfile

When to go
Mendoza has dry summers with wetter winters. Average temperatures for January (summer) are 35°C during the day, and 23°C at night. Temperatures for July (winter) are 12°C by day, and 3°C at night.

Getting there & around
Mendoza's airport, El Plumerillo, has regular connections to Buenos Aires. Aerolíneas Argentinas (www.aerolineas.com.ar) and LAN (www.lan.com) offer daily flights. There are daily buses from Mendoza's bus station, Terminal del Sol (Avenida de Acceso Este and Costanera, Guaymallén), to major destinations, including Buenos Aires, Bariloche and Santiago de Chile.

There are numerous options for travelling around Mendoza. Public transport includes city buses and trolleybuses. Avis (0261 447 0150, www.avis.com) and Budget (0261 425 3114,

www.budget.com) offer car hire, and you can rent a bicycle from a local business in the wine region, such as Mr Hugo in Coquimbito (Urquiza 2288, 0261 497 4067), which is 40 minutes by bus from the town centre.

A taxi is another option. It's best to book ahead through Radiotaxi (0261 430 3300) instead of hailing one on the street.

Tourist information
Medoza Tourist Office Avenida San Martín 1143 (0261 420 2800). Open 8am-9pm Mon-Fri; 9am-9pm Sat, Sun.

Internet
Most hotels have internet access of some kind, and many of the mid-range and high-end lodgings provide Wi-Fi, with connections of varying speeds. Failing that, internet cafés are scattered all over town.

Top: Mendoza Park Hyatt (3). Bottom: Estancia Ancón (3).

Clockwise from top: Parque Nacional Lanín; Junín de los Andes (2); Lago Lácar, San Martín de los Andes.

San Martín de los Andes & Junín de los Andes

Argentina

From seven lakes to a volcanic summit, all in a day's drive.

Ask an Argentinian to lie back and think of Patagonia and the image they conjure up will almost certainly resemble San Martín de los Andes, Junín de los Andes and their hinterlands. Many dream of retiring here – and who can blame them? This is not the mythic, hard-scrabble south of wind-lathed steppe and savage tundra, but the beautiful south of cobalt lakes and whispering forests.

San Martín de los Andes and Junín de los Andes are small islands of urban life in a vast sea of unspoiled natural terrain, much of which is contained in Parque Nacional Lanín, Argentina's third-biggest national park. A sophisticated tourism infrastructure of luxury estancias and gourmet restaurants enables travellers to explore and experience the region in any number of ways. You can saddle up and ride the high country on a horse trek, muck out the stables at a working ranch, dine on locally bagged game in a romantic bistro, ski in winter, fish in summer; it's more a matter of taste than feasibility. You might want to start planning your retirement too...

Explore

SAN MARTÍN DE LOS ANDES

Whether the Ruta de los Siete Lagos (see p182) begins or ends for you here, **San Martín de los Andes** acts as the eastern boundary of Parque Nacional Lanín. This compact town lies in a valley on the eastern shore of Lago Lácar. All around the town are forested slopes from which you can peer down into the profound blue of the water. Even with its high level of tourist infrastructure, the town seems to back away from, or at least fade into, its surroundings – in contrast to Bariloche (see pp179-180), the main tourist hub in the lake region, which can seem to hover just a little aggressively over its lake shore.

The town has two main streets, Avenida San Martín and General Villegas, which run in parallel away from the lake. On these busy thoroughfares you'll find restaurants, cafés, shops and tourist services, plus a few historic sites and museums.

The town's history can be divided into two distinct phases. From 1898, when it was founded, until 1937, San Martín was an obscure military outpost surrounded by farmsteads and sawmills. The second phase started in 1937, when Parque Nacional Lanín was established, setting San Martín on an upward climb to become a popular tourist resort. However, for the native Mapuche – who treasured this area long before the holiday crowd did – the last century has been a story of tragedy and capitulation, not monetary profit and land development.

Those interested in pre-Columbian history should visit the Museo Primeros Pobladores, on Plaza San Martín (Juan Manuel de Rosas 700, 02972 428676). There's also an enjoyable hour-long hike that enters woodlands above Lago Lácar and takes you to a Mapuche village with a great vantage point over the lake. Start downtown at the tourist information office (Avenida San Martín 750). The trail begins a few minutes' walk from here; the staff can point you in the right direction. The path diverges in dozens of directions, but as long as you are going up, you will eventually reach the main indigenous village, where there is a gate and an entrance booth. A small fee is required to enter.

Another good trek is the route to Mirador Arrayán, which also starts within walking distance of downtown. From the town centre, head to the waterfront, turn left and continue until you see the left-hand turning for RP 19. The viewpoint is an hour-long walk each way, or a short drive, on this half-paved, half-dirt road.

Within ten to 15 minutes of leaving town, you start to see views of Lago Lácar – and they get better as the ascent continues. As a bonus, there's a tea-house at its finish (it's generally open from 4pm to 8pm, but hours vary; check at the tourist information office before setting out).

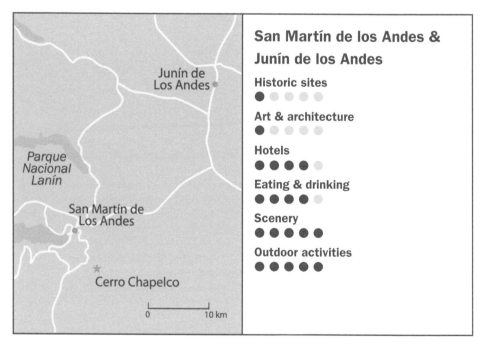

San Martín de los Andes & Junín de los Andes

Historic sites
● ○ ○ ○ ○

Art & architecture
● ○ ○ ○ ○

Hotels
● ● ● ● ○

Eating & drinking
● ● ● ● ○

Scenery
● ● ● ● ●

Outdoor activities
● ● ● ● ●

Clockwise from bottom left: Junín de los Andes (3); Parque Nacional Lanín (2).

The real outdoor action, however, begins a little further afield. San Martín is close to several popular lake beaches, namely playas Catritre, Quila Quina and Yuco (all on Lago Lácar) and Playa Bonita (on Lago Lolog), which can be reached by boat (leaving from the downtown port) or car. This is where forested peninsula meets sandy lake shore. There are also many trekking, rafting and biking options. (Cycling the entire Ruta de los Siete Lagos is an unforgettable experience, but only for those who are prepared to rough it in a tent at night.) The best rafting, which will take you to Chile, is done on Río Hua Hum, 48 kilometres out of town on RP 48.

A great day trip to make from San Martín (though it can also be made just as easily from Junín de los Andes) is to start out on RP 62 to Lago Lolog, on a circuit that will take you into Parque Nacional Lanín. Once you reach the intersection with RP 52, turn left and continue on the lake circuit past Lago Curruhué Chico, Lago Curruhué Grande and Lago Epulafquen. The most recent sign of volcanic activity in the area, a 7.5-kilometre solidified-lava river, the Escorial, appears after the two Curruhué lakes. The lava was laid 400 years ago, and trees have already conquered it, growing right through the rock.

A short drive further along the lake circuit will bring you to a thermal spa, Lahuen Co Spa Termal de Montaña (02972 424709, www.lahuen co.com). These baths can also be accessed by driving from Junín de los Andes to Puerto Canoa, a tiny town inside the national park on RP 61. Boat tours, including a stop for a natural bath, leave from Puerto Canoa. There is a year-round eco-resort at the thermal baths, managed in conjunction with the national park service, which offers yoga classes, massages and mud baths as well as a restaurant. The main spring, which feeds the pools, has a constant temperature of 17°C. Children under 15 are not permitted to bathe in the spring.

Only 18 kilometres from San Martín lies the ski resort of Cerro Chapelco (open from July to September). It has more than 20 runs, and is popular with snowboarders and off-piste skiers. There are also a number of cross-country ski trails. (See p183 **Off the beaten slopes**.)

JUNÍN DE LOS ANDES

A visitor to **Junín de los Andes** can exhaust the on-foot touring options in town in around 15 minutes. It's fortunate, then, that the third-largest national park in Argentina is on the doorstep. Another former military outpost, Junín is now the best jumping-off point for the vast wilderness of **Parque Nacional Lanín**.

A little time spent in Junín de los Andes before setting off for the true wilderness will reward the patient traveller. It's an easy-going, sprawling town (population 10,000) that sits in the furrow of a green valley. Town life revolves around the central square, Plaza General San Martín, on which flourishes a tiny copse. Built on the banks of the Río Chimehuín, the town is known as Argentina's 'trout capital', and if you have some time to spare, head for the riverside, which locals turn into a festive watering hole in summer.

The closest spots to Volcán Lanín, the volcano after which the national park is named, are accessed by a two- to three-hour drive on RP 61, which starts paved but then becomes a dirt road. You can climb the 3,776-metre summit of Volcán Lanín from December to April. According to local mythology, the only way to the summit was on condor wings, and then only for the daughters of chieftains. These days, in the absence of a condor, you can climb to the top with the aid of a good guide and good equipment.

Even if you don't aspire to the summit, you can still traipse much of the 4,210 square kilometres of the national park, which encompasses 35 lakes, dozens of native communities, waterfalls and several species of rare tree, including the monkey-puzzle (*araucaria*).

"Ring the bell hanging from a post by the church and a Mapuche family will send someone to row you across the narrow stretch of lake."

The best trailhead is in Puerto Canoa, across from the ranger station. A four- to six-hour round-trip hike will take you to the end of the trees and the beginning of the ice, to stare straight up at the south face of Lanín's cone. The other day-hike begins at the white church in Puerto Canoa. Ring the bell hanging from a post near the church and a Mapuche family living on on the other side of this narrow stretch of lake will send someone to row you across the water. From behind their property, a four-hour round-trip trail leads into one of the few remaining homesteads in the area, perched on a hillside and with a perfect view of the volcano back across the lake. Also accessed from Puerto Canoa is the 90-minute round-trip trail to the waterfall, Cascada el Saltillo.

The north face of Volcán Lanín, on Lago Tromen and accessed by driving RP 60, is where many hikers heading for the summit start out. There is also a 90-minute river walk in a forest of monkey-puzzle trees. From there, you can walk another 45 minutes to the base of the north-face ascent of the volcano.

Coach class with a difference

Bus travel in Argentina is a world away from the trials of travelling by Eurolines, National Express or Greyhound. Forget the knees-against-your-chest syndrome in a seat that appears designed to cause backaches and shin cramps; this is a country where they have fully honed the long-distance bus experience. Well, they've had to, really, in a country so vast that overnight journeys (or longer) are normal.

Tickets are sold in four classes. *Común* offers the cheapest seats, which are not unlike every bus seat you've ever seen before, although sometimes offering optional air-conditioning. The ones to look out for are *semi-cama* (literally, semi bed), *cama-ejecutivo* and *cama-suite*, which resemble what you would find in business class on an aeroplane.

The difference between *semi-cama* and *cama-ejecutivo* is the size of the seats and how far they recline. Meanwhile, the *cama-suite* seats recline almost horizontally (around 85 per cent), promising the possibility of a good night's sleep, even for the fussy. All of the higher-class seats tend to be broad and comfortable, with arm, neck and foot rests, and often come with a fleece blanket for night-time (and be warned, the air-conditioning is often on full-blast at night, so wrap up). To top it off, there are films

to watch, plus a steward who wobbles down the aisle to serve snacks, hot meals and wine.

Unfortunately, the airline business-class comparisons only apply to the angle of the seat recline. With a few exceptions, the food is more akin to that found in economy class in the 1980s. Vegetarians should travel prepared, as there are no alternative options and limited service-station stops.

When reserving a ticket, always be sure to consider the following: is the service direct? (otherwise, it can be many hours longer, with harshly illuminated interruptions to your slumber); are meals served, not just snacks?; which class do I want? (for journeys over six hours, *semi-cama* is highly recommended – and if if you can, splurge on *cama-suite* for overnight journeys). If possible, avoid travelling on *feriados* (national holidays).

Bus companies tend to specialise in a few routes, and the quality of service they offer varies. However, travelling by bus in Argentina is an experience in its own right, providing an opportunity to get an idea of the scale of this vast country and to take in the scenery you'd miss out on from the air.

For more information on bus travel, *see p382* **Need to know**.

Top: Río Hermoso Hotel de Montaña (2). Right: steak at Ruca Hueney. Middle: Paihuen (2). Bottom: La Araucana Lodge.

OUTDOOR ACTIVITIES

This region keeps adding extreme race events to its calendar, such as the planned 2010 TransAndes Challenge, a punishing cycling and running event in which competitors will cross the Andes from Argentina into Chile and back again. Those not tempted by the prospect of trying to get a bicycle over a ravine will still find plenty to do. You can take your pick from fishing, rafting, horse riding, trekking, mountain and volcano climbing, skiing, hunting, birdwatching, biking, rock climbing and kayaking. Most of the higher-end hotels and all of the estancias organise their own activities or coordinate tours with local adventure companies. An adventure operator for all seasons, covering all of the Ruta de los Siete Lagos area, is Bariloche-based Meridies (02944 462675, www.meridies.com.ar).

You can get your adrenaline fix here in spring and summer (October to March) by flinging your body through the air on zip lines. Fine weather in San Martín also means the avid golfer can play Chapelco Golf & Resort's 18-hole course, designed by Jack Nicklaus and his son. Its lush fairways and greens look incongruous amid the multi-hued earth tones of the high Andes, but those who play the course rate it highly. Two accommodations serve the resort: Loi Suites (02972 410304, www.loisuites.com.ar) and the smaller El Casco Viejo (02972 427713, www.chapelcogolf.com).

Eat

Dining in the two 'los Andes' could not be more different. In Junín, options are limited and straightforward: Argentinian grills, pasta and seafood. The best food is served in the rural estancias or lodges outside town, where you can enjoy riverside barbecues and open fire-pit *asados*. San Martín, on the other hand, packs the gastronomic excitement of Bariloche into a restaurant scene a fraction of the size.

Caleuche

San Martín de los Andes *Ruta 234, km 78 (02972 428154/www.paihuen.com.ar). Open 1-3.30pm Mon; 1-3.30pm, 8.30-11.30pm Tue-Sun. ££££. Modern.*
This restaurant, located at the highest point of the Paihuen hilltop resort (*see p224*), is also one of the high points of San Martín gastronomy. Located 4km from town, this is a top-class establishment, thanks to the talents of chef Pablo Buzzo. His food looks as good as it tastes, with portions outlined in fine lines of sauce that resemble calligraphy, meats stacked high like edible architecture and soups served in carved-out gourds. You'll have your work cut out choosing the wine: the cellar stocks 3,000 varietals, 250 from Argentina alone.

Ku de los Andes

San Martín de los Andes *Avenida San Martín 1053 (02972 427039/www.kudelosandes.com.ar). Open noon-3pm, 8pm-midnight daily. £££. International/Modern.*
The homely dark-wood ambience of Ku is at odds with the way-beyond-rustic aspirations of its kitchen. All around the Siete Lagos, you will have ample opportunities to sample local deer, wild boar, trout and just about everything else that once ran, flew or swam in Patagonia. In Ku, you can try it all prepared with a flair that far surpasses the regional standard. The deer served with Patagonian fruits, and the trout ceviche, are standout dishes. The long dining room, with table nooks set into the sides of the log frame, is an attractive visual complement to the unusual combination of regional flavours arriving at the table. There's also a Ku parrilla branch at RP 234 and Callejón de Bello (02972 425953).

> ## "At La Reserva, lamb is skewered Middle-Eastern style, and a full tapas menu gives the Spanish treatment to wild boar."

La Reserva

San Martín de los Andes *Belgrano 940 (02972 428734/www.lareservarestaurant.com.ar). Open 12.30-3pm, 7.30pm-midnight Mon-Sat; 7.30pm-midnight Sun. £££. International.*
Any reservations about dressing up the region's best meat in international styles will be put to rest by this menu. The ubiquitous regional trout swims inside layers of Italian ravioli; lamb arrives at the table skewered Middle-Eastern style; and a full tapas menu gives the Spanish treatment to wild boar, among other local delicacies. A selection of artisanal beers offers a welcome reprieve for ale drinkers marooned in the land of malbec. Many of the dishes and home-made breads at La Reserva are prepared using a special stone oven.

Ruca Hueney

Junín de Los Andes *Padre Milanesio & Coronel Suárez (02972 491113/www.ruca-hueney.com.ar). Open noon-3pm, 8pm-1am daily. £££. Parrilla/Traditional.*
Chequered tablecloths, a spacious dining room, a laid-back atmosphere, chunks of red meat cooking fiercely over a hot grill: Ruca Hueney's philosophy seems to be, 'If it ain't broke…' Large portions of fresh meat and fish are accompanied by basic side dishes and moderately priced wines at this Junín institution. This is the place to head if you want to dine around the town's main square. Ask if deer is in season, as it is often as good as the famed Argentinian steak in this region.

Stay

Most of Junín's best lodgings are a short drive from town or the Chapelco airport. Most in-town options are modest, though pleasantly situated close to the river. San Martín de los Andes provides plenty of places to bed down in luxury, on the ski slopes, in the quaint downtown area or, further afield, under the forests' pine trees.

La Araucana Lodge

San Martín de los Andes *RN 234, km 66 (011 4719 7113/www.laaraucanalodge.com). Open Nov-May. ££. No credit cards.*

Located just a few miles from San Martin, this is one of the most intimate options for the summer season. It only has five rooms, accommodating ten people at most, so service is attentive and personalised. The location, up in the mountains on ten hectares of private land, contributes to an overall atmosphere that is more private mansion than hotel. This is pure adult pampering: children under 15 are not permitted. Rates are highest in January and February.

"Play cattle rancher for a day at Estancia Huechahue, then unwind in the hot tub while ruminating on the possibility that full-time ranching is not for you."

Estancia Huechahue

30km E of Junín de Los Andes *Parallel 40 & Río Collun Cura (no phone/www.huechahue.com). Open Nov-April. ££££. No credit cards.*

A working cattle ranch run by a British expat, this estancia is famous for its horseback excursions, which range from short trots to 11-day expeditions over the Andes and into Chile. The horse caravans, led by owner Jane, have become a top draw among the many competing get-away-from-it-all options in this region. There is plenty to keep anyone not interested in the gaucho existence busy here too. Situated on Río Aluminé, the ranch is a great place for trout fishing, rafting, barbecues on the river, or hiking to indigenous burial caves and a spot where condors with a wing-span of almost four metres land for the evening. You can even play cattle rancher for a day, and later unwind in the sauna and hot tub while ruminating on the possibility that full-time cattle ranching is not for you. There are three guest lodges with a total of eight double rooms, all with private bath and communal sitting rooms; but the focus here is on the wilderness without, not the mod cons within.

Hostería Chimehuín

Junín de Los Andes *Coronel Suárez & 25 de Mayo (02972 491132/www.interpatagonia.com/hosteria chimehuin). ££.*

This *hostería* is neither modern nor flashy, but its setting – a few blocks from the main square, and right along the banks of the river – makes it a good option for an overnight stay in town. The sprawling grounds are lovely, and the common areas of the main house are straight out of *Snow White and the Seven Dwarfs*: you can imagine a butterfly or jay landing on your shoulder at any moment. This place smells as good as it looks, with pies baking or jams stewing in the kitchen all day – home-made treats which can be sampled at breakfast. The simple rooms in the main house are a little faded; much better to go for one of the cottage-like suites situated in the grounds.

Hostería La Cheminée

San Martín de Los Andes *General Roca & Mariano Moreno (02972 427617/www.hosterialacheminee. com.ar). £££.*

This mid-sized, centrally located Alpine-style property, at its prettiest in winter when its many gables are caked in thick snow, is one of the best lodgings in downtown San Martin. Spacious rooms with wood beams and open fireplaces may be de rigueur for this region, but large indoor heated pools, jacuzzis and saunas, all of which you'll find at La Cheminée, are not.

Paihuen

San Martín de los Andes *RN 234, km 78 (02972 428154/www.paihuen.com.ar). Open July-April. £££.*

Birdsong rather than an alarm call rouses guests at this luxury woodland cabin complex. The property consists of 33 individual cabins of various sizes, the largest of which can accommodate ten at a squeeze (three couples plus kids). The shared amenities include a spa, sauna, outdoor swimming pool and a small art gallery. The on-site restaurant, Caleuche (*see p223*), is one of the best in the region. Ideal for families.

Río Dorado Lodge

Junín de Los Andes *Pedro Illera 448 (02972 491548/www.riodorado.com.ar). £££.*

Reeling in the trout-fishing fraternity, this lodge is also the most comfortable choice close to Junin (about 4km from downtown) without being right in the centre of town. If your stay in the area is not predicated on wilderness-bound wanderlust, this is the best option. The main lodge has a charming dining room, complete with afternoon tea service. While the lodge may not be designer luxury, the spacious rooms with barn-like, log-beam ceilings are as fully outfitted as the renowned on-site fly-fishing shop, with minibar, internet, individually controlled heating and air-conditioning, phone and cable TV.

Río Hermoso Hotel de Montaña

San Martín de los Andes *RP 63, km 67 (02972 410485/www.riohermoso.com). ££££.*

As gorgeous as its name (meaning 'beautiful river') suggests, Río Hermoso is picturesquely set on the shore of

Lago Meliquina. Instead of the retro-wilderness look so common in this region, this hotel's design would do nicely for any sleek urban hotel, with the bonus of views out on to peaks, pines and the lake. The hotel organises ski trips to Chapelco in the winter, while summer activities include fly-fishing, golf, trekking and birdwatching. Its restaurant, in keeping with the interior design, combines contemporary flair with traditional local ingredients.

"San Huberto offers the opportunity to lodge smack dab in the middle of landscapes one would think inhospitable to the well-heeled traveller."

San Huberto Lodge
30km NE of Junín de Los Andes *Ruta Internacional a Chile (02972 421875/www.sanhubertolodge.com.ar). £££. No credit cards.*
The Junín area offers opportunities to lodge smack dab in the middle of landscapes one would think inhospitable to the well-heeled traveller. With Volcán Lanín as its backdrop,

this family-run lodge on private land remains very popular with fishers and hunters, but it's a great place for any travellers who simply want to suck in some fresh air and unwind. This is also a prime spot for birdwatching and horse riding excursions into the national park. Massages, meals prepared with ingredients from the family's own farm and garden, and a wood-panelled jacuzzi are all part of the San Huberto experience. Be warned that the lodge only has room for 16 guests, and is often dominated by fishing groups.

Tipiliuke
22km S of Junín de los Andes *Valle de Río Chimehuín (02972 429466/www.tipiliuke.com). Open Oct-May (July-Sept for private groups). ££££.*
Tipiliuke is a lucky find for those in search of rural luxury, and the fact that it's the only lodge in the area with an 'art consultant' should alert you both to its pretensions and its attention to detail. A maximum of 18 guests at any one time can stay on this 20,000-hectare private estancia, managed by the grandchildren of its 1909 founder. The main lodge has nine elegant bedrooms of classic design, and three common rooms: a fireside lounge, a dining room and a diminutive but inviting bar, all decorated with carefully selected works of native art. A separate five-bedroom house with its own swimming pool can be rented out to families or groups. The lodge owners run the usual panoply of outdoor pursuits, from horseback riding and skiing to trekking, birdwatching and rafting, but this estancia's charms may make you reluctant to wander too far from the comforts of its interior.

Factfile

When to go
The trout-fishing season typically lasts from November until April. The December to February late spring and summer months are great for national park wanderers, but bugs can be a pest, so bring long-sleeved tops, trousers and insect repellent. The peak ski months are typically July and August, but the ski season can start as early as June and last until October, depending on snow conditions.

Getting there
Buses run from Buenos Aires direct to Junín and San Martín de los Andes, but these are long overnight trips, and most travellers prefer to fly from BA's domestic airport, Jorge Newbery, to either Bariloche's Aeropuerto Internacional San Carlos de Bariloche Teniente Luis Candelaria or Chapelco airport (Aeropuerto Aviador Carlos Campos), 20 kilometres from San Martín. Both Aerolíneas Argentinas and LAN offer flights throughout the year. From Bariloche, San Martín is a three-and-a-half-hour bus ride, while Junín is three hours. Both journeys take around one hour less if starting from Villa La Angostura.

Getting around
Most travel through the Junín/San Martín area can be combined with a trip to Bariloche and Villa La Angostura. Junín is only 40 kilometres north of San Martín. There's a bus service between the towns, but renting a car at Bariloche or Chapelco airport, or in any of the towns, is the best option for convenient travel in between towns and national parks.

Tourist information
San Martín Tourist Office Avenida San Martín 750 (02972 427347, www.sanmartindelos andes.gov.ar/turismo). Open 8am-8.30pm daily. **Junín de los Andes Tourist Office** corner of Padre Milanesio & Coronel Suárez (02972 491160, www.junindelosandes.com). Open 8am-9pm daily.

Internet
Junín has one internet café, two doors down from the tourist information office, alongside the main plaza. San Martín has around a dozen internet spots, with at least five located within the 700 to 900 blocks of Avenida San Martín.

Coast

Clockwise from above left: Cabo Polonio (3); Punta del Diablo (2).

Cabo Polonio & Punta del Diablo

Uruguay

Rustic fishing villages with golden sands and crashing surf.

Straddling a rocky peninsula, with dramatic views across the roiling Atlantic, Cabo Polonio is wild, windy and pleasingly under-developed. On either side of the iconic lighthouse, two beaches stretch out for miles and a hundred or so jerry-built houses sit in the crevasses of the surrounding dunes.

In the 1960s, bohemians and hippies, disenchanted with the restrictions of Uruguayan law, crossed the dunes and discovered this lost paradise. Today, most visitors are backpackers, holidaying Uruguayans and carefree Europeans looking to rekindle a spirit that disappeared from the Mediterranean many years ago. By the end of the summer, however, the population whittles down to a clutch of hardened fishermen. Officially, there are just 68 residents and 72 dogs.

Further north, less than an hour's drive from the Brazilian border, Punta del Diablo is a small clutch of brightly painted buildings, with vast golden beaches surrounding the eponymous peninsula. Nearby, colourful fishing boats line the shore. However, it's the waves that attract most visitors – Punta del Diablo has some of the longest beaches and best breaks in Uruguay.

Unlike its more popular neighbours, Punta del Diablo's shores aren't dotted with tourist traps and high-rise buildings. You also won't find a bank or a garage – or, in Cabo Polonio's case, electricity or running water – so arrive prepared.

Explore

CABO POLONIO

There are no main roads into **Cabo Polonio**. Instead, visitors have to board colourfully painted 4x4 trucks from the nearest main road and head across the dunes to the entrance of the village (UR$117). The centre of Cabo Polonia consists of one sandy road running parallel with the coastline. The *calle principal* (main road) is lined with restaurants, shops and posadas, as well as scores of hippies plying their trades. At the tip of the headland, a stunning lighthouse stands tall above the rocks. For a couple of pesos, you can ascend its 132 steps. From the crowning balcony, breathtaking views unfold: to the north, Playa de La Calavera and, in the distance, the seaside village of Valizas; to the south, the sweeping bay of Playa Sur; below, hundreds of sea lions groaning and slipping over the rocks. At the bottom of the lighthouse, you'll find the village's only public toilet with running water.

Playa de la Calavera (*calavera* is Spanish for skull) has the strongest winds and, as a result, attracts windsurfers and kite surfers. It was along this beach that French buccaneer Etienne Moreau used to load cattle on to his ships – cows that had been stolen by the indigenous communities from the invading Spanish and Portuguese.

It's a beach of extreme beauty, crashing waves and vicious undercurrents. You can walk along its five-kilometre sands to the first rocky outcrop and turn back, or continue around the corner and walk to the village of Valizas. For a change of scenery, walk back via the sandy dunes and, if you still have enough energy, climb up the highest dune, Cerro Buena Vista, for panoramic views out across the Atlantic.

Behind the dunes is the Bosque Nativo, a dense forest of ombu trees that's great for exploring or for simply flopping down in the shade with a few friends and a picnic. You can reach the forest by walking the several kilometres from Cabo Polonio, or rent a horse from local residents El Chula or Popeye for a mere UR$350 an hour. (Just ask around for these two well-known local characters.)

On the other side of the village, Playa Sur, with its seemingly never-ending band of white sands, has long been a draw for sun-worshippers and families. Running along the coastline and around the tip of the peninsula are the resort's most sophisticated *ranchos* (*see p237*). Protected from the wind, Playa Sur is an excellent spot for bathing and beach games. A dip in the sea with *toninas* (Commerson's dolphins) is one of the moments that makes a stay here very special.

Located just a hundred metres out to sea is La Isla de Lobos. For UR$350 per person, small boats zip out from Playa de la Calavera to visit a massive colony of sea lions and elephant seals.

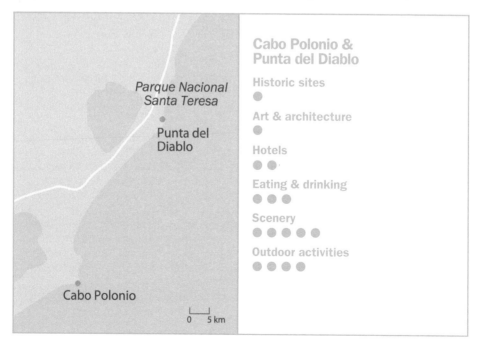

Cabo Polonio & Punta del Diablo

Historic sites
●

Art & architecture
●

Hotels
● ●

Eating & drinking
● ● ●

Scenery
● ● ● ● ●

Outdoor activities
● ● ● ●

Cabo Polonio.

Dolphins, and sometimes sperm whales, can be sighted off the coast during the months of October and November.

PUNTA DEL DIABLO

There's one main street running through the tiny village of **Punta del Diablo** (Devil's Point). This sandy lane, General San Martín, wends its way down to the shore, flanked by unpretentious restaurants, ice-cream vendors and the occasional mini supermarket.

> "There are only 650 permanent residents in Punta del Diablo, mainly fishermen, artists and the odd tradesman."

There are two main beaches: Playa del Rivero, to the north, and Playa de la Viuda (Widow's Beach), situated on the southern, windier side of the village. Playa del Rivero is more sheltered, and popular with sunbathers. In the summer, makeshift bars – serving beer and cocktails and blaring out Latino tunes – materialise from out of the dunes on both sides of the point. Sitting snug between these two beaches is a small bay known as Playa de los Pescadores (Fishermen's Beach), which, as the name suggests, is where you will find wooden fishing boats lined up along the shore. Fishermen founded Punta del Diablo in the 1930s, and today they still ply their trade off the coast using traditional methods of weighted nets and rods. In the afternoon, the smell of fresh fish wafts from the cabins overlooking the bay.

There are only around 650 permanent residents in Punta del Diablo, mainly fishermen, artists and the odd tradesman. However, this number can swell dramatically during the summer, when a bohemian crowd of sun-and-surf-seeking tourists fills the brightly coloured homes and *cabañas*.

There's a small yet vibrant nightlife in the summer months, but typically for this part of the world, partying starts late and finishes well after dawn. The place to be after midnight is the nightclub in the forest, Bitacora. Take street Number 7 and head for the hills. During the day, the club looks like a large barn and corral, but in the wee hours, it's got a happening vibe. There has been talk of a new location, so ask around before venturing out. There's also El Pico, a disco with live reggae and rock music near Playa de la Viuda.

There's not much in the way of shopping in the village, though on the street heading out towards the point overlooking Playa de los Pescadores, a handful of market stalls sell local handicrafts and souvenirs. Very few restaurants and only some of the hotels accept credit cards. There is a currency exchange on the main street, but there is no garage or bank, so fill up your tank and your wallet before you arrive. The nearest ATM is an hour away in Chuy, and it can be temperamental at times.

An easy two-kilometre hike north of Punta del Diablo are the dunes of **Parque Nacional Santa Teresa**. This beachfront reserve spreads over 1,050 hectares and has around 60 kilometres of hiking trails. Santa Teresa is home not only to Uruguayan flora, but also plants from around the world. For the visiting flower enthusiast, there's a garden with over 330 different species of rose. The park is also well known for its diverse fauna, including toucans and monkeys.

Most Uruguayans and Brazilians visit Santa Teresa for the uncrowded beaches and basic forest camping. There are campsites sprinkled throughout the park, but only a few have power supplies. There are also various grades of cabin available for rent, some just 50 metres from the beach; prices range from UR$350 to UR$2,800 per night, depending on the season. Campers will find all the services they need, from a bakery and restaurant to a doctor. You can reserve a campsite or cabin, and find maps and trail information, at www.parquesantateresa.com.uy or by calling 0477 2101.

The hilltop Fortaleza de Santa Teresa is the centrepiece of Parque Nacional Santa Teresa. The fort was initially built by the Portuguese in 1762 but was captured and finished by the Spaniards several years later. This was just the start of a succession of conquests; it was not until 1825 that the newly formed nation of Uruguay finally captured and held the fort. It has played a vital role in many civil wars and is considered Uruguay's most enduring vestige of the past. Inside the thick stone walls there is a chapel and a museum with a collection of weapons, as well as an area recreating the soldiers' kitchen area, complete with menus.

The enormous Laguna Negra, a birdwatcher's paradise and home to over 120 avian species, is also in the park. Marshlands, palm groves and native woods surround the lake, unofficially known as 'the lagoon of death' for its proximity to 3,000-year-old burial grounds. From Laguna Negra, you can take a boat to the biological station of Potrerillo, a protected area where it is possible to observe nature in its most virgin state. To arrange a tour, call 0470 6028.

OUTDOOR ACTIVITIES

Surfing is one of the big draws in these parts. There is relatively consistent surf year-round, but the best periods are September to November

Clockwise from top: Valizas;
Cabo Polonio; Isla de Lobos.

Punta del Diablo.

and March to May. Surfers from around the region come here for the exposed beach breaks and two-metre swells. If you are not a strong swimmer, you should be careful of rip currents, which make surfing here moderately dangerous. The beach north of Cabo Polonio has particularly strong tides, but there are lifeguards on both the village's beaches.

In Cabo Polonio, boards and a wetsuit can be hired out, and resident boarder Marito will happily teach you all the moves. (Find him in front of El Parador, on the south beach.)

In Punta del Diablo, there is a small surf shop on General San Martín where you can hire boards by the day or by the hour. The shops also sells wetsuits and surf accessories such as wax and leg ropes. La Surfera is a surf school at the end of street Number 7, overlooking the southern end of Playa del Rivero (099 111 931 mobile). It caters to beginners of all ages, and you can opt for group or individual lessons. The school is open between November and March.

If you're feeling adventurous in Punto del Diablo, you can also try sandboarding on the mammoth dunes at Playa de la Viuda or Playa del Rivero. Dune boards can be rented out from the surf shops. In summer, explore the beaches and forest on horseback. Horses are available with or without a guide, by the hour. There is a small shop on General San Martín – Caballos – where you can enquire about horse riding tours in the medium and high seasons.

Eat

Not surprisingly, simple seafood fare is what these coastal resorts do best. Try the omnipresent *rabas* (fried squid), *milanesas de cazón* (breaded baby-shark steaks), mussels and the surprisingly tasty *buñuelos de algae* (battered seaweed balls). In Punta del Diablo, the local fishermen sell their catch in the afternoons along the shore near the main beach, so you can rest assured your purchase will be fresh.

New restaurants and bars swell in numbers in high season (December to February). While a fair few last only for one season, the places listed below were all thriving at the time of going to press – though there is every chance they could change ownership and therefore name. Opening hours are also not set in stone.

During the high season, restaurants often mutate into bars once the final plates have been cleared from the tables. During the low season (April to November) in Cabo Polonio, only Sargento García and Lo de Joselo are open, and then just at weekends. Note that most restaurants only accept cash; ATMs and credit cards belong to another world.

El Diablo Tranquilo

Punta del Diablo *La Corvina, no number (0477 2647/www.eldiablotranquilo.com). Open Restaurant 9am-1.30am daily. Bar 24hrs daily. ££. International/ Modern.*

Although it's situated off the main strip, El Diablo Tranquilo, which is open year-round, has wonderful views, especially from the third floor; if you want to dine alfresco, you can be served on the beach. After dark, the place turns into a happening late-night bar frequented by young hipsters and backpackers. The owners also have a hostel of the same name, located on the other side of the road, a little further from the beach.

La Estación

Cabo Polonio *calle principal (no phone). Open 7pm-6am daily. ££. No credit cards. Bar.*

Rough, ready and perennially busy, this spit-and-sawdust bar attracts everyone from backpackers and surfers to the odd local fisherman. At the back of the bar, there's a beaten-up pool table, while up front a projector screens everything from Hollywood classics to radical surfing competitions. Surprisingly tasty burgers are cooked on the patio.

La Golosa

Cabo Polonio *calle principal (no phone). Open noon-4am daily. £££. International.*

This candlelit, gay-friendly restaurant, where shoes are forbidden and dishes are served in old crockery, is perfect for a romantic night out. The food is mainly international, with an occasional nod to the Middle East. We recommend the houmous and the home-made ravioli, baked in the oven, as well as the excellent *moqueca de pescado* (creamy fish stew). A private salon allows privacy for groups, while on a calm night you can eat outside at one of the terrace tables.

Kiosco Alba

Punta del Diablo *Playa de los Pescadores (no phone). Open Summer 11am-9pm daily. Winter lunch only Sat, Sun. £. No credit cards. Traditional.*

The best empanadas in town can be found at this hole-in-the-wall shack just off Playa de los Pescadores. There are actually three empanada shacks, run by three sisters, within close proximity of each other. Our favourite is the one closest to the point, furthest away from the main street. Pull up a plastic chair and enjoy the specialities – empanadas with fish and cheese, or mussels. Whatever you choose, it will be best chased with an ice-cold Patricia beer. The stall is open daily in summer, but hours can be sporadic off-season.

Lo de Joselo

Cabo Polonio *calle principal (no phone). Open noon-6am daily. ££. No credit cards. Traditional.*

Featured in Anthony Bourdain's food-focused travel show, *No Reservations*, this intimate restaurant has tables set out under climbing vines in a courtyard filled with candles. Lo de Joselo's remarkable blind owner lives and sleeps in this bar, supplying punters with everything from shots of Licor de Butia (made from the extracts of a palm tree) to vegetarian sandwiches, while his pet penguin waddles around entertaining the customers.

Top: El Diablo Tranquilo. Middle: Nativos Posada & Hostel (2). Bottom: Cabo Polonio.

HELADERIA ARTESANAL

Nativos

Punta del Diablo *Avenida Santa Teresa, no number (0477 2524/www.nativos.com.uy). Open mid Dec-Mar noon-5pm, 7pm-2am daily. ££. Traditional.*

Nativos is possibly the best restaurant in Punta del Diablo. It has connections to La Corte, a renowned restaurant in Montevideo with an emphasis on simple yet sophisticated cooking. The focus of the menu is on excellent seasonal produce such as lamb, wild boar and rhea. You'll find a hearty seafood pasta and a very reasonably priced fish of the day. The squid is outstanding. Amazingly, meals are only a fraction more expensive than dishes at many of the pizza places on the main strip. There's also a boutique hotel attached (*see right*), which is surrounded by trees and set near a stream.

El Parador

Cabo Polonio *Playa Sur (no phone). Open from noon daily. ££. No credit cards. Traditional.*

As the sun sets, anyone vaguely in the know heads to El Parador (or La Puesta, as it is commonly known), a wooden, multi-deck bar and restaurant where you can sip on caipirinhas, capirioskas and ice-cold beers. The good-looking staff serve up a range of fresh salads, along with battered squid and sandwiches. The *licuados* (smoothies), made with fresh fruit, are highly recommended. A local favourite, located 100m from the beach entrance, this place manages to be classy, cool and laid-back.

Sargento Garcia

Cabo Polonio *Playa de la Calavera (099 616 486 mobile). Open 9am-6am daily. ££. No credit cards. Traditional.*

Named after the podgy Mexican boozer in the TV series *Zorro*, this is a beachside classic. Punters drift in throughout the day: first, for the all-inclusive booze-absorbing breakfast; and then for lunch, when chunky hamburgers, seafood salads and the delicious *bondiola* (pork) sandwich and chips are served. During the day, it is always worth waiting for a table on the terrace, which is an ideal spot from which to watch the fishermen come and go. Around midnight, Sargento Garcia becomes the resort's focal point for after-dinner revelry, as scores of tipsy visitors and locals drop in for a chat and a dance. The bar often books DJs and performing artists. Sargento Garcia may be changing ownership in the near future, so details are subject to change.

El Viejo y el Mar

Punta del Diablo *Playa de la Viuda (099 149 704 mobile). Open Dec-Easter 10am-2am daily. Apr-Nov 10am-2pm, 6-10pm daily. £. No credit cards. Seafood.*

Open year-round, this small restaurant is located right beside the ocean (take the tiny access road off General San Martin towards the beach). Fishing nets hang from the rafters and seafaring paraphernalia adorns the walls; the chef is a charismatic old fisherman called Ernesto, and you'll be eating whatever he feels like cooking. The emphasis here is on traditional, home-cooked meals. The seafood dishes draw on influences from French, Spanish and Italian cuisine, but are made with locally sourced produce. Musicians play here from time to time.

Stay

Many visitors to Punta del Diablo – particularly Argentinians and Uruguayans – rent out a small house (or *rancho,* as they are commonly known). A typical *rancho*, with space to sleep up to five or six people, will cost significantly less in low season.

The set-up in Cabo Polonio is much more basic, but what the village lacks in facilities – water, electricity, telephone and home comforts – is more than compensated for by the joy of being so close to nature.

Posadas and *ranchos* in Cabo Polonio can be booked online through www.cabo-polonio.com and www.cabopolonio.com – or you can simply turn up and ask around.

For Punta del Diabo, the Portal del Diablo website (www.portaldeldiablo.com.uy) has the most comprehensive listing of homes and cabins on offer, with different sizes, locations and price bands. Use the site to book ahead for summer stays. Most houses display a hand-painted sign with a contact phone number, and pretty much every house in town is available to rent during January. Generally, visitors start reserving high-season spaces in September.

Aquarella Pousada de Charme

Punta del Diablo *La Corvina, no number (0477 2400/ www.hotelaquarella.com). ££. No credit cards.*

Billed as an apart-hotel, the Aquarella offers rooms and suites with Wi-Fi, air-conditioning and views overlooking Playa del Rivero; the suites also have a daily maid service. The hotel has its own restaurant, and is one of the few properties in Punta del Diablo with a pool. You couldn't ask for a better location, just a few steps from the main beach. It's advisable to book early, especially if you are planning to visit in the summer.

Nativos Posada & Hostel

Punta del Diablo *Avenida Santa Teresa, no number (0477 2524/www.nativos.com.uy). ££.*

Consisting of four charming, tranquil cabins, in a back-to-nature setting just before the last bend of the road towards Playa de la Viuda, Nativos is more boutique hotel than rustic hostel. Each room is individually decorated with chunky, hand-made wooden furniture, and you can enjoy the sound of the local bird life from the hammocks slung up on the balconies. There's maid service in the rooms and Wi-Fi internet access throughout, and towels and bedding are provided.

La Perla

Cabo Polonio *Playa de la Calavera (0470 5125/ www.laperladelcabo.com). ££.*

If hot water, an electricity supply (albeit only until midnight) and a neatly-made bed are more important to you than that rustic feel, you might well want to stay in this hotel in the second building on the beach. The 12 guest rooms all have en-suite bathrooms, though only half have views over the beach; the rest look out on to the lighthouse or, less excitingly, the interior. Book well in advance to secure an ocean view. The decoration is simple and homely, with basic wooden furnishings and sand on the reception floor.

Posada de los Corvinos
Cabo Polonio *Playa de la Calavera (098 565 966 mobile). £. No credit cards.*
Owned and run by the ever-friendly Matias and Laura, Posada de los Corvinos, which is 100m from the beach, ticks all the right boxes: clean rooms, easy access to the beach and the village centre, and a cool and relaxed vibe. There are three private rooms with a sea view and one shared room offering a maximum of four bunks, all equipped with hot showers (a rarity in Cabo) generated by solar power. The swinging hammocks are perfect for indulging in an afternoon siesta.

Posada Mariemar
Cabo Polonio *Playa de la Calavera (0470 5164/ 0470 5241). ££. No credit cards.*

With over 40 years in the business, this two-storey posada offers almost identical facilities and views across the Atlantic as La Perla (*see p237*). There are four double rooms and three triples, all with private bathrooms. It's an unpretentious hotel: the paint is bright and the design distinctively 1970s, with wooden furnishings and basic amenities. The restaurant is reputed to have the freshest fish and – set just a few metres from the beach – the best views in the village. It's also the only eaterie in which you can find meat on the menu.

Posada La Viuda del Diablo
Punta del Diablo *Playa de la Viuda (098 640 792 mobile/www.laviudadeldiablo.com). £££. No credit cards.*
One of the newest hotels in Punta del Diablo, La Viuda del Diablo is surrounded by dunes on the more exposed of the village's two beaches, just outside of town (follow Nueva Granada to the beach and turn left). The bright, tastefully decorated suites have in-room jacuzzis, air-conditioning, balconies and ocean views. There's also a small restaurant and bar, and parking spaces are available.

Factfile

When to go
The high season runs from mid December to the end of February, with accommodation prices peaking from Christmas until the end of January. By the end of February, many of the restaurants and shops are closed. Either side of the peak season, between November and March, is the ideal time to go to avoid the crowds. The weather usually remains good until the end of March, though even in the height of summer you should make sure you pack a woolly jumper for the chilly evenings. Punta del Diablo has a small amount of year-round trade, but Cabo Polonio is battened down from June until early October.

Getting there & around
Punta del Diablo is three hours east of Montevideo's Aeropuerto Internacional de Carrasco, along Uruguay's coastal highway and scenic Ruta 9. It's an hour away from Punta del Este, or a 40-minute drive from the Brazilian border town of Chuy. There are daily buses from main cities like Montevideo (four hours 30 minutes), Rocha (one hour 30 minutes) and Chuy (one hour). Consult the schedules at Terminal Tres Cruces (www.trescruces.com.uy) in Montevideo. A number of bus companies service the route to Punta del Diablo, including Rutas del Sol (02 402 5451) and Cynsa (02 402 5363).

If you want more flexibility, it's better to rent a car. Though Punta del Diablo itself is small enough to traverse on foot (mainly barefoot), a

car is convenient for day trips to the nearby Parque Nacional Santa Teresa, or Chuy for food supplies and banks with ATMs.

From the main Montevideo bus station, Rutas del Sol buses head out to Cabo Polonio four times a day. Most will stop off along the way in San Carlos and La Pedrera, before continuing up to Cabo Polonio and Valizas. At the entrance to the village, you need to hop on one of the trucks that will take you across the dunes and into the village. The entire trip takes approximately five hours. For details of costs and times of the buses, check out www.trescruces.com.uy.

Tourist information
The best resource is www.portaldeldiablo.com.uy, a website produced by a group of professionals in Punta del Diablo. This portal offers information in English on lodgings and restaurants and there are lots of photos as well as maps.

Neither Cabo Polonia nor Punta del Diablo has a tourist information office per se, but you'll find that locals are extremely friendly and knowledgeable. The website of the Uruguayan tourist board is www.turismo.gub.uy.

Internet
In Cabo Polonio, there's a very slow and expensive service in the main supermarket, Lujambio's. There are several cyber cafés in Punta del Diablo, and almost all lodgings have either wireless access or a shared terminal.

Clockwise from top: Aquarella Pousada de Charme; Posada la Viuda del Diablo; Cabo Polonio (2).

Punta del Este.

José Ignacio & Punta del Este

Uruguay

Hip beach resorts where the jet set roam.

Surrounded on three sides by the South Atlantic, Uruguay's idyllic village of José Ignacio is paradoxically both catatonically low-key and an extremely glamourous place to park your flip-flops. No high-rise towers, no discos, no ugly people. The tallest building by several stories is the iconic 1877 lighthouse, which sits on a rocky promontory at the town's windswept edge. From there, you can spy José Ignacio's thatched roofs, tidy gardens and dressed-down celebs.

A slight hill that rises from the beaches lends each of the village's dozen sandy streets an ocean view. Strict zoning laws mandate low-rise, single-family dwellings, meaning there are only about 300 lucky inhabitants and 50 hotel rooms. Out of season, the village reveals its peaceful pre-Hollywood appeal, with plenty of opportunities to enjoy the unspoiled surroundings in complete tranquillity. High season, however, brings an influx of A-listers, meaning mere mortals may have a hard time making reservations.

José Ignacio is often lumped into the stretch of the 'Uruguayan Riviera' loosely referred to as Punta del Este. But Punta proper is on its own peninsula an hour to the south, just beyond the reach of the gaping Río de la Plata. Punta del Este is where you find those concrete towers, casinos, nightclubs and impressive breast implants. You'll also find plenty of photo opportunities: a yacht-packed marina; schools of sea lions, obese from devouring fishmongers' scraps; and a sculpture of giant fingers playfully emerging from the sand. For those who like to split the difference, the midpoint town of La Barra mixes Punta del Este's action with José Ignacio's tranquillity. Beach-hopping encouraged.

The hotel of everyones' dreams
when planning a trip: intimate, cozy,
and with an exceptional location
facing the ocean. The Style of the
saloons and bedrooms have the
atmosphere and charm of a country
house. Our hotel and unforgettable
holidays are awaiting you.

You deserve it!

Ruta 10 Km 160 La Barra
Punta del Este Uruguay
Tel (59842) 770021
alaposta@adinet.com.uy
www.lapostadelcangrejo.com

Explore

JOSÉ IGNACIO

A one-time pirate hideout where fishermen still quietly ply their trade, the tiny settlement of **José Ignacio** has become the place to go for a sophisticated crowd seeking an alternative to the more party-oriented atmosphere of Punta del Este, 40 kilometres south.

José Ignacio offers lazy summer evenings, impressive sunsets and outstanding food. In the last few years, its low-key luxury has attracted some famous names (Naomi Campbell, Martin Amis, Gisele Bündchen), who have all been seduced by the village's natural beauty, with its long, wide expanses of sand bordered by white dunes and deep pine forests.

The village itself is made up of small, one- and two-storey stucco buildings, bars and restaurants, and the odd millionaire's beach-facing pad. Land prices here have rocketed up in the last few years, but somehow the village – with the help of strict building laws – is still hanging on to its rugged charm. For an overview, visit the main tourist attraction, the José Ignacio lighthouse, which stands over 32 metres tall. You can climb up anytime between 10am and sunset.

José Ignacio offers two sorts of seashore: the tranquil waters of Playa Mansa to the south, and the rougher Playa Brava to the north. Kitesurfers favour **Laguna Garzón**, which lies around four kilometres further north.

The focal hangout for the jet set is La Huella (*see p247*). More than a beachside restaurant, it is an institution unto itself. In high season (November to March), it is capable of effortlessly turning over 1,000 covers a day – and it serves, without a doubt, the best cocktails you'll find anywhere along the Uruguayan coast.

PUNTA DEL ESTE

It may be bigger and brasher than José Ignacio, but **Punta del Este** still stands proud as a watering hole of the rich and famous. With the calm Río de la Plata on one side of the peninsula and the choppier Atlantic on the other, it offers a string of beaches for swimming or surfing.

Getting your bearings here is easy: just remember which area you're in and the number of the *parada*, or 'stop', that you are at. These numbered sections of the beach run from the centre of the peninsula and continue in both directions along the coast; at each *parada*, *paradores* (beach clubs) offer various services. Most places have sunshades and sun-loungers for hire, and can rustle up the standard steak sandwich (*chivito*) or prepare a refreshing *licuado* (fruit smoothie).

In the height of the season, when evening falls the throngs descend on the main drag, Avenida

Laguna Garzón

José Ignacio

La Barra

Punta del Este

ATLANTIC OCEAN

0   5 km

José Ignacio & Punta del Este

Historic sites
●

Art & architecture
● ●

Hotels
● ● ● ● ●

Eating & drinking
● ● ● ● ●

Scenery
● ● ● ● ●

Outdoor activities
● ● ● ●

Gorlero, and the surrounding streets. A typical night begins with a late dinner in one of the many seafood or Italian restaurants, before things hot up in the area's famed nightspots and stay that way until sunrise.

Casapueblo

Punta Ballena, Maldonado (042 578041/www.carlos paezvilaro.com). Open 10am-sunset daily. Admission UR$117; free under-11s.

Punta del Este's most iconic and surreal construction took 36 years to complete. This unique building in Punta Ballena houses the workshop and museum of artist Carlos Páez Vilaró, the man behind the masterpiece. Visitors can wander through the warrens of whitewashed structures that recall Mediterranean architecture, and visit the artist's gallery. Classical music concerts take place at sunset in the summer, and you can also spend a night in the hotel (*see p251*).

LA BARRA

Ten kilometres north of Punta's concrete jungle, **La Barra** is continuing its transformation from quiet village to international playground. The expanding array of galleries and gastronomic spots offers an alternative to beachside bronzing, and a number of businesses are capitalising on the popularity of this area outside of peak season with year-round opening hours.

"Surfers trip up and down La Barra's main strip, while 'Bikini Beach' is the focal point for a catwalk show of sun worshippers."

The local landmark is Puente Leonel Viera, situated at the entrance to La Barra and spanning the Río Maldonado. The stomach-drop sensation you get as you pass over the undulating structure gave it the nickname *el puente de la risa* (the bridge of laughter). Nobel-winning Chilean poet Pablo Neruda was inspired to write an ode to the La Barra bridge.

By day, surfers trip up and down La Barra's main strip, while Playa Bikini (or Bikini Beach) is the focal point for the catwalk show of sun worshippers. There are chic boutiques and cool café-bars, and, come night-time, it's pure, unadulterated revelry in one of the innumerable clubs. With names and venues changing from one season to the next, it's always best to ask around to discover the summer's hottest location. When in doubt, you should be able to find some scene stalwarts in and around La Barra.

Popular with music-savvy clubbers, Crobar (Complejo Purple, Camino Urquiza) attracts the biggest DJs from overseas, while in the centre of La Barra, Tequila Bar (Ruta 10, km 161.5) is the favoured playground of the rich and famous. At the other end of the scale, tiny Diablito (Ruta 10, km 160) has a back patio that regularly hosts DJ sessions.

OUTDOOR ACTIVITIES

Water sports are practised up and down the coast. Playa Brava in Punta del Este is the perfect surf beach, and Parada 3 on Playa la Olla is where you'll find Punta Surf School (042 481388), a good place for beginners. At Laguna Garzón, Laura Moñino runs a windsurfing and kitesurfing school (094 420704, www.kitey windsurflaura.com), with classes for novices as well as for those who are a little more steady on a board. Jet ski and watercraft rental outfits abound here, and can be found along most strips of beach.

Punta del Este has excellent golf and tennis facilities. Tenis del Este (Marne and Marselle, Parada 7 at Avenida Roosevelt, 042 485300, www.tenispuntadeleste.com) offers courses and tournaments for all ages, as does José Ignacio's Club de Mar (048 62137, www.club demar.com.uy). For golf, try the Cantegril Country Club (042 223211, www.cantegril.org.uy), Club del Lago Golf (042 578423, www.lagogolf.com) or Barrio Parque del Golf (042 480840, www. rinconclub.com.ar).

At Haras Godiva, Austrian Carolin Mallmann's prestigious stud farm in José Ignacio, seasoned veterans organise horse riding treks (048 06112, www.harasgodiva.com). Meanwhile, more laid-back and less costly horse riding excursions can be arranged through Posada Laguna Anastasio, based in the countryside close to Laguna Garzón (098 601191, www.posadaanastasio.com).

Eat

Fish and seafood are the obvious specialities in the area – specifically, *mejillones* (mussels), *rabas* (squid), *chipirones* (baby squid), *corvina* (sea bass) and seafood salads – while carnivores won't be disappointed by the steaks.

Many restaurants shut down for good from one season to the next, with new eateries springing up each summer to replace them. Places get very busy, and reservations are essential in high season. If you arrive in the quiet season between April and October, you'd be wise to ensure you have your own kitchen, as open restaurants are few and far between.

Bed and barbecue

Francis Mallmann and Punta del Este go together like cheese and crackers. Or grilled steak and *chimichurri*. Or – let's not play around – leg of lamb smeared with Dijon mustard, roasted swiftly between two fires, and served with roast potatoes and almonds.

That last dish is a Mallmann speciality, typical of the kind of high-end, deceptively complex comfort food that has, over a three-decade career, made him Argentina's best-known chef and restaurateur. He's also a television star, an author and an unashamed romantic who bedecks the walls of his restaurants with English poetry and needs little encouragement to wax lyrical on the relationship between food and sex.

Mallmann has been in the restaurant business since the late 1970s, but it wasn't until the '90s, when Punta del Este was transforming from exclusive enclave to sprawling resort, that his star truly began to shine. Los Negros, Mallmann's flagship restaurant in José Ignacio, became legendary, as much for its international celebrity clientele and steep prices as for its outstanding food. Those who say Mallmann put tiny José Ignacio 'on the map' have a point.

Tiring of the hype and hullabaloo he had helped create, Mallmann sold Los Negros in 2006 and moved his Uruguayan operation away from the coast to El Garzón, a sleepy ex-railway village he'd first stumbled upon in the 1970s.

These days, it isn't so sleepy. Hotel Garzón (*see p252*), Mallmann's five-room luxury posada and restaurant, has tempted some of the in-crowd inland, and a slew of property developments around the town and Laguna Garzón, the nearby lake, are turning the village into... well, what José Ignacio was 20 years ago.

No shortage of buzz, then; but is Hotel Garzón as good as it sounds? For those who can afford it, the answer is a resounding '*¡Si!*' The rates are high but genuinely all-inclusive, covering breakfast, lunch, afternoon tea, supper and an open bar (with wines from partner Finca La Anita), as well as the use of bicycles and horses. The five rooms – with their dark-wood fittings, free-standing tubs and king-size beds with floral bedspreads – are soothing and stylish, and exactly what modern urbanites expect from a country retreat. The food, including the speciality lamb, is predictably sublime, and the staff are young, multilingual and attractive. (For hard-bitten, veteran gauchos, look elsewhere.)

This collision of cool and quality has led many to speculate that the Laguna Garzón area will be Uruguay's 'next big thing'. This is Punta del Este, mind, where tonight's happening spot is tomorrow morning's 'that place is so, like, over', so you should ink this into your itinerary now. There's a leg of lamb with your name on it.

● *Francis Mallmann's latest book,* Seven Fires, *is published by Artisan Books.*

Top & bottom: Punta del Este.
Middle: José Ignacio (2).

Baby Gouda
La Barra *Ruta 10, km 161, at Los Romances (042 771874). Open Dec-Feb 11am-late daily. £££. International.*
Sitting proudly at the brow of La Barra, Baby Gouda is a popular stop-off point after the short but vertiginous climb from the beach. Kitsch and cool with a Moroccan twist, this spacious and spectacularly colourful deli stocks an excellent spread of olives, cheeses and fresh salmon. The adjoining restaurant serves simple but tasty food, with typical dishes including prosciutto, pâté and generous *picadas* (cold meat and cheese platters), which can be shared between two to four people.

La Bourgogne
Punta del Este *Pedragosa Sierra & Avenida del Mar (042 482007/www.labourgogne.com.uy). Open Easter-Nov from 11am Thur-Sun. Dec-Easter from 11am daily. ££££. French.*
Many years ago, Jean Paul Bondoux arrived in Uruguay with a rucksack and some very ambitious ideas. Using his charm, grit and polished culinary skills, he soon became one of the region's leading chefs, setting up restaurants in both Buenos Aires and Punta del Este. Ever the perfectionist, Bondoux uses vegetables grown on his nearby plot of land. Naturally, the food is top-notch; you'll find everything from imported Russian caviar to Bondoux signature dishes, including *magret au poivre vert* (duck with green pepper) and a fabulous *marmite* (a fish stew of fresh vegetables and the best of the day's catch). Reservations are a must in high season.

Cactus y Pescados
La Barra *Descent to Playa Bikini (042 774782). Open Apr-Nov 10am-1am Fri-Sun. Dec-Mar 10am-1am daily. £££. Seafood.*
Cactus y Pescados has an excellent view of Playa Bikini and the steady stream of bronzed bodies heading to and from the sea. Lunch choices are Punta del Este standards – mainly *chivitos*, battered squid and salads – but the range of fruity *licuados* (smoothies) and cold beers make this a good spot to soak up the scene, either before or after a dip in the sea.

El Franchute
La Barra *Ruta 10, km 168.5 (042 775677/www.elfranchute.com). Mar-Nov from 8.30pm Thur-Sat. Dec-Feb from 9pm daily. ££££. No credit cards. French.*
Chef Laurent Lainé presents French classics on a prix-fixe menu that's updated daily, depending on the availability of seasonal products. The Uruguayan wine selection is impeccable, as is El Franchute's atmosphere. The menu can be viewed on the website, which also features step-by-step instructions for making some of the chef's delicious recipes. Tables are available by reservation only.

La Huella
José Ignacio *Playa Brava (048 62279). Open Easter-Nov 12.30-2pm, 8.30pm-midnight Fri, Sat; 12.30-2pm Sun. Dec-Easter 12.30pm-12.30am daily. ££££. Modern.*

Without doubt the coolest restaurant in José Ignacio, La Huella is the favoured hangout of every actor, model, wealthy businessman or wannabe celebrity you can imagine. Not bad for an overgrown fish shack with bare wooden beams and a thatched roof. When you've had your fill of people-watching, you'll find plenty to grab your attention on the Mediterranean-inspired menu, which includes grilled octopus and barbecued sea bass, along with perfectly executed caipiroskas and bloody marys. Add atmospheric music and dinner by candlelight, and you've got yourself a memorable José Ignacio experience. The small terrace overlooking the beach is not to be missed, although if you're planning to visit in January, you'll need the patience of a saint; the place goes crazy during this time of year.

Lo de Charlie
Punta del Este *Calle 12 819 (042 444183). Open Apr-Nov from 7.30pm Thur, Fri; 11.30am-4pm, from 7.30pm Sat, Sun. Mid Dec-Mar 11.30am-4pm, from 7.30pm daily. £££. Seafood.*
With walls painted by Carlos Páez Vilaró, the man responsible for Casapueblo (see p244), Lo de Charlie's bold colours and vibrant character help make this spot one of the major players in the Punta restaurant scene. Mediterranean-inspired dishes feature fresh, local products, and the time that owner Charlie spent training in kitchens across Europe and the US is evident in every mouthful. A variety of meats, seafood and pasta are on offer, but the must-try dish is *chipirones a la plancha* (grilled baby squid). Booking ahead is essential during the busy summer months.

> "Lit by candles, log fires and, on most nights, a starry sky, Marismo is hidden from the crowds."

Lucy
José Ignacio *Garzas & Golondrinas (048 62090). Open Apr-Nov from 10am Fri-Sun. Dec-Mar 9am-midnight daily. £££. Traditional.*
This restaurant doesn't even attempt to compete with the minimalist fashion predominant elsewhere on the coast – probably because it doesn't need to. Its recipe for success is thanks to the eponymous Lucy, who oversees the authentic home-cooking; don't miss out on her mango duck. The offerings have recently expanded to include special-edition Inés Berton teas and a tempting range of desserts, such as chocolate cake with *turrón* or nut tart with tangy citrus ice-cream.

Marismo
José Ignacio *Ruta 10, km 185 (048 62273). Open Dec-Feb & Easter from 9pm daily. ££££. No credit cards. Modern.*

Pölder

Punta del Este
naturally sophisticated

All the sites, all the possibilities.
Punta del Este is a seaside resort full of
contrasts. A series of oceanic beaches
blended with woods, buildings and luxurious
villas make Punta del Este an ideal place for
leisure. Its natural and architectural beauty,
its infrastructure and services create a
balance between nature and man's work.

Maldonado
URUGUAY

www.maldonado.gub.uy

Lit by candles, log fires and, on most nights, a starry sky, this exquisite restaurant is hidden among white sand dunes, far from the crowds. You won't find starchy white tablecloths here; instead, well-worn wooden tables and chairs are assembled haphazardly in groups under the open sky, while covered eating areas offer low seating and tables arranged beneath white fabric canopies. Baby squid, pizza, fresh fish and the delicious lamb (cooked for four hours) emerge piping hot from two large mud ovens. As it is slightly hidden and out of the way, Marismo is best found by letting a taxi do the work.

Namm

José Ignacio *Ruta 10, km 185. (048 62526). Open Dec-Feb 8pm-late daily. ££££. No credit cards. Modern.*
Specialising in sushi, roast lamb and grilled meats, Namm is hidden just off a dirt road in the woods behind José Ignacio (keep an eye out for the sign). Constructed in stone, with a glass front and a good-sized wooden deck, it offers a memorable eating experience, complete with bonfires and moonlit dining. Outside, the tree-house booths are perfect for large parties.

Novecento

La Barra *Ruta 10 & Las Sirenas (042 772363/ www.bistronovecento.com). Open Dec-Mar from 7pm daily. ££££. International.*
Set in the heart of La Barra, Novecento is one of the preferred meeting spots for the young and wealthy. The reach of the original BA institution now stretches as far as New York and Miami. While the bistro-inspired restaurant has French and North American influences, it is first and foremost Argentinian – so the menu doesn't fail to include the classic *ojo de bife* (ribeye steak). Look out for the usually fantastic dishes of the day.

O'Farrell

La Barra *Calle Punta del Este & Ruta 10, km 164.5 (042 774331). Open Mar-mid Dec from 8pm Sat, Sun. Late Dec-Feb from 8pm daily. ££££. Modern.*
This romantic restaurant with ocean views is considered among the best on the local gastro scene. The menu, characterised by French and Mediterranean touches, features dishes such as duck foie gras with caramelised pear, shrimp and sweetbread with guacamole and jalapeños, and grilled sea bass with seafood rice. Dishes can be accompanied by your bottle of choice from the impressive wine list, featuring around 200 labels.

El Palenque

Punta del Este *Avenida Roosevelt, Parada 6 (042 494257/www.elpalenque.com.uy). Open Apr-July, Sept-Nov noon-4pm Wed; noon-4pm, from 8pm Thur-Sun. Dec-Mar noon-2am daily. ££££. Traditional.*
This classic Uruguayan restaurant – the original Montevideo branch has been in business since the late 1950s – is famous for its peerless cuts of beef and fish, which hit the parrilla with a glorious sizzle. Among the eaterie's many specialities, you'll find suckling pig, lamb tripe, baby beef, paella and pasta. There's also a fantastic selection of Argentinian, Spanish, Chilean, French and even Australian wines.

Restaurant T (Hernán Taiana)

La Barra *Ruta 10, km 162.5 (042 771356/ www.hernantaiana.com). Open Sept-Nov from 8.30pm Fri, Sat. Dec-Mar from 8.30pm daily. ££££. Modern.*
Ten years after opening this restaurant, head chef and owner Hernán Taiana continues to pop up among the tables, eager to tell diners about the entrées. When he's not doing that, he's travelling the world looking for new ideas. As a result, the menu is wonderfully eclectic, ranging from ravioli stuffed with prawns and leeks to tuna steaks doused in ginger and honey, and, a customer favourite, lamb with sweetbreads. Your best bet when ordering is to go with the chef's recommendations; he won't disappoint.

"Isolated and bohemian, Tercer Ojo attracts some illustrious guests, hoping to evade roaming paparazzi lenses."

Tercer Ojo

José Ignacio *Avenida República Argentina & Las Toninas, km 181 (048 62411/094 967957 mobile). Open noon-3pm, 9pm-midnight daily. £££. No credit cards. Modern.*
This quiet and isolated spot attracts illustrious guests looking to escape roaming paparazzi lenses. The bohemian restaurant is essentially the top floor of the owner's house, so the vibe is cosily familial, with kids' paintings taped up on the walls and holiday snaps among the crockery. The food is as colourful and creative as the decor, with specialities including black forest cake, profiteroles, ceviche, lamb and even the odd wild boar. Reservations are required.

Stay

In José Ignacio, places tend to close for the winter, but most Punta del Este hotels stay open during low season, regardless of the weather, meaning Punta del Este maintains a permanent – albeit small – community year-round.

If you are considering renting a private beach house or villa instead of staying in a hotel, like many holidaymakers in the region, it's wise to book well ahead. Some options for private rentals include Buenos Aires' Curiocity Villas (011 4803 1113, www.curiocityvillas.com), US-based Time & Place Homes (+1 866 244 1800, + 1 214 393 2839, www.timeandplace.com) and Ignacio Ruibal (0486 2228, 094 430 2224, www.ignacioruibal.com).

At the time of writing, the finishing touches were being put to the Hotel Fasano Las Piedras

VAN DER BRÜIN

agathes quartzs & semi-precious stones

vdbstones@gmail.com
www.vanderbruin.com.uy

ALL PUNTA DEL DIABLO
ON INTERNET

www. PORTAL
DEL DIABLO.COM.UY

FOLLOW US ON TWITTER
www.twitter.com/portaldeldiablo

lo de Charlie

La Pedrera:
Rambla lado este hacia el barco undido
Cel . 00598. 96. 231809

Punta del Este:
Calle 12 N° 819 Puerto de Punta del Este
(00598. 42) 444183

(Camino Egusquíza, www.laspiedrasvillasfasano. com). With 20 luxury bungalows spread out over 480 hectares, the hotel, which is located eight kilometres from La Barra, has myriad facilities that include a restaurant, bar, spa, tennis courts and even a polo field.

Note that prices for accommodation soar in high season, but cheaper deals can be found during off-peak periods.

Arbol Casa Loft

José Ignacio *Teros, between Golondrinas & Tordos (011 4803 1113 in BA/www.arbolcasaloft.com). ££££. No credit cards.*

Just a few blocks from José Ignacio's iconic lighthouse, Arbol Casa Loft's six luxury suites feature Malaysian and Indonesian furniture, and luxuries that include 32-inch LCD TVs and Wi-Fi. Some suites have spacious balconies with ocean views, and others have access to the gardens or private patios. Shared facilities include a swimming pool and lounge area complete with home theatre. For a more private seaside retreat, you can rent out the entire property.

L'Auberge

Punta del Este *Carnoustie & Avenida del Agua, Barrio Parque de Golf (042 482601/www.lauberge hotel.com). £££.*

Over 50 years old, L'Auberge is located in Punta del Este's distinguished Parque de Golf neighbourhood. Six types of room are available, all furnished in an elegant, European style, with some set within the hotel's famed water tower. Although rooms in the tower tend to be on the small side, choice antiques and breathtaking views more than compensate. Meanwhile, the comforts of the more spacious suites and deluxe rooms can include a balcony with garden view, fireplace and jacuzzi. Belgian waffles are the speciality in the tea room, which is open daily from December to March, and Saturdays year-round.

La Ballenera

La Barra *Ruta 10, km 162 (042 771079/ www.ballenera.blogspot.com). £££. No credit cards.*

Owner Florencia has an inimitable knack for making guests feel right at home at this five-bedroom guesthouse, which is surrounded by pine trees yet close enough to the beach for you to hear the waves crashing against the shore. The rooms are spacious, quaint and named after whales – Austral, Humpback, Blue, Minke and Sei. Some of the second-floor rooms feature ocean views, fireplaces and private balconies, while others face the garden.

La Bluette

La Barra *Ruta 10, Parada 49 (042 770947/ www.hotellabluette.com). £££.*

Decorated in French-Riviera style, this boutique hotel is an affordable option for those wanting a relaxed and informal stay without compromising on comfort. It's an intimate operation, and the owners will bend over backwards to help with any reasonable request. Each of the 13 suites is decorated according to a different theme, though all have ocean views and private terraces, where guests can enjoy

meals cooked by the hotel chef. Impromptu parrillas in summer and crackling fires in winter tend to unite guests for spirited chat over some good wine.

> ## "Sample authentic Spanish tapas at Le Club, accompanied by a delicious *clericó* (white sangria) made with fresh fruit."

Le Club

La Barra *Avenida de los Cangrejos & Avenida del Mar (042 772082/011 4815 0669 in BA/www.leclubposada. com). ££££.*

At the peak of high season, it seems as if most of La Barra's population stops by here for a sunset cocktail, and it's easy to see why. A modern take on Casapueblo (*see p244*), Le Club is a hotel, bar and restaurant dedicated to good living. The rooms are minimally decorated in a predominantly white palette, and some have individual decks and ocean views. The restaurant's innovative, Mediterranean-inspired dishes are largely seafood-based, although you can also sample a variety of authentic Spanish tapas and a delicious *clericó* (white sangria) prepared with fresh fruit. Over the years, Le Club has attracted a stellar international clientele – including Sophia Loren and Antonio Banderas – for either an aperitif or a weekend sojourn.

Club Hotel Casapueblo

Punta Ballena, 12km NW of Punta del Este *Ruta Panorámica (042 578611/www.clubhotel.com.ar). ££.*

This white, Mediterranean-style construction, the work of Uruguayan artist Carlos Páez Vilaró, is 12km from Punta del Este. Spread out across the cliff side, it features 70 fully equipped apartments with terraces facing the sea – all the better to appreciate the legendary sunsets. Rooms vary slightly in size and decor, though all feature white adobe walls and plush beds. Note that there is a three-night minimum stay from mid December to March.

Hotel Art & Spa Las Cumbres

Laguna del Sauce, 18km NW of Punta del Este *Ruta 12, km 3.9 (042 578689/www.cumbres.com.uy). £££.*

Located deep in the woods surrounding Punta del Este and run by a family of keen travellers, this boutique art-hotel displays a fascinating collection of objets d'art from around the world. The 28 spacious, comfortable rooms and suites offer stunning views of the peninsula, ocean, *laguna*, forest or fields: if you're staying in the Star Suite, the panoramic views include all five. Each room is equipped with various high-tech comforts, such as a Bang & Olufsen audio system, a plasma TV and an iPod shuffle or mini. Most rooms also feature whirlpool tubs and fireplaces. Non-residents can enjoy the views and a splendid spread of cakes by dropping in for afternoon tea from 4.30pm.

Hotel Garzón

35km N of José Ignacio *Camino de la Capilla & Ruta a José Ignacio (0410 2809/0410 2811/www.restaurant garzon.com). ££££.*
Run by celebrity chef Francis Mallmann (*see p245* **Bed and barbeque**), this inland country hotel offers five beautifully-appointed rooms, each with its own wood-burning stove. The Nordic-style decor is impeccably tasteful and luxurious, and the king-size beds wonderfully comfortable. Rates include all meals; the complex is also home to one of the area's finest restaurants.

Posada Azul Marino

José Ignacio *Ruta 10, km 185 (048 62363/ www.azulmarino.com.uy). ££££.*
An isolated location, five kilometres from Laguna Garzón and just a few metres from the sea, makes this small posada the perfect spot to unwind. Nine minimally furnished, ocean-front rooms each come with a private deck and home comforts, including cable TV and Wi-Fi, while the superior suite has a large terrace and open-air jacuzzi. Relax by the pool, or try the surf-and-turf menu in the restaurant.

La Posada del Faro

José Ignacio *Calle de la Bahia & Timonel (0486 2110/ www.posadadelfaro.com). ££££.*
La Posada del Faro is still the hippest place to stay in this unique fishing village. Perfect for a romantic getaway or an escape from the daily grind, the hotel's 15 rooms are decorated in minimalist white, relieved by a few restrained details in sober shades. Most rooms come with private terraces and several also have fireplaces, making a winter sojourn an enjoyable experience. The pool has a fully stocked bar right in the middle, and is the ideal place to watch the incredible sunsets. Prices rise dramatically in high season, when there is a ten-night minimum stay; book well in advance.

La Posta del Cangrejo

La Barra *Ruta 10, km 160.5 (042 770021/ www.lapostadelcangrejo.com). ££££.*
This La Barra classic has drawn a string of famous guests with its prime beachfront location and fine French dining. Country-style rooms have ocean or garden views, comfortable beds and large, flatscreen TVs; some have a fireplace and jacuzzi tub. A spectacular poolside terrace overlooking the ocean provides a relaxing retreat. Centrally located to most La Barra goings-on, the hotel is within walking distance of shops, bars and restaurants.

Factfile

When to go

'The Season', as it's rather grandly known in the area, is short and generally runs from 20 December to 10 January. During this time Punta del Este, José Ignacio and La Barra's populations swell hugely; the atmosphere is at its peak, but so are the prices. For a more relaxing time, early December or late February to early March are ideal, when the weather is still nice and hotel rates are lower.

Prices are halved in colder months, but be forewarned: services are cut as well. Many restaurants and discos only bother to open their doors during prime beach weather.

Getting there

Punta del Este's airport is 16 kilometres from the town. Many visitors first fly into Buenos Aires, then switch to Aerolíneas Argentinas (www. aerolineas.com.ar) or Pluna (www.flypluna.com) for a connecting flight to Punta del Este.

Another option from Buenos Aires is to take the Buquebús ferry to either Montevideo or Colonia, then continue by bus (02 916 1910 Uruguay, 011 4316 6500 Argentina, www. buquebus.com). Bus companies COT (02 409 4949, www.cot.com.uy) and Copsa (02 1975, www.copsa.com.uy) offer services between Montevideo and Punta del Este.

Getting around

Within Punta del Este, most things are within walking distance, though it's best to hire a car if you want to spend time in La Barra or José Ignacio as well. Some good rental companies are Europcar (Calle Gorlero & Calle 30, 042 495017, www.europcar.com.uy), Avis (Calle 31, 042 442020, www.avis.com.uy) and Punta Car (02 900 2772, www.puntacar.com.uy).

For short-distance travel, taxis are best. Reliable companies include Punta Shopping (042 484704), Parada 5 (042 490302) and Aeropuerto (042 559100). Alternatively, COT (042 409 4949) runs a bus service up and down the coast.

For motorcycle and bicycle rentals, try Golden Bike (corner of calles 29 & 24, 042 447394).

Tourist information

Punta del Este Tourist Information Avenida Gorlero, between calles 25 & 23 (042 446519). Open Mar-Nov 9am-6pm daily. Dec-Feb 8am-midnight daily.

Internet

Internet is typically slow and expensive, but is offered at some hotels. A handful of cyber cafés have cropped up in Punta, and ANCAP service stations offer free Wi-Fi.

From top: Hotel Fasano
Las Piedras; Le Club;
Club Hotel Casapueblo;
Baby Gouda.

Clockwise from top left: birdlife on Península Valdés; the peninsula's coastline; sea lions; Magellanic penguins; Southern right whale; Trelew.

Península Valdés & Around

Argentina

An other-worldly coastline full of exotic Patagonian wildlife.

A startling fountain of spray rises from the inky-blue Atlantic, shortly followed by a giant, forked tail, hovering gracefully for all to see and then slapping down into obscurity with a jolting thud. If there's one place on Earth where you're going to feel small, this is it. Southern right whales are among the planet's biggest mammals, and, fortunately for nature-lovers, their size brings showmanship.

In the stark landscape of Península Valdés, visitors flock to see wildlife perform dramatic displays they've only ever seen on screen. Some get the chance to watch orca whales skid up on to the beach and pick off unsuspecting sea lions from the sand in a torrent of spray. Here, the circle of life plays out before your eyes and, as the cute ones get snapped up mercilessly, it's definitely not the Disney version.

The enclosed warm waters of the Golfo San José and the Golfo Nuevo make the area an ideal breeding ground for a host of marine mammals. Protected by forbidding cliffs, huge troops of elephant seals and sea lions sun themselves on the beaches; inquisitive dolphins jump playfully through the surf; and over at nearby Punta Tombo, the world's largest colony of Magellanic penguins hops to its own beat.

Puerto Madryn is a good base from which to visit Península Valdés. Those looking to get even closer can arrange boat trips from Puerto Pirámides, before taking a day trip to the colonial outposts of Trelew and Gaiman, where you can refuel in a traditional Welsh tea shop over 10,000 kilometres from the residents' ancestral homeland.

There's certainly no other place quite like this windswept coastline. Where else can you find a region so wild and desolate, yet so brimming with life?

Explore

PUERTO MADRYN

Puerto Madryn is the typical starting point for exploring the Reserva Faunística Península Valdés. Quiet in summer, the town livens up in winter and spring (June to December), when whale activity peaks. The main part of town is located around Avenida Julio A Roca, which runs parallel to the beachfront. This is where you will find most of the hotels, restaurants and tour companies. Time spent here is all about organising tours to the peninsula, or arranging diving and snorkelling excursions. The town is also a place to scout for whales, which you can see from the beach or high on a cliff at the end of town. That's also where you'll find Ecocentro (Julio Verne 3784, 02965 457470, www.eco centro.org.ar), which features a tower for viewing whales and a touch-pool with live sea creatures. Days in Puerto Madryn are typically spent strolling lazily along the long stretch of wide, sandy beach, which runs from one end of town to the other. There's also the option of renting a bike to visit a nearby colony of sea lions at Punta Lomo.

Slightly further out of town, attractions include Playa el Doradillo (20 kilometres to the north). This is the best place to see whales from the beach: water close to the coast is so deep that they can come within 20 metres of the shoreline.

If you want to walk among elephant seals and even lie next to them, Punta Ninfas is the place. It's located around 75 kilometres south-east of Puerto Madryn.

"If you want to walk among elephant seals and even lie next to them, Punta Ninfas is the place."

RESERVA FAUNÍSTICA PENÍNSULA VALDÉS

Declared a UNESCO World Heritage Site in 1999, the **Reserva Faunística Península Valdés** (admission AR$45) is one of the most important ecosystems on the planet, covering over 4,000 square kilometres. It is made up of arid land, rocky cliffs, wide sandy bays, mud flats and salt pans, with an abundance of different species of animals, including guanacos (camelid animals), *choique* (like ostriches), *maras* (Patagonian hares), armadillos and grey foxes. However, the main attraction is, without a doubt, the marine life that inhabits the reserve's coastline.

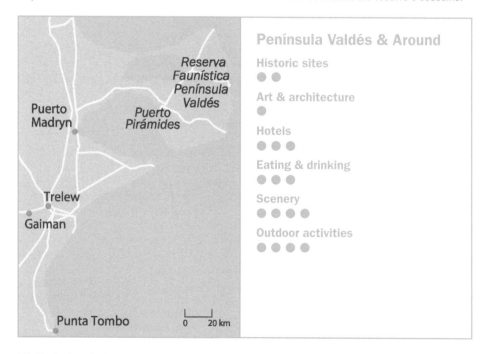

Península Valdés & Around

Historic sites
● ●

Art & architecture
●

Hotels
● ● ●

Eating & drinking
● ● ●

Scenery
● ● ● ●

Outdoor activities
● ● ● ●

Península Valdés.

A must-see is Punta Delgada, where you can look out from a rocky perch to the frothy sea swirling below and to the large colonies of elephant seals and sea lions gathering by the shore. Sea lions can also be seen at Punta Cantor and Punta Norte, where the ferocious orca whales hunt from February to April.

A worthwhile stop is Isla de los Pájaros, an important seabird colony on an island just off the coast; peak viewing times are between September and December. Although you are not allowed to go on to the island, park rangers have set up telescopes and binoculars along the coast. The Isla de los Pájaros was part of Antoine de Saint-Exupéry's inspiration for *Le Petit Prince* (*The Little Prince*), a novel loved by both children and adults. It is said that Saint-Exupéry, who lived in Argentina from 1929 to 1931, flew over the island and decided it resembled a boa constrictor that had just eaten an elephant – an image he then wrote into the tale.

"You don't need to worry about finding your sea legs: from the shore at Puerto Pirámides you can observe dolphins and whales jumping and slapping their tails."

Whale-watching tours typically start in **Puerto Pirámides**, a village set in a small bay hidden by rocks, with a gorgeous long, sandy beach. You don't need to worry about finding your sea legs here: from the shore, you can observe dolphins and whales jumping and slapping their tails. The village is small but offers countless activities, including diving, snorkelling and kayaking (*see p260*).

All of the main points on the peninsula can be visited in one day, but bear in mind that the majority of your day trip will be spent in a minibus. To spend more time in the reserve, hire your own car and stay in Puerto Pirámides or one of the estancias on the peninsula itself.

Located at the entrance of the reserve, the Centro de Visitantes Istmo C Ameghino (visitors' centre) is open daily from 8am to 8pm. It's worthwhile making this your first port of call before heading into the reserve, as the centre provides detailed information about all resident animals and marine life. There is also a whale skeleton and information about the mammal's breeding and feeding patterns. Park guides are on hand to dispense maps of the reserve and answer any questions you might have. The centre also has a viewing tower, where you can relax into a comfortable sofa and enjoy vast vistas over the peninsula. Admission is free.

TRELEW

In 1886, Welsh immigrants began construction of a railway, which, in turn, brought about the creation of the town of **Trelew**. Vestiges of Trelew's Welsh past can still be seen today through its museums, statues and the occasional Welsh speaker. A day trip to Trelew will suffice to see the best of its sights.

Trelew has had a few famous visitors, including American outlaws Butch Cassidy and the Sundance Kid, who fled to Bolivia and then Patagonia at the turn of the 20th century after a series of bank robberies across the US, including one that became the inspiration for the eponymous movie. Butch and The Kid stayed at the Hotel Touring Club (Avenida Fontana 240) in the town centre. The hotel bar is a good place to stop for a drink and admire the artefacts and black and white photographs from Trelew's past. While you are there, you can ask to see the room in which the infamous pair slept, along with photos and other memorabilia from their six-month stay in the town. Just ask the bar staff when you go in.

Some 16 kilometres from Trelew, Playa Unión is the playground of the locals, who come here to laze on the beach during summer, while Puerto Rawson attracts the tourists for dolphin-watching tours (*see p260*).

Museo Paleontológico Egidio Feruglio (MEF)

Avenida Fontana 140 (02965 432100/www.mef.org.ar). Open Sept-Mar 9am-8pm daily. Apr-Aug 10am-6pm Mon-Fri; 10am-8pm Sat, Sun. Admission AR$25.
This is an excellent museum – and Trelew's best. It exhibits the bones and fossils of prehistoric horses and rhinos, as well as dinosaurs such as the mythological-sounding giganotosaurus and titanosaurus, which have been found in the area. The displays are innovative and engaging, and there is a fantastic video explaining how life began on our planet. Children will love the large-scale dinosaur sculptures and glass floors with fossils inside. Information is provided in English and Spanish.

Museo Pueblo de Luis

Avenida 9 de Julio & Avenida Fontana (02965 424062). Open 8am-8pm Mon-Fri; 2-8pm Sun. Admission AR$2.
This museum is housed in the town's original train station. It follows the history of the town, from the dwellings of the native Tehuelche people to the building of the railway and the Welsh colonisation. It features photographs and artefacts, including old typewriters and stoves. Most of the descriptions are in Spanish, but non-Spanish speakers will still find it worth a visit.

Clockwise from top:
Museo Paleontológico
Egidio Feruglio; Península
Valdés; Gaiman tea-house.

PUNTA TOMBO

This three-kilometre-long peninsula, covered in sand and gravel, is open from October to March (admission AR$35 adults, AR$17.50 children). A desolate-looking place, it is home to the world's largest Magellanic penguin colony. Over half a million penguins arrive here to breed every year between September and March, when the weather gets warmer. The nests are built under bushes or in small burrows, which are visible to onlookers. Magellanic penguins are monogamous and meet up with their partner year after year to breed together, females being able to identify their partners through their unique calls.

The reserve is located around 180 kilometres south of Trelew. At the entrance, there is an information booth and some food stands. Make sure you follow the designated paths and use the special viewing areas so as not to disturb the penguins. The reserve is also home to guanacos, *choique* and seabirds such as cormorants and petrels. Tours to visit Punta Tombo can be organised from Puerto Madryn or Trelew.

GAIMAN

After Welsh settlers founded the town of Trelew, they carried on building the railroad to the area that became **Gaiman**. They built the first house here in 1874, and lived peacefully alongside the native Tehuelche people. The word 'Tehuelche' means 'stony' or 'rocky point', so the Welsh called their village Gaiman, which is the equivalent Welsh word.

Pretty tea-houses and stone cottages make up this quaint village. The villagers here are very proud of their Welsh heritage, and are actively working to perpetuate the language and culture. The tourist information office has an excellent map showing a route around all the historic houses and buildings in the area. Housed in the old train station, the Museo Regional Galés (28 de Julio 705, closed Mon) is also worth a stop to gain some insight into the town's history. The museum has machinery, tools and clothing on display.

Parque Paleontológico Bryn Gwyn

Zona Rural de Bryn Gwyn (02965 432100/www.mef. org.ar). Open Mar-Sept 11am-5pm (last entry 3pm) daily. Oct-Feb 10am-6pm (last entry 4pm) daily. Admission AR$10; AR$5 children; free under-6s.
Situated 8km from the town centre, this outdoor park is maintained by the MEF museum in Trelew (*see p258*). A two-hour trek will take you past the different fossils and bones found in the area, which belonged to prehistoric mammals and fishes as well as dinosaurs. Make sure you take warm clothes in the winter, and water and sunscreen in the summer, as there is no shade or shelter along the way. The park sometimes closes due to bad weather, so it is best to check with MEF beforehand.

OUTDOOR ACTIVITIES

Most tour companies are located on the main road parallel to the beach in Puerto Madryn. They typically offer trips to Península Valdés, Punta Tombo (the best place to see penguins), Punta Ninfas, and to Puerto Rawson to see the Commerson's dolphins (*tonina*). Recommended operators include Bottazzi (Boulevard Almirante Brown 85, 02965 474110, www.titobottazzi.com) and Cuyun Co (Avenida Julio A Roca 165, 02965 451845, www.cuyunco.com.ar).

Tours of the peninsula last all day and stop at all of the main points. Standard prices don't include entrance to the park, whale-watching tours or lunch.

> "If you're lucky, you might even get to see whales and dolphins while sea kayaking in the bay."

Whale-watching excursions can be arranged by Hydrosport (Puerto Pirámides, Primer Bajada, 02965 495065, www.hydrosport.com.ar) or Bottazzi, either at its Puerto Madryn office (*see above*) or in Puerto Pirámides (Primer Bajada, 02965 495050). Most tours of the peninsula will stop in Puerto Pirámides for a few hours so that people can take a whale-watching tour.

Diving and snorkelling are also big pastimes here. Most companies offer diving with sea lions, night dives, beginners' dives and courses; enquire at Lobo Larsen (Puerto Madryn, Avenida Julio A Roca 885, shop 2, 02965 470277, www.lobolarsen.com) or Aquatours Buceo (Puerto Madryn, Avenida Julio A Roca 550, 02965 451954, www.aquatours.com.ar).

Sea kayaking tours leave from Puerto Pirámides and explore the bay, usually passing colonies of elephant seals and sea lions. If you're lucky, you might even get to see whales and dolphins. Try Patagonia Explorers (Avenida de las Bellenas, Puerto Pirámides, 02965 15 416843 mobile, www.patagoniaexplorers.com). Kayaks can also be hired on the beach in Puerto Madryn.

Puerto Rawson is where you can go to see the Commerson's dolphins. One company that offers specific excursions to see these creatures is Estación Marítima (02965 498508, www. estacionmaritima.com.ar). Note that whale diving is illegal, and anyone caught doing it could face time in prison.

For horse riding tours around the area, call Laura or Juan Pablo (02965 15 573638 mobile, 02965 15 654997 mobile).

Magellanic penguins
in Punta Tombo.

Estancia Rincón Chico.

Eat

Cantina El Náutico

Puerto Madryn *Avenida Julio A Roca 790 (02965 471404/www.cantinaelnautico.com.ar). Open noon-2.45pm, 8-11.45pm daily. ££. Seafood/Modern.*
This fun restaurant, filled with nautical paraphernalia, is a local favourite. The food ranges from seafood paella and oregano chicken to grilled lobster. Don't forget to check out the large selection of desserts, such as flamed pancake with rum, or *queso con dulce* (cheese with sweet potato jelly). The restaurant is also a favourite among Argentinian celebrities, as the photos covering the walls attest.

Las Dunas

Puerto Madryn *Boulevard Almirante Brown 1900 (02965 457403). Open noon-3.30pm, 8pm-midnight daily. ££. Italian/Traditional.*
This very popular beachfront pizzeria has a funky vibe, with red walls, white beach-style furniture and traditional Argentinian music. The pizzas here are delicious and fresh; some diners insist they're the best in town. Varied topping options include rocket and walnuts or eggs and bacon. The menu also includes *ñoquis* (gnocchi), *ravioles* and *canelones* with a choice of sauces, as well as a handful of seafood and meat dishes.

> "Mediterráneo offers the tastiest seafood in town, with sea views complemented by dishes such as peppered octopus and salmon with almonds."

Estela

Puerto Madryn *Roque Sáenz Peña 27 (02965 451573). Open noon-2.30pm, 8pm-midnight Tue-Sun. ££. Parrilla.*
Set back from the road in a wooden Swiss-style chalet and decorated with Welsh knick-knacks, Estela provides an intimate setting to enjoy excellently prepared barbecued meats. Dishes include beef roll with apple, and grilled fish with blue cheese. Of the home-made pastas, the spaghetti bake is particularly good.

Margarita

Puerto Madryn *Roque Sáenz Peña 15 (02965 470885). Open 10am-4pm, 7pm-5am daily. £££. Modern.*
This traditional yet sophisticated pub is a great place to go out for a few glasses of wine or a cocktail or two. Choose a small table next to the window or a romantic booth on the upper level. The kitchen serves nicely presented roasted meats and grilled fish, as well as a large selection of pizzas. On Friday and Saturday nights, there is a DJ and dancing for added entertainment value.

Mediterráneo

Puerto Madryn *Boulevard Almirante Brown 1040 (02965 458145). Open noon-3.30pm, 8pm-midnight Mon-Sat. £££. Seafood.*
This bright and cheery restaurant, which serves some of the tastiest seafood in town, offers great sea views to perfectly complement dishes such as peppered octopus and salmon with almonds. It also has a good selection of wines, and there's an area where kids can play while the adults imbibe. In summer, umbrellas and deckchairs are set up on the beach, and food can be ordered outside as well.

La Taska Beltza

Puerto Madryn *9 de Julio 461 (02965 474003). Open noon-3pm, 7pm-midnight Tue-Sun. £££. No credit cards. Traditional.*
This classic Basque restaurant has an intimate atmosphere, with iron fixtures and soft lighting. Elegant and romantic, it serves some beautifully-prepared Patagonian delicacies. Try the black ravioli stuffed with spider-crab, hake with red pepper sauce, or crunchy bruschetta with Patagonian lamb. Top it off with a delicious dessert such as home-made banana ice-cream smothered in caramel and dark chocolate.

Ty Cymraeg

Gaiman *Abraham Matthews 74 (02965 491010). Open 2-7.30pm daily. £££. Café.*
This spacious riverside tea-house comes complete with lace tablecloths and tea-cosies. The owner, Mónica, is very proud of her Welsh heritage and has numerous photos and Welsh heirlooms on display. There are eight different kinds of cakes on the menu, including Welsh fruitcake and a nut cake with mocha cream, as well as home-made scones, bread and jam. If you don't finish it all – which is likely – Monica will wrap it up in a doggy bag for you.

Ty Nain

Gaiman *Hipólito Yrigoyen 283 (02965 491126). Open 4-6.30pm daily. £££. No credit cards. Café.*
For a more intimate Welsh tea, far from the tour groups (they're not allowed), try this sweet little tea-house, set in a whitewashed stone cottage with ivy growing up the walls. Here, you can enjoy a Welsh tea of cakes, scones and home-made jams, surrounded by frilly white lace and delicate china teacups. There's also a small museum filled with Welsh artefacts.

El Viejo Molino

Trelew *Gales 250 (02965 428019). Open noon-3pm, 8pm-midnight daily. £££. Parrilla/Traditional.*
Set in an 1800s mill, this chic restaurant is in a class of its own in the city of Trelew. It's two storeys high, with ornate lights hanging from the ceilings, and tender meats roasting in an open glass parrilla below. There are *folklore* and tango shows on Saturday nights.

Stay

La Casona del Río

5km S of Trelew *Establecimiento Rural Chacra 105, access via Calle Capitán Murga (02965 438343/ www.lacasonadelrio.com.ar). ££.*
This charming farmhouse, with its green turret roof and vines and roses climbing up the brick walls, is the perfect spot for a relaxing, peaceful stay. It is set among golden fields and green forests, with a burbling river at the back. Yanina (the Argentinian owner) and her family are wonderful hosts. They enjoy entertaining guests with traditional folk music, and make delicious home-cooked meals such as roasted lamb or rabbit, followed by apple pie made to Yanina's mother's recipe. Thai massages, horse riding and tennis are also offered.

La Elvira

Península Valdés *Hipólito Yrigoyen 257, office 2 (02965 474248/www.laelvira.com.ar). Open Sept-late Apr. ££££. No credit cards.*
This modern, working sheep estancia provides eight double rooms, decorated in floral patterns and pastel colours. The big, white building stands out against the flat landscape and features a library with a large selection of books, and an outdoor deck with a swimming pool. There is also a country barn, which serves as the hotel's restaurant, with roasted estancia-raised lamb on the menu. Guided tours of the reserve and talks on the area can be arranged, and guests can try their hand at sheep shearing. There are options for breakfast only, or half and full board. The breakfast is exceptionally good, featuring a range of sweets that includes regional jams, pies, pastries and fudge brownies.

"Miles of empty golden terrain stretch along one side of Faro Punta Delgada, while the wild, whipped-up sea lies on the other."

Estancia Rincón Chico

Península Valdés *Boulevard Almirante Brown 1783 (02965 471733/www.rinconchico.com.ar). Open mid Sept-mid Apr. ££££. No credit cards.*
Expect to find escapism of the highest order on the remote plains surrounding Estancia Rincón Chico. There are great views from the wood and glass building, whose veranda is ideal for watching wildlife and the spectacularly colourful sunsets. The eight rooms are light and bright, each with en suite bathrooms, snug duvets and mountains of pillows. Hire a bicycle to explore the area, go on a guided tour around the reserve, or take advantage of the private 15km beach.

Faro Punta Delgada – Hotel de Campo

Península Valdés *Punta Delgada (02965 458444/ www.puntadelgada.com). ££££.*
Miles of empty golden terrain stretch along one side of this large hotel complex, while the wild, whipped-up sea and rocks lie on the other. It is located on the Península Valdés, in a remote location that is perfect for breezy cliff-top walks to the local lighthouse or to view the elephant seals. The complex includes a traditional wood-lined restaurant that serves local dishes such as barbecued meats. There is also a pub with a pool table and intimate seating areas that are perfect for relaxing after a day exploring the peninsula. The hotel offers 27 basic but warmly decorated rooms. Trekking, horse riding excursions and 4x4 tours can also be arranged.

Hostal El Cuenco

Gaiman *Fontana 300 (02965 15 505963 mobile/ www.hostalelcuenco.com.ar). £££. No credit cards.*
Surrounded by willow trees, these Swiss-style, triangular chalets are located in the countryside just outside Gaiman. The wood-panelled interiors come complete with self-catering kitchens and lounges with rustic, open fireplaces. The upstairs bedrooms are small but have charm, with the added bonus of balconies overlooking the gardens. There are also parrillas for making your own Argentinian *asado*.

Hostería Paradise

Puerto Pirámides *Segunda Bajada (02965 495030/www.hosteriaparadise.com.ar). £££.*
A small and intimate place, Hostería Paradise is set in the village of Puerto Pirámides. The white tower with brightly painted sea life at the front may verge on tacky, but the rooms are cosy and have lots of character. The only drawback is that some of the rooms only have partial sea views; the suites provide the best views, and come with their own jacuzzi. The attached restaurant, a cheery affair decorated with fishing paraphernalia and serving fresh seafood, is one of the best in Puerto Pirámides. Try the trout with lemon purée, or the grilled stingray.

Hostería Ty'r Haul

Gaiman *Sarmiento 121 (02965 491880/ www.hosteriatyrhaul.com.ar). £. No credit cards.*
This Welsh-style B&B is set in a beautiful building that was built in 1907 and, years later, was restored to its former glory. At the top of the house is a gold-coloured dome, which gives the place its Welsh name, meaning 'sun house'. The interior spaces are decorated in shades of red and orange, with wrought-iron lamps and antique furniture. The rooms are simple, with soft lighting and bare brick walls. The B&B also features its own tea room, where you can tuck into Welsh cakes in front of the open fireplaces.

Posada Los Mimbres

Gaiman *Chacra 211 (02965 491299/ www.posadalosmimbres.com.ar). £. No credit cards.*
This delightful little B&B is located in the farmland just outside Gaiman. You can choose to stay in the old or new house, both of which are filled with comfortable furniture and have big fireplaces to keep you warm during the cold winters. The restaurant offers traditional Patagonian food,

featuring ingredients picked fresh from the orchard. Bike rentals and organised local tours are also available.

"Beautiful sea views abound at Territorio Hotel; whales can be seen, and even heard, from the bedrooms."

Las Restingas Hotel de Mar
Puerto Pirámides *Primera Bajada (02965 495101/ 011 4519 2526/www.lasrestingas.com). ££££.*

The only hotel on the beachfront in Puerto Pirámides, Las Restingas has 12 rooms, each with a choice of sea or village views. All the rooms are bright and feature exposed brick walls and private balconies or terraces. The hotel has an excellent restaurant, with a terrace overlooking the sea that is great for sundowners. There is also a spa, gym and swimming pool facing outwards towards the sea.

Territorio Hotel
Puerto Madryn *Boulevard Almirante Brown 3251 (02965 470050/www.hotelterritorio.com.ar). £££.*
First appearances can be deceiving with this large, warehouse-like waterfront hotel. The interior comes as a pleasant surprise, with its rustic furniture, local sculptures and photographs and warm colours. Beautiful sea views abound; from June to December, whales can be seen – and even heard – from the bedrooms. Services include a full spa, bar and restaurant serving a fresh, seasonal menu.

Factfile

When to go
Try to time your visit to coincide with the whale season (June to mid December). At this time, you will be able to see penguins, which breed in Punta Tombo from around October to March, as well as the many types of birds that inhabit Isla de los Pájaros from September to December. Outside these periods, you can still see elephant seals and sea lions, which stay all year round, as well as orcas from February to April.

From June to September, the weather is typically cold and windy. At the beginning of October, temperatures start to warm up, with the hottest months being December, January and February. Outside of the whale season and during the coldest months, many estancias and rural hotels, as well as some restaurants, are closed.

Getting there
By car or bus from Buenos Aires, the journey to Puerto Madryn takes between 18 and 20 hours. Bus services are offered by Don Otto (011 4315 7700, www.donotto.com.ar), Andesmar (0261 405 4300, www.andesmar.com) and Expreso Que Bus (011 4311 9229, www.quebus.com.ar). All go to Puerto Madryn from Retiro bus station in Buenos Aires. Most trips are overnight.

Aerolíneas Argentinas (www.aerolineas.com.ar) flies to Trelew from Aeroparque Jorge Newbery in Buenos Aires. Direct flights take approximately two hours.

Getting around
Local bus services go between Puerto Madryn and Trelew, and between Trelew and Gaiman or Rawson. The companies 28 de Julio and Mar y Valle run hourly departures from Puerto Madryn to Trelew, and take one hour. Buses to Gaiman and Rawson leave frequently from the Trelew bus station. Once in Rawson, you can take the Bahía bus or a local taxi to Playa Unión and Puerto Rawson. Buses also travel between Puerto Madryn and Puerto Pirámides twice a day, once in the morning and once in the evening.

Be aware that as Puerto Pirámides is within the limits of a national park, you will have to pay the AR$45 entrance fee even if you are only staying in the village.

Tourist information
Puerto Madryn Avenida Julio A Roca 223 (02965 453504, www.madryn.gov.ar). Open 7am-9pm Mon-Fri; 8am-9pm Sat, Sun.
Puerto Pirámides Avenida de las Ballenas (02965 495048, www.puertopiramides.gov.ar). Open 8am-6pm daily.
Puerto Rawson & Playa Unión Avenida Guillermo Rawson (02965 496887). Open 8am-8pm Mon-Fri; 10am-8pm Sat, Sun.
Trelew Mitre 387 (02965 420139, www.trelew patagonia.gov.ar). Open 8am-8pm Mon-Fri; 9am-9pm Sat, Sun.
Gaiman Belgrano 571 (02965 491571, www.gaiman.gov.ar). Open high season 9am-8pm Mon-Sat; 11am-8pm Sun. Low season 9am-6pm Mon-Sat; 11am-6pm Sun.

Internet
Many hotels have internet or Wi-Fi. There is a large internet café in Puerto Madryn on Avenida Roca & 28 de Julio. Trelew has internet cafés located around the main square and Plaza Independencia, and Gaiman has a few dotted along its main street, Avenida E Tello.

Left & below: Mar de las Pampas; right: birdlife in Cariló.

Pinamar, Cariló & Mar de las Pampas

Argentina

Upmarket beach towns, set amid a pine forest.

Giving off a haughty alpine air despite their sea-level location, Pinamar, Cariló and Mar de las Pampas have the humble pine cone to thank for their success. Seeds sown 80 years ago stabilised the dunes along this 20-kilometre stretch of Atlantic coast, and pine trees now stand to attention, guarding the wide, sandy beaches. You can't help but unwind here: the pine scent revitalises the weariest of minds, while traipsing the sands provides a free pedicure for sore city feet.

A four-hour hop from the capital, the towns of Pinamar and Cariló, with Valeria del Mar sandwiched between them, and Mar de las Pampas 25 kilometres south, are a summertime playground of the smart set, including Argentinian A-listers and former presidents. Cranking up in December, the area awakens from its winter slumbers and the dunes and forest spring back to life.

The past few years have seen a construction boom along this stretch of coastline, with alpine chalets and modern apart-hotels popping up like the large edible mushrooms found under the pines after a dousing of rain. Unlike the crowded resort of Mar del Plata, where you'll fight for a patch of sand at the height of summer, the Costa Verde (or Green Coast, as the area is sometimes known) is a much classier affair, with beaches extending to 300 metres wide in places, providing ample space to stretch out. Beach and turf polo competitions bring in the world's best players, while every day can seem like Friday with fresh Atlantic fish on the menu.

But deciding to visit the Costa Verde isn't quite as easy as it sounds. One enduring conundrum remains: should you take advantage of 15 hours of daily summer sun from January to March, or enjoy blustery winter walks on deserted beaches followed by tea next to a roaring log fire? That choice is yours.

Explore

PINAMAR

The summer experience in **Pinamar** is all about glitz and glamour in a small beachside town. Although getting back to nature with a forest walk or a round of golf at the 18-hole Links course (Shaw 1640, 02254 491815, www.linkspinamar.com.ar) features on many agendas here, most visitors tend to be of the young and rich variety, and are more interested in good times. Come November, rustic shopping malls such as Paseo el Reloj (Bunge & Libertador) open their doors, beach clubs set up their *carpas* (tents) and Argentina's fashionably famous pop down to be papped.

Founded in the 1960s, Pinamar has succumbed to little more than a handful of high-rise builds, meaning visitor numbers are kept in check. More 24-hour than Cariló or Mar de las Pampas, the town leaps to attention in January and February: beachside catwalk shows lure top models down from Buenos Aires; car companies will spin you across the northern dunes; surf schools set up shacks; and the sophisticated *buena onda* (good vibe) reverberates from beach to forest.

Nightlife in summer is lively but not outrageous, with enough going on to pick and mix as you please. Those looking for a good time go bar-hopping along the main street, Avenida Bunge (pronounced Boon-gay, thanks to its Belgian founder), before ending the night at Ku (Quintana and Corso) for *cumbia* and house music. Summer attracts big-name national DJs to the beachside club.

Pinamar is also the perfect bolt-hole for a winter weekend. You can get the best table without reserving, tea rooms rustle up calorie-laden delicacies and the town relives its giddy summer memories. Except this time everyone's wearing clothes – and plenty of them.

Casa Museo Víctor Magariños D

Del Libertador, between Picaflores & Odisea (02254 488623). Open Jan-Feb 6-8pm daily. Admission free.
Painter and architect Victor Magariño's former home was built in the middle of nowhere back in 1967. Since his death in 1993, the little wooden studio with a beautiful wild garden has housed his abstract paintings and installations. Wander the studio at your leisure; tea is provided, should you need refreshment. Note that the opening hours can be sporadic, so it is best to call ahead or check with the Pinamar tourist office (*see p277*).

CARILÓ

An enchanted forest springs to mind as you drive down Cerezo (Cherry Tree Road), the sandy drag into **Cariló**, Argentina's most upmarket beach resort. Pines and eucalyptus trees embrace this not-so-main road, which leads to the town centre.

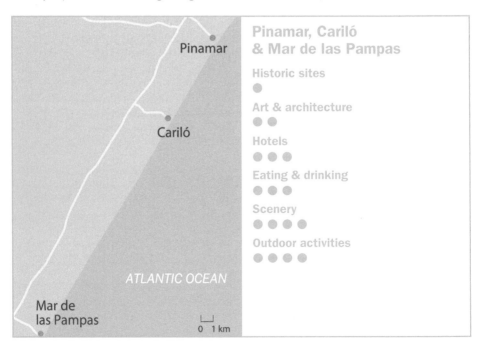

Pinamar, Cariló & Mar de las Pampas

Historic sites
●

Art & architecture
● ●

Hotels
● ● ●

Eating & drinking
● ● ●

Scenery
● ● ● ●

Outdoor activities
● ● ● ●

Pinamar.

In summer, Cariló (which means 'green dune' in the Mapuche language) is all about upper-crust families spending quality time together: teens too cool for their parents are bundled off to Pinamar, while younger kids and their grandparents do their bonding here. This is the main reason why wealthier Argentinians tend to rent private accommodation rather than hotel rooms.

Roads in Cariló are romantically named after trees, such as Paraíso (paradise), or birds (Gaviota, meaning seagull). The architecture is a blend of rustic and modern, with the odd Spanish villa thrown in. The floor-reaching Alpine roof previously in fashion has been substituted for box-like homes combining wood with grey stone.

> ## "Director Francis Ford Coppola chose this stretch of coast to replicate the Hamptons for his film *Tetro*."

Cariló's expansive, dune-surrounded beaches are golden, clean and laden with pretty violet shells. In winter 2008, director Francis Ford Coppola chose this stretch of coast to replicate the Hamptons for his film *Tetro*. Street lights and overhead cables are notably absent, as is asphalt, which residents believe would turn Cariló into just another beach town (*see right* **It's not easy being green**).

MAR DE LAS PAMPAS

In 1957, three Argentinian accountants purchased the land that comprises **Mar de las Pampas**, Las Gaviotas and Mar Azul and, by hand, they planted a pine forest to stabilise the dunes. Mar de las Pampas town was founded just 16 years ago, so it adopted the best characteristics of older sisters Pinamar and Cariló – namely the sandy roads and detached, rustic houses built with quebracho wood. In this ultra-relaxed resort, city dwellers manage to leave their neuroses back in Buenos Aires. The town attracts everyone from families with pre-teenage children to gay couples, all with the common aim of unwinding amid the natural beauty; it's hard to feel hemmed in in a town covered 70 per cent by forest.

Mónica García, guide to the Museo Histórico in the nearby town of Villa Gesell, says, 'Mar de las Pampas is like a natural spa. Walking barefoot on sand helps your circulation, and the seawater is medicinal and can even help to cure a cold.' García gives talks on the area's ecology and environment, as well as organising birdwatching activities, helping visitors to recognise the importance of maintaining a natural harmony in the area. For groups of ten or more, she can provide a translator (to book, email monica mar24@hotmail.com, with 'guided visit Mar de las Pampas' as the subject line; the cost is AR$35).

Faro Querandí
12km S of Mar de las Pampas. Open Dec-Mar 2-5pm daily. Admission AR$2.

A black and white edifice built in 1922, the Querandi lighthouse can be seen from up to 38 kilometres away. Vertigo suffers probably shouldn't attempt the staircase, but others can puff their way to the top and step out on to the rather rickety deck, where the biting wind may be ferocious but the views are phenomenal: think Sahara meets oasis meets Atlantic. For a real bone-shaking experience, take a door-to-door guided tour with English speaker Edi Ferrari (02255 463118) in one of his 4x4 vehicles – he's been roaming the dunes for around 30 years and knows the area like the back of his hand. En route to the lighthouse, you'll drive through the sandy streets of neighbouring villages Las Gaviotas and Mar Azul, before crossing on to the beach (where the use of vehicles is permitted). Note that the Faro Querandi nature reserve is only accessible from the beach.

OUTDOOR ACTIVITIES

The Costa Verde is an ideal spot for some sea-fishing. A standard four-hour trip (bait and rods included) involves joining a weather-beaten sea dog and his crew for a trip out into the Atlantic, where you can expect to catch native fish such as pejerrey and dorado, even if you're a novice. Sharks can be seen from October, so bring a camera to prove you grappled with one. You'll find a number of operators in Pinamar at Avenida del Mar and the pier, including Sólo Pesca (02254 495063) and Tulumei (02254 488696).

For golf, stick to Cariló, where the club is the town's nucleus (Cariló Golf Club, Ñandú & Perdiz, 02254 470044). Players can enjoy 26-yard fairways on an 18-hole course in the heart of the forest. Lessons are available.

An off-road adventure will take you to places others can't – and don't know how to – reach. In Cariló, try Giant Jeep (Boyero & Casuarina, 02254 487951, 02267 15 522216 mobile). Once you get to the beach, give sandboarding in the dunes a shot. Alternatively, there's quad biking in Pinamar (Hannibal, Júpiter 971, 02254 494555) or Cariló (Motorrad, Boyero & Cerezo, 02254 470437). But avoid using these mean machines in Mar de Las Pampas, where their presence is not welcome.

You can also take a horse riding trip over the dunes; note that although hard hats are not usually worn, they are readily available. In Cariló, try Dos Montes on Zorzal and Cedro (02254 480045, dosmontes@telpin.com.ar).

It's not easy being green

The Costa Verde and its unique beach-forest combination is the jewel – or should that be emerald – in the Atlantic Coast's crown. The area's 20,000 residents actively try to maintain its green airs and graces, and they regularly take action to make their voices heard.

Around 200 families live in Cariló on a permanent basis. In 2005, they marched down the sandy streets to demonstrate against the local council, which had been muttering about asphalting calles Cerezo and Divisadero, the two arteries leading in and out of the town. The principal streets in Pinamar and nearby towns Valeria del Mar and Ostende had already succumbed to this fate, which made Cariló's residents even more adamant about retaining its element of rusticity.

Driving slowly down Cariló's sandy roads is a necessity, so pedestrians can wander about safely, carbon footprint in mind, day and night. Access can become an issue when it rains because the sand turns into sticky, muddy craters, but visitors continue to choose Cariló above other towns specifically to get an injection of nature into their system.

Although the area is now going through a construction boom, architects' plans are closely scrutinised. Houses are meant to be designed bearing nature in mind, and permission from the council is required before any pine tree can be cut down. That's not to say that some property owners, eager to maximise the sunlight, don't encourage illicit chopping.

Lumberjacks have been known to run off into the night, mid-fell, when confronted by police.

In 2006, people-power struck again in Cariló, bringing the construction of a cinema complex to a standstill. This time, the Sociedad de Fomento (neighbours' association) took out an injunction against the developers so that building work ceased for two years, leaving an enormous, half-built construction standing in the heart of town. A compromise was eventually reached, and in December 2008 the two-storey Galería Cilene, wooden and rustic-looking, finally opened. The battle, not the war, had been won.

In Mar de las Pampas, residents are equally feisty, but their bugbear is the quad bike. While Cariló and Pinamar are more accepting of the four-wheeled machine buzzing about, Mar de las Pampas is firmly against it. It is forbidden to take quad bikes on to the beach as the vibrations they create is detrimental to the dune system. Locals will wag their fingers in disapproval and shout 'No!' at any driver they see going through town.

In addition, Mar de las Pampas' beach club was recently rebuilt in order to facilitate the shifting sands. The owners not only had to move the building a few metres, but also had to reconstruct it on stilts because the neighbours' association demanded it so. Permission will not be granted for additional beach clubs in the town, much to the delight of the area's residents and discerning tourists.

Mar de las Pampas.

A day at a beach club (*balneario*) is a summer staple, and Pinamar and Cariló have their fair share of such places. The clubs have excellent facilities, including restaurants, swimming pools masseurs and exercise classes. Pinamar's centrally located Posta Sur (Avenida del Mar & De Los Tritones, 02254 400690) is owned and run by English-speaker Marcela Crespo, and offers t'ai chi chu'an and swimming classes, among other activities. At Cariló's Divisadero (Acacia & the beach, 02254 570381), you can lounge about on a large white pouffe, before taking a dip in the pool, then the ocean.

In summer, there is no shortage of surf schools. Take a class at Cariló's Escuela de Surf, in front of Cozumel beach club (Acacia & the beach, 02254 470246), or at Parador Robinson Crusoe in Pinamar (Avenida del Mar Sur & Simbad el Marinero, 02254 401657), then spend the evening lounging in a hammock, listening to reggae and ska bands.

Eat

Camelia Sensi

Cariló *Boyero 1471 (02254 571157). Open 11am-4pm, 7pm-midnight daily. £££. Café/Modern.*
Fondue is one speciality at this multi-level hidey-hole, run by the owners of Valeria del Mar's classic steak house Santoro (Espora & Bouchard, 02254 401231). As service can suffer at busy times, an alternative is to pop in at teatime for a hefty piece of cake and a *submarino* (a glass of hot milk with a baton of chocolate stirred in).

> "For the area's best calamares, lightly battered and fresh out of the pan, head to the locals' favourite beach club, Cozumel."

La Casa del Mar

Mar de las Pampas *El Lucero y Roca (02255 454700). Open Dec-Easter 12.30-4pm, 8pm-1am daily. Apr-Nov 12.30-4pm; 8pm-1am Fri-Sun. £££. No credit cards. Modern.*
The European-influenced menu here comes from husband-and-wife team Juan and Fernanda, who previously lived in Spain. Dishes change every few weeks, and have an imaginative edge that sets them apart from standard Argentinian meals. Baked corvine fish or salmon sashimi salad are outstanding; try the accompanying edible flowers.

Casa del Sol

Mar de las Pampas *Cuyo, between Virazón & Roca (02255 453311). Open Dec-Mar noon-4pm, 8pm-midnight daily. Apr-Nov noon-4pm, 8pm-midnight Sat, Sun. £££. No credit cards. Modern.*
Lizzy Tochetto, one of the first residents to set up camp in Mar de las Pampas, runs this former literary café. Share a caprese salad, but ask for extra basil. Follow up with pork *matambre* and sweet potatoes, or the seafood tripod with its succulent prawns. The fruit platter with chocolate fondue is a battle between good and evil.

Cozumel

Cariló *Acacia & the beach (02254 470246). Mar-Easter 9am-9pm daily. Easter-Feb 9am-6pm Fri-Sun. £££. Modern/Seafood.*
For the area's best calamares, lightly battered and fresh out of the pan, head to the locals' favourite beach club, Cozumel, for lunch. A tomato-based fish soup, complete with a floating poached egg and chips for dipping, may not be the healthiest option, but the taste is worth the extra calories. The loaded seafood salad is a lighter alternative. Add a jug of sangria or *clericot*, made with white wine, for a lunch in true summer style.

De Mi Campo

Cariló *Avellano 181 (02254 572862). Open high season noon-3.30pm, 8pm-midnight daily. Low season noon-3pm, 8pm-midnight Fri-Sun. £££. Parrilla.*
With a salad bar to keep the most discerning vegetarian content, this modern and comfortable steak house makes it far too easy to turn a lunch into a whole afternoon of eating and boozing. Watch the world pass by from the front garden, where you're likely to find the friendly resident terrier eager for scraps.

El Dorado

Pinamar *Avenida del Mar, between Bunge & De las Gaviotas (02254 400387/www.eldoradopinamar.com.ar). Open high season 9am-1am daily. Low season 10am-midnight daily. £££. Italian/Seafood.*
A five-star beach club with a fine sea view, El Dorado is known for its attention to detail and extremely high level of service, with career waiters attending to your every whim. Sample home-made pasta, fresh seafood, fish and red meats in its elegant, modern interior. A comprehensive wine list, headed by El Esteco bodega, rounds off an excellent gastronomic experience.

El Granero

Mar de las Pampas *Joaquin V González & Hudson (02255 479548). Open Dec-Easter noon-4pm, 8pm-midnight daily. Easter-Nov noon-4pm, 8pm-midnight Fri-Sun. ££. Parrilla.*
A reservation at this family-run, family-oriented parrilla, which is packed on Saturday nights, is essential in summer. Originally a hotel, this place is home to the only traditional *asador* in town. The mouth-wateringly tasty fried beef empanada has an interesting chive twist, and should be followed by the challenging *parrillada* – a sizzling platter of various meat cuts.

Jalisco

Cariló *Divisadero 1510, Galería Terrazas (02254 571717). Open Dec-Easter 11am-4pm, 7pm-2am daily. Easter-Nov noon-4pm, 8pm-midnight Sat, Sun. ££. International.*
Dishing up larger-than-life tortillas – stuffed with chicken, beef or prawns – that most diners struggle to finish off, Jalisco puts the *picante* back into an otherwise spice-free life on the coast. Ask the chef to ramp up the heat, if you're in urgent need of a wave. There's another branch in Pinamar (Bunge 478, 02254 493166).

El Más Allá

Pinamar *Libertador, 1.5km from the end of the street. (011 15 4478 2820 mobile/www.elmasalla.com.ar). Open Dec-Mar 9am-4pm daily. Apr-Nov 9am-midnight Fri-Sun. ££. No credit cards. Café/Modern.*
If you're without a 4x4 and don't fancy walking, call ahead and the restaurant will send someone to pick you up. This remote and hexagonal beach club, complete with Hawaiian umbrellas, is abuzz with trendy couples and families who demand top-notch facilities, but at a distance from the central beaches. Tuck into a cheese or chocolate fondue, or simply sip a cocktail while watching the waves break.

"Tulumei's own fishermen bring in the catches of the day, which are served on wooden trays with wedges of lemon."

Ona Refugio

Mar de las Pampas *Miguel Cané, no number, between El Lucero & El Ceibo (02255 454414). Open Dec-Easter noon-4pm, 9pm-midnight daily. Easter-Nov noon-4pm, 8pm-midnight Sat, Sun. £££. Italian.*
Kick off proceedings with prosciutto and stuffed fried olives, then move on to the rabbit agnolotti, a meaty pasta dish with a three-mushroom sauce. If you still have a small space, indulge in the *marquis de chocolate*. These hearty modern dishes are cooked by a knowledgeable chef and presented in charming surroundings, with tables set out under the pine trees.

Sociedad Italiana

Pinamar *Eneas 200, between Cazón & Rivadavia (02254 484555). Open high season noon-3pm, 8.30pm-1.30am daily. Low season 8.30pm-midnight Wed-Mon. ££. No credit cards. Italian.*
Inexpensive, simple pasta at the Sociedad Italiana (Italian Society) offers locals a satisfying slice of Italy. Doubling as a language school in winter months, this large restaurant sees queues around the block come summer, and for good

reason. The handmade gnocchi with mushroom sauce is ample for two smaller appetites.

Tamarisco

Valeria del Mar, 2.5km NE of Cariló *Corbeta Cefiro 38 (02254 486656). Open Dec-Easter 9pm-1am daily. Apr-Nov 8.30pm-midnight. ££££. Seafood.*
When the foghorn reverberates around the dunes at 9pm sharp, it's time for a fishy supper. Tamarisco's owner and chef hand-picks his produce each day from Pinamar's Pinapez fishmonger, so the best reaches your plate. Service isn't always on the ball, but the scallops are beyond delectable and the main courses inventive and delicious.

Tulumei

Pinamar *Bunge 64 (02254 488696). Open Nov-Apr noon-4pm, 8pm-1am daily. May-Oct noon-4pm, 8pm-midnight Mon, Thur-Sun. £££. No credit cards. Seafood.*
Tulumei's own fishermen bring in the catches of the day, typically prawns and squid, which are served on wooden trays, with plenty of lemon wedges with which to douse them. Food here is as authentic and fresh as the pine air, and the restaurant is warm and inviting.

La Vieja Ventola

Cariló *Castaño 1551 (02254 572222). Open Dec-Easter noon-3pm, 8pm-midnight daily. ££££. Seafood.*
Owned by the folks behind Cariló Village (*see p276*), this gourmet fish restaurant delivers exactly what it promises: fresh fish, lobster and shellfish galore. Though this ultra-upmarket place is located a few blocks from the main action of the town centre, it still gets absolutely packed; be sure to book ahead in summer.

Viejos Tiempos

Mar de las Pampas *Leoncio Paina, between Cruz del Sur & Peñaloza (02255 479524). Open Oct-Easter noon-midnight daily. Easter-Sept noon-midnight Sat, Sun. £££. No credit cards. International/Traditional.*
Perched on a sand dune, this kitsch Hansel-and-Gretel cottage opened in 1989. Despite the restaurant's deceptive exterior, it specialises in Mexican food, so tuck into enchiladas, nachos and tacos until your stomach screams, '¡Basta! Enough corn-based food!' Make a beeline here in winter for gooey cakes and toasted sandwiches. Defrost your frozen feet by the fire that owner Dardo will whip up out of a single pine cone as soon as you dare to shiver.

Stay

Staying in this lush green coastal area means you're likely to get a beach view and a sunrise to boot. Apart-hotels catering to small groups ensure privacy and the emphasis is always on relaxation, so spas are usually part and parcel of the deal.

Hotels tend to rank between three and four stars and offer great service; but as there are so many restaurants and bars to try in the area,

Above: La Mansion del Bosque. Below: Runa Moraira.

a breakfast-only deal is your best bet. Note that prices in winter can be half the summer rate.

From one-bed chalets to rustic two-bed log cabins and beachfront mansions, private rentals are a popular option for families or groups of friends, offering privacy and space away from the masses. An upfront deposit of up to 50 per cent of the total is normal, and an additional damages deposit may also be required.

A few options are Cariló Casa (Paraíso 665, 02254 570569, 02254 15 457468 mobile, www.carilo-casa.com), La Compañia de Cariló (Local 5, Divisadero 1526, 02254 579040, www.lacompaniadecarilo.com.ar) and Agenda de Cariló (Boyero, between Cerezo & Avellano, 02254 570645).

Bear in mind that it is customary to rent a house for a two-week period in January and February, but easy to rent for just a weekend throughout the rest of the year.

"Just one sand dune away from the beach, Runa Moraira offers eight luxurious stone cabins, and inviting poolside gazebos."

Altos de Ostende Apart & Spa

Ostende, 2km S of Pinamar *Robette & Cherburgo (02254 470244/www.altosdeostende.com.ar). £££. No credit cards.*
Comprising eight apartments, this intimate wood and stone apart-hotel nestles on the outskirts of Pinamar. It's a cost-effective option that still allows for the luxury of a spa, complete with two pools, a jacuzzi and a solarium. Although the accommodation is self-catering, a breakfast with bread baked freshly on the premises is delivered to you at the time of your choice. Guests in the apartments with two-plus rooms can snuggle beside a log fire. Children are made welcome.

Cariló Village

Cariló *Carpintero 1640 (02254 570417/www.carilovillage.com.ar). £££.*
Luxurious log cabins circle an outdoor swimming pool, while peacocks strut on the patio at the first apart-hotel to be built in Cariló. A central forest location means access to local shops and restaurants is easy, and the beach is three sandy blocks away. The excellent La Ronda restaurant – offering buffet and à la carte – may prevent you from ever leaving the two-hectare resort. One sniff of the invigorating, orange-scented incense used in the spa will leave you feeling utterly relaxed.

Casa Grande

Cariló *Aromo 255 (02254 470739/www.casagrandecarilo.com.ar). £££. No credit cards.*
You'll be in the lap of modern luxury at this centrally located apart-hotel. Offering 12 apartments, each with a jacuzzi, fireplace and barbecue for budding *asado* experts, this place allows you to relax in style with the latest technology at your fingertips, should you choose not to leave the forest-side hotel. The health club offers all the standard spa conveniences, including an indoor-outdoor swimming pool, a Finnish bath, sauna and gym.

Hostería la Forêt

Mar de las Pampas *Los Andes & Virazón (02255 472708/www.hosterialaforet.com). ££. No credit cards.*
Set in the middle of the forest, 150m from the water, this no-smoking, adults-only hotel has just eight rooms. Run by hands-on owner Diego, the sleekly modern building is surrounded by a wooden deck, which creates an outdoor living room. Pine trees and evergreens have been incorporated into the construction, keeping nature at the hotel's heart. Superior suites have the luxury of a 180° view of the forest, and a hydromassage bath.

Hotel Costa Cariló

Cariló *Albatros 20, at Jacarandá (02254 572322/www.costacarilo.com). £££.*
Staying at this self-catering beachside apart-hotel makes for a wonderfully peaceful getaway. You can admire the sea views from the balcony of the compact, basic apartments, or sit in the eight-person jacuzzi while gazing up at the forest canopy, courtesy of the glass roof that covers the indoor pool area. Note that children under the age of 14 are not allowed to stay here.

La Mansion del Bosque

Mar de las Pampas *Juez Repetto & R Peñaloza (02255 479555/www.lamansiondelbosque.com). £££.*
It's said that the best materials along the Argentinian coast were used in the construction of Mansion del Bosque, as it was originally slated to be the presidential summer home. When those plans fell through, the mansion was converted into a luxury hotel and spa. As it's situated in the heart of the forest, guests can fall asleep to the sound of pine cones falling on the hardwood floor of the courtyard, and wake up to the incessant chatter of birds. It's worth calling ahead, though, as the hotel has been known to close for a month in September.

Pillmayken Cabañas & Spa

Mar de las Pampas *Julio Roca, between Cuyo & Victoria (02255 461700/www.pillmayken.com.ar). £££.*
Some 40m from the beach and a stone's throw away from the action, this hotel is surrounded by pine and olive trees, and has a touch of the *Flintstones* in its styling. The mix of stone and cypress wood originates from Patagonia, and has been adopted along the Atlantic coast. Submerging yourself in the heated indoor pool or Finnish bath are just two ways to relax in the spa, while reflexology and aromatherapy are among the specialised treatments available.

Puerto Hamlet

Cariló *Cerezo 101, at Avurtarda (02254 570623/ www.puertohamlet.com). ££.*

With fireplaces and carob-wood furnishings in each basic but comfortable log cabin, Puerto Hamlet is an ideal winter choice; on inclement days, you can squirrel yourself away in the cosy clubhouse and spend an afternoon browsing through books in the reading corner. Friendly service adds to the accommodation's popularity with families. It's just one block from the sea, and has an enormous garden that's home to over 100 tree species.

Runa Moraira

Mar de las Pampas *Victoria, between Roca & Virazón (02255 466522/www.runamoraira.com.ar). £££.*

Just one sand dune separates this small complex from the beach – as close to the sands as is legally allowed. There are eight luxurious stone cabins, and inviting poolside gazebos out in the garden. Built in 2004, Runa Moraria means 'love and energy among the pines' – and even if you've forgotten your crystals, comfort levels are high, with modern amenities incorporated in a rustic, attractive environment. The spacious, high-ceilinged apartments are perfect for a good night's sleep, and floor to ceiling windows offer dune views.

El Tennis

Pinamar *Fragata Victoria 4300 (011 5352 9320/ www.eltennis.com). £££.*

If you forget your racket, well, it's game, set and match. This hotel was designed with the next David Nalbandian in mind, so make the most of the ten clay courts, set amid verdant gardens. This sporty beachside resort has 50 log cabins, each with a private terrace with a barbecue. The health club features indoor and outdoor pools and a gym; less active types can sweat it out in the sauna, or indulge in all manner of massages and mud therapies in the spa.

Terrazas al Mar

Pinamar *Avenida del Mar & De las Gaviotas (02254 480900/www.terrazasalmar.com). £££.*

It's a dilemma: you're about to slide into the pool and you glimpse the Atlantic in front of you. What do you do? Dive in, or run ten metres down to the beach? Terrazas al Mar has the coast on its doorstep, indoor and outdoor pools, and is situated just a few metres away from buzzing Avenida Bunge. It also has an excellent modern European restaurant and countless spa and beauty treatments. The rooms are decorated in muted colours and plain furniture, but the scene-stealing sea views more than make up for that. Suites have hot tubs and ocean views.

Factfile

When to go

The area is in full bloom come December. Temperatures reach 30°C during the summer months of January and February, when water-sport activities, fishing trips and fashion shows are at their height – perfect for visitors who are looking for a busy, buzzy holiday. By March, activities start to taper off, and in April you can claim the beach as your own.

Winter (July to September) is all about bracing, blustery beach walks followed up with cake and hot chocolate in a wooden forest tea-house. Many hotels offer spa facilities, so you can have the best of both the great indoors and the great outdoors.

Getting there

By car from Buenos Aires, the journey takes three to four hours and there are two tolls once leaving the capital.

Coach companies El Rápido (011 4314 8799), Plaza (011 4312 9328) and Plusmar (011 4315 3424) run several daily services from Retiro bus station to Pinamar, which take around four hours 30 minutes. Book ahead in summer.

For Mar de las Pampas, it's a five-hour trip by coach to Villa Gesell and a taxi ride from there. You can also fly: Aeródromo Villa Gesell (02255 457301, 02255 454657) is around 14 kilometres from Pinamar. Flights from Aeroparque

Jorge Newbery in Buenos Aires are more frequent during the summer.

Getting around

The journey between Pinamar and Cariló takes around an hour by local bus. Taxis and private hire cabs are reasonable, although prices are significantly higher in summer.

Tourist information

Cariló Boyero & Castaño (02254 570773). Open Jan, Feb 8am-10pm daily. Mar-Dec 10am-5pm Mon, Tue, Thur-Sun.
Mar de las Pampas (central office) Avenida 3 820, between streets 108 & 109, Villa Gesell (02255 478042, www.villagesell.gov.ar). Open Apr-Nov 9am-8pm daily. Dec-Mar 8am-midnight daily.
South office: Paseo 173, at Avenida 3, Villa Gesell (02255 470324). Open Apr-Nov 10am-4pm Thur-Mon; Dec-Mar 10am-6pm daily.
Pinamar Shaw 18 (02254 491680, www. pinamar.gov.ar). Open Jan, Feb 8am-10pm daily. Mar-Dec 8am-10pm Mon-Sat; 10am-6pm Sun.

Internet

Most hotels and many cafés have Wi-Fi. However, in summer the service is often unreliable. In Pinamar, head to Ojalá (Bunge 1107, 02254 480626), which is open from 8am to 2am daily.

Dramatic Landscapes

Top: Barreal del Leoncito. Middle: rafting. Bottom right: Alameda trees. Bottom left: river in Barreal.

Barreal

Argentina

Stargazing in an Andean oasis.

Isolated and unspoilt, Barreal is the tail-end town of the longitudinal Valle de
Calingasta, a gash of green hemmed in by two massive mountain ranges: the
Andean cordillera to the west and the eastern Sierra del Tontal, or *precordillera*,
that separates the region from the provincial capital of San Juan.

Living in the furrowed brow of this seismic zone is a challenge rewarded by
spectacular scenery. Nourished by mineral-rich waters from mountain springs,
the fertile land spills forth with fruits and herbs that perfume the air. The white-
tipped spine of the age-old Andes stands out against a cerulean sky so clear that
the area is home to two astronomical observatories.

In Barreal, life is peaceful and unhurried. The siesta is still observed and doors
are left unlocked. There is no public transport, and the quiet streets are bordered
by poplars and willows; the ring of a bicycle bell is a cheery salutation rather than a
manifestation of road rage. The settlement peters out into the *precordillera* – which
turns from ochre-coloured to rust in the Cuyan sun – while Barreal del Leoncito, a
shimmering dried-out lake bed, laps at its southern extremes.

But Barreal is not all about solemn contemplation of nature's magnificence.
It's also home to a host of adventure-tourism opportunities: you can hurtle through
a torrent of Andean meltwater or skim across the surface of a sun-baked lake bed at
high speed. If you are tempted to abandon civilisation entirely, you can take off on
horseback through mountain passes in the shadow of the mighty Cerro Mercedario.
It's not so bad being stuck between a rock and a hard place.

Explore

The unnumbered streets and somewhat scattered premises of **Barreal** may prove a little baffling to hardened city-dwellers, but losing yourself in the pleasant lanes is all part of the town's appeal. (Addresses have been given here, where possible, with the closest intersection.) Plaza San Martín, where the tourist office is located, is the central hub; wander one kilometre east and you're in the gingerbread peaks of the *precordillera*, or Sierra del Tontal; set off west and you reach Río de los Patos, in the shadow of the indomitable Andes. The main thoroughfare, Avenida Presidente Roca, is where you'll find the town's only bank and a temperamental ATM machine that occasionally runs out of readies.

At the intersection of Avenida Presidente Roca and Florida, you'll find Iglesia Jesús de la Buena Esperanza. This humble, adobe-walled church, constructed in the late 1930s by Chilean engineer Julio Alamos Cuadra, sits on a leafy plot of land in the southern end of town. Beneath the reed roof of the unassuming structure is a curious statue of Christ, unconventionally represented in a seated position, which some residents suggest reflects the rather laid-back nature of the Barrealinos themselves.

AROUND BARREAL

Some 25 kilometres south of Barreal, opposite the Barreal del Leoncito, an unnamed but obvious road leads eastwards to Parque Nacional El Leoncito (02648 441240, www.parques nacionales.gov.ar). Situated approximately 12 kilometres along this turn-off is the ranger's office, where you can enquire about trekking in the reserve. This protected landscape, spread in and around the slopes of the Sierra del Tontal range, is dotted with plants such as the aromatic *ajenjo*, used in traditional medicine.

The cloudless canopy overhead is home to the scarlet-breasted long-tailed meadowlark as well as earth's fastest mover, the peregrine falcon, while groups of guanacos and the suri cordillerano (a type of rhea) patrol the higher reaches of the park. Visitors can saddle up and take in the views of the Andes, the *precordillera* and the processions of poplars that appear gilded in the autumn sun, or strike out on foot along the Paisajes de Agua path towards El Rincón waterfall.

In front of the entrance to Parque Nacional El Leoncito lies the Barreal del Leoncito. Seen from afar, this dried-out lake bed could be mistaken for a body of water glinting in the harsh sun. If a curious array of sails is discernible, the illusion is doubly convincing. Up close, the 12- by five-kilometre expanse of mineral-rich clay, also

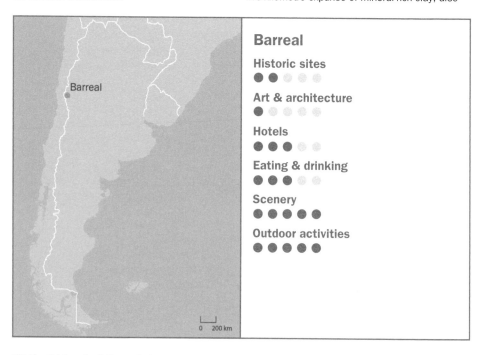

Barreal

Barreal

Historic sites
●● ○ ○ ○

Art & architecture
● ○ ○ ○ ○

Hotels
●●● ○ ○

Eating & drinking
●●●● ○

Scenery
●●●●●

Outdoor activities
●●●●●

0   200 km

Clockwise from top:
Cerro Alcazar; a *capilla*;
sand carting.

known as the Pampa del Leoncito, or simply El Barreal Blanco, is decidedly dry, and the sails belong to three-wheeled vehicles used in the practice of *carrovelismo*, or land sailing. Propelled by the local wind – nicknamed El Conchabado (the servant) – that makes a regular appearance in the late afternoon, the *carrovelas* speed across the barren surface of the *barreal*, reaching speeds of up to 120 kilometres an hour. Not just for spectators, the sport can be practised here in the company of an expert instructor.

The Laguna Blanca, or white lagoon, is situated 85 kilometres from Barreal and some 3,200 metres above sea level. It resembles a giant mirror, reflecting the boundless blue sky and surrounding snowy summits, beneath the majesty of Cerro Mercedario. Up here, the silence is almost eerie and the views uninterrupted, except for the occasional guanaco. The journey into the cordillera is equally stunning: the sinuous road criss-crosses the Río de los Patos within territory navigated by herdsmen leading their livestock along the arduous route. To reach Laguna Blanca, take the western turn-off – which also leads to Las Hornillas – just beyond La Querencia Posada on RN 149. Exploring the area as part of an organised excursion is advised, as the mountainous terrain makes for challenging driving. At La Junta, you are required to sign your life away in a visitors' register. Note that only off-road vehicles are permitted beyond this point.

Halfway between Barreal and the small town of Calingasta on the RN 149, a small sign indicates a side road leading off 200 metres into the *precordillera*. The unpaved track comes to a halt at the foot of the imposing turret-like forms of Cerro Alcazar. This impressive geological whim, whittled by the wind over thousands of years, dates to the same era as the spectacular rock formations of San Juan's Valle de la Luna (*see p287* **Rock of ages**). At 1,600 metres, its summit affords great views of the surrounding area and beyond. Just across the main road are the Ruinas de Hilario, the remains of a major metal foundry dating from the 1860s.

It is worth stopping off in Calingasta, which lies 40 kilometres north of Barreal on RN 149, to visit the Capilla de Catalve, a Jesuit church that dates from the 17th century and contains some of the oldest bells in the country. Also known as the Capilla de Nuestra Señora del Carmen, this simple, whitewashed adobe construction looks out towards the Andes; local legend has it that independence hero José de San Martín stopped by while searching for a spot to cross the *cordillera*. Ask at the Cora Esquivel del Toro museum (Aldo Cantoni, no phone) about viewing the antique dresses embroidered with gold and silver threads that adorn the statue of the Virgen del Carmen. You'll find the church 350 metres from the main town square.

"Stargazing in this corner of the world is easy: skies remain cloudless almost 300 nights a year."

Complejo Astronómico El Leoncito (CASLEO)

Parque Nacional El Leoncito, 37km SE of Barreal, RN 149 (02648 441088/www.casleo.gov.ar). Open 10am-noon, 3-5.30pm daily. Admission AR$10; free under-14s. No credit cards.

Far from the atmospheric contamination and luminescent interference of populous settlements, and against a backdrop of snow-capped Andean peaks, sits one of the Southern Cone's most important astronomical observatories. Stargazing in this corner of the world is easy: the incredibly clear skies remain cloudless almost 300 nights a year. Located within Parque Nacional El Leoncito, CASLEO offers guided tours around the compound (wear something warm, as the interior is chilly) and you can view the massive 40-ton telescope used by the scientists. The ideal option is, of course, a night-time visit, when observations are conducted with more manageable telescopes. Nocturnal tours must be arranged in advance and can include dinner at the communal eating quarters and lodging in the modest on-site accommodation.

OUTDOOR ACTIVITIES

Adventure-tourism options abound in Barreal. At Las Hornillas there are excellent opportunities for trout-fishing, and the hills are alive with the sound of excited shrieks as thrill-seekers raft down the river in the company of Pablo Schlögl from Hostel Barreal (02648 441144).

Trekking can be as easy or as challenging as you like; you are spoilt for choice with the *precordillera* and the Andes themselves. Many mountaineers consider scaling Cerro Mercedario more satisfying than big sister Aconcagua, which stands just outside Mendoza (*see p209*).

Brothers Diego and Ramón Ossa's treks on horseback are recommended (02648 441004, 0264 15 503 2008 mobile, www.exploraparques.com), and their father, Ramón Ossa Sr (0264 15 4040913 mobile, www.fortunaviajes.com.ar), organises horse treks through the Andes following the Ruta Sanmartiniana.

For a fast-paced, adrenaline-filled afternoon, have a crack at *carrovelismo* with local expert Rogelio Toro (0264 15 671 7196 mobile). Ask at your accommodation for details of off-road excursions; plenty of places offer, or can arrange, these services.

Top: Barreal del Leoncito.
Middle: woods around
Barreal. Bottom: Complejo
Astronómico El Leoncito.

Eat

Options for eating out in Barreal are currently limited. The town's relative isolation means there is an emphasis on seasonal local produce, and jams, chutneys and desserts made from locally-grown fruits should not be missed. For a break from the *bife*, try some freshly caught trout, accompanied by one of the excellent wines from the province. Opening hours are often flexible, so it is best to call in advance.

Posada San Eduardo (*see p288*) also has a recommended restaurant (open 11am-2.30pm, 8-10pm daily).

"El Alemán's snug interior is decorated with beer tankards, and out on the patio you can sample artisanal brews."

El Alemán

Los Huarpes, no number (02648 441193). Open high season noon-3pm, 8-11pm daily. Low season noon-2.30pm, 8-10pm Tue-Sat; noon-2.30pm Sun. ££. International.

Typical German dishes such as *kassler* (smoked and salted pork) and *fleischkäse* (similar to meat loaf) are served along with smoked trout, salmon and top-quality steak at this well-respected establishment. The snug, informal interior is decorated with an assortment of beer tankards, and out on the shady patio you can sample some preservative-free, artisanal brews; try a glass of the extra-strong, demonically monikered Diablo.

Doña Pipa

Mariano Moreno & Hipólito Yrigoyen (02648 441004/ www.cdpbarreal.com.ar). Open noon-2.30pm, 8-11pm daily. ££. International.

Simple, unpretentious home-cooking is what you can expect at this rustic-style restaurant. Although the menu changes monthly, dishes don't stray far from the tried-and-tested trinity of pasta, meat and poultry. The succulent *suprema de pollo al vapor con salsa de champignon* (steamed breast of chicken in a mushroom sauce) is a fixture, as are the regional wines from the Callia bodega. Those with a sweet tooth should save some room for the *dulce de alcayota*, a sugary local speciality made from a type of squash.

El Mercedario

Avenida Presidente Roca & Calle de los Enamorados (02648 441167/www.elmercedario.com.ar). Open 11am-2pm, 8pm-midnight daily. ££. No credit cards. Traditional.

In the dining room of this posada, tasty vegetables fresh from the garden are offered alongside conventional parrilla fare, such as *morcilla* (black pudding), chorizo and slabs of steak. The simple house salad, made with home-grown organic produce, is abundant and full of flavour, and the *papa à la Barrealina* (baked potato with garlic, olive oil and aromatic herbs) does spuds proud. Start with a glass of syrah, a juicy Cuyan empanada, *humita en chala* (a seasoned, maize-based purée wrapped in corn husks), or the house *picada*, which includes home-made salami and artisanal cheese made with milk from resident cow Aurora.

Shop

As yet unblemished by chain stores and tacky souvenir shops, the town's main shopping attraction is the artisan fair held at weekends around the central Plaza San Martín. Resident craftspeople, like Silvia de Marchi and Sonia Vidal, sell directly from their homes. Look out for hand-painted signs advertising *dulces* (sweets) or *artesanías* (crafts), and pick up colourful shawls, wooden figurines or home-made preserves.

De mi Campo

Avenida Presidente Roca, no number (02648 441125/www.demicampo.com.ar). Open 8am-noon, 2.30-6pm daily.

Set within an idyllic country estate full of rose bushes and lavender plantations, De mi Campo stocks a range of beauty products as well as teas, compotes, condiments and other gourmet delicacies, all created with organic crops harvested on-site. Among the aromatic options are rosemary and camomile shampoos, and body sprays perfumed with wild rose or apple. The sun-dried tomatoes in malbec, and the *alcayota* jam, will appeal to gastronomes.

Stay

As a base camp for fans of outdoor pursuits, Barreal's accommodation scene has traditionally been more functional than five-star. However, in recent years, a number of charming lodgings have opened their doors. Advance booking is advised.

Cabañas Doña Pipa

Mariano Moreno & Hipólito Yrigoyen (02648 441004/ www.cdpbarreal.com.ar). £.

Set within a tree-flanked complex, these simple, spartan cabins may not be fresh from the pages of an interiors magazine, but they are spacious, spotless and ideal for self-catering (for a maximum of six guests). The ample grounds contain a swimming pool, shaded areas and parrillas (barbeques), as well as a restaurant serving breakfast, lunch and dinner. The friendly owners can organise all sorts of excursions and activities through their sister operation, Explora Parques.

Rock of ages

In the sun-drenched north-east of San Juan, a vast expanse of bone-filled badlands known as Valle de la Luna (Valley of the Moon) stretches along the provincial frontier. Officially it's known as Parque Provincial Ischigualasto, but the park's popular moniker refers to the peculiar lunar landscapes contained within the 150 square kilometres of protected reserve. Surreal rock formations, shaped by wind, rain and time, stand stark against an azure horizon. A curtain of red sandstone mountains offsets the cinder-coloured earth and provides an introduction to Parque Nacional Talampaya, 80 kilometres to the north in the neighbouring province of La Rioja.

These contiguous parks – equally impressive and astonishingly different – were declared a UNESCO World Heritage Site by at the turn of the millennium. Their incredible scenery has drawn comparisons with the USA's Bryce Canyon and the startling topography of Turkey's Cappadocia, but the area's photogenic facet is just one of its attributes.

Valle de la Luna's rocks are said to offer completely uninterrupted documentation of the Triassic period, a geological era of approximately 50 million years. Such comprehensive archaeological evidence has yet to be revealed anywhere else on the planet. Palaeontologists have also unearthed remains of a herrerasaurus, a massive carnivore, and of one of the earliest known dinosaurs, the eoraptor (or dawn plunderer), a dinky specimen that inhabited the earth between 230 and 225 million years ago.

Visits to Valle de la Luna involve travelling in convoy in your own vehicle, or that of a tour operator, along a defined route. A park ranger leads the excursion, and stops are made at the park's celebrated natural structures, which include the gravity-defying El Hongo (the Mushroom) and El Submarino (the Submarine), and the fascinating Cancha de Bochas (the Ball Court), with its mysterious spherical forms. Many tour operators offering day trips to Valle de la Luna include Parque Talampaya in the itinerary; its relative proximity to Ischigualasto and its awe-inspiring terracotta-coloured cliffs, which are guaranteed to make you feel immensely insignificant, mean that this park should not be missed.

The pleasant town of San Agustín de Valle Fértil, approximately 80 kilometres south of Valle de la Luna and 250 kilometres north-east of San Juan's capital city, serves as a base for those exploring the parks. Accommodation is improving; the satisfactory Hostería Valle Fértil (www.alkazarhotel.com.ar/vallefertil), overlooking the town's reservoir, and the secluded Finca la Media Luna (www.finca lamedialuna.com.ar), in the nearby mountain village of La Majadita, are currently two of the best options.

La Querencia.

Eco-Posada El Mercedario
Avenida Presidente Roca & Calle de los Enamorados (02648 441167/www.elmercedario.com.ar). £.
Three kilometres outside the centre of town, the open doors of El Mercedario reveal the rustic interiors of this late-1920s, traditional adobe structure. Free from any ostentation – not to mention minibars and flatscreen TVs – the sober bedrooms feature wood-burning stoves and decor inspired by national culture and native flora and fauna. The property has some admirable green twists, including the solar-powered heater to provide hot water, and the organic residue from the posada's restaurant that is converted into fertiliser for the fruits and vegetables grown on the small farm.

Hospedaje El Alemán
Huarpes & Gualino (02648 441193). £.
To really get away from it all, try one of these four cottage-style buildings, close to Río de los Patos. Designed for double or triple occupancy, the red-brick buildings with log-beam ceilings combine a rural aesthetic with modern facilities: each has a kitchenette and electric heating. Affable owners Bernhard and Perla have plans for a private restaurant for guests, as well as a parrilla and a small bar.

Posada San Eduardo
Avenida San Martín & Calle de los Enamorados (02648 441046). £.
Owner Ricardo Zunino, a former Formula One driver, swapped the tracks for tranquillity when he retired to Barreal. The guest rooms in this carefully restored farmhouse display tasteful minimalism and, in some cases, welcoming adobe fireplaces. In the extensive grounds, which are planted with poplars and peach trees, guests can wander undisturbed, take a dip in the pool, or trot about the estate on horseback.

La Querencia
Florida via Belgrano & RN 149 (0264 15 436 4699 mobile/www.laquerenciaposada.com.ar). ££.
In a town where amazing vistas are a dime a dozen, La Querencia goes one step further: from the pool, in the middle of a grassy garden bordered by poplars and willows, the imposing Andes are inescapable. The six rooms are kitted out with fireplaces to combat chilly nights, when the only discernable sound is the crackle of firewood. Convivial hostess Adela's attention to detail is evident throughout – especially in her delicious breakfasts, featuring home-made yoghurt, jams and delicate pastries.

El Rancho de Carmen
Avenida Presidente Roca, no number (02648 441076/ www.elranchodecarmen.com). ££.
A delightfully secluded guesthouse facing the Andes, this is just the place for an intimate weekend. The large, open kitchen and living room area, complete with an enormous fireplace, plump-cushioned sofas and wooden beams hung with lavender, evoke the rural elegance of a Provençal farmhouse. Spend a night here in one of the two pretty, barley-coloured bedrooms, wake up to the smell of freshly baked bread from the clay oven, and you may just want to take up permanent residence.

Factfile

When to go
Spring and summer, from September to March, are the seasons for rafting, land sailing and trekking the Ruta Sanmartiniana, but these are popular periods and summer temperatures can be exhausting.

The usually verdant surroundings glow golden in autumn (April to June), when days are pleasant and perfect for trekking or horse riding, though nights are chilly. Escape to Barreal in winter (July to September) for languorous evenings in front of log fires and to enjoy the spectacle of the snow-covered Andes.

Getting there & around
El Triunfo (0264 422 4925) has two daily bus services to Barreal from the provincial capital of San Juan. Return journey departure times can be confirmed at Barreal's 24-hour service station on the northern end of Avenida Presidente Roca, and tickets should be bought here in advance.

Two *combi* (minivan) companies run services from San Juan to Barreal and must be booked ahead: Combis José Luis (0264 434 2317) and Combis Silvio (0264 425 2370). By bus or *combi*, the journey takes approximately five hours. You will need your own transport or a hired driver and vehicle for exploring much of the area – 4x4s are strongly recommended, and are essential for trips to Laguna Blanca and other isolated locations.

The tourist office can provide information on companies offering both tours and transportation. Valle Castaño Expediciones (0264 15 407 0419 mobile, vallecastano4x4@gmail.com), based in San Juan, offers vehicles with guides for trips around the region.

Tourist information
Dirección de Turismo de la Municipalidad de Calingasta Avenida Presidente Roca & Las Heras (0264 844 1066 ext 28, www.calingasta turismo.gov.ar). Open 10am-10pm Mon-Fri; 9am-midnight Sat, Sun.

Internet
Ciber W Soler & Las Heras (no phone). Open 10am-1.30am daily. Internet access in town is limited and speed is often slow.

Glaciar Perito Moreno.

El Calafate

Argentina

Jaw-dropping glaciers amid the Patagonian wilderness.

El Calafate, a small, remote town in the province of Santa Cruz, is the base for visitors to Patagonia's most famous glacier, Glaciar Perito Moreno, one of the most emblematic, wildly impressive landscapes in Argentina. Seen from afar, it is breathtaking – but it's the chance to observe its spectacular, translucent bulk at close range, gazing up at its frozen walls from a boat, from the nearby walkway, or even standing on it, that makes a visit unforgettable.

It's only when you get up close that you discover the glacier is a soundscape as well as a landscape. You soon get used to the constant echo of explosions of varying degrees, from gunfire-like crackles to deafening cannon volleys. Violent storms and secret wars seem to be taking place in the glacier's depths, all interspersed with peaceful lulls that bring nothing more than the murmur of water and the whirr of the wind rushing past.

From a base in El Calafate, you can also visit other lesser-known glaciers, such as the Upsala and the Spegazzini, or head off on horseback or in a 4x4 into the deserted mountains. You can fish for giant trout and visit traditional Patagonian estancias, which seem lost in the immensity of the steppe. Yet the main attraction for most visitors here remains the celestial radiance of the glaciers – a thrilling universe unto themselves.

EOLO
PATAGONIA'S SPIRIT

WELCOME TO THE
SPIRIT OF PATAGONIA.

A UNIQUE AND EXCLUSIVE LODGE
LOCATED BETWEEN EL CALAFATE
AND THE PERITO MORENO GLACIER.

www.eolo.com.ar
reservas@eolo.com.ar
(+5411) 4700-0075
El Calafate - Santa Cruz
Patagonia - Argentina

RELAIS &
CHATEAUX

SAY HUEQUE
Tours in Argentina & Chile

the travel agency for
independent
travellers

Downtown: Viamonte 749 6° of. "1" – Tel/ Fax:
(+5411) 5199 2517/20. Palermo: Guatemala 4845 1° of "4"
Tel /Fax: (+5411) 4775 7862. Bs. As. – Argentina.
info@sayhueque.com - www.sayhueque.com

To advertise in the next edition of…

Email: guidesadvertising@timeout.com Call: +44 (0)20 7813 6020

Explore

Founded in 1927, deep in the heart of the Patagonian steppe, **El Calafate** is a town of 20,000 inhabitants that, over the last few decades, has become an increasingly important tourist destination. Fortunately, it maintains much of its small-town Patagonian atmosphere, bisected by dirt roads and with no building higher than three storeys.

The centre of the town is a narrow, tree-lined boulevard called Avenida Libertador San Martín, which is home to a number of tour operators, shops and restaurants, as well as the casino and one of the town's four banks. Several hotels can be found within two or three blocks of this avenue, with the rest no more than a ten-minute drive by taxi.

Windswept and somewhat dusty, El Calafate has little of the particular charm that would recommend it as a destination in its own right. Still, the quality of its hotels – some of which are equipped with modern spas and truly spectacular views across the sapphire surface of Lago Argentino – provide some compensation. But no one flies to nearly the end of the vast American continent just to see El Calafate: it's all about the surrounding landscape, which is one of the most dazzlingly beautiful sights in all of Patagonia.

AROUND EL CALAFATE

GLACIAR PERITO MORENO

The Perito Moreno glacier is situated 78 kilometres west of El Calafate on Ruta 11. As you enter **Parque Nacional los Glaciares** by road, you'll drive past long expanses of lenga forest before the first flash of white ice appears. In the final 500 metres before reaching the car park, the road rises and you can see the glacier's immense four-kilometre breadth, snaking up the valley like a huge tongue of ice.

This glacier is in a continuous process of renewal, and is one of only a few advancing glaciers in the world. It crumbles and regenerates constantly; first growing steadily until it hits the rocky shore of a peninsula, then forming a dam that finally succumbs to the pressure of the water trapped behind it and collapsing violently. Then it grows again. This extraordinary natural collapse is known as 'the rupture' and occurs every two to four years, with film crews and eager spectators camping out to witness it.

The most common excursion at Glaciar Perito Moreno consists of walking along a set of raised walkways built directly in front of the glacier. You can walk their looping length in about two unhurried hours. The ice show is incessant, and the chances of witnessing a tower come crashing down will increase the longer you stick around.

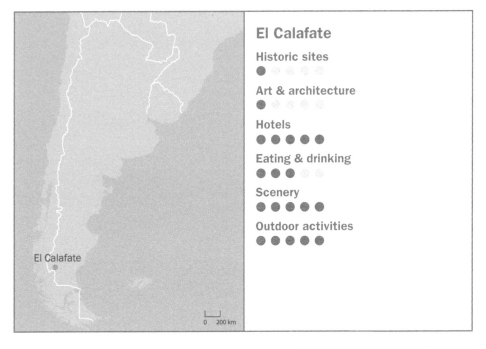

El Calafate

Historic sites
● ◌ ◌ ◌ ◌

Art & architecture
● ◌ ◌ ◌ ◌

Hotels
● ● ● ● ●

Eating & drinking
● ● ● ◌ ◌

Scenery
● ● ● ● ●

Outdoor activities
● ● ● ● ●

El Calafate

0   200 km

There are wooden benches and a snack bar for those happy to settle in for a while to admire the majestic panorama.

Group tours generally consist of a half-day excursion starting in the morning. Those who stay on for the afternoon can take a trip in a 110-seat passenger boat, which follows an hour-long navigation through icebergs to observe the glacier's immensity close-up; trips depart hourly from 10.15am to 4pm every day with Hielo & Aventura (02902 492205, www.hieloyaventura.com). Alternatively, you can take the so-called 'Mini-trekking' excursion on the ice to complete a full day at the glacier. The hike allows you to trek directly on its surface with the aid of crampons strapped to your shoes or boots. It consists of a two-hour walk – an excursion that requires a bare minimum of physical fitness, and is recommended for reasonably healthy people from ten to 65 years of age.

A second option is the 'Big Ice' excursion, a more demanding seven-hour hike over the ice. Both hikes are organised by Hielo y Aventura and should be booked in advance. The glacier trek is rounded off with a glass of whiskey on the rocks – the rocks, in this case, being sparklingly clear and beautiful glacial ice, chipped off as you watch.

If you don't mind splashing some cash, a two-day cruise on the small vessel *Marpatag* offers a more in-depth way of appreciating Perito Moreno up close, and of seeing other glaciers such as Upsala and Spegazzini. The boat has 22 double rooms, and the trip consists of two nights and two days enjoying the icy landscapes from every possible angle, in the comfort of a floating living/dining room with large panoramic windows. In a deluxe cabin, two days and two nights on board, including meals, costs around US$1,000 per person (011 4312 4427, www.cruceros marpatag.com).

Alternatively, if you'd rather avoid tours altogether and make your own way there in your own time, you can simply travel to the glacier and its walkways by bus (*see p301*).

GLACIAR UPSALA

Another unmissable excursion from El Calafate is a voyage across Lago Argentino, through hundreds of drifting icebergs, to Glaciar Upsala. A bus makes the rounds of the hotels each morning to take visitors to Puerto Bandera, inside Parque Nacional los Glaciares, where a 180-seater catamaran with large windows awaits. As it slides through the lake's milky waters, icebergs of every shape and size loom on either side of the boat, some of them almost five times its size. Some have pointed peaks and pyramid forms; others look like submarines, just breaking the surface of the water with their frozen periscopes.

After a two-hour voyage, the catamaran reaches the face of the Upsala, which is 60 kilometres long and ten kilometres wide. Passengers disembark for a brief walk through the forest leading to Onelli Bay. Here, you can witness one of the loveliest views in Patagonia: surrounded by an amphitheatre of mountains, three glaciers descend the slopes into a lake crammed with blue and white icebergs.

"As the boat slides through the lake's milky waters, icebergs of every shape and size appear."

BOSQUE PETRIFICADO LA LEONA

North of El Calafate (120 kilometres) stands Bosque Petrificado la Leona – not to be confused with the famous, much larger petrified forest in the north of Santa Cruz province (*see p343*). Andes Expeditions (02902 492075, www.losglaciares.com/bosquepetrificado) conducts excursions to La Leona. After driving to Santa Teresa estancia, groups set off on a four-hour walk through an extremely arid landscape, reaching an eight-square-kilometre dip in the earth's surface that looks like a lunar crater. Inside, among sandstone canyons, is a forest of 20 petrified tree trunks that extend from one to five metres in length. They are the weird remnants of a forest dating from 60 to 90 million years ago, when Patagonia was a vibrant, life-filled forest and the habitat of dinosaurs. Along the way, walkers can spot a dinosaur bone, one and a half metres long, sitting next to the path.

OUTDOOR ACTIVITIES

One of the best non-glacier-related excursions in El Calafate's surroundings is the 'Balcón de El Calafate' (02902 491446, www.miloutdoor.com). A 4x4 vehicle whisks you across curious lunar landscapes to a 'balcony' on the mountain peak, with a dazzling view of Lago Argentino. A similar excursion, on which you can choose segments of horse riding or trekking, climbs Frías hill (02902 492808, www.cerrofrias.com). If horse riding particularly appeals, one of the best options is around Lago Roca (02902 495447, www.cabal gatasdelglaciar.com). For fishing, Lago Strobel is at the heart of a far-flung estancia, where you have to stay a minimum of two nights to make the most of a trip on which you might catch dozens of huge rainbow trout, which can weigh up to ten kilograms apiece (02902 493311, www.calafatefishing.com).

Ice trekking on Glaciar
Perito Moreno.

Eat

The most noteworthy element of El Calafate's cuisine is the famous Patagonian lamb, thought by some to be the best *cordero* in the entire region. It's usually prepared by being wired to an iron cross and barbecued for a number of hours, ensuring that much of the fat runs off to leave crispy-edged, delicious meat that needs nothing but salt for seasoning. The secret is in the feeding – the animals are raised on a diet of native coirón grass and acquire a flavour rather different from that of European sheep, brought to perfection by the slow-cooking method. More sophisticated lamb-based dishes, served with various sauces and accompaniments, are also part of the local cuisine, as are salmon and trout. In low season, restaurants have been known to spontaneously close for a month. Ask at your hotel to be sure your chosen eaterie is open.

Casimiro Biguá

Avenida Libertador 993 & 963 (02902 492590/ www.casimirobigua.com). Open restaurant noon-midnight daily. Parrilla 11am-4pm, 7pm-1am daily. ££££. International/Parrilla.

This restaurant has two branches. The parilla specialises in grilled and roasted meat, while the other outpost is more of a restaurant/wine bar affair. In the former, traditional Patagonian lamb is served roasted; at the latter, it turns up in rather more sophisticated dishes, preceded by starters such as trout ceviche with julienne vegetables, mango and a touch of coriander, or lamb carpaccio with a vinaigrette of port and herbs. Lamb in an almond crust is served on a purée of garlic and basil, with vinegared bouquet garni and mustard sauce; or try the *merluza negra* (Chilean sea bass) on a bed of leeks with olive oil, vegetable coulis and flakes of serrano ham. Home-made pastas, risottos and salads round out the restaurant's extensive menu. An exceptional wine list includes over 250 Argentinian labels, as well as various imported wines and numerous liqueurs, ports, whiskies and cocktails. You can round off proceedings with a choice of Cuban cigars.

Mi Viejo

Avenida Libertador 1111 (02902 491691). Open noon-3.30pm, 7.30pm-midnight daily. £££. Parrilla.

Just a glimpse of roasting lamb through the window of Mi Viejo, and its heady accompanying aroma, is usually enough to lure passers-by through the doors of another of the town's classic parrillas. For starters, there's cured meat or fish: options include hare, trout, lamb and *choique* (rhea), a small, native ostrich-like bird. If you'd rather proceed straight to a main course, the pasta speciality is giant crab ravioli with four-cheese sauce. Spinach crêpes with salmon in pink sauce are another light option, or try some rhea, served as a casserole or stuffed into empanadas. You can't go far wrong with the lamb, though, roasted with a deliciously crispy layer of fat, or served with mushroom sauce and Spanish-style potatoes.

Pascasio M

25 de Mayo 52 (02902 492055/www.pascasiom.com.ar). Open 11am-4pm, 7pm-1am daily. ££££. Modern/ International.

This restaurant has come on in leaps and bounds in recent years, consolidating its gastronomic good name on the basis of regional products such as giant crab, trout, hare, lamb and rhea. The platter of smoked meats and fish is a popular choice and consists of venison, wild boar, trout and sheep's cheese, as well as imported duck, rabbit and salmon. Lamb, of course, also figures, and can be ordered in the form of a carpaccio prepared with lemon, capers, oil, cheese and vinegar. As a main course, the lamb can be roasted with chardonnay sauce, or rolled and steamed with mushrooms and served with fresh tomato sauce. The atmosphere owes its laid-back vibe to the low jazz in the background, and an interesting display of photographs on the walls shows off some of the area's loveliest landscapes.

La Tablita

Coronel Rosales 28, opposite El Calafate bridge (02902 491065). Open noon-3.30pm, 7.30pm-midnight daily. £££. Parrilla.

This is the best known and also the oldest of the town's parrillas, dating from 1968. La Tablita's name refers to the classic wooden boards from which roasted meat is traditionally eaten in Argentina. These days, it's plates all the way here, although the cooks – or *parrilleros* – have stayed the same for years. Flavoursome Patagonian lamb is served, as well as incredibly tender meat of both the red and white variety, and trout and salmon dishes, all complemented by a very good wine list. For dessert, the home-made Calafate berry ice-cream is highly recommended.

Shop

Cruz del Sur

Avenida del Libertador 1064 (02902 491590). Open 10am-1.30pm, 4.30-9pm daily.

Deeply aromatic inside, as only a shop piled high with sumptuous leather goods like this can be, Cruz del Sur is quite a find. As well as various high-quality souvenirs in metal, bone and horn, there are gorgeous bags, boots and clothing fashioned from different kinds of leather, including the attractively mottled *carpincho* leather, which is made from the skin of the capybara, the world's largest known rodent.

Paseo de los Artesanos

Avenida del Libertador & 9 de Julio. Open high season 9am-10pm daily.

Open in peak season, this centrally located crafts market is a good spot to pick up locally made handicrafts, and a great way to support hard-working artisans. Leather, silver and nickel goods are generally good bets when buying from Argentinian craftspeople, but don't miss the vibrant, inexpensive beaded jewellery. You'll also find assorted elves and gnomes, which are crafts-market staples – shaped with varying degrees of care and skill.

Clockwise from top:
Perito Moreno (2);
trekking; Ruta Nacional
40; Lago Argentino.

Top: Los Notros. Middle:
Esplendor El Calafate (2).
Bottom: Eolo.

Stay

Due to the enduring attractions of the glacier and the spectacular local scenery, El Calafate has developed a good range of accommodation, including a five-star hotel with a spa and luxurious hotels with views over Glaciar Perito Moreno. There is also the option of staying outside town, at one of the area's historic ranches in the heart of the immense steppe. If you stay at one of these lodges you can take part in the same range of excursions you'd find in town. Bear in mind, though, that most are miles from town, so you might not be able to pop into El Calafate for dinner. On the other hand, the food at most estancias is excellent, as is the profound tranquillity you'll experience.

"Interior-design quirks at Casa Los Sauces range from empty birdcages to tables made from recycled sheep pens."

Casa Los Sauces
Los Gauchos 1352 (02902 495854/ www.casalossauces.com). ££££.
Laid out in the style of a Patagonian ranch, this member of the Small Luxury Hotels of the World group features a decor of exposed stone walls and striking paintings and sculptures. An observatory, a feng-shui spa, a gourmet restaurant and splendid, large-windowed suites are key features. Its location, handily close to the centre of town, is also a bonus. However, the most interesting twist is that the hotel is owned by Argentina's power couple, Néstor and Cristina Kirchner, the former and current president, respectively. Mrs President is said to have personally selected all the interior-design quirks, which range from empty birdcages to tables made from recycled sheep pens. The couple have their personal residence just next door.

Design Suites
Calle 94, 190 (02902 494525/ www.designsuites.com). £££.
Located high up on the Nimes Peninsula, with a magnificent view of Lago Argentino below, this hotel has 60 rooms equipped with the latest technology, as well as spa services, a heated indoor-outdoor pool, a sauna and an art gallery. Its airy, stripped-down decor sees local woods and stone seamlessly combined with the sleek lines of a modern hotel.

Eolo
30km S of Calafate *RP 11, km 23 (02902 492042/ www.eolo.com.ar). ££££.*
Eolo (also known as Aeolus) is the name of the keeper of the winds in Greek mythology, and the moniker is appropriate for this far-flung lodge, deep in the kingdom of wind and solitude. To one side, the horizon stretches across the steppe to the blue smudge of Lago Argentino, and to the other, in the distance, you can see the far-off peaks of Torres del Paine (*see p301*). The lateral limits of the great, elongated plain on which Eolo is set are marked by two ranges of mountains running parallel to one another – an immense landscape whose dimensions come to seem almost abstract as you gaze at the panorama from your room or from the picture windows in the lounge. Hiking, mountain biking or taking a dip in the small heated pool are some of the diversions that await visitors to Eolo, which has the silhouette and wooden beams of a typical Patagonian ranch. Services include a bar, restaurant, library, sauna, massage room and Wi-Fi in all 17 rooms.

Esplendor El Calafate
Perón 1143 (02902 492488/www.esplendor hoteles.com).£££.
Located on a promontory overlooking the town, this boutique hotel set a new standard in El Calafate when it opened in 2005. Neatly avoiding all the clichés of the typical rustic interior, the hotel meshes a modern urban design with elements inspired by its Patagonian location, including the use of materials such as stone and sand, hand-woven textiles, fragrant woods and incense. Scattered about are eye-catching glass sculptures that brilliantly emulate the glacier's turquoise colour, as well as light fittings in the shape of antlers. The hotel has 50 rooms, with views of Lago Argentino and Cerro Calafate.

Estancia Cristina
Parque Nacional los Glaciares *(02902 491133/ www.estanciacristina.com). £££.*
You can visit this estancia, built in 1914, as part of a day-long excursion that takes you through the bobbing icebergs of Lago Argentino, or you can simply come and stay. From the ranch, which is inside Parque Nacional los Glaciares, you can then set off in a 4x4 or on horseback to visit Glaciar Upsala before heading back to one of the estancia's eight rooms, decorated in the Patagonian style, with views on to huge, snowy mountains. There's also a museum that tells the story of Percy and Jessy Masters, who arrived from England in 1900 and founded the estancia as a sheep farm.

Estancia Nibepo Aike
56km from El Calafate *RP 15 (02966 436010/ 02966 422626/www.nibepoaike.com.ar). £££.*
This 128-square kilometre ranch, created in 1901 and set inside Parque Nacional los Glaciares, can be visited as a staying guest or as a day-tripper. An old-fashioned sheep-shearing shed is one attraction, as are the horse riding excursions and Patagonian lamb *asados*. Located in a valley carved out by glaciers, the English-style house, built in 1921, is protected from the wind by a row of poplars. Its grooved, sloping roof, typical of Patagonian houses, is designed to

Meanwhile, in Chile...

If you get this far south in your Patagonian adventure, why stop at a mere border? Across the way in Chile, Parque Nacional Torres del Paine draws thousands of hikers every year with its milky-green lakes, steep valleys, granite mountains, grassy meadows, pre-Andean desert, lush forests and yet more giant, creaking glaciers – all arranged, as if by some omnipotent set designer, around the Paine mountain range.

Puerto Natales is the jumping-off point for Torres del Paine. A weathered settlement of battered tin roofs and sleepy streets, this remote waterside outpost is the picture of solitude. However, just like El Calafate, people don't stick around in the town itself for long.

Aside from its string of natural jewels, the beauty of trekking in the Torres del Paine park is its accessibility – guides aren't necessary, and anyone with good all-round fitness, basic common sense and decent outdoor gear can take on the challenge independently.

It is now theoretically possible to do the entire Paine circuit without a tent, hopping from one *refugio*, or mountain cabin, to the next (book in advance at www.fantasticosur.com). For the ultimate treat, incorporate a stay at Patagonia Camp (+56 2334 9255, www.patagoniacamp. com), which offers luxury yurts with king-size beds and private bathrooms.

The park's star trek is the ten-day Paine Circuit, which circles the entire Paine range. This challenging walk, a shoo-in on any list of the world's top-ten treks, offers constantly changing views of the massif. For those with a little less time – or stamina – the 'W' circuit (four to five days), named after the shape it traces on a map, allows you to skip the 'less exciting' sections through the forest and pampas, taking you straight to the big hits:

Glaciar Grey emptying into an iceberg-spotted lake; the vertiginous path up the Valle Francés; the striped, 2,600-metre Cuernos del Paine; and the majestic, needle-like Torres del Paine.

Glaciar Grey, the largest glacier in the park, is a clear highlight. Chunks of ice the colour of blue curaçao float on the lake, like an accidental paint spillage over the otherwise subdued Patagonian palette. There are no hordes, no railings, no dedicated 'photo op' spots here. Glaciar Grey enters into view without fanfare, its variegated blue-grey crevasses and cuts appearing to each hiker like a thrilling private discovery.

A perfectly planned trek ends with a towering finale: the three polished granite spires known as the Torres del Paine. After a knee-grinding boulder ascent, which happens to be the toughest section of the trek, you are repaid with one of the world's most dramatic spectacles: a trio of granite spires soaring above a cirque, neatly carved with picture-perfect precision by millennia of glaciation.

Back in Puerto Natales, consider checking in for some post-trek pampering at Indigo (+56 6141 3609, www.indigopatagonia.com), where rainforest showers, sleek design and fluffy white towels await, as well as rooftop hot tubs with a view back towards Torres del Paine.

To reach Puerto Natales from El Calafate, most visitors opt for the short charter flights offered by Aerovías Dap (+56 6161 6100, www.aeroviasdap.cl). Buses and transfer services also run across the Argentinian–Chilean border. Either should be booked in advance. From Puerto Natales, it's a 120-kilometre journey to Parque Nacional Torres del Paine. Official maps of the area are available online at www.pntp.cl.

deal with snow in a no-nonsense way. The interior, preserved exactly as it was when it was a working ranch, is as snug as it is functional, with lenga-beech panelling and antique furniture.

Hotel Posada Los Alamos
Guatti 1135 (02902 491144/ www.posadalosalamos.com). £££.
This was the town's first five-star hotel, and it's still one of the best, with 144 rooms, a bar and restaurant. Its three main parts are separated by large gardens, with one of the wings featuring a spa (complete with a full gymnasium), a swimming pool and a view of the golf course. Protected by a wall of poplars, the hotel has an alpine look, with pointed roofs and wood-panelled interiors. Its homely rooms come with chunky furniture and extra-snug bedding.

Miyazato Inn
Egidio Feruglio 150, Zona de Chacras (02902 491953/www.losglaciares.com/miyazatoinn). ££.
In a peaceful setting among the mountains that surround El Calafate, this modern farmhouse contains five quiet rooms with private bathrooms, bright wooden floors, exposed brick walls and furniture made of local *algarrobo* (carob) wood. The location, less than a ten-minute drive from the town centre, puts it in walking distance of Laguna Nimes, which, in summer, is aflutter with geese and flamingos.

"At Los Notros, you can relax in the jacuzzi while gazing out at the ice."

Los Notros
Parque Nacional Los Glaciares (011 5277 8200/ www.losnotros.com). Open Sept-May. £££.
One of the most spectacular views in all of Patagonia is the unique selling point of deluxe hotel Los Notros; it's the proud owner of an uninterrupted vista of Glaciar Perito Moreno. The 32 comfortable, wood-floored rooms each have a glacier view, so you can be relaxing in your bathroom's jacuzzi while gazing out at brilliant white ice. There's also gourmet food and a well-stocked wine cellar.

Xelena Hotel
Favaloro 3548 (02902 496201/www.xelena.com.ar). £££.
With 71 very spacious rooms, each with a king-size bed, flatscreen TV, home theatre and Wi-Fi, Xelena is topped off to perfection by its splendid views of Lago Argentino. There are two restaurants and a spa, complete with a pool, a dry sauna and, in a nod to the faraway northern hemisphere, Finnish baths.

Factfile

When to go
You can visit El Calafate all year round, but be aware that in winter (June to September) the temperature drops considerably and the walkways alongside the glacier are sometimes covered in snow. In July, there is no trekking on the glacier itself, but all the other excursions are still available, and it's perfectly possible, if you pack enough warm clothes, to visit El Calafate comfortably. High season starts in November and lasts through the summer until the beginning of April; it's always advisable to bring warm clothing, since the wind often picks up in the late afternoon. Autumn and spring are also good times to visit, with fewer tourists and less wind.

Getting there
El Calafate has a modern airport, and most visitors arrive by air, sometimes by way of Bariloche or Tierra del Fuego. A smaller number arrives by car along RN 40, from the north of Santa Cruz province. There are comfortable buses, too, but distances are enormous.

Getting around
For most excursions, you can be picked up from your hotel at no extra charge. To reach Glaciar Perito Moreno, aside from the organised trips,

you can take local buses, which run at various times throughout the day, depending on the time of year.
The three companies that can take you to the glacier without a guide are Chalten Travel (02902 491833, www.chaltentravel.com), Taqsa (02902 491843, www.taqsa.com.ar) and Cal-tur (02902 491842).

Tourist information
Buenos Aires Tourist Information Centre Suipacha 1120 (011 4325 3098, 011 4325 3102, www.santacruzpatagonia.gob.ar). Open 10am-5pm Mon-Fri. The province's tourist office in Buenos Aires offers English-speaking assistance, and the website is also excellent; you can even make enquiries via an online 'chat' function.
El Calafate Tourist Office Coronel Rosales (02902 491090, www.elcalafate.gob.ar/turismo). Open 8am-8pm daily.

Internet
Most hotels have computers available with free internet for guests, and Wi-Fi is now common. There are a number of cyber cafés on Avenida Libertador and adjacent streets, the largest being the one inside the Cooperativa Telefónica (Avenida Libertador 761).

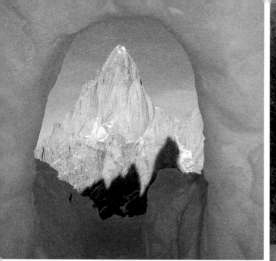

Monte Fitz Roy, El Chaltén & the surrounding area.

El Chaltén

Argentina

Jagged peaks ripe for hiking.

Resembling glistening white vampire's teeth and craggy granite fangs, Monte Fitz Roy and the surrounding peaks are the most dramatic in the Argentinian Andes, rising from the Patagonian steppe like a formidable witch's castle in a children's fantasy film. At the base of this castle, in a wind-battered river valley 212 kilometres north-west of El Calafate, lies El Chaltén – Argentina's trekking and climbing capital.

Built inside the northern sector of Parque Nacional Los Glaciares, El Chaltén was established in 1985 to trump Chile's claim to the Lago del Desierto area. These days, tourism rather than geopolitics is El Chaltén's raison d'être, as evidenced by the thousands of trekkers, technical climbers, mountaineers, birdwatchers and nature-lovers who come here every summer.

Outdoor activities lie right on El Chaltén's doorstep, spread out like a sumptuous, all-you-can-eat wilderness smörgåsbord: there's hiking through ancient beech forests, ice-trekking on crevice-etched glaciers, leisurely sailing on azure glacial lakes, and the conquering of life-claiming peaks such as Monte Fitz Roy (3,405 metres) and Cerro Torre (3,128 metres). This is Patagonia in all its raw, windswept beauty – devoid of casinos and garish souvenir stores. El Chaltén expands and contracts depending on the season; its year-round stalwarts are fewer than a thousand locals, who are as warm and generous as the winters are cold and bitter.

Named after the indigenous Tehuelche word for Fitz Roy, Chaltén translates as 'smoking mountain'; perhaps the Tehuelche misinterpreted the ribbons of cloud around its peak as smoke, or perhaps, at sunrise, with Fitz Roy's peaks illuminated a fiery red, the mountain really did resemble an active volcano. Whatever the reason, on a clear morning, El Chaltén has a wow factor that will take your breath away.

Explore

El Chaltén is still very much a work in progress – main roads have only just been paved, an ATM recently installed and a bus station built. Consisting of a motley collection of A-frame buildings, the rapidly developing town fans out in dusty, grid-like fashion from the two principal streets, Avenidas Güemes and San Martín. Unlike Torres del Paine in Chile (*see p300* **Meanwhile, in Chile…**), to which the Fitz Roy sector of Parque Nacional Los Glaciares bears an uncanny resemblance, hiking trails commence right in town, and there are plenty of exciting day-trekking possibilities.

The town lies within Parque Nacional Los Glaciares, where self-guided hiking trails range from short, scenic strolls to multi-day treks that snake their way past glacial lakes and mountain chains. The park office (*see p311*) provides free hiking maps and information on park flora, fauna, regulations and safety.

If you have only one day to gorge on the park's glorious scenery, the 15-kilometre return hike to Laguna Torre affords an easy taste of some of the park's northern highlights, including unbeatable views of Cerro Torre's precipitous spire reflected in a silty lake dotted with icebergs calved off the Glaciar Grande. For something with tougher gradients, the 25-kilometre return trail to the emerald-hued Laguna de Los Tres is the closest most mortals get to Fitz Roy's granite face, and affords one of the most dazzling views in the entire park.

Two of the lesser-trodden routes from El Chaltén include the Laguna Toro trail, a 30-kilometre return hike which requires spending the night at a lakeside campsite with head-on views of the continental ice cap; and the 24-kilometre Lomo del Pliegue Tumbado trail. The latter's uphill slog climaxes in the best panorama in the area – on a clear day you can see Lago Viedma, Laguna Toro and Fitz Roy.

If time or endurance levels are lacking, try the walk to the Mirador de Los Cóndores. This two-kilometre return hike starts from behind the national park office and offers a condor's-eye view of the town and valley. Just off the RP 23, about three kilometres north of town, the Chorrillo del Salto trail leads to a 20-metre waterfall. For multi-day hiking options, ask the park office about trails that link up. Back-to-nature urges can be indulged via the park's handful of free campsites.

Located 37 kilometres north of town and once the subject of a bitter border dispute between Argentina and Chile (an international commission granted Argentina sovereignty in 1995), Lago del Desierto is an elongated, turquoise lake flanked by dense Patagonian forest. Boat excursions sail to the lake's northern shore and back, while easy

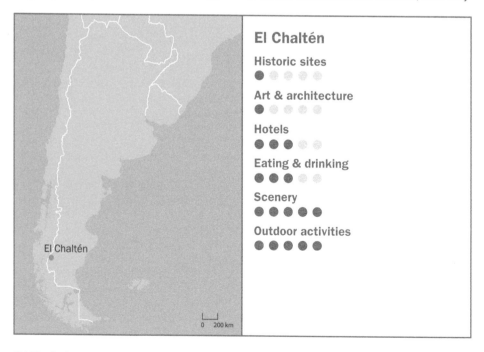

El Chaltén

Historic sites
● ◦ ◦ ◦ ◦

Art & architecture
● ◦ ◦ ◦ ◦

Hotels
● ● ● ◦ ◦

Eating & drinking
● ● ● ◦ ◦

Scenery
● ● ● ● ●

Outdoor activities
● ● ● ● ●

El Chaltén

0   200 km

Fitz Roy.

lakeside trails lead to lookouts with views of Fitz Roy, Laguna Huemul and the hanging Glaciar Huemul. An 11-kilometre hiking trail traces the lake's eastern shore to the north, where there is a free campsite. For those with a tent, boots made for walking, or a mountain bike, a 16-kilometre path heads from the lake's north shore over the border to Chile. The journey involves two nights of camping, two passport stampings and a lake crossing (in summer, boats ply Lago O'Higgins twice weekly to the Chilean hamlet of Villa O'Higgins).

A cruise on Lago Viedma, 18 kilometres south of El Chaltén, offers an opportunity to hold frozen court with the awe-inspiring Glaciar Viedma, Argentina's largest glacier. Leaving from Bahía Túnel on the lake's northern shore, boats sail past icebergs calved off Viedma's icy-blue walls and down the breadth of its 40-metre face. For a closer look, strap on a pair of crampons and experience Viedma's ice caves, crevasses and lakes on an ice-trekking or ice-climbing tour. As with most glaciers in Parque Nacional Los Glaciares, climate change is taking its toll, and Viedma is receding fast.

"Long before it was Argentina's trekking capital, El Chaltén was an exclusive playground for technical climbers lured by the sky-puncturing peaks."

OUTDOOR ACTIVITIES

Long before it was Argentina's trekking capital, El Chaltén was an exclusive playground for technical climbers lured by the sky-puncturing peaks of Torre (3,102 metres), Fitz Roy (3,405 metres), Egger (2,900 metres), Solo (2,121 metres) and Poincenot (3,002 metres). They still turn up every summer (mainly between mid February and March, when the winds are gentler) to attempt record-breaking ascents of sheer granite peaks whose cloud-shrouded walls are prone to crumbling. Climbing permits can be picked up at the park office.

For those new to ice-trekking, many companies in town offer one-day treks on Glaciar Torre, which might whet your appetite for a more challenging multi-day expedition, complete with harnesses, crampons and ice axes, into the little-explored continental ice field – the planet's

third largest ice mass, after Antarctica and Greenland. Try Fitz Roy Expediciones (San Martín 56, 02962 493017, www.fitzroyexpediciones.com.ar), which is open from October to April. The company runs mountain-climbing, glacier-trekking and ice-climbing excursions, as well as expeditions on the continental ice field with specialist guides.

For good old-fashioned rock-climbing, contact Mountaineering Patagonia (San Martín 16, 02962 493194, www.mountaineeringpatagonia.com) or Casa de Guías (Avenida San Martín, no number, 02962 493118, www.casadeguias.com.ar).

A good all-round company for ice-trekking, climbing, boat trips on Lago Viedma and excursions into the national park is Patagonia Aventura (San Martín 56, 02962 493110, www.patagonia-aventura.com).

Eat

You'll come for the hiking, but you'll want to stay for the food. Sophistication and creativity are in abundance, and many chefs try to source ingredients locally. As elsewhere in Patagonia, lamb is a recurring theme and is invariably good. Restaurant prices may seem inflated, but after a bottle of boutique wine and a night of amicable service, all will be forgiven.

El Bodegón Cervecería
San Martín 568 (02962 493109). Open Oct-June noon-3am daily. ££. Traditional/International.
This bustling, driftwood-decorated brewpub is where the party's at. Glass after foaming glass of Czech-style Pilsner – direct from the microbrewery out back – is served with complimentary popcorn and peanuts. Strangers strike up tipsy conversations at the long wooden tables, and guitars are pulled out for impromptu jam sessions, while stomach-lining corn-based stew, empanadas, soup, pasta, pizza and chocolate brownies are dished out by the jovial staff. Once you've managed to score a seat here, you won't be giving it up in a hurry.

Domo Blanco
Güemes 120, Shop 3 (02962 493173). Open Oct, Nov, Mar-Easter 3-11pm daily. Dec-Feb 2pm-midnight daily. ££. Café.
The husband and wife team who've had the town's monopoly on *helado artesanal* (home-made ice-cream) for more than a decade try as much as possible to source ingredients locally. As a result, there are twice as many flavours to choose from in summer (almost 30), including Calafate berry, raspberry and strawberry. Even if you're feeling fruity, opt for at least one scoop of Domo Blanco's crowd-pleasing namesake – a *dulce de leche* base with walnuts, white chocolate and rum. Cave in and order the 1kg tub. If you don't want to brave the elements, they can deliver it to your door.

Road tripping

Ruta Nacional 40 (RN 40) – usually referred to as 'La Ruta Cuarenta' – is the Route 66 of Argentina. The highway hasn't yet been celebrated in a famous pop song, but it has a sort of mythic quality: to drive it is to explore Argentina's history, culture and national character. What is certain is that RN 40 gives drivers (not to mention cyclists and hitchhikers) a keen sense of the country's bewildering scale. It runs for 5,028 kilometres, from the Strait of Magellan to the high plains of northern Argentina. More than 50 per cent of the road has been paved in the last 20 years, but there are still plenty of potholes, meandering (and barrier-free) bends and bad drivers to make even the asphalted sections far more interesting than your average country road.

Heading south to north is an epic journey that takes you from sheep-farming Anglo-Argentinian Patagonia through some of the most remote, least populated corners of the country, into the vineyards and rain-shadow deserts of the central zone, and then on to the largely indigenous regions of the Andean northwest. Of course, 'remote' is relative, but if you have been in Buenos Aires and need a break from city people and taxi smoke, you could do worse than embark on an RN 40 adventure.

RN 40 seems most at home in lonely Patagonia. Out of the car window, all you see is a scrub of tough grasses, sturdy little bushes and not a single tree between the road and the horizon. Then you pass parks filled with frigid green lakes, jagged mountains and huge glaciers. RN 40 is a comfort zone in this bleak terrain, giving you a taste of the end of the world, but with the option of driving on to the next compact town.

Don't try travelling the road without a spare can of petrol, a good map and a stock of yerba mate – you can't drive this most iconic of roads without the quintessential pot of green tea. A four-wheel drive vehicle is ideal, although its carburettors may need adjusting for high altitudes. In gravelled areas, a metal cage is recommended for the windscreen and, when things get muddy (especially in the north-west during summer), tyre-chains may be required.

Hopping around Argentina by jet to tick off Ruta 40's glaciers, peaks, waterfalls, forests and colourful Andean towns means you miss the vastness, the rhythm and the whole idea of the country. RN 40 is an access road to the soul of the nation, to its country inns and estancias, to its diverse and dramatic topographies. Most roads in Argentina are like bicycle spokes heading for the clamour of the capital; 'La Ruta Cuarenta' shuns the big city and leads its explorers into an older, simpler, slower, far more beautiful country. The thrill of travelling RN 40 is not only in the sheer joy of embarking on a long drive, but in knowing that a slight detour might lead you into a world not featured in the guidebooks.

Los Cerros.

Estepa

Cerro Solo & Antonio Rojo. (02962 493069). Open Oct-Easter noon-1am daily. £££. Italian/Traditional.

Patagonia meets Italy in this softly-lit restaurant – think wood-fired pizzas, lamb ravioli, beef soaked in malbec, lamb with Calafate-berry sauce and aubergine lasagna. There are superb views of Fitz Roy from the back garden, which is an ideal spot to lunch or knock back a pisco sour in the waning evening sun. Later, the action moves indoors, where musicians frequently serenade diners. The tiramisu and white chocolate ganache tips the meal over the edge from delicious to dangerously decadent.

Josh Aike

Lago del Desierto 104 (02962 493008). Open Nov-Easter 11am-11pm daily. Café.

A Patagonian town without a chocolate shop is like Buenos Aires' La Boca without tango, but Josh Aike is no generic cliché-filler. Nothing but first-rate chocolate is bitten into, melted over and stirred at this rickety wooden two-storey *chocolatería*. The bittersweet hot chocolate (ask for it spiked with whiskey or Baileys) and house-made *alfajores* (cornflower biscuits) come highly recommended. For more substantial fare, try the cheese or chocolate fondue for two. Grab a window seat upstairs for a superb view of Fitz Roy.

El Muro

San Martín 912 (02962 493248). Open noon-midnight Mon, Tue, Thur-Sun. £££. Parrilla/International.

North of the centre, you'll recognise El Muro by its exterior climbing wall, which serves as an excellent appetite-builder. Inside, it's all spacious, stylish timber and soft lighting, and there are plenty of people-watching opportunities to be had from the large picture windows. *Carne* sizzles to perfection on the *asador*, while pizza à la parrilla, lamb goulash and salmon *sorrentinos* (stuffed pasta parcels) keep things varied. There's also a 20-strong wine list to consider. If you're in El Chaltén over the winter, you might end up making a few visits here, as it's one of the few restaurants open year-round.

Patagonicus

Güemes 57, Shop 1 (02962 493025). Open Nov-Easter 10am-midnight daily. ££. Italian.

When you're hankering for a quality hit of Italian carbs, the pizzas and pastas here won't disappoint. Hunger pangs are relieved around large wooden tables within walls adorned with black and white photos of pioneering climbing expeditions and the owner's mountaineer father, Cesarino Fava. At night, this place is buzzing – and after a few El Bolsón-brewed beers, you will be too.

Ruca Mahuida

Lionel Terray 104 (02962 493018). Open Nov-March 11.30am-3pm, 7-11pm daily. £££. Modern.

After a chilly day on the trails, this is the culinary equivalent of slipping into a muscle-melting jacuzzi. It's an intimate, five-table affair housed in a sweet wooden-roofed cottage, and just the ticket if you're looking to impress (although you'll impress no one if you forget to book). In a town of quality restaurants, Ruca Mahuida manages to steal the prize for imagination, fusing traditional South American fare with local, Patagonian ingredients. The tenderloin in malbec with quinoa mushroom risotto and sweet potato is the brightest star on a menu that also offers fish, home-made pastas and vegetarian options such as stuffed green pumpkin. Whatever you order, pair it with a bottle of fine *vino* and save room for a round of chocolate marquise.

La Tapera

Antonio Rojo & Cabo Garcia (02962 493138). Open Oct-Easter 3pm-midnight daily. ££. Modern.

Chipo, the exuberant Argentinian owner, runs the heartiest and happiest eaterie in town. So successful was his cosy main-street restaurant, La Tapera – where ravenous diners shared tables with strangers and became life-long friends by dessert – that it was only a matter of time before it moved up in the world to larger premises. Now set in a spacious wooden *cabaña* with a crackling fire, the menu may have quadrupled in size, but the intimacy and *campo* vibe is still here. Start with the soup – the best in El Chaltén, with a rotating cast of vegetable, tomato, onion, spinach and pumpkin – then move on to the lamb and lentil stew, which satisfies the most bottomless of pits. Go out with a bang with La Bomba de Tiempo (literally 'the time bomb'), a crêpe with *dulce de leche*, raspberries, orange, chocolate and cream.

Shop

A word of advice: don't leave your souvenir shopping to be done in El Chaltén. You'll only be disappointed. You'll find what limited shopping the town has concentrated along the two main streets, Avenidas Güemes and San Martín.

El Viento Nos Amontona

San Martín 320, Shop 2 (02962 493241). Open Oct-Apr 10am-1pm, 3-10pm daily. May, June, Aug, Sept 3-8pm daily.

With a name meaning 'the wind brings us together', this brightly painted shop is a little slice of Buenos Aires cool in remote Patagonia. Everything is by Argentinian designers, including locally made handicrafts, aprons, bags, jewellery, clothing, cosmetics, *mate* paraphernalia and other random objects. If nothing else, you'll walk out with a smile on your face.

Rincón del Sur

Lago del Desierto 265 (02962 493301). Open 10am-midnight daily.

This wine bar is the hottest thing to arrive in El Chaltén since central heating. Wind-battered climbers and thirsty hikers come to drink through 130 Argentinian vintages and 30 speciality brews. Half the shop is a delicatessen, stocked with gourmet picnic staples such as prosciutto, cheese, olives and sun-dried tomatoes, while the other half is a bar, where you can park yourself at a wooden table and tuck into a plate of *picadas* (cold meat and cheese platter). Tango bands spice things up on occasion.

Viento Oeste

San Martín 898 (02962 493200). Open Oct-April 10am-1pm, 3-8pm daily. May-Sept reduced hours.
This outdoor-equipment store is a one-stop shop for all your nature-loving needs: hire or buy a tent, sleeping bag, backpack or gas stove. It also stocks hiking boots, waterproof clothing, trekking guides, park maps, postcards and assorted souvenirs.

Stay

Whether you are a fickle flashpacker or a high-end traveller, El Chaltén has a bed for you. Regardless of what you pay and where you stay, a gobsmacking view will probably be part of the package. Book well in advance if you're visiting in January or February, and note that most places close between Easter and October. If you're willing to compromise on convenience, a couple of the best establishments lie a few kilometres outside of town. Few hotels offer internet, although Wi-Fi – albeit torturously slow – is starting to make an appearance.

Albergue Patagonia

San Martín 493 (02962 493301/patagoniahostel@ yahoo.com.ar). Open Oct-May. £. No credit cards.
For outstanding service, bang for your buck and the company of other travellers, you can't do better than this split-personality hostel. Alongside the grungy hostel dorms and doubles in the two-storey main house, you'll find more salubrious digs in the neighbouring building, which is more upmarket B&B than backpackers' haunt. Here, you'll find a selection of generously sized, tastefully furnished doubles and triples, complete with spotless en suites. Breakfast is included in the price, and, best of all, guests can hang out in the main house with its communal kitchen, laundry room, book exchange and comfortable lounge. The staff are knowledgeable and conscientious, and do an expert job of arranging tours.

"Rooms at Los Cerros have king-sized beds, stellar views of the Río de la Vueltas and soak-till-you-prune jacuzzis."

Los Cerros

San Martín 260 (02962 493182/www.experience patagonia.com). Open Oct-Easter. £££.
Despite its large, conspicuous red presence on a plateau in the centre of town, Los Cerros is a book not to be judged by its cover. If money is no object, this is the place to bunk

down. Its 34 rooms, painted in deep red hues, are immaculately decorated, with king-sized beds, stellar views of the Río de la Vueltas valley and soak-till-you-prune jacuzzis. You could venture out for activities with the hotel's personal guides, or just stay indoors all day, indulging in pampering spa treatments, using the internet, going through the DVD collection, or attending talks on local flora and fauna. Two-for-one drinks and all-you-can-eat *picadas* are offered at the bar's 7-8pm happy hour. Don't overindulge, though; the restaurant knows how to give wild Patagonian game, lamb and seafood the gourmet treatment (AR$170 for three courses), and the sommelier, who has 80 Argentinian wines at his disposal, is quite the matchmaker.

Estancia La Quinta

2km S of El Chaltén *off RP 23 (02962 493012/ www.estancialaquinta.com.ar). Open Oct-April. £££.*
For a taste of the Patagonia of yesteryear, try this working cattle ranch for size. One of the oldest settlements in the area (it has been in the same family for four generations), it's run by Alfredo and Patricia, a charming bilingual pair who know how to lay on the hospitality. Their favourite subjects are local history (they've turned the original cottage into a museum) and flora and fauna (keep your eyes peeled for guanacos, woodpeckers and foxes). The modern main building is where you'll find the 30 comfortable bedrooms. Those facing east look out on Fitz Roy, four have disabled access and 20 have jacuzzis – the perfect elixir for post-hiking muscle pain. Three communal living areas let you curl up in front of a fireplace and natter to fellow guests. In the evening, you're spared the trek into town, thanks to an on-site chef who sources beef from the property and fish from Lago del Desierto, and caters for the fussiest of dietary requirements.

Hostería El Pilar

17km N of El Chaltén *on RP 23 (02962 493002/ www.hosteriaelpilar.com.ar). Open Nov-Easter. ££. No credit cards.*
If you've come to Patagonia to get away from it all, this place is an ideal hideaway. Along a bumpy gravel road just beyond the boundary of Parque Nacional Los Glaciares, this re-creation of an old corrugated-iron estancia is ringed by forest and feels wonderfully remote. A wood stove crackles cheerfully away in the living area, while guests retreat to the ten quaint bedrooms, decorated in warm autumnal shades with rustic wall hangings and those all-important mountain views. The kitchen, bar and library operate a help-yourself policy, and the restaurant menu changes daily. Free transfers are offered to and from El Chaltén, and public buses ply the route a few times daily. If you just want to hang out locally, however, a fine hiking trail leads from the guesthouse to the stunning Glaciar Piedras Blancas.

Hostería El Puma

Lionel Terray 212 (02293 436424/www.hosteriael puma.com.ar). Open Oct-April. £££.
An upmarket lodge owned by climber Alberto del Castillo, this 12-room guesthouse occupies a quiet spot just north

of the centre. The spartan but stylish rooms go heavy on the rustic charm, with wooden floorboards and beams, exposed-brick walls and fine valley views. Guests have access to Wi-Fi internet, a luminous living area with an open fireplace, and a first-rate restaurant, Terray, whose Patagonian-flavoured menu is complemented by a choice of 30 vintages hailing from the San Juan, Mendoza and Salta provinces.

Inlandsis
Lago del Desierto 480 (02962 493276/www.inlandsis. com.ar). Open Nov-Easter. £.
This boutique bed and breakfast has welcoming, super-helpful English-speaking staff, free internet and Wi-Fi, and killer mountain and valley views from the eight stylish bedrooms. Thoughtful little touches – such as stylish exposed brickwork, excellent insulation, piping-hot showers and mattresses an osteopath could love – make all the difference. The staff can put together a wholesome packed lunch on request, while beer, wine, toasted sandwiches and cheese fondue can be ordered throughout the day. The generous breakfast includes home-made jams and cakes. With very reasonable starting prices, this place is quite a find.

"Timber reigns supreme at Nothofagus, along with rustic decorative touches and Mapuche-style wall hangings."

Nothofagus Bed & Breakfast
Hensen & Riquelme (02962 493087/www.nothofagus bb.com.ar). Open Oct-May. £.
A sky-blue house dolled up like a chalet, Nothofagus has seven light-filled rooms, five with phenomenal views of Fitz Roy and three with private bathrooms (the rest are shared). Timber reigns supreme in the immaculate accommodation, with rustic decorative touches and Mapuche-style wall hangings. The walls might feel a little thin if you score noisy neighbours, but the Wi-Fi service, bright communal area and homely atmosphere more than compensate.

Factfile

When to go
November to Easter is the best time to visit El Chaltén. Winters (July to September) are chilly and inhospitable, and most businesses close after Easter and open again in mid October. January and February are high season (book ahead), and even in midsummer, the weather can change from balmy and clear to biting snowstorm in the space of hours, so pack accordingly. March and April are idyllic months. November and December are blustery.

Getting there
The nearest airport is in El Calafate, 212 kilometres south-east of El Chaltén. From El Calafate, it's a two hour and 30 minute drive along the paved RN 40 and the mostly paved RN 23. Buses run between El Calafate and El Chaltén (three hours 30 minutes) up to six times daily from October to June, and once daily the rest of the year. El Chaltén's bus station, opposite the tourist office on Güemes and Perito Moreno, was almost complete at the time of going to print. Bus companies TAQSA, Cal-tur, Trans Patagonia Servicios, Las Lengas and Chaltén Travel have plans to operate out of the station.

From El Chaltén, there are services to Piedra Buena for connections to Puerto Madryn, and along RN 40 via Perito Moreno (13 hours) to Esquel (29 hours) and Bariloche (34 hours). Companies include Chaltén Travel (02962 493092, www.chaltentravel.com), which operates from November to April, and TAQSA (02962 493130, www.taqsa.com.ar), which has services from October to April.

Getting around
El Chaltén is small enough to navigate on foot. If you're staying outside the village or need a taxi, try Tere Torres (Ricardo Arbilla 40, 02962 493202). Albergue Patagonia (*see p310*) rents out mountain bikes.

From October to Easter, there are three bus transfers daily to Lago del Desierto (one hour 30 minutes) with bus companies El Huemul Transfer (02962 493312) and Las Lengas (02962 493023), via El Pilar (30 minutes).

Tourist information
El Chaltén Güemes 21 (02962 493270, www.elchalten.com). Open Oct-Easter 8am-8pm Mon-Fri; 9am-9pm Sat, Sun. Easter-Sept 8am-3pm Mon-Fri. Note that the town's only ATM is next door.

Internet
Chalté-Net Güemes 120, Shop 5 (02962 493249). Open Oct-Apr 9am-10pm daily. May-Sept 4.30-9pm Mon-Sat.
Note that the town's satellite internet connection is very sluggish. Wi-Fi services are slowly being introduced in hotels.

Clockwise from top left: bridge to Garganta del Diablo; Parque Nacional Iguazú; Guaraní tribesman; falls from the Argentinian side; kayaking on the river.

Iguazú

Argentina

Roaring waterfalls and colourful wildlife.

When it comes to destinations to see before you die, the Cataratas del Iguazú should rank near the top of the list. There's nothing quite like this towering mass of spray and sound, which can be found straddling two countries amid 2,250 square kilometres of parkland.

Some 275 waterfalls punctuate this stretch of river. At its largest and most dramatic conjunction, the water is churned into thick creamy clouds that tumble through rainbows of light, while bright butterflies and birds dart through the mist. The resulting spray rises for so many metres that, from a distance, the falls can almost seem to be travelling in two directions.

'Iguazú' refers to the attraction in its entirety, but it is usually divided into four distinct areas, with a small town and national park on each side of the falls. On the Argentinian side, Puerto Iguazú offers a surprisingly tasteful answer to a typical tourist town, while a few kilometres east, Parque Nacional Iguazú surrounds Argentina's share of the legendary falls. This is not to be confused with Parque Nacional do Iguaçu, which is the Brazilian slice of the waterworks, with its own tourist gateway in the town of Foz do Iguaçu.

Both sides of the waterfalls have their advantages, with most visitors agreeing that a better all-round panorama is to be had in Brazil, but the ultimate glory – the sensational Garganta del Diablo, or 'Devil's Throat' – belongs to Argentina.

Explore

PUERTO IGUAZÚ

Despite being, to all intents and purposes, a tourist town, **Puerto Iguazú** handles its captive audience with characteristic Argentinian flair. The modest town centre has a gaggle of refreshingly upbeat tourist restaurants, several tasteful souvenir stalls and some excellent-value accommodation. The main action is centred around the hub of Avenida Victoria Aguirre and Avenida Brasil, where streets filled with shops and restaurants branch out in several directions.

Heading north on Avenida Brasil will take you into a less touristy enclave, with a local market and several eateries favoured by residents rather than visitors. Those looking to make a longer circuit of the town could head to El Hito (Avenida Costanera and Avenida Tres Fronteras). This small and unremarkable obelisk, a kilometre or so west of the main shopping streets, marks the meeting point of the Iguazú and Paraná rivers. From here, you can see Argentina, Paraguay and Brazil.

PARQUE NACIONAL IGUAZÚ

Parque Nacional Iguazú offers its visitors a well-planned and environmentally-minded walk through the falls. Local buses pull up to the main gates, leaving visitors to make their way to the beginning of the waterfalls proper on foot (entry AR$60). You can then decide whether to continue the walk through several short and attractive trails, or hop on an electrically powered train to cut some of the distance between the park's watery attractions.

From the first station, Estación Central, one option is to walk the El Sendero Macuco trail. A seven-kilometre round trip through lush vegetation and trees, the trail routinely crosses wildlife not often seen in the main park areas; if you're lucky, you might spot a toucan or two en route. It ends at a secluded waterfall, the Salto Arrechea – admittedly not as dramatic as the main falls, but nowhere near as busy either. With parts of the trail involving the slippery negotiation of rocks, it is likely to take the better part of a morning or afternoon.

The second stop on the train – or a pleasant 20-minute stroll from the park entrance, heading through the jungle along the aptly-named Sendero Verde (green trail) – is Estación Cataratas. The station is the departure point for two of the three main routes to the falls, the Circuito Superior (upper circuit) and Circuito Inferior (lower circuit). The former is a short but rewarding walkway that takes in several viewing platforms, from which visitors can appreciate the massive scale of the waterfalls below, and admire the panoramic views. The Circuito Inferior traces a longer 4,200-metre route around the bottom of the falls, allowing walkers to dip their toes

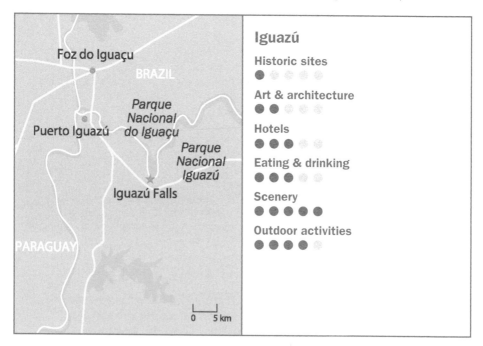

Iguazú

Historic sites
● ◉ ◉ ◉ ◉

Art & architecture
● ● ◉ ◉ ◉

Hotels
● ● ● ◉ ◉

Eating & drinking
● ● ● ◉ ◉

Scenery
● ● ● ● ●

Outdoor activities
● ● ● ● ◉

Parque Nacional Iguazú.

into jets of spouting water, douse themselves in spray and ignore warnings not to feed the coatis (fluffy, raccoon-like animals that enjoy a well-fed existence through scavenging tourists' scraps).

At the end of the trail, you can take a boat ride across the river to the Isla San Martín, to continue exploring this part of the falls. Boats leave roughly every 20 minutes and cost AR$20 for a standard trip, or up to AR$45 when teamed with extra 'explorer' activities, which involve guided tours of the island's verdant interior and longer forays into the nearby waters.

Best left until last is the truly spectacular Garganta del Diablo, or 'Devil's Throat' – the biggest of the park's waterfalls, and a definite highlight. Getting there entails either a short train ride to the Estación Garganta del Diablo, followed by a 15-minute walk to the lookout point, or a longer stroll along the river.

Expect to see tumbling water on an incredible scale, teamed with thousands of colourful butterflies. The sheer scale of the thundering, horseshoe-shaped falls is breathtaking; when Eleanor Roosevelt visited, she was heard to mutter 'poor Niagara'.

"Time your visit during the five-day window of a full moon, and a midnight rainbow can sometimes be made out from the rising spray."

If you find yourself at Iguazú during the five-day window of a full moon, a moonlight tour, organised by the park itself (03757 491469, reservas@iguazuargentina.com), is unmissable. Although no replacement for seeing the mighty falls during the daytime, visiting at the dead of night adds a new, otherworldly perspective to the landscape. On a good night, a 'midnight rainbow' can be made out from the rising spray.

The tour begins with an optional dinner in the park at La Selva Restaurant (see p318), followed by three departures, at 8pm, 8.45pm or 9.30pm. The experience lasts about three hours, with the last departure giving visitors the chance to arrive at the falls around midnight. The best views, however, are usually to be had during the earlier tour, when the moon is lower in the sky. A full-moon schedule can be found online at www.iguazuargentina.com. The tour, with dinner included, costs AR$130; without dinner, it is AR$80.

PARQUE NACIONAL DO IGUAÇU, BRAZIL

Clearly more deliberately set up for tour parties, and with an obvious focus on selling activities outside the ticket price, the Brazilian side of the falls is very different to its Argentinean counterpart. While the latter sculpts tasteful walkways through the forest and jungle, the former ploughs a wide road directly through the centre. What's more, the park bus thoughtfully stops off to plug two tourist trips before arriving at the falls proper.

Depending on your preferences, Brazil is a better option if you're looking to get wet and wild with boat trips, rafting, helicopter ascents and so forth. The hard sell begins straight away, as tour companies surround the main entrance to plug their many activities. Helisul (+55 45 3529 7474, www.helisul.com) offers helicopter rides, while Macuco Safari (+55 45 3574 4244, www.macuco safari.com.br) runs various boating, rafting and jungle exploration trips.

In order to explore the Brazilian side comprehensively, you should probably opt for a boat trip or tour, as not doing so means just taking in the view before boarding the bus for the long journey back to the entrance.

That said, some visitors feel that the trips are not particularly good value for money, and a 20-minute stroll at the end of the bus tour could well be enough to justify your entry fee (AR$45). At the final point of disembarking, tourists tramp along a long metal walkway, past several pre-ordained photo opportunities, before arriving at the ultimate vista. It's an awe-inspiring sight, as the viewing platform leads right to the edge of the most stunning area of the falls. There's a great view of Garganta del Diablo in the distance; immersed in the spray, it's surprisingly easy to forget that you're surrounded by fellow tourists.

A further walkway leads to an elevator that will lift you to an even higher panorama, but nothing beats standing among the barrelling columns of water on the lower deck.

FOZ DO IGUAÇU, BRAZIL

Depending on your perspective, **Foz do Iguaçu** is either a nondescript border town or a refreshingly real stop in a land otherwise built for tourists. The centre may lack the tourist restaurants and bars of nearby Puerto Iguazú, but if you've had one parrilla too many and are keen to hear some non-English speakers, it's a great chance to soak up a bit of Brazilian atmosphere.

The central Avenida Brazil is lined with restaurants and snack bars, providing a welcome break for those looking to sample some local cuisine and drinks at considerably lower prices than in more touristy joints. East of town is a brash stretch of hotels and casinos, which could keep visitors comfortably immured from the town proper if they so wished.

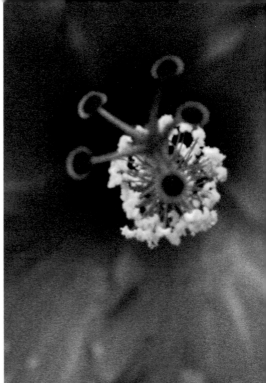

Top: local flora and fauna.
Bottom: Loi Suites Iguazú.

Eat

The best establishments can be found in Puerto Iguazú. Argentina's Parque Nacional Iguazú has a few snack bars clustered around Estación Central and Estación Garganta del Diablo, with additional snack bars and restaurants lining the walkway from the entrance to the first station.

In Brazil's Parque Nacional do Iguaçu, a number of snack bars, and one or two restaurants, can be found at the tour buses' final stop. Many visitors choose to bring their own packed lunches, which must be consumed in designated areas near the other eateries.

Aqva Restaurant
Puerto Iguazú *Avenida Córdoba 135, & Carlos Thays (03757 422064/www.aqvarestaurant.com). Open noon-midnight daily. ££. Italian.*
Set on a street packed with tourist restaurants, this place manages to attract both visitors from around the globe and local regulars. Part of the appeal stems from its thoughtful little touches – a complimentary glass of sparkling wine on paying the bill, for example – and superb service. But the light, classic Argentinian dishes are the main attraction. The menu includes fresh pastas and gnocchi, pizzas and grilled meats, along with a decent selection of vegetarian options.

Argentina
Puerto Iguazú *Felix de Azara, no number, & Avenida Brasil (no phone). Open noon-11pm daily. £. Café/Traditional.*
If you're hoping for a local offering in a town rooted firmly in the tourist trade, this ramshackle bar is a great choice. It's one of a handful of no-frills eateries surrounding Puerto Iguazú's market area, which is a haven for residents stocking up on their favourite cheeses, olives and pickles. The bar has a small television as well as a storefront packed with home-made fare, from outsized jars of pickled peaches to a colourful selection of liqueurs (the favourite in these parts being sweet and spicy Lei, an Italian-style aperitif with cinnamon overtones). From these tempting wares, the bar owner's wife can prepare a platter of *picada*, featuring cheeses, cured meats and olives. Teamed with a cold beer and a football match on TV, it makes for a classic Argentinian evening.

La Esquina
Puerto Iguazú *Avenida Córdoba 148 (03757 420633/www.hotelsaintgeorge.com). Open noon-3pm, 7pm-midnight daily. £££. International/Parrilla.*
Adjoining the Hotel Saint George (*see p320*), this intimate restaurant is perfect for romantic dinners à deux. The superb meals are a cut above the fare typically offered on Argentinian menus, and there's an excellent selection of wines. The grilled river fish is recommended, but the star of the show is the parrilla, complete with succulent slabs of *bife de chorizo* (sirloin).

Porto Canoas
Parque Nacional do Iguaçu *Last tour-bus stop (+55 45 3521 4400/reservas@cataratasdoiguacu.com.br). Open noon-6pm daily. £££. International.*
If you've worked up an appetite climbing the park's trails, head here for a more comprehensive buffet meal than you'll find in the standard snack bars. Porto Canoas offers a magnificent spread, which more than justifies the price. Thanks to an incredible location opposite the falls, the views are sublime; diners can admire them from the air-conditioned glass-walled interior, or opt for a table out on the lovely riverside terrace.

> ## "Fish, plucked fresh from nearby tropical waters, is grilled to perfection over La Rueda's charcoal."

La Rueda
Puerto Iguazú *Avenida Córdoba 28 (03757 422531/www.larueda1975.com). Open noon-3.30pm, Tue, Wed, Fri-Sun; 6pm-midnight daily. £££. Seafood/International.*
Consistently winning rave reviews, this is the restaurant that locals are most likely to recommend. What's more, it lives up to its sterling reputation. While the menu offers the standard Argentinian meats and *asado* selection, it's the excellent river fish, plucked fresh from nearby tropical waters, that is the main draw. The selection is dependent on the season, but might include such delicacies as dorado – an enormous and supremely ugly river fish, which, grilled to perfection over La Rueda's charcoal, is a flavoursome match for a glass or two of good red wine. A word of warning: only American Express credit cards are accepted at present, although the owners thoughtfully keep a scooter on standby to whizz customers in need of cash to a nearby bank.

La Selva
Parque Nacional Iguazú *Near park entrance (03757 491469). Open 11.30am-3pm daily. ££££. Traditional.*
Despite being based in the prime tourist-trap territory of Parque Nacional Iguazú, this restaurant doesn't take advantage of its captive audience. While others of its ilk might ply diners with unimaginative, poor-quality tourist fodder, charging premium prices for the privilege, La Selva offers a genuinely diverse buffet. Spanning the breadth of some 30 food platters (and that's before you've hit the parrilla or desserts), there's something for everyone, from crunchy salads to fresh pasta. Add to this this parrilla options, from which the staff will shave you juicy chunks of steak, lamb, pork or chicken direct from the griddle, and you're more than set for even the most challenging of nature trails.

La Aldea de la Selva
Lodge & Spa.

Yuca Bar

Puerto Iguazú *Avenida Brasil 136 (no phone). Open 1pm-midnight Mon-Thur, Sun; 2pm-midnight Fri, Sat. £. Café.*

A great halfway house if you're looking for a less formal option to the restaurants around town. This atmospheric bar is perfect for laid-back lounging, and serves pizzas, pastas, sandwiches and excellent *picadas*. The warm interior lends itself to intimate drinks, but with outdoor seating near the main nightlife spots, it's also a great place to watch the world go by.

Stay

La Aldea de la Selva Lodge & Spa

7km SE of Puerto Iguazú *Selva Iriapú (03757 425777/www.laaldeadelaselva.com). £££.*

Located just a few miles from Puerto Iguazú, La Aldea is an excellent option for those who want to combine the jungle-lodge experience with visits to the falls. Guests sleep in attractive log cabins, each of which has a private balcony (plus hammock) overlooking the trees. Unlike in some of the more remote lodges, the rooms here come with mod cons such as cable TV and air-conditioning (though no Wi-Fi at time of writing). Several short and well-defined trails allow guests to explore the property's small patch of rainforest, where flocks of raucous parakeets and the occasional toucan can be spotted. Activities such as rappelling and zip-lining are offered as part of the hotel's 'Jungle Fly' programme.

"At Loi Suites Iguazù, hidden in the Iryapù jungle, the wildlife seems so close it might just take over the hotel."

Hotel das Cataratas

Parque Nacional do Iguaçu *Paraná, Brazil (+55 45 2102 7000/www.hoteldascataratas.com). ££.*

Like a looming nemesis to the cream-coloured Sheraton on the opposite side of the falls, the baby-pink Hotel das Cataratas is far closer to the action– though arguably at the cost of the Argentinian panorama. Conveniently situated on the main road into the park, and only a short walk (or shuttle bus) from the main viewing platform, this venue has the edge on its Argentinian counterpart when it comes to accommodation set within the parks proper. The 1970s decor and aging facilities in many rooms may be off-putting for some guests, but there is an attractive pool area, tennis courts and guided walks into the nearby jungle. The hotel was under extensive renovation at the time of writing and may be due some further glory.

Hotel Esturión

Puerto Iguazú *Avenida Tres Fronteras 650 (03757 420100/www.hotelesturion.com). £.*

Located a short distance from the centre of town, the Esturión caters to visitors who prefer to be at a slight remove from the action. The spacious pool area is perfect for all-day lounging, while the extensive grounds are scattered with luxurious, shaded day-beds. The rooms are coolly contemporary and well appointed, and the adjoining restaurant offers a good choice of lighter lunchtime specials, as well as good-value dinner options. Breakfast, while extensive, may disappoint those hoping for some savoury options – this is the sweet-toothed Argentinian *desayuno* on a grand scale.

Hotel Saint George

Puerto Iguazú *Avenida Córdoba 148 (03757 420633/www.hotelsaintgeorge.com). ££.*

The grand old dame of town, Hotel St George is located in the centre of Puerto Iguazú. The attractive lobby heralds the interior spaces to come – enormous bedrooms with spacious en suite bathrooms and tasteful, classic decor. Some of the older rooms are looking slightly worn these days, and if you're here for a quiet few nights, the central location might be a little loud for your tastes. But the lovely pool area, reasonable rates and well-regarded restaurant (*see p318*) more than compensate.

Iguazú Grand

Puerto Iguazú *Ruta 12, km 1640 (0800 444 8298/ www.iguazugrandhotel.com). ££££.*

Situated between the town of Puerto Iguazú and Parque Nacional Iguazú, this hotel is ideal for those dedicated to getting the most from the falls. With an enormous expanse of land to play with, the Grand offers a spacious pool area, spa, café, restaurant and even an on-site casino. The rooms are classically styled and very comfortable, although the gold furnishings in the high-end 'panoramic suite' are a little bit over the top.

Iguazú Panoramic

Puerto Iguazú *Paraguay 372 (03757 498133/ www.panoramic-hoteliguazu.com). £££.*

Despite sounding more like a 3D cinema than a hotel, the Panoramic is the classiest option in Puerto Iguazú. Situated at a discreet distance from the main action, this is the place to go for sumptuously styled interiors, top-notch cuisine, endless landscaped grounds and a great panoramic view out on to the nearby river. With a collection of restaurants, cafés and bars, plus 24-hour room service, a modest on-site casino and other indulgent touches, it's got all bases covered for a relaxing stay.

Loi Suites Iguazú

Puerto Iguazú *Selva Iriapú, no number (03757 498300/www.loisuites.com.ar). £££.*

Hidden in the Iryapú jungle and connected to Parque Nacional Iguazú, Loi Suites Iguazú's five buildings are interconnected by suspended bridges, elevated walkways and dirt paths. The wildlife, even seen from inside, seems so close it might just take over the hotel. You can sometimes spot monkeys and other small animals in the tall trees, making you almost forget there's civilisation not too far off. There are 154 elegantly-styled rooms with jungle views, and eight beautiful villas with outdoor jacuzzi tubs and views of the Río Iguazú. With a spa, three pools surrounded by wooden decking and greenery, a bar, a restaurant and a selection of outdoor activities on hand, who needs civilisation anyway?

Marco Polo

Puerto Iguazú *Avenida Córdoba 158 (03757 425559/ www.marcopoloinniguazu.com). £. No credit cards.*
If you're keen to do the backpacker thing without forfeiting any comforts, this is an excellent choice. Right in the centre of town, with a relaxed vibe and accommodation to rival that of a boutique hotel, the Marco Polo is a hostel doing everything right. The rooms are simple but stylish, with wooden floors and bright furnishings. There's also a street-side bar to rival the best in the area, a great pool area and

a jacuzzi, making this place stellar value for money. The onsite travel agency also offers some of the best deals for Iguazú excursions.

Sheraton International Iguazú

Parque Nacional Iguazú *(03757 491800/ www.starwoodhotels.com). £££.*
Unbeatable purely for its location opposite the world's greatest waterfalls, the Sheraton's high-end venue is the choice of honeymooners and big spenders. Those staying here are still a little distance on foot or by train from any of the falls proper, although this could be an advantage, as the wildlife feels a little freer to venture into the grounds, with poolside guests frequently treated to visits from hummingbirds, butterflies and all manner of exotic creatures. The whole setup feels a little tired nowadays, as the original styling hasn't yet been revamped, but it's a quality spot nonetheless, and great for a cocktail even if you're not staying the night.

Factfile

When to go
A visit to Iguazú is likely to be rewarding at any time of year. In the milder months of October to December and April to June, you'll enjoy a far more pleasant stroll through the trails and falls. But during the rainy season of November to March, you'll see Iguazú at its torrential best. Summer (January to March) is hot and humid, but there is plenty of wildlife.

Getting there
Three flights a day to Puerto Iguazú are offered by both Aerolíneas (www.aerolineas.com) and LAN (www.lan.com); the latter tends to be cheaper. Buses leave regularly from Buenos Aires to make the 18-hour trip to Puerto Iguazú. From Posadas, a bus trip takes five to six hours. American and Australian visitors should note that they will need a visa to enter Brazil.

Getting around
You can save yourself time by taking taxis (Puerto Iguazú to Parque Nacional Iguazú, or Foz do Iguaçu to Puerto Iguazú). Drivers can make any given trip ten or 20 minutes faster than the buses. On the Argentinian side of the falls, battered yellow *colectivos* (buses) make the rattling journey between Puerto Iguazú and Parque Nacional Iguazú every 20 minutes or so. They leave from several spots along the main road, Avenida Victoria Aguirre, detouring at the central bus station. Technically, you want the number 21, but it's easier to look for the sign in the window that says 'cataratas' (waterfalls). The trip from Puerto Iguazú to Parque Nacional Iguazú takes 30 to 40 minutes.

To get to the Brazilian side, you'll need to take a bus from Puerto Iguazú's central bus terminal. Head to the section for local departures (clearly signed), where the last stand has departures for Foz do Iguaçu every 30 minutes or so. These buses will drive you through the border, where day visitors can enter unofficially without a stamp, although you'll still need your passport.

Unless you're planning on heading into Foz do Iguaçu, inform the driver that you want to go to the 'cataratas'. He'll deposit you at the intersection, where you can catch a bus en route from Foz do Iguaçu to Parque Nacional do Iguaçu. There's also likely be a taxi or two waiting to whisk you into the Brazilian park if you'd rather not wait for the bus.

If you are a day visitor and plan on taking the bus back, note that the last departure is at 7.30pm. Otherwise, a taxi can take you back over the border and into Puerto Iguazú.

Tourist information
Puerto Iguazú Avenida Victoria Aguirre 396 (03757 420800, www.iguazuargentina.com). Open 7am-9pm Mon-Fri; 8am-noon, 4-8pm Sat, Sun.
Foz do Iguaçu Praça Getúlio Vargas (+55 45 3521 1455, www.fozdoiguacu.pr.gov.br). Open 7am-8pm daily.

Internet
Both the Brazilian and Argentinian side offer plenty of internet and telephone cabins. In Puerto Iguazú, Telecentro Internet (Avenida Victoria Aguirre & Eppens) is a large, air-conditioned facility that's open daily.

Yacutinga Lodge & surrounding jungle.

Misiones

Argentina

Welcome to the jungle.

Dense forests fan out in all directions, a monotony of lush green. Above the trees, dark carrion birds circle in lazy holding patterns. Rivers and streams pierce the jungle. Most of the time, they flow glittering and soundless towards the Atlantic, but in places they run straight off a cliff in a furore of noise and spray. And beneath all this, the famous soil – the iron-rich, rust-coloured, pungent clay that gives this land its nickname: *tierra colorada* (red earth). It makes termite mounds glow in the dark, stains hubcaps for good and cakes the boots of travellers long departed.

This is Misiones, in the extreme north-east of Argentina. Its borders are principally defined by three rivers, the Paraná, Iguazú and Uruguay. Its shape resembles a crooked finger beckoning at Brazil. Most travellers only visit the tip of the finger for the Iguazú falls, a household name among natural wonders and a must see before you expire, if ever there was one. But why stop there? Misiones' sub-tropical topography is unique in Argentina and its culture, in which indigenous and immigrant influences have collided and combined, is as rich as its soil. There are rustic lodges in which to unwind, Jesuit ruins to explore, remote waterfalls to discover and *yerba mate* plantations to stroll through. Above all, there is the forest, ancient yet fragile, whose dark interior exerts an irresistible magnetism.

Explore

POSADAS

Hugging the south bank of the Río Paraná, Misiones's provincial capital was founded in 1879. It is a lively, welcoming city, albeit one with few obvious tourist attractions. Its centre is the palm-adorned Plaza 9 de Julio, overlooked by the neo-Gothic cathedral and the colonial-style Government House. There are several places of interest within walking distance of the square, among them the Museo de Bellas Artes y Centro Cultural Juan Yaparí (Sarmiento 319, 03752 447375), where the region's best art is on permanent display; the Museo Histórico Aníbal Cambas (Alberdi 600, 03752 422860), which holds an important collection of indigenous arts, crafts and tools dating back to 10,000 BC; and the excellent artisan market in Paseo Bossetti, which is open daily.

Ten blocks north of the centre is the city's waterfront, which affords terrific views of Encarnación, **Posadas**' Paraguayan 'twin' on the other bank. From here, you can also see the impressive suspension bridge that connects the two cities. This area once hummed with trade, in the era when Posadas was a flourishing river port, before falling into decline in the mid-20th century. Now, thanks to heavy investment, the *costanera* has been spruced up and rebranded as a leisure quarter, with an inline skater-friendly esplanade and a stretch of restaurants and bars (none of which is good for anything except the view, sadly, but it's still early days).

THE JESUIT RUINS

The missions of San Ignacio Miní, Santa Ana and Loreto form part of one of three man-made UNESCO World Heritage sites in Argentina (the others being the Jesuit Block and estancias in Córdoba, *see p121*; and La Cueva de las Manos in Santa Cruz, *see p343)*. Their crumbling walls and buildings, still magnificent in places, are the last traces of a vanished, indeed vanquished, society.

The three missions were founded in the 17th century as part of the group of 30 Jesuit Guaraní missions that spanned the borders of what are now three countries – Argentina, Paraguay and Brazil. Each mission functioned as a self-sufficient village with thousands of inhabitants. Life revolved around the central square, still easily recognisable at each site, on which stood the church, the town hall and the living quarters of the most important Guaraní. The Jesuit fathers lived in buildings laid out around a square adjacent to the church. There were also workshops, cemeteries, kitchen gardens for the community's daily subsistence, and large *yerba mate* plantations that accounted for the bulk of the settlement's income.

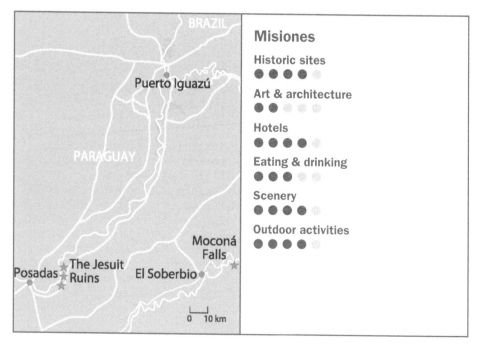

Misiones

Historic sites
● ● ● ● ◦

Art & architecture
● ● ◦ ◦ ◦

Hotels
● ● ● ● ◦

Eating & drinking
● ● ● ◦ ◦

Scenery
● ● ● ● ◦

Outdoor activities
● ● ● ● ◦

But what was most remarkable about the missions was their sophisticated architecture. The most spectacular building was the church of San Ignacio Miní, designed by Italian architect José Brasanelli. Although nothing of its richly painted and gilded interior remains, the portal still stands as a monument to the scale and grandeur of the original construction.

After the expulsion of the Jesuits in 1767, the missions were first abandoned, then ransacked, then swallowed up by the jungle, before being rediscovered in the early 20th century. While repairs have been carried out at San Ignacio Miní, the sites of Santa Ana and Loreto are still overgrown with thick vegetation. However, it's worth taking time to explore these missions to see the remains of the intricate irrigation systems, prisons and once-extensive orchards.

San Ignacio Miní is easy to get to from Posadas; the other missions, less so. If you want to see all of the ruins – including the Trinidad complex across the river in Paraguay – in one fell swoop, the best option is to take an organised excursion. Try Guayrá (www.guayra.com.ar) or Turismo Verde (www.viajesturismoverde.com.ar).

"One of Argentina's best kept secrets is Moconá Falls, where one half of the river falls sideways into the other half – to spectacular effect."

THE ATLANTIC RAINFOREST

Aside from isolated patches in southern Brazil and Paraguay, Misiones's large tracts of Atlantic rainforest are all that remain of the mighty jungle that once swathed the entire region. Agriculture and logging – legal or otherwise – have caused large-scale deforestation; were it not for the province's network of private reserves and public parks, the jungle's years would be numbered.

The largest and most important protected area is Parque Nacional Iguazú (see p312-321) in the northernmost tip of the province (**Puerto Iguazú** is around 300 kilometres from Posadas). South-west of here are provincial parks of Uruguaí and Salto Encantado, the former a verdant forest, the latter a drier lowland with panoramic vistas. In the centre of Misiones, along the Río Uruguay and near the city of **El Soberbio**, is one of the province's best known parks, Reserva Biosfera Yabotí. Here, wild strains of yerba mate and strangler fig create a dense undergrowth. South

of here is one of Argentina's best kept secrets – **Saltos de Moconá**, or the Moconá waterfalls. Stretching for almost two kilometres along the Río Uruguay, these falls are unique in that they run parallel to the river, rather than across it. Put simply, one half of the river falls sideways into the other half – to spectacular effect.

Dramatic though these geological anomalies are, the main reason for visiting the rainforest is to experience one of the planet's most precious and diverse ecosystems. Of the 1,000 or so distinct bird species identified in Argentina, around half are indigenous to Misiones, a province that occupies a mere one per cent of the country's land mass. While toucans are the show-stealers around here, there are multiple species of kingfisher, parakeet, parrot, hummingbird, eagle and vulture to spot too.

Mammals prefer to be heard and not seen, but with the help of a good guide you stand a chance of spying howler monkeys, anteaters, tapir and deer. And maybe, just maybe, you'll find yourself staring into the dark forest and seeing a pair of bright green eyes staring back at you. The good news is that you've seen either a puma or a jaguar. The bad news is that no one will believe you.

Eat

This is the right time to take a break from steak; the meat in Misiones tends to be as chewy and tasteless as the meat in central Argentina is tender and flavourful. Concentrate on regional specialities instead, such as torta frita (a floury, round biscuit that is deep-fried and often served for breakfast), stuffed vegetables, fruit preserves and river fish like pacú and surubí. One ingredient that's hard to avoid is manioc, or cassava root, known as mandioca in Spanish. If you can do it with a potato, you can do it with mandioca.

Thanks to the high percentage of the population descended from German or Polish immigrants, sauerkraut and smoked sausage often lurk somewhere on the menu too.

La Querencia
Posadas Bolívar 322 (03752 434955). Open noon-3pm, 7.30pm-1am Mon-Sat; noon-3pm Sun. ££. Parrilla/Traditional.
Famous restaurants are usually a let-down, so by the time you've heard the tenth person tell you that no one who's anyone passes through Misiones without eating at La Querencia, you'll be girding yourself for disappointment. No chance. This Posadas institution is a terrific parrilla that specialises in bringing patrons more grilled protein than they could feasibly consume. Try the chicken galeto – stuffed thigh and breast with parma ham, roast pepper and chimichurri that comes sizzling on a huge spit.

Stay

Most of the properties listed below are jungle lodges or estancias that include full board and some excursions in their rates (usually charged per person rather than per room). Transfers and alcoholic drinks are rarely included.

Posadas is not set up for tourism, and hotels in the city tend to be cheap and soulless. The best of a bland bunch is the four-star Hotel Julio César (Entre Ríos 1951, 03752 427930). Most people visit the Jesuit ruins on a day trip, but if you do want to stay overnight in San Ignacio, try Hotel San Ignacio (San Martín 823, 03752 470422).

Don Enrique Lodge
40km NE of El Soberbio *Paraje La Bonita (011 4790 7096/www.donenriquelodge.com.ar). £££. No credit cards.*
In the east of the province, Don Enrique is a classy jungle hideaway that's popular with enterprising honeymooners and upscale birdwatchers. The lodge lies on the banks of the Río Paraíso. Directly to the north is the Reserva Biosfera Yabotí, a reserve that protects 2,500sq km of Atlantic rainforest. But the biggest draw in this neck of the woods is the Saltos de Moconá, which are easily accessible by boat from the lodge. Other outdoor activities include walks with Guaraní guides, kayaking and photographic safaris.

"Stroll through the Estancia Santa Inés' patch of rainforest, ride through yerba plantations or swim in the stone pool."

Estancia Santa Cecilia
30km E of Posadas *RN 12 (03752 493018/ www.santa-cecilia.com.ar). £££££. No credit cards.*
This is a grand estancia whose whitewashed and stylishly symmetrical main house dates from 1908. The four spacious guest rooms contain original furniture and fittings and, unusually for an Argentinian ranch, are air-conditioned. The grounds are extensive and a joy to stroll around. Horse riding is on offer, and the staff will arrange excursions to the nearby Jesuit ruins. If you can't stay overnight, you can visit for a day-long *día de campo*, which includes the obligatory belt-warping *asado*.

Estancia Santa Inés
20km S of Posadas *RN 105, km 8.5 (03752 15 660456 mobile/www.estancia-santaines.com.ar). ££. No credit cards.*

The Núñez family will be your hosts at this historic estancia, a century-old *mate* plantation that, in its heyday, was one of the biggest producers of *yerba* leaves in the country. It's still a working farm, though the multi-storey red-brick workshops and drying houses that once hummed with activity are now silent and empty. The stunning main house, with its twin half-timbered gables and broad eaves sheltering a continuous gallery, contains five atmospheric guest rooms full of faded family photos, antique silver *mate* gourds, musty books and ornamental weaponry. You can stroll through the estate's patch of rainforest, take long horse-rides through the *yerba* fields (where wild rhea can often be spotted) or swim in the volcanic stone pool. Then again, you might prefer to simply sit on the terrace with a *mate* and watch as hummingbirds raid the trumpet vines.

Posada La Bonita
34km NE of El Soberbio *(011 15 5842 8386 mobile/03755 15 680380 mobile/www.posadala bonita.com.ar). £££.*
One of a select number of lodgings able to list 'private waterfall' among their amenities, Posada La Bonita offers rustic cabins set right in the heart of the rainforest, on the banks of the Río Uruguay. The aforementioned cascade, Salto La Bonita, burbles away just 200m from the cabins. Various trails pierce the dense woods surrounding the falls; these can be enjoyed on foot, on horseback or by 4x4. Longer excursions include treks in the adjacent Reserva Biosfera Yabotí and boat trips to Saltos de Moconá.

Posada Puerto Bemberg
Puerto Libertad, 35km S of Puerto Iguazú *(011 4152 5266/www.puertobemberg.com). ££££.*
Owned by a branch of the illustrious Bemberg family (best known for founding the Quilmes brewing empire in the late 19th century), this large and attractive property is pitched at visitors who want to experience the Misiones jungle without getting their fingernails too dirty. The main house, built in the 1940s but completely renovated since then, comprises 14 guest rooms (one is a suite), a restaurant serving regional specialities (try the grilled pacú river fish), a well-stocked library, and an equally well-stocked wine cellar. Recycled wood plays an important role in the posada's design scheme: the colourful headboards were sourced from derelict *conventillos* (tenement houses) in La Boca, and most of the furniture in the living room had a former life as the cheap seats at Newell's Old Boys football stadium in Rosario. The guided walks through the property's strip of private rainforest, led by biologist Emilio White, are fascinating.

Tacuapí Lodge
110km NE of Posadas *16km NE of Aristóbulo del Valle (03743 420335/www.tacuapi.com.ar). £££.*
The Salto Encantado provincial park, which contains the 60m-high waterfall of the same name, has the virtue of being one of the least touristy reserves in Misiones; and Tacuapí Lodge is right next to it. The five split-level cabins, which accomodate either four or six guests, have attractive hardwood furnishings and balconies overlooking giant

Top: Posada Puerto Bemberg (4). Bottom: Don Enrique Lodge (3).

ferns and lianas that pre-date World War I. The lodge's activities programme consists of guided walks of varying duration and difficulty, from low-key strolls along the decked paths of the hotel's own property to sweaty treks deep into the Encantado reserve in search of secret clearings and hidden cataracts. The lodge's optional excursions include visits to local Guarani communities and tours of leafy *yerba mate* plantations.

"Yacutinga Lodge blends wood, stone and varicoloured glass to create an effect that is part Gaudi, part *Lord of the Rings*."

Yacaratiá Lodge

9km S of El Soberbio *Paraje Perito Moreno* (011 15 3008 2343 mobile/www.yacaratia.com). *££*. No credit cards.

Remote, rustic and air-conditioned, Yacaratiá is ideal for high-maintenance jungle explorers. The property's main house, built from locally quarried stone, is set on an incline;

around it are seven discrete wood-and-stone cabins, each with its own deck gallery. Meals (included in the rates – expect fresh fish, seasonal fruits and plenty of manioc) can be consumed either in the house or outside your cabin. The property's other shared facilities include an outside pool and a sauna for up to eight people. If you can tear yourself away from this idyll for a few hours, you'll want to take an excursion to the nearby Moconá Falls, which can be accessed by boat or 4x4. Note that all excursions are outsourced to an independent company, and are not included in the rates.

Yacutinga Lodge

60km E of Puerto Iguazú *near Colonia Andresito* (03757 15 544493 mobile/www.yacutinga.com). *££££*.

As much a labour of love as a lodging, Yacutinga is set in a huge private reserve of Atlantic rainforest that juts out into the Río Iguazú. A range of all-action programmes are offered, the most popular of which is a two-nighter that includes several guided walks and – the highlight – a kayaking expedition on the broad, empty river, where kingfishers skim across the glittering waters. The lodge's buildings, half obscured by ancient rosewood trees and knotted lianas, are an architectural marvel, blending local wood and stone and varicoloured glass to create an effect that is part Gaudi, part *Lord of the Rings*. They're also built for comfort – no *Mosquito Coast*-style roughing it here. But what really lifts Yacutinga on to the top shelf of South American eco-lodges is the zeal and expertise of its staff.

Factfile

When to go

Misiones is a year-round destination, with tourism peaking in spring (October to December) and autumn (April to June). It has a subtropical climate, which means that there is no dry season. Expect humidity and dampness, but not necessarily heat: owing to its altitude and proximity to the Atlantic, Misiones can be bitterly cold in winter (July to September) with night-time temperatures often dropping below zero.

Getting there

Most travellers arrive by plane. Misiones has two international airports – Aeropuerto Internacional Puerto Iguazú (03757 421996), near Puerto Iguazú, and General José de San Martín (03752 457413), near Posadas. Flights operate daily from both Buenos Aires (Aerolíneas Argentinas and LAN) and Salta (Andes Líneas Aéreas).

Those wishing to arrive by bus can choose from a number of reliable operators. We recommend Flechabus (011 4000 5200, www.flechabus. com.ar), Vía Bariloche (0800 333 7575, www.viabariloche.com.ar) and Crucero del Norte

(011 5258 5000, www.crucerodelnorte.com.ar). It takes around 14 hours to get from BA to Posadas, and around 18 hours to reach Puerto Iguazú.

Getting around

Those staying at a jungle lodge are likely to have all their transfers arranged by the lodging (ask about the surcharge). Car hire companies in Posadas include Budget (Colón 1909, 03752 435484) and Europcar (Junín & San Martín, 03752 432245). A bus ride from Posadas to Puerto Iguazú lasts four to six hours. Buses going to San Ignacio leave hourly from Posadas bus station; the journey takes one hour.

Tourist information

Posadas Colón 1985 (03752 447539, www.turismo.misiones.gov.ar). Open 7am-8pm daily. You'll find extremely helpful staff at the main tourist information office.

Internet

Check in advance with your accommodation about internet access: it is by no means universal. Any wireless connection is likely to be sluggish.

Tea time

Not for all the tea in China would Argentinians part with *mate*. They drink it so frequently, in such large quantities, and so unselfconsciously that they often forget they're even doing it. Asking an Argentinian if he drinks a lot of *mate* is rather like asking a Frenchman if he eats a lot of cheese – the question is likely to elicit a puzzled, perhaps even a pitying, stare.

To make *mate*, you need three items of hardware and two items of software. The hardware consists of a hollow vessel, also called a *mate* and usually ovoid in shape; a straw (originally a bamboo joint but now usually made from metal) through which the liquid will be sucked, known as the *bombilla*; and a thermos flask to keep the water hot. The software comprises hot, but not boiling, water, and the tea itself, known as *yerba mate*. The latter comes from the evergreen *Ilex paraguensis* tree, regarded as a gift from the gods by the Guaraní, who first drank *mate*, and as a cash crop by the Jesuits of Misiones, who first worked out how to cultivate the trees.

Combining these components to make a good *mate* is a skill that supposedly takes years to acquire, but in fact takes around 15 minutes. Add *yerba* to the gourd until it is two-thirds full. Insert the *bombilla* at an oblique angle. Slowly pour the hot water into the hole created around the *bombilla*. Suck. Repeat.

This process is managed by – and only by – the server (*cebador*). The *mate* is circulated clockwise around the group and always returned to the server for replenishment after each serving – one person, one *mate*. The server

may or may not add sugar, depending on the taste of the next recipient. People in the interior provinces tend to take *mate* straight (*amargo*), while those in Buenos Aires – *porteños* are notoriously sweet toothed – add sugar.

You've got the gear and the know-how. Now you need a group. People who drink *mate* alone do so out of necessity. Students swear by its mild stimulative effect to help them through a long night's cramming. Long-distance truck drivers, who use oversized *mate* gourds to reduce the number of refills, drink it for the same reason. But *mate* drinking is essentially a social activity, a non-verbal assertion of friendship. You might offer your mortal enemy a cigarette, but you'd never pass him the *mate*.

Mate is an acquired taste – not everyone's cup of tea. However, most visitors want to take a gourd home with them, if only as an evocative memento. There are a myriad of styles available, from the classic natural gourd (fruit of the *Lagenaria vulgaris* climbing plant) to ornate silver-plated chalices and the tourist-friendly 'cow hoof'. (Argentinians are about as likely to drink *mate* from one of the latter as they are to run a Chilean flag up the Obelisco.) Street markets and weekend fairs are good places to hunt for traditional, simple gourds. 'Designer' *mates* are increasingly in vogue: if you're in the market for a neon-hued gourd, or one made from transparent acrylic, try design shops such as Nobrand (Gorriti 5876, 011 4776 7288), Capital (Honduras 4958, 011 4834 6555) and Calma Chicha (Honduras 4909, 011 4831 1818) in BA's Palermo Viejo.

Parque Nacional Sierra de las Quijadas.

Parque Sierra de las Quijadas

Argentina

Dramatic red canyons and dinosaur footprints.

A barely noticeable jagged ridge on the horizon suggests little of the majesty awaiting visitors to Parque Nacional Sierra de las Quijadas. Million-year-old tectonic activity thrust this mass of rock above the ground, allowing water and wind to shape it into a network of burnt-red canyons and valleys. In the park's centre, the rising land suddenly collapses into the Potrero de la Aguada, a basin criss-crossed by dry river beds and surrounded by cliff walls and temple-like rock formations. Occasional rain and wind uncover the ancient traces of humanity and its Jurassic forebears that lie hidden below the surface. Fossilised invertebrates and the footprints of dinosaurs emerge from smooth banks of stone, while the imprints of man appear in the circular remains of the Huarpe people's ovens.

Nearby San Luis is a lively provincial capital that acts as the gateway to the park and the surrounding sierras. In the pretty hill country, visitors can ride horses through the woods, enjoy the lake at Potrero de los Funes and pan for gold in the hills at La Carolina. Parque Nacional Sierra de las Quijadas makes an ideal one- or two-night stopover on the way to Mendoza, but its stunning landscapes, friendly city and year-round sunny climate will leave you feeling it's a lot more than just a detour.

Explore

The main attraction around San Luis for foreign tourists is undoubtedly **Parque Nacional Sierra de las Quijadas**. Unless staying at La Aguada (*see p335*), visitors have to base themselves in or around San Luis and arrange transport from there. The town of San Luis offers little in the way of sightseeing apart from some museums of provincial interest. Visitors will find more entertainment by people-watching around the shady plaza or exploring the pedestrianised shopping street, Rivadavia, and the various bars and restaurants.

PARQUE NACIONAL SIERRA DE LAS QUIJADAS

Parque Nacional Sierra de las Quijadas is situated 116 kilometres north of San Luis, along Ruta 47 (02652 445141, www.parques nacionales.gov.ar). Some visitors enter the park with a travel agency that supplies its own guide, but this often entails a very basic trip to the park. Most visitors are instead shown around by the Gauchos de las Quijadas, a cooperative of local guides. They're a friendly, knowledgeable bunch, and most travellers are pleased to know that their money goes directly to the families who live in the area. Entrance to the park (open 8am-6pm daily) costs AR$25.

Arriving at the park entrance, visitors can either drive or walk the 12-kilometre road that leads to the campsite and the starting point for the various hiking circuits. The most notable aspect of this first stretch of parkland is the Hornillos Huarpes, which are remains of the Huarpe people's ovens, dating from AD 1000. The circular foundations, just visible in the clay, mark out where this indigenous tribe cooked food and produced clay pots, perhaps on a large scale. The Huarpe once thrived in this region, but forced labour imposed by the Spanish destroyed many of the communities and, tragically, the diversion of water for agriculture dried up a vast, shallow lake to the west of the park, where many Huarpe lived on the fish they caught.

The park's centrepiece is the Potrero de la Aguada. This natural amphitheatre acted like a *potrero*, or corral, for the first ranchers who grazed their cattle on the valley floor, with the towering cliffs and hills preventing the animals from straying. It was the partial remains of these cattle that would provide the park's name: the numerous bands of outlaws who used the network of remote canyons as a hideaway killed the cattle for food, and ranchers would find traces of their illegal *asados* (barbecues) through the discarded jawbones, or *quijadas*. This gave rise to the outlaws being known as the *gauchos de las quijadas*.

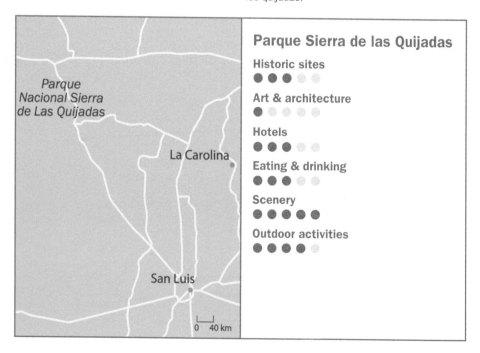

Parque Sierra de las Quijadas

Historic sites
● ● ● ◌ ◌

Art & architecture
● ◌ ◌ ◌ ◌

Hotels
● ● ● ◌ ◌

Eating & drinking
● ● ● ◌ ◌

Scenery
● ● ● ● ●

Outdoor activities
● ● ● ● ◌

From Potrero de la Aguada, visitors have four route options for exploring the park: Miradores (viewpoints), Las Huellas del Pasado (footprints of the past), Farallones (cliffs) and Guanacos (wild llamas). The guided tours leave at particular hours of the day, and may be cancelled during extreme heat or rain. Call the park to confirm times before visiting.

"The path follows the rim of the canyon, offering spectacular views over the red rock formations at sunset."

The Miradores route is an easy one-hour walk for which a guide is not required. The path follows the rim of the canyon, offering spectacular views over the valley and red rock formations, particularly at sunset.

Las Huellas del Pasado involves a two-and-a-half hour guided trek down from the Miradores to an escarpment that juts into the valley. On the way, walkers can see one of the area's best examples of a chica, a small tree that has existed since the time of the dinosaurs and is considered a living fossil. With its extensive system of roots that absorb the minimal moisture in the soil, and a lack of foliage that prevents transpiration, this warped and thorny tree is one of the few plants to thrive in the arid landscape. However, its slow growth rate and use as firewood has reduced it to a threatened species.

Further on, in a fenced-off area, are the trace fossils of various invertebrates, visible on the exposed rock. The first huellas, or footprints, are a deep three-toed imprint, believed to have been made by an ornithopod (a two-legged, duck-billed herbivore), some time between 110 and 120 million years ago. To see the next footprint, visitors must lean over a fence to view a section of rock on the point of collapsing into a gorge. The elephant-like mark was left by a sauropod, an extremely large and long-tailed herbivore – though the size of the print makes it likely that this was not a fully grown specimen.

The park is most famous among palaeontologists for the discovery, in 1970, of pterodaustro guiñazui, a flamingo-like reptile that lived 100 million years ago. The almost perfectly intact fossil showed the adults to have had a wing-span of over two metres, and it is believed that colonies of the reptiles inhabited the many lakes that once characterised the area.

Las Quijadas is not only home to petrified animal life. The fastest creature on earth, the peregrine falcon, may, if you are very lucky, be seen diving at up to 350 kilometres per hour to catch its prey. The giant Patagonian cavy, a large hare-like mammal, also makes its home here and is preyed on by the numerous pumas that live in the far reaches of the reserve. The area is also inhabited by guanacos, and the lesser fairy armadillo. Just 15 centimetres long, this tiny species stands out from other armadillos thanks to the ring of soft white hair that hangs below its shell. Plant-lovers can follow the one-hour, self-guided 'native flora trail' near the Huarpe ovens, which has information panels about 22 species of local plants.

The third trail, Farallones, or cliffs, is the longest, taking between three and five hours, depending on the group. The trail crosses the dry river-beds and gullies of the Potrero de la Aguada valley floor, before ascending up to the canyon walls on the other side. Visitors can walk between these wonders of erosion and marvel at the tower-like, sheer rock walls, some soaring hundreds of metres upward. The Guanacos trail is a shorter version of the Farallones trail and offers a panoramic view over the cliffs rather than a walk among them, as well as the possibility of spotting a rare guanaco.

Good walking footwear, a hat, sunscreen and at least a litre of water are highly recommended when visiting the park as temperatures, particularly in summer, can get very high.

Twice a month, between October and May, Luciano Franchi (Caseros 869, San Luis, 02652 15 212271 mobile, www.lucianofranchi.com.ar) offers a wonderful trip to Las Quijadas, which includes a visit to the dinosaur footprints, an asado in the campsite and a beautiful night walk to see the dramatic Potrero de la Aguada glowing under the full moon (check full moon dates beforehand). The cost is AR$185.

FURTHER AFIELD

Although the park is the major tourist attraction in the San Luis area, there are a few other interesting activities that are worth considering.

La Carolina, set on a hilltop 80 kilometres from San Luis, is a pretty mining village founded by the Spanish and later mined by the English for its gold deposits. Tours of the abandoned mines are fascinating, but panning for your own gold in the nearby streams is even more fun. To arrange a trip, contact Bernardo Spürgin (02652 494171, www.campolasierra.com.ar).

The Salinas de Bebedero salt flats, 42 kilometres south-west of San Luis via RN 7 and RP 15, though not as impressive as those in the north-west of the country, are still a sight to behold. Contact Gimaturs (Avenida Presidente Illia 305, San Luis, 02652 435751) to arrange private or group trips to the salt flats, from AR$60 per person.

Eat

Bar Morrison
San Luis *Pringles 830 (02652 440818). Open 7am-1am daily. ££. No credit cards. Café.*
Old rock concert posters and slatted wooden-booth seating create the atmosphere of a 1950s American diner. The rock theme reaches its zenith on weekends, when local bands strut their stuff. It's a great place for an informal bite to eat at any time of day, or for an atmospheric snack in the evening. The steak sandwiches and pizzas go down well with a bottle of beer. Daylight hours are more peaceful, and reliable Wi-Fi makes it a good place to surf the net.

By Resto
San Luis *Avenida España 602 (02652 435439). Open noon-3pm, 9pm-midnight Tue-Sun. ££. Modern.*
The modern decor of By Resto is tastefully offset by a traditional layout and very friendly service. The menu is almost worryingly broad, but unusual dishes, such as pork chops with cherry and date sauce, are perfectly cooked and provide a welcome respite from grilled meat. Although it is within walking distance of town, it might be worth hailing a cab on the way back if you have overindulged.

Infinito
San Luis *Hotel Vista Suites, Avenida Presidente Illia 526 (02652 425794). Open noon-3pm, 8pm-midnight daily. £££. Modern.*
Vista Suites' gourmet restaurant is certainly one of the better establishments in town, and the chef is dedicated enough to produce almost everything in-house, including some delicious breads. The menu changes regularly, running the gamut from juicy roast *chivito* (kid goat) to a killer mushroom and chicken chow mein. The stylish surroundings of the hotel make this a great spot to dine, and it is very convenient if you happen to be staying in the hotel, or in the Quintana next door.

Pampa
San Luis *Pedernera 426 (02652 423209). Open 12.30-3pm, 8.30pm-1.30am Mon-Sat; 12.30-3pm Sun. ££. Parrilla/Traditional.*
This is an ultra-traditional steakhouse, where older waiters serve excellent meat with a decent selection of wine. The restaurant is relatively new, and is set in a renovated townhouse with exposed brick walls. With tables spread through several rooms of the old building, it's a pleasant and intimate atmosphere in which to dine. If you're feeling steaked-out, ravioli stuffed with salmon is a great alternative, and there is a reasonable selection of salads.

Los Robles
San Luis *Colón 684 (02652 436767). Open 12.30-3pm, 9pm-12.30am Mon-Sat; 12.30-3pm Sun. £££. Traditional.*
Los Robles is a bastion of excellence in San Luis; every local will point you in its direction if you ask for a recommendation. Though the space itself feels a little cramped, the decor is cheerfully modern and the service is very professional. There is a faultless parrilla, as well as a selection of dishes that are hard to find in these parts, such as a fantastic seafood casserole and scallops. The temperature-controlled wine cellar has the best selection in San Luis, with some excellent vintages from Rutini, Zuccardi and Nieto Senetiner. Los Robles is busy almost every night, so it's advisable to make a reservation.

Uovo
San Luis *Las Heras & Colón (02652 447319). Open 1-3pm, 9pm-12.30am Tue-Sat. ££. International.*
This bar and lounge would probably feel more at home in the capital's chic Palermo Soho district, but its green plastic bar, chandeliers and trendy wallpaper add a bit of spice to San Luis's generally conservative restaurant scene. The menu includes decent pastas, a selection of meat and some reasonable attempts at oriental dishes. On weekends, part of the venue turns into a lounge bar, and the broad range of quality label spirits are put to good use in some excellent cocktails, including Uovo Night, a mixture of rum, peach juice and champagne. Next door is Panna, an ice-cream shop run by the same owner, which comes in handy for picking up dessert or sampling a booze-free nightcap.

Stay

If you're visiting Parque Nacional Sierra de las Quijadas and the surrounding area, note that most decent lodgings are set in and around the provincial capital, San Luis – with the exception of La Aguada. Although San Luis's hotel scene has leaped forward in recent years, much of its stock is still not geared towards the foreign market.

As tourism is very seasonal, bargains can often be negotiated outside the peak summer months of January and February.

La Aguada
16km N of Parque de las Quijadas *Ruta 20, km 396 (011 15 5247 4049 mobile/www.laaguada.com). ££. No credit cards.*
Sitting in the middle of a giant emptiness, with the red peaks of the park visible on the horizon, this is the only accommodation close to the isolated Parque Nacional Sierra de las Quijadas. Its location means there is no mobile phone coverage or landline, and the four hours of electricity per day come from an on-site generator. However, satellite internet is available when the electricity is turned on. Although further construction is in the pipeline, at the time of writing only two cabañas were offered, so book well in advance. The pleasant rustic buildings have two bedrooms, as well as a sitting room and kitchen, and can sleep up to six people. The food is delicious – which is fortunate, considering you don't have the option of eating anywhere else. There is a pool, but the scarcity of water makes maintenance slightly tricky, and it can be a little on the green side. Confirm your arrival time in advance, or you might have to walk several kilometres if the gate on the main road is locked.

Parque Sierra de las Quijadas Clockwise from top: Parque Nacional Sierra de las Quijadas (2); La Aguada; Parque Nacional Sierra de las Quijadas.

Campo la Sierra

San Luis *Ruta 20, km 19.5, El Volcán (02652 494171/www.campolasierra.com.ar). ££.*
With its pleasant grounds and jovial German owner Bernardo, this ranch is a great place to experience life in the green sierras just outside San Luis. The six comfortable, well-maintained cottages scattered throughout the wooded property sleep between two and eight people. Bernardo is an excellent cook, producing wholesome German dishes such as goulash or pork with sauerkraut, which he serves in his home in the evenings. Depending on the season, you may get the chance to savour local *jabalí* (wild boar), possibly skewered by your host using one of his impressive collection of hunting bows. Archery practice and horse riding excursions across the hills can be arranged, along with 4x4 trips to regional attractions, including Parque Nacional Sierra de las Quijadas and the gold-panning village of La Carolina. All in all, it's an homely, welcoming place to stay.

Hotel Potrero de los Funes

San Luis *Ruta 18, km 16, Potrero de los Funes (02652 423898/www.hotelpotrero.sanluis.gov.ar). £££.*
With aspirations to become Argentina's Monte Carlo, the broad racetrack that surrounds the Potrero de los Funes reservoir was, at the time of writing, preparing for Formula One test drives. Though perhaps not up to the standard of Monte Carlo's luxury accommodation, Hotel Potrero de los Funes provides a high level of comfort and services. Paying a little extra for a view over the water is worth it. Pedal boats and kayaks are on hand to splash about in, and there are giant, walk-in, inflatable balls for rolling about on the lake like a hamster. The large terrace is a great spot to catch some rays, and there is also a swimming pool, sauna, putting green and tennis courts to keep guests entertained. The on-site restaurant is a good place to get stuck into some *chivito* (kid goat).

Hotel Quintana

San Luis *Avenida Presidente Illia 546 (02652 438400/ www.hotelquintanasanluis.com). £££.*
The Quintana is San Luis's establishment hotel. The air-conditioned rooms are equipped with all the basic comforts and there's a decent-sized pool and sauna to relax in, as well as a bar and lounge. The reliable restaurant, which serves gourmet Argentinian cuisine, is one of the better options in and around town. Be warned, though: the size and efficiency of this hotel make it a popular venue for local wedding receptions, so be prepared to share the premises with a large part of someone else's family.

Vista Suites

San Luis *Avenida Presidente Illia 526 (02652 425794/ www.vistasuites.com.ar). £££.*
In a city where 'chic' and 'luxury' are about as hard to find as the elusive guanacos in the nearby national park, the contemporary decor of Vista Suites is a welcome surprise. The five categories of suites offer sophisticated and extremely comfortable accommodation, some with pretty views over the sierras beyond the city. The glass-fronted penthouse spa contains the best pool in town as well as a sauna and gym, and offers hydro-massage and a range of other massage therapies. The very helpful staff can arrange excursions to Las Quijadas and elsewhere. The stylish, stripped-down Infinito restaurant and bar (*see p335*) are also highly recommended.

Factfile

When to go

San Luis has a dry continental climate, with year-round sunshine; what little rain there is generally falls between October and March. The best times to visit are October to December and April to June, when there is little chance of rain or cold. From January to March, occasional temperatures of up to 42°C and heavy rain can cause the park to close. Check beforehand.

Getting there

A number of bus companies run daily services between Buenos Aires and the San Luis bus station (Avenida España 990, 02652 424021), and other destinations. Try CATA (02615 241699, www.catainternacional.com) or Auto Transporte San Juan (02652 424998, www.atsj.com.ar). San Luis is about eight hours 30 minutes from Buenos Aires by bus, and three hours from Mendoza.

There is one flight per day from Buenos Aires to San Luis's airport (Avenida Fuerza Aérea 3095, 02652 422427) with Aerolíneas Argentinas (0810 2228 6527, www.aerolineas.com.ar).

Getting around

To get to the park, you can hire a car from Budget (Hotel Belgrano San Luis, Belgrano 1440, 02652 440288), or contact a travel agent, such as Dasso Viajes (Rivadavia 444, 02652 421017), who can arrange transfers to the park and back in minibuses, as well as trips to the hills around San Luis and to other sights.

Tourist information

San Luis Tourist Information Avenida Presidente Illia & Junín (02652 423957, www.turismo.san luis.gov.ar). Open 8am-8pm daily.

Internet

Wi-Fi is available in most hotels in San Luis and in upmarket ones in the surrounding area. Web Bar, on the corner of Pringles and Peatonal Rivadavia, offers decent broadband.

Top: Ría Deseado. Middle: Monumento Natural Bosques Petrificados. Bottom left: Cueva de las Manos. Bottom right: Miradores Darwin.

Puerto Deseado & Around

Argentina

A lost world uncovered.

Spanning almost as much territory as the entire United Kingdom, the province of Santa Cruz's vast landscapes range from icy brilliance and exuberant forests to the stark aridity of the steppe. Many visitors to Argentina see a small corner of the province when visiting the glaciers around El Calafate, but the more isolated north, though a relative stranger to mass tourism, guards some of Patagonia's most fascinating treasures.

The small fishing town of Puerto Deseado lays claim to one of the world's strangest geological formations, the Ría Deseado. This shimmering, blue estuary lines the dried-up bed of an ancient river and has become a breeding ground for a vast array of seabirds and mammals, including oystercatchers, sea lions and a colony of exotic rock-hopper penguins, which, with their Charlie Chaplin-like gait and distinctive spikey yellow feathers, prove endlessly entertaining to those lucky enough to take a boat to Isla Pingüino.

Venturing further into the surrounding plains, other little-visited highlights include the Monumento Natural Bosques Petrificados, with its 150-million-year-old tree trunks, and the archaeological site of Cueva de las Manos, or 'Cave of the Hands', where hundreds of handprints have been immortalised for over 9,000 years.

Charles Darwin, on visiting Puerto Deseado in the 1830s, declared that he had never seen so isolated an area in his life. Not much has changed. With very few inhabitants in the hundreds of surrounding kilometres, staying in one of the area's estancias is a sure-fire way to achieve absolute tranquillity. Yes, you'll have to bypass luxury hotels and high-end cuisine, but the right type of traveller will find this refreshing in its own way. A brief look out of the window and you could easily come to the conclusion that the true luxury here is the outdoors.

Explore

PUERTO DESEADO

Resembling an oasis in the middle of a desert, **Puerto Deseado** is surrounded by deep canyons and sedimentary cliffs that date back to the Jurassic period. Home to 20,000 people, it lays claim to being the most important fishing port in Patagonia. Driving into town, you'll be struck by a bright-blue estuary that suddenly appears on the flat, ochre-coloured landscape. This body of water, the **Ría Deseado**, is by far Puerto Deseado's biggest draw. Once an ancient river, it dried up, leaving a stark void that was later filled with seawater, seeping 42 kilometres inland. Today, the seawater remains, rising and falling four times a day with the tides.

Sailing across the estuary is a dream ride for wildlife-lovers. Isla Chaffers is home to the largest of the area's seven penguin colonies, with more than 40,000 resident Magellan penguins, along with various types of seagull, stormy petrels and blackish oystercatchers. Other local highlights include Isla Elena, home to hundreds of grey cormorants, and Isla de los Pájaros (the Island of Birds), where passengers can observe the resident penguins. Look out, too, for tonina; freshwater dolphins with the colouring of a killer whale.

A typical boat trip takes some two hours and can be extended to include the Miradores de Darwin viewpoint, which lies towards the end of the 42-kilometre estuary. At this spot, the width of the estuary's banks begins to narrow, most signs of fauna disappear, and you're left with the same strange, desolate beauty that so impressed Darwin as he rowed through the estuary 175 years ago, during his research for *The Origin of Species*.

A little further on, an unusual triangle-shaped mass of land rises up in the middle of the estuary. This is the spot to disembark to view a cave where the hands of aborigines from several thousand years ago are painted on the walls. It's worth a visit, particularly if you are unable to make it to the more impressive Cueva de las Manos (*see p343*).

Located 25 kilometres south of Puerto Deseado, Isla Pingüino is home to Patagonia's only colony of rock-hopper penguins, distinctive for their long, black and yellow feathers, which look like unruly eyebrows, and their showy way of hopping with both feet together. A tour allows you to observe the penguins feeding their young or working to build their nests. The island is also home to the more common Magellan penguins, sea lions and elephant seals, and you're likely to spot enormous jaegers (seabirds) flying close overhead. Be warned that in high winds, boat trips in the area are often cancelled.

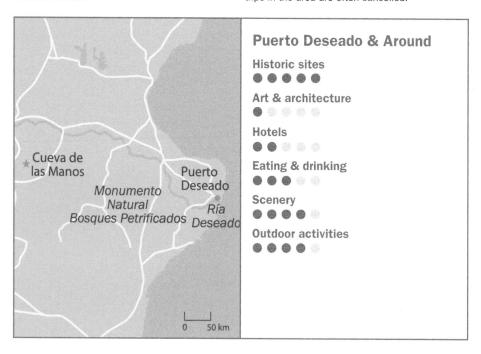

Puerto Deseado & Around

Historic sites
●●●●●

Art & architecture
●◦◦◦◦

Hotels
●●◦◦◦

Eating & drinking
●●●◦◦

Scenery
●●●●◦

Outdoor activities
●●●●◦

Isla Pingüino lighthouse.

Clockwise from top: rock-hopper penguin; grey cormorants; Estancia Telken.

EL MONUMENTO NATURAL BOSQUES PETRIFICADOS

Situated 257 kilometres west of Puerto Deseado, **El Monumento Natural Bosques Petrificados**, or the petrified forest, is a sand desert which has shifted to reveal a series of huge, 150-million-year-old tree trunks. It's a magnificent, if slightly eerie, sight. A half-day trip from Puerto Deseado usually gives visitors about an hour to walk among the remains.

This bleak landscape, almost devoid of vegetation and where guanacos run wild, is the opposite of what Patagonia was like in the Jurassic period, when these trees last stood tall. Back then, Patagonia was covered in vast swampy forests where dinosaurs roamed. But then the Andes mountain range sprang up, and the humid Pacific winds were met with a new natural barrier, where today they unload all their rain, leaving these plains extremely dry. This lost world has now reappeared thanks to wind erosion, which has exposed the majestic 30-metre-long trunks as well as fossilised rocks.

The reserve is open daily from 9am to 7pm October to March, and 10am to 5pm from April to September. Admission is free. If you don't take a tour, carry water and food; there are no shops in the area, and the nearest town is 200 kilometres away down a dirt road.

CUEVA DE LAS MANOS

Lost in the immensity of the steppe, 561 kilometres from Puerto Deseado, **Cueva de las Manos** is the most important archaeological site in Argentina. The small UNESCO-listed cave has 829 hands painted on its walls and eaves, the oldest dating from 9,355 years ago – some 5,000 years before Stonehenge was erected. The multicoloured hands appear to have been painted yesterday, and can clearly be seen without even entering the cave, as they are well illuminated by the sun.

Situated above a huge rocky canyon, the cave can be accessed from its principal entrance or via a moderately demanding trek from the nearby Estancia Cueva de las Manos (see p344), crossing the Río Pinturas by a suspension bridge. This can be done without a guide and is highly recommended, as it allows you to experience the true magnificence of the landscape, which can be lost when entering the cave from the main entrance on the other side of the river.

The admission price to the cave is AR$50. Due to its remote location, excursions to Cueva de las Manos are not sold from Puerto Deseado. Instead, trips can be arranged through Estancia Cueva de las Manos. Alternatively, the cave can be reached via the town of Perito Moreno, in the province's north-west corner, where you can sign up for a tour with Zoyen Turismo (02963 432207, www.zoyenturismo.com.ar).

Eat

Outside of Puerto Deseado, most of your meals will be eaten at your host estancia. An *asado* of beef or Patagonian lamb is standard fare, as is grilled trout, freshly caught from one of the area's lagoons. Generally, dishes are simple, traditional and abundant. There are very few places to eat on the road, except for modest snack bars at some filling stations, so plan ahead and pack provisions.

Lo de Armando

Puerto Deseado *San Martín y Sarmiento (0297 487 1399). Open 11am-3.30pm, 8pm-1am Mon-Sat. ££. No credit cards. Italian.*
The top draw of this restaurant is its mix of pastas and seafood, such as sorrentinos filled with oyster or king crab. It has two salons, big windows looking on to the city square, walls covered in maps and shelves packed with wine bottles.

"Puerto Cristal specialises in seafood, brought directly from local shores."

Puerto Cristal

Puerto Deseado *España 1698 (0297 487 0387). Open 11am-3.30pm, 8-11.30pm daily. ££. Seafood.*
Appropriately enough, given its large windows looking over the port and the Laguna de Prefectura, Puerto Cristal specialises in fresh seafood, brought directly from local shores. Order a plate of seafood *picada* (featuring scallops, mussels, king crab, calamari, lobster, clam, squid and octopus), the *cazuela de mariscos* (seafood stew) or the *merluza negra* (Chilean sea bass). For die-hard carnivores, roasted Patagonian lamb is also on the menu.

Stay

Puerto Deseado has only emerged as a tourist destination in the last few years, and its relatively short tourist season (October to April) means there is a shortage of hotels. For this reason, it is advisable to make your hotel reservations a few months ahead, especially for January and February.

The best way to book estancias in the area is through Estancias de Santa Cruz, in Buenos Aires (Viamonte 920, 5H, 011 5237 4043, www.estanciasdesantacruz.com), where English is spoken. Estancia guests can expect activities to include trout fishing and horseback riding.

Cabañas Las Nubes

Puerto Deseado *Ameghino 1351 (0297 15 403 2677 mobile/www.cabanaslasnubes.com.ar). ££. No credit cards.*

At the highest point of Puerto Deseado, on a rocky cliff by the coast of the Ria Deseado, this complex of 15 Alpine-style cabins is the newest accommodation option in town. The two-storey cabins have roomy interiors, and were built with wood and exposed bricks. They are equipped with a refrigerator, a microwave and a TV.

Estancia Cueva de las Manos

5km from La Cueva de las Manos *RN 40 (02963 432319/www.cuevadelasmanos.net). Open Nov-Easter. ££.*

This estancia is conveniently situated for a visit to Cueva de las Manos. The accommodation may be a world away from its well-heeled counterparts just outside Buenos Aires, but too much pampering would spoil the rugged-living experience. Instead, expect no-frills comforts, including a restaurant with big windows looking out on to the deserted terrain, comfortable double and triple rooms with private bathrooms, a cabin for six and two dormitory rooms. Guests can also take trips to Charcamata – a similar cave to Cueva de las Manos, but set in an even more desolate landscape.

Estancia Telken

145km from Cueva de las Manos *Ruta 40 (02963 432079/telkenpatagonia@yahoo.com.ar). Open Oct-Easter. ££.*

A New Zealander dedicated to raising sheep, John Campbell Clack founded this estancia after settling here in 1915. It covers 210sq km and is home to 6,000 sheep, 40 cows and more than a hundred horses, as well as a *laguna* with hundreds of birds, including flamingos, black-necked and coscoroba swans, upland geese, red shoveler ruddy ducks and the rare hooded grebe. There are six rooms with private bathrooms, all decorated like a family home, with antique furniture. The main building is constructed entirely from wood, and is surrounded by a little garden. Guests usually use the estancia as a base for visiting Cueva de las Manos.

Hotel Los Acantilados

Puerto Deseado *España 1611 (0297 487 2168/ 0297 487 2070/www.hotelesenpatagonia.com.ar). £.*

The city's best hotel, Los Acantilados is a volcanic-stone and wood construction, perched on a cliff top site with beautiful views of the port and the Ria Deseado. Although somewhat past its peak, it retains a warm, inviting atmosphere, with 40 rooms and a full bar with large windows facing the estuary.

Factfile

When to go

The best times to visit Puerto Deseado are in the spring and summer (from October to March) and at the beginning of autumn (from April to June). Winters are cold and windy. Excursions to see the rock-hopper penguins run from the beginning of October to the beginning of April. Estancias open between October and April, closing after Easter.

Getting there & around

In general, visitors to Puerto Deseado fly from Buenos Aires to Comodoro Rivadavia, 360 kilometres from Puerto Deseado, with Aerolíneas Argentinas (0810 2228 6527, www.aerolineas.com.ar). The journey from Comodoro Rivadavia airport to Puerto Deseado takes two hours 30 minutes by car, and just over three hours by bus. From Puerto Madryn to Comodoro Rivadavia, buses take six hours and cars four; from Península Valdés, it takes an extra hour and a half.

Several companies sail across the Ría Deseado to Isla Pingüino: Los Vikingos (0297 487 0020, www.losvikingos.com.ar) and Darwin Expeditions (0297 15 624 7554 mobile, www.darwin-expeditions.com) both offer excursions.

Overland excursions to the Monumento Natural Bosques Petrificados and Miradores de Darwin can be arranged through a travel agency, such as Cis Tours (0297 487 2864, www.cistours.com.ar).

Car hire is available in Comodoro Rivadavia through Hertz (Aeropuerto General Mosconi, 0297 454 8999), Localiza Rent a Car (Aeropuerto General Mosconi, 0800 999 2999) and Avis (Aeropuerto General Mosconi, 0297 454 9471).

While main roads are well paved or have stretches of hardened rubble, estancia access roads are generally unpaved and can become muddy and hard to navigate when it rains (a pretty infrequent occurrence).

Tourist information

Buenos Aires Tourist Information Centre (Suipacha 1120, 011 4325 3098, 011 4325 3102, www.santacruzpatagonia.gob.ar). Open 10am-5pm Mon-Fri. The province's tourist information centre in Buenos Aires is the best place to get information on northern Santa Cruz, and has helpful, English-speaking staff.
Puerto Deseado Dirección de Turismo San Martín 1525 (0297 487 0220, www.turismo.deseado.gov.ar). Open Apr-Oct 9am-7pm Mon-Fri; noon-4pm Sat, Sun. Nov-Mar 9am-7pm daily.

Internet

Estancias generally do not have internet access. There is a cyber café in downtown Puerto Deseado: Nuevo Centro Shop (Almirante Brown 559, 0297 4870777), open 9am-10pm daily.

Miradores Darwin.

Top: Jujuy landscape. Middle: Salinas Grandes. Bottom left: street market, Quebrada de Purmamarca. Bottom right: Cabildo, Salta.

Salta & Jujuy
Argentina

Spectacular valleys, colonial towns and Andean culture.

Salta and Jujuy blow every pampas/glass-lake stereotype of Argentina right out of the water. Here, the familiar tapestry of the country's European heritage begins to unravel as the land rises up towards the Andes. Through llama herds and polychromatic ponchos, the ancient cultures of the Andean peoples reach down from Peru and Bolivia, while some of the nation's oldest remnants of the conquering Spanish can be found in heart-rending *folklore* ballads and time-warped adobe and wood churches. Even the gauchos, stalwart bastions of Argentinian heritage, look different in their blood-red ponchos and *guardamontes* (winged chaps).

The city of Salta, with its slow pace of life and colonial architecture, is brimming with boutique hotels, and restaurants serving regional and modern cuisine. It's surrounded by places offering every imaginable adventure sport, from paragliding to bungee jumping. Further south, Cachi and the Valles Calchaquíes showcase some of the most varied and dramatic landscapes in the country. Gorges rise to desert plateaus before dropping back into valleys dotted with white colonial villages. In sleepy Cafayate, you can sip some of the continent's best vintages at the world's highest vineyards, while simultaneously enjoying warm sun and unrivalled views. Heading north to the Quebrada de Humahuaca in Jujuy (pronounced 'hoo-hooey'), visitors find themselves surrounded by a network of ravines where the descendants of Andean peoples are as colourful as the rock formations that surround them. To the east and west lie the climatic extremes of the lush Yungas forests and the tantalising desolation of the vast, dry Puna, created by the rain shadow of the Andes.

The twin forces of history and geology have combined to produce a region so rich in microclimates, historic sights and culture that you could spend months exploring it. However, manageable distances allow visitors to cover a lot in a short space of time, with the dramatic journeys being as much of a draw as the destinations.

Explore

The city of **Salta** is conveniently situated near the border between the provinces of Salta and Jujuy, making it a good place to begin from or even to use as a base to make day trips to the various attractions. Although distances are not enormous, having a car is definitely the most enjoyable way of getting about, not least because much of what there is to see is en route. The majority of sights (except **Cachi** and around) are accessed by good paved roads, and the drives themselves are spectacular – though nervous or acrophobic drivers might prefer someone else to take the wheel.

SALTA

Sitting at the northern end of the fertile Valle de Lerma, the city of Salta is surrounded on all sides by lushly forested mountains, which dramatically rise up to the dry slopes of the Andes in the west. Its colonial buildings and palm-planted plazas give the city a wonderfully exotic flavour.

Founded in 1582 by Hernando de Lerma, after whom the valley is named, Salta boomed under Spanish rule during the 17th and 18th centuries as a trading stop on the route between Buenos Aires and the colonial HQ in Lima, Peru. After stagnating for much of the last two centuries, the city is currently undergoing a resurgence

on the back of an agricultural and tourism boom. In the process, many of the older buildings have been replaced with unattractive high-rises – but the city is now cleaner and better organised, and money has been pumped into arts and culture.

Salta is a very manageable city to explore, with many of the sights within walking distance of the central plaza, 9 de Julio. To get a feel of the city, walk east from Plaza 9 de Julio down Caseros street, taking in the Basílica San Francisco and its beautiful church tower, San Bernardo convent and the old townhouses en route. Continue on Caseros until you reach Avenida Hipolito Yrigoyen, then turn right. Take a trip on the *teleférico* (*see p350*) before heading west on San Martin, taking in the Parque San Martin and its craft stalls. A stroll north on pedestrianised Juan B Alberdi takes you back to Plaza 9 de Julio. Sip a coffee in one of the cafés that surround the tree-covered plaza, and slip into the laid-back rhythm of the city.

If you feel like a little action after the sedentary pace of Salta life, head to calle Balcarce, a street a few blocks north of the main plaza. Located next to the train station, this was where the original immigrant workers arrived and rented rooms. Night was playtime, and their folk music turned the area into a riotous strip of bars and *peñas* (folk bars and eateries, *see p351* **Female folk stars**). Abandoned for years, the old houses have been revamped, some traditionally and others decked out in rather incongruous neon

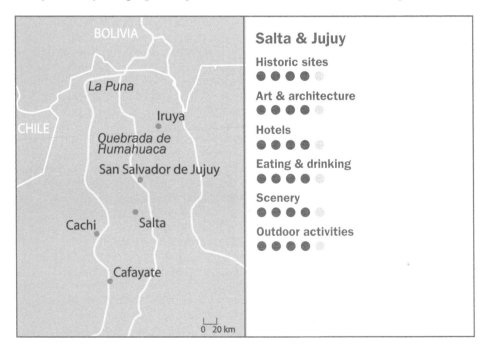

Salta & Jujuy

Historic sites
● ● ● ● ◉

Art & architecture
● ● ● ● ◉

Hotels
● ● ● ● ◉

Eating & drinking
● ● ● ● ◉

Scenery
◉ ● ● ● ◉

Outdoor activities
● ● ● ● ◉

Clockwise from top:
Purmamarca market
(2); Cafayate.

and aluminum. Although the area is highly commercialised, it's very entertaining and is aimed at locals as well as tourists, giving it some sense of authenticity. The Sunday street market here (10am-8pm), where you can pick up crafts from all over the region, is also worth a visit.

The Tren a las Nubes is one of the most publicised attractions in Salta (www.trenalas nubes.com.ar). As train journeys go, it is pretty dramatic. Winding their way up from Salta toward the Chilean border, the three carriages traverse sharp switchbacks to gain altitude, pass through 21 tunnels and cross 13 viaducts and 29 bridges, before reaching an altitude of 4,200 metres. All this takes place in one of the driest and most striking landscapes on earth. However, it doesn't come cheap (expect to pay up to US$140), and the lunch of cold rice and meat may not appear to be a good indication of value for money. Altitude sickness can be a problem, and if you suffer from cabin fever, note that the trip is 15 hours and much of the return journey is in the dark.

Around 20 kilometres outside Salta, and once a weekend retreat for the local aristocracy, the pretty town of San Lorenzo is now Salta's Beverly Hills for the merchant class. Set against forested hillsides, its shady streets and higher altitude provide a welcome break from the city. The privately owned Quebrada de San Lorenzo reserve offers visitors a chance to experience the lush forests around Salta. For one of the best rides in the country, across the open grasslands of Loma Balcón hillside, call Joaquín Castellanos (0387 492 2516, 0387 492 1606) to arrange horses and an optional guide.

Cabildo
Caseros 549 (0387 421 5340). 9am-6pm Tue-Fri; 9am-1.30pm Sat, Sun. Admission AR$3. No credit cards.
On the corner of the main plaza, opposite the cathedral, is the old colonial Cabildo (town hall), now the Museo Histórico del Norte. The section charting pre-Columbian life in Salta is a fascinating reminder that there was, of course, a Salta long before the Spanish came. Petrol-heads will be intrigued to come across the largest car ever made by Renault, a very early limousine formerly belonging to the governor of Tucumán. If a collection of curiosities is not your cup of tea, the entrance charge is still worth it just to admire the beautiful adobe and wood architecture.

Catedral
España 558 (www.catedralsalta.org). Open 7.30am-12.30pm, 5-8.30pm daily. Admission free.
Notable for its baroque extravagance and blinding golden altar area, God's mailing address in Salta is also home to the Lord and Virgin of the Miracles, two statues that are venerated for apparently saving the city from destruction by earthquake on three separate occasions. If you're in the area on 15 September, don't miss the annual celebrations, when mass parades and up to 300,000 devotees fill the city, and various aircrafts perform flypasts in their honour.

MAAM
Mitre 77 (0387 437 0499/www.maam.org.ar). Open 11am-8pm Tue-Sun. Admission AR$30. No credit cards.
MAAM, which stands for Museo de Arqueología de Alta Montaña (Museum of the High Mountains), was created after the remains of three sacrificed Inca children were discovered almost 7km above sea level in Salta's western Puna region in the late 1990s. An interesting display of artefacts and audiovisuals about the discovery precede the museum's centrepiece: the mummified remains of a young child. (At the time of writing, only one of the three cadavers found by the research team was on display.) The driest climate on earth has left the little body perfectly intact, as if it were dozing in the sun.

Teleférico
Avenida San Martín & Avenida Hipólito Yrigoyen (0387 431 0641/www.teleferico.elturistaperiodico.com). Open 10am-7pm daily. Admission AR$20. No credit cards.
Although a distinct lack of snow makes skiing back down unlikely, a trip in Salta's *teleférico*, or chair-lift, affords a spectacular panorama of the city. Relax in the gardens at the top and plan your next sightseeing conquest from on high, before stopping at the café to fortify your stomach for the return journey.

CAFAYATE
Two hundred kilometres south of Salta – a two-and-a-half hour drive – is **Cafayate**, an increasingly popular town that is famous for its wines. There are enough bodegas, restaurants and good hotels to make this a destination worth spending a few days in, perhaps as part of a trip that also takes in Cachi and its surroundings. Unlike Mendoza, this wine region is small – so visitors can focus on the wine itself rather than the wine trail.

South of Salta, the crops and pastures of the Valle de Lerma continue as far as the area around Coronel Moldes and Cabra Corral, a vast and incredibly deep reservoir that has been developed as a location for adventure sports. More attractive than the artificial lake is the surrounding landscape, which deviates from Salta's archetypal extremes in its lush, bucolic understatement. Fields of corn and tobacco are bordered by hedgerows, and little brick houses peek out through flower-filled gardens. Finca Santa Anita (*see p362*) is the perfect stop for lunch – or a night – on the way to Cafayate.

Soon, the terrain changes dramatically, as the mountains close in on the valley. Agriculture gives way to dry, narrow and near-deserted valleys, towered over by rocky, red slopes. Look out for signs on the left for the Anfiteatro (amphitheatre), 40 kilometres or so before Cafayate. A vast cylindrical cave, open to the sky, this masterpiece of erosion has acoustics that are impressive enough to have attracted various orchestras.

Female folk stars

You'd be hard pressed not to hear folk music when visiting Argentina's north-west. The deep throbbing of bombo drums and the stamp of dances echo from *peñas* (folk clubs) by night; on weekends, melancholic love ballads can be heard floating above the trees from rural homesteads. From middle-class students to the ancient gauchos and llama herders of La Puna, the music is a vital part of the region's identity.

Argentinian *folklore* (pronounced folk-lore-ay) has been shaped by the history and geography of different parts of the country. The extreme landscapes of the north-west have proved to be a rich source of talented composers and lyricists, including Gustavo 'Cuchi' Leguizamón and Manuel J Castilla. *Folklore* music and lyrics convey social and personal issues, as well as reflecting the often harsh and lonely environments. A form of expression for a conservative society of Spanish settlers, it initially excluded women, their rightful place being considered the kitchen.

But in the early 20th century, as *folklore* evolved from being a tradition of anonymous songs handed down over the generations to becoming a musical genre characterised by celebrities, women were finally given their opportunity to shine.

The first female to really hit the big time was Patrocinio Díaz, when she was given a lucky break in Santiago del Estero by Andrés Chazarreta, who allowed her to sing in his group. Concert audiences, at first shocked that a lady should be allowed out at such an hour, were soon to become accustomed to seeing women performing on stage.

At first limited to performing other people's songs, female musicians such as poet and writer María Elena Walsh were soon composing their own work. Today, women are as much a part of *folklore* as their male counterparts, and female superstars, including Mercedes Sosa, have won international renown.

Some women to look out for on the contemporary *folklore* scene in the north-west are Melania Peréz, Julia Elena Dávalos and Paola Arias (*pictured*), all very accomplished musicians from Salta, and Mariana Cayón from Cafayate, who recently became the first woman to play the *quena* (a traditional type of flute), for which she has won national *folklore* awards.

Balcarce street in Salta has a number of *peñas*, such as La Vieja Estación (Balcarce 885, 0387 421 7727), where *folklore* can be watched – or participated in, by volunteering to stumble about with elegantly dancing gauchos and ladies in traditional costume. For a less touristy option, make your way to restaurant and *peña* La Casona del Molino (Luis Bulera 1, 0387 434 2835).

To see indigenous *folklore* performances, head to Quebrada de Humahuaca (*see p354*). During many religious celebrations in the region (particularly Easter), groups of musicians called 'Sikuris', who are named for the pan pipes they play, fill the valleys with music as they wind their way among vast pilgrimages and processions. Call the Jujuy tourist office (03882 428153) for dates and locations. Many restaurants, bars and hotels also regularly host *folklore* performances, so you are unlikely to miss a taste, even if you don't actively seek it out.

Top: Colomé.
Bottom: Cachi.

Two hours from Salta, the road leaves the canyons and enters the valley of Cafayate. As you cross a plain of spiralling dust devils and sand dunes, it's quite startling to suddenly find yourself on an elegant, tree-lined avenue, with vineyards stretching towards the mountains on either side. Irrigation in the 19th century turned this barren area into a region that now produces some of the country's best, most distinctive wines.

The sunny climate, attractive architecture and sleepy atmosphere lend the town a Provençal ambience. The broad, leafy town square is a nice place for a stroll at any time of day, and there are some interesting sights within a short distance of Cafayate, including the impressive ruins at Quilmes, 55 kilometres to the south in Tucumán province (*see p120*).

"It is miraculous that this parched landscape produces such an exuberant harvest."

There's really no denying, however, that Cafayate's top attraction is the grape. The source of the wine's quality lies in the altitude, glut of sunshine and arid climate. Torrontés, a small white grape that thrives here like nowhere else, is the region's speciality. The combination of its crispness and rich, fruity aroma is a living metaphor of the parched landscape that miraculously produces such an exuberant harvest. Cabernet sauvignon and malbec grow well on the higher slopes above the town, and produce excellent and distinctive vintages.

Many of the big bodegas are located in the town itself or on its outskirts, and receive daily bus loads of tourists for guided tours around what, in reality, are industrialised agricultural processing plants. It's worth seeing one as a contrast to the smaller bodegas, which tend to focus on quality rather than quantity.

Wine can be bought wholesale at the bodegas, and is often significantly cheaper than in Salta city and definitely better value than the wine shops in Cafayate. Don't miss a taste of the delicious torrontés- and cabernet-flavoured ice-creams at Helados Miranda (Güemes Norte 170).

For a glimpse of how local plonk was produced before Cafayate's potential was recognised and exploited, head for the village of Angastaco, an hour's drive along the road to Cachi. Ask around for Juan Cruz, who lives near the old church and informally shows visitors his antiquated winery. It's fascinating to see inside one of the old adobe houses, normally only glimpsed from the car window en route to Cachi or Cafayate.

Bodega Domingo Hermanos
Avenida Güemes & 25 de Mayo (03868 421225/ www.domingohermanos.com). Open 9am-12.30pm, 3-6.30pm Mon-Fri; 9am-12.30pm Sat; 10.30am-12.30pm Sun. Tours run according to demand.
Domingo Hermanos has been corking bottles in the valley since the '60s. The diversity of the wines here is produced by the distinct terroirs and altitudes of the vineyards, which extend to the valley floor, the slopes of Yacochuya and the lunar-like desert of the Quebrada de Las Flechas on the road to Cachi. Visitors to the bodega receive the standard free tour, a selection of cheeses and a tasting of the torrontés and cabernet malbecs from Domingo Hermanos's dependable and good-value line. However, to get a real taste of what this fantastic bodega is producing, buy a bottle of its structured and highly citric torrontés, the most unusual in Cafayate, or the award-winning malbec, with its mature tannins and red berry flavours. If you have extra cash, try getting your hands on a rare bottle of 2003 Palo Domingo.

Bodega El Esteco
Ruta 40, 100m from junction with Ruta 68 at entrance to Cafayate (03868 15 566019 mobile/www.elesteco. com.ar). Open 10am-noon, 2.30-6.30pm Mon-Fri; 10am-noon Sat, Sun. Tours 10am, 11am, noon, then half-hourly from 2.30-6.30pm Mon-Fri; 10am, 11am, noon Sat, Sun. Tour price AR$20-$650.
Adjoining the hotel Patios de Cafayate (*see p365*) is the imposing Bodega El Esteco. The winery produces a huge array of wines, which you will see on the shelves of practically every supermarket in Argentina. The standard one-hour tour involves a visit to the bodega and a tasting of the red and white wines from the Elementos range. The tour is interesting, if only to realise that this type of wine production is essentially an agribusiness where every stage is mechanised with the latest technology. Longer tours and multi-line tastings can be arranged beforehand. For take-away purposes, the Don David and Elementos lines are a good choice. Alternatively, they can be sampled next door in the hotel restaurant – though perhaps due to Patios de Cafayate's luxury status, the wines are triple the price they're sold at in other restaurants or shops.

Bodega José L Mounier
South of town on Ruta 68, take right for El Divisadero, signposted after 10km (03868 422129/www.bodega mounier.com). Open 9.30am-5pm Mon-Sat. Tours run according to demand. Tour price AR$15.
The eponymous owner of this attractive homestead, with its gleaming white buildings and 25 hectares of vineyard, grew up in a vinicultural family in Mendoza. Visitors can tour the vineyard as well as taste some of the finished products, and purchase some of the best value bottles in town. The fruity torrontés is excellent and scarily addictive. The Finca las Nubes cabernet malbec is a wonderful example of the rich, peppery reds that characterise this region, and the reserve, with its added tannat and softer tannins, tops the lot. With 48 hours' notice, you can book a lunch and savour the wines in situ. And, if you're visiting in March, you can put your gloves on and help out with the harvest.

San Pedro de Yacochuya

Yacochuya. Just north of junction between RN 40 &
RN 68, branch left on RP 2 and follow signs for 6km
(03868 421233/www.sanpedrodeyacochuya.com.ar).
Open 10am-5pm Mon-Fri; 10am-1pm Sat. Tours run
according to demand.

Perched on the valley slopes above Cafayate, this boutique
bodega has stunning views, which are themselves just a
backdrop to some of Argentina's finest wines. Arnaldo
Etchart and world-renowned oenologist Michel Rolland
were attracted to this unique terroir ten years ago, and
created a vineyard focused on producing a small quantity
of very fine wine. The irrigated, furrowed slopes provide
ideal conditions for producing incredible reds like the
malbec-cabernet sauvignon blend. At 15.7% alcohol, this
meaty and complex wine will have you smelling red berries
for days, though its smooth tannins settle well on the palate.
Standard tours are free, while a lunch package (AR$240)
comprises a tour of the bodega, a bottle of red and white
wine, *picadas* and lunch. The wonderfully aromatic and dry
torrontés is served with a plate of cheeses, raisins and olives,
while Arnaldo's charming wife, Inés, tells the story of the
bodega and its wines. Lunch is presented in the old estancia
and usually involves hearty meat dishes, which still struggle
to match the awesome San Pedro de Yacochuya red.

CACHI AND AROUND

Burned lunar landscapes, vast cactuses, death-
defying mountain roads, colonial villages – the
Valles Calchaquíes have it all, and a journey
across this strange series of microclimates is
worth the sometimes precarious drive. In the
valleys, named after one of the fierce tribes who
for a century resisted Spanish rule, it feels as if
the locals are as determined to keep modernity
at bay as their ancestors were the conquistadors.

Heading south from Salta, Ruta 68 branches
right on to Ruta 33 at El Carril. Leaving the
tobacco plantations behind, it passes through
canyon country before reaching one of Argentina's
most spectacular ascents, the Cuesta del
Obispo, and the beginning of Parque Nacional
Los Cardones. In the first section, the vegetation
gives way to dramatic, green mountain slopes
and stomach-knotting precipices. If you're
travelling by car, pull over at one of the lay-bys
and peer down at the road below, winding its way
into the distance. You may be lucky enough to
spot a condor soaring over a distant peak.

On reaching the summit, the ground levels off
and a new landscape of wind-blasted plateau
opens up. This soon gives way to the home of
Parque Nacional Los Cardones' namesake – an
area famed for its blanket of cardón cactuses,
which appear like sentinels standing guard over
the desert. For the local Andean people, this
cactus has been used as a source of water and
food, and its wood provides a durable building
material. The park is a haven for wildlife, and
offers refuge to the puma, guanaco, Andean
deer and red fox, among others.

Ten kilometres before Cachi is the pre-
Columbian town of Payagasta, once a stopover
on the Inca road that ran south from the empire's
heartland in Peru. The next stop, **Cachi**, a town
of gleaming white adobe buildings and towering
pavements is situated 2,100 metres above sea
level. Its 16th-century church contains good
examples of cardón-wood construction.

Around 11 kilometres outside town is La
Paya, one of the few excavated remains of an
Incan settlement in an area that once formed
part of the Cusco-centred Tawantinsuyo empire.
For more information, pay a visit to the town's
archaeological museum (Pasaje Juan Calchaquí,
03868 491080, open 8.30am-6.30pm Mon-Fri,
10am-1pm Sun).

South of Cachi, Ruta 40 leads to peaceful
Molinos, an immaculately preserved town of
ancient adobe streets that is home to San
Pedro de Nolasco, one of the region's finest
examples of colonial-era ecclesiastical
architecture, as well as the old governor's
house, now the Hacienda del Molinos hotel
(*see p362*). The increasingly bumpy route
carries on into a series of spectacular valleys,
where fertile green fields and hillsides covered
in drying red peppers are overshadowed by
jagged dry ridges. After exiting the Quebrada
de las Flechas, a canyon where wind and water
have carved out an eerie lunar landscape, the
road eventually leads to the tranquil wine
country of Cafayate.

QUEBRADA DE HUMAHUACA

In 2003, its 10,000 years of human history
and unique blend of pre-Columbian, colonial
and natural heritage earned the **Quebrada de
Humahuaca** UNESCO World Heritage Site status.
Although the resulting surge in visitor numbers
has inevitably altered the peaceful atmosphere
of the 200 kilometre-long network of valleys,
infrastructure improvements mean that it is now
far easier to explore. At two hours 30 minutes
north of Salta, a basic day trip is one possibility,
but spending a night or two soaking up the
unique environment is highly recommended.

The journey from Salta follows Ruta 34 north
before joining Ruta 9, which begins the ascent
out of Jujuy's lush lowlands into the arid sierras.
On entering the Quebrada proper, medieval-
looking patchworks of alfalfa, lavender and
tobacco surrounded by molle and willow trees
cover the narrow valley floor, their delicacy
enhanced by the craggy, multicoloured slopes
that rise up on either side. One kilometre from
the main valley is the village of **Purmamarca**, with
pretty streets of adobe houses overshadowed by
a spectacular mound of orange and purple rock.
Bargain-hunters are advised to shop in Salta,
however, as the market in Purmamarca is
notoriously inauthentic and overpriced.

Llamas on Ruta 33 to Cachi.

An hour north of Purmamarca lie the spectacular salt flats of Salinas Grandes. A visit to this alien-looking, profoundly silent landscape is a unique experience. Outside the unfinished restaurant by the roadside, traders sell objects carved out of salt; opposite are the water pools where salt is sustainably extracted for commercial purposes. The route to the salt flats, from which you can spot vicuñas and wild donkeys, is wonderfully atmospheric in its own right. The road zig zags up through an increasingly barren landscape to a chest-tightening altitude of 4,200 metres, one of the highest points reached by any paved road in the north-west.

Back in the main valley, Maimará is home to the Paleta del Pintor (Painter's Palette), an undulating rock formation displaying a sweep of reds, purples and yellows created by the area's copper and iron deposits. The village's cemetery, with its hillside tombs, sits by the roadside like an exposed vault of safety-deposit boxes for the dead. **Tilcara**, the hippyish but attractive tourist hub of the Quebrada de Humahuaca, has an excellent selection of bars, restaurants and hotels, and makes a good base to explore the area. The Pucará, or fort, is a must-see. Further north is the equally attractive but less-visited town of Humahuaca. The Iglesia de la Candelaria church contains some rare canvasses of the prophets, painted in 1764 by Cusco School maestro Marcos Zapaca.

Pucará de Tilcara

1km S of Tilcara, *across the Río Huasamayo bridge (0388 4955006). Open 9am-6pm daily. Admission AR$10.* The Pucará (fort) de Tilcara on the southern edge of the town is the only archæological sight that is publicly accessible in the Quebrada de Humahuaca. A tribe called the Tilcaras sited the fort here 900 years ago for its natural defensive position overlooking the valley. At its peak, it was home to over 2,000 inhabitants who lived in small, windowless stone buildings. The fort was conquered by the Incas, who maintained its use as a defensive structure before the invading Spanish got their hands on the Pucará and eventually abandoned it. In the early 20th century, it was excavated and has been partially reconstructed to show how its inhabitants lived. The museum is a good resource of pre-Columbian and Spanish history, and the adjoining high-altitude botanical gardens are attractive and fascinating for those interested in the region's plant life.

FURTHER AFIELD

IRUYA

To escape the world for a few days or to get a glimpse of life in the isolated villages of the north-west, **Iruya** is the number-one choice. It lies 26 kilometres to the north of Humahuaca on Ruta 9. Located in a craggy mountain valley at nearly 2,800 metres above sea level, the village is stunningly beautiful and deservedly features in just about every tourism campaign in Salta. The best accommodation is at the Hostería de Iruya (03887 482002, www.hosteriadeiruya.com.ar).

NATIONAL PARKS IN SALTA & JUJUY

With the exception of Los Cardones, in the Valles Calchaquíes, Salta and Jujuy's national parks are not the easiest places to reach; nonetheless, they are a must-see for nature-lovers. The lush forest of Calilegua and El Rey national parks can be visited from Salta with Tastil (0387 431 1223, www.turismotastil.com.ar), and the flamingos at Laguna de los Pozuelos can form part of a trip to La Puna. Parque Nacional Baritú is more remote, and a trip here is best organised by contacting the tourist office in Jujuy (03882 428153). More information on the national parks can be found at www.parquesnacionales.gov.ar.

LA PUNA

La Puna is a vast semi-desert region that covers Salta and Jujuy's western flanks, and stretches north and west into Chile, Bolivia and Peru. Formed by the rain shadow of the Andes, the region's climate is characterised by extreme temperature differences between day and night and less than 100 millimetres of rainfall per year. The parched yellow landscapes, salt flats and haunting emptiness of the place thrill adventure-seeking travellers. There are few paved roads in this region, so the best way to visit is by four-wheel drive with a professional guide. Federico Norte (0387 436 1844, www.nortetrekking.com) and Socompa (0387 416 9130, www.socompa.com), both based in Salta, offer fixed itineraries or can tailor a trip based on your needs and time constraints. Highlights include one of Argentina's oldest churches (in the village of Susques), the magnificent flamingo-speckled lakes in the Parque Nacional Laguna de Los Pozuelos and the high-altitude volcanic peaks near Tolar Grande.

OUTDOOR ACTIVITIES

Salta and Jujuy's varied and extreme terrain make it ideal for adventure sports. Extreme Games (Buenos Aires 632, Ruta 47, km 11, 0387 421 6780, www.extremegame.todoweb salta.com.ar), based on the bridge over the Cabra Corral reservoir, one hour south of Salta, offers bungee jumping, *puenting* (a sort of upright, swinging bungee) and more.

On the rapids that exit the reservoir, or in the Yungas forests, Salta Rafting (Buenos Aires 88, local 13, 0387 401 0301) will take visitors on trips ranging from an afternoon's paddling to a nine-day epic. Closer to Salta, you can also take to the skies by paragliding from the San Lorenzo hills with Andean Trips (Dean Funes 344, 0387 421 8483, www.andeantrips.com.ar).

Top: Maimará cemetery.
Bottom: Salinas Grandes.

ESTANCIA
EL BORDO DE LAS LANZAS

*Enjoy for a while living
on an authentic Estancia
Discover the spirit of Nothern Argentina*

1609 – 2009 | 400 years of history

Salta . Argentina | Phone: + 54 387 4903070
Agustín Arias: +54 (9) 387 155 041310
mail: info@estanciaelbordo.com | www.turismoelbordo.com

PROMOTING A PRINCIPLED RESPONSE TO TERRORISM
PROTECTING THE RIGHTS OF WOMEN DEFENDING THE
SCOPE OF HUMAN RIGHTS PROTECTION **PROTECTING
CIVILIANS IN WARTIME** SHAPING FOREIGN POLICY
ADVANCING THE INTERNATIONAL JUSTICE SYSTEM
BANNING INDISCRIMINATE WEAPONS OF WAR
LINKING BUSINESS PRACTICES AND HUMAN RIGHTS
RESPONDING FIRST TO HUMAN RIGHTS EMERGENCIES
PROMOTING A PRINCIPLED RESPONSE TO TERRORISM
PROTECTING THE RIGHTS OF WOMEN DEFENDING THE
SCOPE OF HUMAN RIGHTS PROTECTION PROTECTING
CIVILIANS IN WARTIME SHAPING FOREIGN POLICY

HUMAN RIGHTS WATCH
AS LONG AS THERE IS OPPRESSION
TYRANNY HAS A WITNESS
ADVANCING THE INTERNATIONAL JUSTICE SYSTEM
BANNING INDISCRIMINATE WEAPONS OF WAR
LINKING BUSINESS PRACTICES AND HUMAN RIGHTS
RESPONDING FIRST TO HUMAN RIGHTS EMERGENCIES
REPORTING FROM CLOSED SOCIETIES PROMOTING A
PRINCIPLED RESPONSE TO TERRORISM PROTECTING THE
RIGHTS OF WOMEN LINKING BUSINESS PRACTICES AND
HUMAN RIGHTS PROMOTING A PRINCIPLED RESPONSE TO
TERRORISM PROTECTING THE RIGHTS OF WOMEN DEFENDING
THE SCOPE OF HUMAN RIGHTS PROTECTION
RESPONDING FIRST TO HUMAN RIGHTS
EMERGENCIES PROMOTING A PRINCIPLED
RESPONSE TO TERRORISM WWW.HRW.ORG

LEGADO
MÍTICO
Pequeños Hoteles Emblemáticos

Tel/fax: (54 387) 422 8786 / 421 4650 - Mitre 647, (A4400EHM)
Ciudad de Salta. reservassalta@legadomitico.com
Lo invitamos a descubrir también Legado Mítico Buenos Aires.

www.legadomitico.com

For a more traditional form of adventure, contact Caravana de Llamas (0388 495 5326, www.caravanadellamas.com.ar), which arranges spectacular llama treks over the white salt plains or mountains around Tilcara. To ensure that your visit is one long adrenaline rush, Horizonte 4x4 (0387 4901374, www.horizonte-tours.com) rents motorbikes to explore the region at high speed. Alternatively, travel at a more leisurely pace by renting a bicycle from MTB (General Güemes 569, 0387 15 527 1499 mobile, www.mtbsalta.com), or booking a place on one of its bike excursions.

Salta is a fisherman's paradise, with its lakes, fast-running mountain streams and mighty tropical rivers teaming with surubí and dorado. Many companies offer excursions: try Destino Exotico (0387 15 527 1499 mobile, www.destinoexotico. com). Hiking trips offer access to areas which are otherwise impossible to reach. Federico Norte (0387 436 1844, www.nortetrekking.com) offers some of the best tours.

Eat

Bistro 490
Salta *Santa Fe 490 (0387 422 7022). Open 7pm-12.30am Mon-Sat. £££. Modern.*
In keeping with the Buenos Aires fashion of adding allure to your restaurant or bar by hiding it, the *porteña* owner of Bistro 490 has located her establishment in an unassuming-looking house in a quiet area of town. But despite the understated premises, there is nothing modest about the food. With a menu that changes daily, chef Valeria uses seasonal ingredients from local markets and wild herbs from the countryside, as well as bringing in seafood from down south to provide Salta with something special every night. Intense and original flavours enliven traditional meat, chicken and seafood dishes and, depending on the time of year, archaic regional specialities like *achoscha rellena* (stuffed Andean cabbage leaves) may be served. A well-chosen selection of wines from Cafayate, San Juan, Mendoza and Patagonia completes an evening of epicurean pleasure in colourful and comfortable surroundings. Special diets can be catered to with advance warning.

Casa de las Empanadas
Cafayate *Mitre 24 (03868 15 454111 mobile). Open 10am-3pm, 7-11pm Tue-Sun. £. No credit cards. Modern.*
Perhaps due to their sanctified status, empanada fillings in Salta appear to be frozen in a holy trinity of beef, chicken and cheese. The heretical (or perhaps godsend) La Casa de Las Empanadas, which is unexpectedly located in very non-revolutionary Cafayate, offers a delightful selection of its own inventions as well as the sacred three. Vegetarians can gorge on fillings such as goat's cheese, basil, tomatoes and corn, while tuna and salami provide relief for those still craving something meaty. The ecstatic scribbles that cover every inch of wall space say it all.

Casa Moderna
Salta *Vicente López 423 (0387 431 0685). Open 10am-2pm, 6-10pm Mon-Sat. ££. No credit cards. International.*
There are two Casa Modernas in Salta. The original business (España 674) stands completely at odds with its name. Thousands of ancient, dusty beer and wine bottles are stacked to the ceiling, while boxes of imported chocolates, cheeses and other goods fill equally dusty display cases. The gruff manager serves up good empanadas, *picadas* and beer. His wife's new Mediterranean-feel restaurant and delicatessen is much more cheerful, and, despite being located in an old building, noticeably more *moderna*. The owner makes the best bread in Salta and serves it up with delicious hams and cheeses, as well as a good selection of main courses. The deli is Salta's best spot to stock up for a picnic, with excellent local wine and rolls of creamy goat's cheese.

Las Leñitas
Salta *Balcarce 802, & Alsina (0387 421 4865). Open noon-4pm, 8pm-2am daily. ££. Parrilla.*
If you don't fancy being serenaded by boisterous gauchos or dragged away from your food to be publicly humiliated while dancing with a nimble-footed local, then this quiet restaurant, with its less intrusive singing waiters, might be the place for you. It's set in a converted warehouse, whose soaring ceilings ensure the restaurant never feels too crowded, even on busy weekends. The menu offers an excellent selection of meat, and it's a pleasant surprise to find, in the centre of the room, an enormous salad bar. The very friendly staff pick up guitars and drumsticks every now and then and gently regale customers with regional *folklore*, with a few love ballads thrown in for good measure.

MAAM Café
Salta *Mitre 77 (0387 437 0499/www.maam.org.ar). Open 9am-10pm daily. ££. Café.*
The museum eaterie, one of many cafés surrounding the main plaza, is a good spot to grab a breakfast of coffee and *medialunas* (croissants) and watch Salta's daily life played out in the square opposite. A wholesome selection of sandwiches and salads is served.

La Monumental
Salta *Entre Ríos 202, & Vicente López (0387 431 7653). Open noon-3.30pm, 8pm-1am daily. ££. Parrilla/Traditional.*
La Monumental has proven to be so monumentally popular that its owners have now opened four restaurants, all serving exactly the same thing. The meat here is always cooked *a punto* (medium), and dished out in enormous portions. Avoid the pseudo-castle outpost of La Monumental on Entre Ríos and Vicente López, and opt for the more intimate restaurant directly opposite. The *costillas de cerdo* (pork ribs) are excellent, and the *morcilla con arroz* (black pudding with rice) is some of the best you'll find. If you want to feel like a local (or a less well-heeled one, at least), order an aluminum jug of the house wine, which is quite drinkable – although consumption of large quantities is not to be recommended.

El Nuevo Progreso

Tilcara *Lavalle 351 (0388 495 5237). Open 3pm-2am Mon-Sat. ££. Modern.*

Offering a perfect blend of local atmosphere and fantastic food, this place is hidden away from the tourist hordes on the corner of Tilcara's second plaza. The rustic wooden floor and whitewashed walls don't prepare you for the gourmet delights created by the imaginative chef. Local ingredients such as llama, alfalfa, tomatoes and quinoa are used to create delicious traditional dishes. On many evenings, while locals prop up the bar, a duo of folk musicians arrives to strum and hum you into an Andean nirvana.

Pacha Mama

Tilcara *Belgrano 590 (0388 495 5293). Open 11am-3.30pm, 8pm-midnight daily. ££. No credit cards. Traditional.*

The low-key stone and wood surroundings of Pacha Mama are a great spot to taste some of the local specialities, *humitas* and tamales. The former are made from mixing ground sweetcorn with cheese and boiling it in a corn-leaf bundle. For the latter, simply substitute the cheese for meat. These sturdy, ultra-filling packages are made here with just the right combination of texture and flavour; if you're still hungry, you can always follow them up with a llama steak.

El Patio de La Empanada

Salta *San Martín, & Islas Malvinas (0387 434 4336). Open 10am-4pm, 8pm-1am daily. £. Traditional.*

The source of Salta's culinary pride, the empanada can be a dangerous topic in these parts. God forbid making comparisons with empanadas you sampled in Buenos Aires. Suggesting the best spot in town at which to eat them may also be a perilous pursuit, considering the battles that rage over what 'best' involves. Risks of retribution aside, El Patio de la Empanada is heartily recommended. Though a little off the beaten track, you'll find its delicacies worth the hike down calle San Martín. On a busy covered terrace, noticeably free of tourists, several small businesses compete for customers' attention. Choose the outlet to the left when facing the back entrance, go for *empanadas de carne fritas* (the deep-fried meat variety) and complement them with a litre of sugary *gaseosa* (soft drink) or a Quilmes beer.

Plaza de Almas

Salta *Pueyrredón 6, & Caseros (0387 422 8933/ www.plazadealmas.com). Open 8pm-2am daily. ££. No credit cards. International.*

Painted a rich purple, this crafts shop-cum-restaurant, with its floor-to-ceiling wallpaper of books, clothes and art, is a bohemian blip in an otherwise traditional city. The menu comprises an eclectic mix of local and international ingredients that turn out surprisingly well, if a little on the heavy side. Fried beef and local vegetables are mixed with fresh cream and curry sauce to produce *chuy*, a rich and delicious stew-like dish that will keep you going until the next day's lunch. Vegetarians (ready to stab the next cheese empanada they see) can choose from a range of *torres*; crêpes stuffed with fried vegetables and covered in creamy sauce. Vegetarian versions of many of the other dishes on the menu can be rustled up on request.

Terruño

Cafayate *Güemes 28 (03868 422460). Open noon-3.30pm, 7-11.30pm daily. ££. Traditional.*

Cafayate's laid-back atmosphere seems, in many cases, to have filtered into its approach to food, with most restaurants offering the usual assortment of parrilla, pizzas and pasta. Terruño, a little place facing the plaza, is a notable exception. True to its name (which translates as 'terroir'), it offers up an excellent selection of meat and locally produced vegetables, often served in rich, carefully-seasoned sauces. There's also a great selection of wine from local bodegas.

Stay

Bloomers

Salta *Vicente López 129 (0387 422 7449/ www.bloomers-salta.com.ar). £££. No credit cards.*

An old townhouse painted bright purple, Bloomers is one of Salta's new boutique hotels – and definitely the best value. Located three blocks from the main square, the hotel is run by the charming Xibil and Adrián, who offer three doubles and two single rooms. The rooms are simply but tastefully furnished, blending modern design and comfort with the original features of the building. The sunny central garden and spacious sitting room are perfect to relax in after a day exploring the countryside. In a country where breakfasts are invariably continental, the expansive brunch of scrambled eggs with tomatoes, Andean potatoes, toast and *medialunas* (croissants) is a real treat.

El Bordo de Las Lanzas

El Bordo, 60km NE of Salta *via Ruta 9 & Ruta 34. Rivadavia 298 (0387 490 3070/www.turismo elbordo.com.ar). £££.*

An appealing blend of history and untainted beauty, this 400-year-old estancia belongs to the Arias family, descendants of Salta's patriot, Martín Miguel de Güemes. Built in adobe and oak, the beautiful house has eight en-suite rooms decorated with 17th- and 18th-century paintings and furniture. Sipping a gin and tonic on the veranda at sunset, you'll soon feel more of an old friend here than a tourist; local dishes or a superb barbecue are served up on request. Day trips to see everything the region has to offer can be arranged. Alternatively, you can take it easy by the pool or go gaucho and visit the local colony of *yacaras* (alligators) on horseback. El Bordo's location and facilities make it an ideal base from which to explore the whole region, and with all meals and activities included, it's excellent value.

Capricho

Salta *Dean Funes 26 (caprichoreservations@ yahoo.com/www.caprichosalta.com.ar). ££.*

Unlike many city hotels, which try to cram as many bodies in to the square foot as possible, this beautifully restored townhouse offers just three very spacious suites. Outside are three wonderful courtyards of old exposed brick, draped with bougainvillea and jasmine. Monica, the French owner, has put the 'boutique' back into a concept that has become

Top & bottom left: tamales, empanadas and humitas.
Bottom right: Plaza de Almas.

rather tired in recent years, and the rooms, with their antique furniture, rich colours and little mezzanines, are a delight. With five days' notice, cookery courses in how to make proper tamales, *humitas* and, of course, empanadas are available. Bookings are by email only.

Colomé

Molinos *RP 53, km 20, about 5km outside town on Ruta 40 (03868 494940/www.estanciacolome.com). ££££.*
After a dusty, bone-jarring ride, it's a little surreal to have your luggage wheeled off on a brass trolley by a uniformed porter. But that's just the beginning of the extravagance that awaits Colomé's guests. Wine tycoon Donald Hess bought this bodega after spotting potential in its grape, and in the process of promoting the world's highest-altitude wines, he converted the old estancia into one of the country's most renowned hotels. Its nine suites, with spectacular views of the vineyards and surrounding mountains, are the height of contemporary luxury, and there's a cosy living room and a library in which to relax. Wander around the gardens, enjoy an afternoon by the pool, fill up on supper made from fresh ingredients from the estate and end the evening lounging on the terrace, under a brilliant night sky.

El Cortijo

Cachi *Avenida Automóvil Club (0386 849 1034/ www.elcortijohotel.com). ££££.*
Cachi's growing popularity in recent years has resulted in a proliferation of hotels, though many of the nicer ones are located in the surrounding countryside. This pretty, colonial-era family home in the centre of town has been 'recycled', as Argentinians would say (they mean refurbished), and offers 12 comfortable rooms. Brightly coloured textiles are artfully offset by simple white walls, antique furniture and an impressive collection of sacred pieces from the Cusco school of art. A range of cakes, breads and jams are available at breakfast and tea-time; in the evening, cheeses and meats can be enjoyed with a choice of regional wines.

Finca Santa Anita

Coronel Moldes *On Ruta 68 heading south, turn left at Coronel Moldes for Dique Cabra Corral (0387 490 5050/www.santaanita.com.ar). £££.*
This old adobe estancia, painted pink and surrounded by the lush tobacco fields of the southern Valle de Lerma, is a wonderful place to spend a night or two on the way to Cafayate or Cachi, or if visiting the Cabra Corral reservoir. The rooms are old-world and comfortable, and the food, featuring vegetables from the organic garden and award-winning goat's cheese, is excellent. Lunches can be arranged if booked one day in advance.

Hacienda de Molinos

Molinos *opposite San Pedro de Nolasco Church (03868 494094/www.haciendademolinos.com.ar). ££££.*
This beautifully restored hotel is the perfect place to sit back and enjoy an atmosphere of complete peace. Ironically, Hacienda de Molinos was formerly the residence of a brutal provincial governor, whose subterranean emergency escape route remains testimony to his popularity ratings.

The 18 standard and superior rooms are arranged around two patios with dramatic views of the Río Calchaquí and mountains beyond, and the understated decor allows the beautiful simplicity of the adobe and carved wood structure to shine through. The hotel offers reliable Andean and international cuisine, and there's a pool and decent Wi-Fi. Excursions and horse riding can be arranged on request, as can a babysitter.

"Heading down the eucalyptus-lined drive at House of Jasmines, you feel as if you have slipped back in time."

House of Jasmines

15km SW of Salta *RN 51, km 11 (0387 497 2002/ www.houseofjasmines.com). ££££.*
A 20-minute drive outside Salta, House of Jasmines sits amid just over one square kilometre of tree-dotted parkland, with an unrivalled view of the forested hills that surround the city. Entering the eucalyptus-lined driveway, you immediately feel as if you have slipped back in time, and the rough plastered walls and cosy windows of the estancia seem only to confirm the suspicion. Brought into the limelight by its former owner, actor Robert Duval, House of Jasmines offers more than Hollywood glamour. The owners combine the estancia's historical charm with first-rate service and luxury. Some rooms are in the main house, while others occupy a couple of nearby cottages. All are stylishly appointed, with white-painted furniture and extremely comfortable beds. The swimming pool has magnificent views, and there's a delightful little spa.

Legado Mítico

Salta *Mitre 647 (0387 422 8786/ www.legadomitico.com). £££.*
The 11 rooms at this boutique hotel are themed around local historical figures, regions and peoples. The Güemes room contains a traditional gaucho outfit, while the Wichi tribe room is decorated with old photographs and indigenous-style furnishings. Though it can feel slightly contrived, the modern design and furnishings are impeccable, and the hotel offers the type of accommodation rarely found outside Buenos Aires. Plans are afoot to create a pool and spa as well as a restaurant; the hotel currently offers snacks and a reasonable selection of wines.

El Manantial del Silencio

Purmamarca *RN 52, km 3.5 (0388 490 8080/ www.hotelmanantial.com.ar). ££££.*
The oldest hotel in Purmamarca remains the most attractive. Although it's almost shocking to see another colour added to the already rich patchwork of the Quebrada de Humahuaca, its green gardens and pool are a welcome

El Cortijo.

Legado Mítico.

respite from the arid valley outside. The hotel has the feel of an old country house, and the 19 rooms are spacious and comfortable. The hotel can arrange excursions to Salinas Grandes and other local attractions.

Patios de Cafayate
Cafayate *junction of RN 68 & RN 40 (03868 421747/www.patiosdecafayate.com). ££££.*
Adjoining the formidable El Esteco bodega is this grandiose luxury hotel. Converted from the original family home, it's a vision of gleaming wooden rafters, polished antiques and pretty tiled courtyards. The rooms are housed in low white buildings, spread across carefully-tended gardens that must contain at least 90% of arid Cafayate's grass. In the hotel's wine spa, friendly masseuses will scrub you with goat's cheese and quinoa, douse you in cabernet sauvignon and knead out every last knot before leaving you to soak in a hot tub overlooking the mountains. Before jumping gleefully into the 'heated' garden pool, be sure to check that the solar panels are working.

Posada de Luz
Tilcara *Ambrosetti, & Alverro (0388 495 5017/ www.posadadeluz.com.ar). £££.*
It's difficult to imagine there was much debate on agreeing to name this place 'Posada of Light'. As the Quebrada has sunshine practically every day of the year, the whole posada is overflowing with a brilliance that seems to have bleached the stone walls and slender trees of the garden into wonderful, otherworldly shades. The accommodation, in the form of various small buildings and cottages, is spread across a large plot of land, which lies just a few blocks from the centre of town. Rooms, with their own wood-burning stoves, are cosy and tastefully decorated, each one leading on to its own little terrace where you can catch a few rays of your own. Breakfasts are excellent, and the staff extremely helpful.

Viñas de Cafayate
Cafayate *25 de Mayo, Camino al Divisadero, turn right at Bodega Domingo Hermanos on RN 40 heading south (03868 422272/www.cafayatewineresort.com). £££.*
Nestled among hectares of vineyard with an uninterrupted view of the mountains, this is about as close to the soul of Cafayate as you can get, short of curling up in a wine barrel. The 12 standard and deluxe rooms, which each have access to a private balcony overlooking the vines, are arranged around a central courtyard with a garden and swimming pool. An organic garden supplies the basics for a restaurant serving regional and gourmet dishes. The hefty cellar allows guests indisposed to clocking up bodega miles the opportunity to sit and sample a spectrum of local vintages. Excursions to nearby attractions and visits to bodegas can also be arranged.

Factfile

When to go
Salta and Jujuy have sunshine and relatively warm temperatures almost all year round. Rain in the areas around Salta city can be persistent in summer (January to March); May and June are the coldest months. Spring and early summer (September to December) are best for warm weather and greener landscapes.

Getting there
With over seven companies operating between Salta's bus terminal (Avenida Hipólito Yrigoyen 339, 0387 4221580) and Buenos Aires, services are regular. Chevallier (011 4000 5255, www.nuevachevallier.com.ar), Flechabus (011 4000 5200, www.flechabus.com.ar) and La Veloz del Norte (0800 444 8356, www. lavelozcallcenter.com.ar) run bus services from Salta to various destinations nationwide, as well as to Bolivia and Chile.
   There are numerous daily flights from Salta's Martín Miguel de Güemes airport (RN 51, km 5, 0387 424 3115) to Buenos Aires. Aerolíneas Argentinas (0810 222 86527, www.aerolineas. com.ar) flies to Salta. For details of connections to Córdoba and Iguazú from Salta, contact Andes Líneas Aéreas (0810 777 26337, www.andes online.com).

Getting around
Scheduled bus services run to Tilcara, Cachi, Cafayate and elsewhere from Salta's bus terminal. Tastil (Caseros 468, 0387 431 1223, www.turismotastil.com.ar), in Salta, offers day and overnight trips to the major attractions in the area, and its sister company Movi Track (Caseros 468, 0387 4316749, www.movitrack.com.ar) offers similar trips in a range of unusual vehicles.
   Also based in Salta, NOA (Buenos Aires 1, 0387 431 7080, www.noarentacar.com) offers good rental deals on a selection of vehicles, including 4x4s.

Tourist information
Salta Buenos Aires 93 (0387 431 0950, www.turismosalta.gov.ar). Open 8am-9pm daily.
Jujuy Canónigo Juan Ignacio Gorriti 295, San Salvador de Jujuy (0388 422 1325, www. turismo.jujuy.gov.ar). Open 7am-10pm daily.

Internet
The majority of hotels and many bars in Salta offer Wi-Fi. The expensive hotels outside the city normally have internet access, and every town has internet cafés.
   MZ Computación (Córdoba, & España) in Salta offers reliable broadband.

Top left: seal. Top right: Isla de los Pájaros, Beagle Channel. Middle & bottom: Ushuaia.

Ushuaia

Argentina

The historic port at the end of the world.

This is the way the world ends – in a small, unpretentious port on the southern shores of Tierra del Fuego, the ragged exclamation point of the Americas. Beyond Ushuaia there is nothing but the pearl-grey waters of the southern oceans, churning violently around the vast polar continent. These are strange latitudes, where the sun either barely sets or barely rises, where westerly hurricanes blow down off the Andes and twist the trees into permanent deformity, and where the Andean cordillera suddenly ducks its snowy head beneath the ocean.

Only a certain kind of character can thrive in a place like this, but like most people who live at a geographical extreme, Ushuaians are proud of their ne plus ultra status (if you aren't tired of products tagged 'fin del mundo' by the end of your stay, you haven't been looking hard enough). For most tourists, by contrast, Ushuaia is a jumping-off point. Some go south, exploring the scenic inlets and islands of the Beagle Channel, or farther, around Cape Horn, or farther still, to the Antarctic Peninsula, where the Andes rise again. Others strike out northward, to ski down the slopes of Cerro Castor or trek through the ancient lenga forests of the Fuegian backcountry. Some people simply come to eat *centolla* (king crab), which is to the average crustacean what the Piedmont truffle is to the button mushroom.

Whatever you visit for, you'll leave with the sense that you've experienced somewhere unique. During its history, Ushuaia has been terra incognita, an illusory gateway to the spice islands, a penal colony, a tax haven and a tourist resort. Here, sea captains have blown their brains out in despair, while others have won fame and fortune. It was on and around this coastline that Charles Darwin set in train the most profound developments in the natural sciences since Newton was disturbed in the orchard. You'll be amazed by what can happen at the end of the world.

Explore

Getting around **Ushuaia** is a lot easier than pronouncing it ('Ooh-SWY-ya' gets you close). It's a city built on slopes, with steep roads leading away from the water, but much of the action is focused on the main thoroughfare, Avenida San Martín. Here, you'll find chocolate shops, outdoor equipment outlets, several lively drinking holes and a number of tour operators, most of which offer discounted, last-minute berths on Antarctic cruises. From the main drag, the town morphs into a chaotic streetscape that runs from south to north. At the top, the architecture is a mix of neat wooden cabins and A-frame chalets; at the bottom, the waterfront is a focus for seafood restaurants and two-star hotels. East along calle Maipú, the docks are sprawling and messy, although the passenger port, Puerto de Ushuaia, is more orderly. Large cruise liners bound for Antarctica dock here, though even the grandest of these – and some of them look like toppled *art moderne* skyscrapers – seem puny when set against the granite steeples of Cerro Martial, which glower over the town from the north.

All sights in downtown Ushuaia are within easy walking distance of each other, although you may need to take a taxi from your hotel to get to the town centre.

Museo del Fin del Mundo

Avenida Maipú 173 (02901 421863/www.museo delfindelmundo.org.ar). Open Oct-Apr 9am-8pm daily. May-Sept noon-7pm daily. Admission AR$20; AR$8 reductions; free under-14s.

Established in 1979, this museum traces the history of the region's indigenous peoples, the settlers and the old grocery shops that were once the town's commercial lifeblood, as well as its bird life and maritime heritage. The latter section features the figurehead from the prow of the *Duchess of Albany*, which ran aground off Tierra del Fuego in 1893. The remains of the ship can be seen on the shore. A little bookshop stocks literature relating to the area, while anyone wishing to send a postcard from 'the end of the world' may do so at the post office.

Museo Marítimo y Presidio de Ushuaia

Yaganes & Gobernador Paz (02901 437481/ www.museomaritimo.com). Open Oct-Mar 9am-8pm daily. Apr-Sept 10am-8pm daily. Admission AR$45; AR$30 reductions; free under-12s. No credit cards.

Two wings of the former prison – closed to convicts for more than half a century – have been converted into this large museum complex. Partly devoted to maritime exhibits (including scale models of FitzRoy's *Beagle* and Magellan's *Trinidad*), the big attraction here is the prison building itself and its reconstruction of prison life. In the jail's 'heyday', its 380 cells housed 600 inmates, who were put to work locally as bakers, electricians, carpenters, firemen and printers. Infamous for its grim austerity, the prison was shut down by president Juan Domingo Perón in 1947.

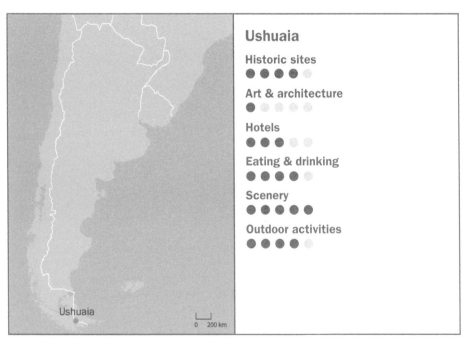

Ushuaia

Historic sites
●●●●◌

Art & architecture
●◌◌◌◌

Hotels
●●●◌◌

Eating & drinking
●●●●◌

Scenery
●●●●●

Outdoor activities
●●●●

Ushuaia

0   200 km

Isla de los Pájaros,
Beagle Channel.

Museo de Maquetas Mundo Yámana

Rivadavia 56 (02901 422874). Open 10am-8pm daily.
Admission AR$9; AR$4 reductions. No credit cards.
Amid all the tales of nautical derring-do and painstaking colonisation, it is easy to forget that Tierra del Fuego was inhabited long before Magellan rounded Cape Horn. This private museum – obviously a labour of love – exhibits excellent scale models depicting Yámana dwellings and activities. You'll also find interesting information about the other tribes that populated the archipelago, such as the Selk'nam and the Haus.

AROUND USHUAIA

If weather permits, be sure to take a boat trip into the exquisite Beagle Channel, named for the brig-sloop that brought Robert FitzRoy and a young, obscure naturalist named Charles Darwin to the tip of South America in 1831 (*see right* **Evolution's captain**). Tickets for excursions can be purchased either at the Muelle Turístico (tourist pier) near the port, or in advance from outfits such as Rumbo Sur (02901 422275, www.rumbosur.com.ar) or Canal Fun & Nature (02901 437395, www.canal fun.com). Your hotel will be glad to help with all excursion bookings.

All boats leave from the passenger port and head out into the channel, past the hillsides studded with lenga trees and on to the Les Eclaireurs lighthouse, stopping off at the Isla de los Lobos (sea lion colony) and the Isla de los Pájaros (bird colony). These tours typically last between three and five hours. Longer excursions go to Estancia Harberton, perhaps the most famous farm in the entire country. The estancia, 85 kilometres east of Ushuaia, is an isolated ranch perched on the very edge of the continent. It was built by the English missionary Thomas Bridges, and is still lived in and worked by his direct descendants. Nowadays, guided tours in English and Spanish take you to the family cemetery, gardens and sheep-shearing sheds.

If you're visiting Ushuaia during the winter months (June to September), you're probably here to ski. While the slopes overlooking the town at Cerro Martial are perfect for beginners, the more serious option is Cerro Castor (www.cerrocastor.com), 26 kilometres from Ushuaia. The resort has 24 pistes, three ski lifts, two teleskis and one bambi lift, and is the southernmost ski centre in the world. The season climaxes on 17 August with the annual Marcha Blanca (White March), a re-enactment of independence hero José de San Martín's crossing of the Andes.

For a condor's-eye view of Ushuaia and the glittering bay beyond, head up to Glaciar Martial, above Cerro Martial. Apart from being a beautiful natural wonder, this colossal chunk of ice also supplies Ushuaia with most of its drinking water. If you're feeling particularly energetic, you can try walking the seven kilometres from town, though the more sensible option is to take a taxi to the base station of the Centro Recreativo Glaciar Martial's chairlift. Ride part of the way up, then clamber up to the base of the glacier. Just don't put it off until next time: experts predict that the receding glacier will disappear entirely over the next 50 years. You can stop off at the base for a rejuvenating pot of tea and cakes at La Cabaña (Luis Fernando Martial 3560, 02901 434699).

"For a condor's-eye view of Ushuaia and the glittering bay beyond, head up to the beautiful Glaciar Martial."

Parque Nacional Tierra del Fuego

11km W of Ushuaia *on RN 3, km 3047 (no phone).*
Open 24hrs daily. Admission Jan-Mar AR$50; free under-16s. July-Sept free to all. No credit cards.
While large sections of the Tierra del Fuego national park are off-limits to hikers, it's still one of the area's essential day trips. While wandering through its forests – snow-laden in winter, aflame with colour in autumn – you may be lucky enough to see guanaco, grey foxes, beavers (imported from Canada, and now a pest), steamer ducks, oystercatchers and the austral parakeet (the world's southernmost parrot). If you hear a sound like a semi-automatic weapon, there's no need to duck for cover – it's a Magellenic woodpecker, digging its nest. Most treks are short and easy. The Senda Costera offers thrilling views over the Bahía Ensenada, Isla Estorbo and Isla Redonda; many of the more ambitious treks can be combined with kayaking to these islands.

Tren del Fin del Mundo

8km W of Ushuaia *on RN 3, km 3042 (02901 431600/www.trendelfindelmundo.com.ar). Open Jan-Mar at least 3 services per day. July-Sept at least 2 services per day. Check website for departure & return times. Rates from AR$90.*
One of the most popular ways of getting to and from the national park is aboard one of these cute and colourful steam locomotives (all they need are faces to resemble characters in the Reverend WV Awdry's *Thomas* series), which run along a short stretch of narrow-gauge railway. The original train tracks were laid by prisoners in 1896 to link the jail to the nearby forests. The railway fell into disuse when the prison closed down in 1947, but reopened in 1994 as a tourist attraction. Passengers can travel in tourist or first class, or can rent the President's Wagon, which seats eight for a king crab and champagne dinner (from US$80 per person). The scenic five-kilometre trip takes 45 minutes and stops off at a reconstruction of a Yámana settlement.

Evolution's captain

Charles Darwin was a naturalist, a travel writer, an eminent Victorian and, as even his fiercest critics will concede, one of the most influential thinkers of the modern age. But had it not been for Robert FitzRoy, he might have ended up an anonymous clergyman in a country parsonage.

A complex man with a Byronic temperament, FitzRoy was captain of HMS *Beagle*, which was re-commissioned in 1831 to complete a second mapping expedition along the southern Patagonian coastline. Darwin, then studying at Cambridge and seemingly destined for the Church, heard FitzRoy was looking for a naturalist to join him, and leapt at the chance.

By this point, FitzRoy had already seen how such an expedition could break even the toughest of men; the *Beagle*'s first captain had become so fed up with the barren landscapes and wretched climate of Tierra del Fuego that he had shot himself in the head.

When you're building an empire, these things happen. But something far stranger had occurred during that first voyage: FitzRoy had ended up kidnapping four natives and bringing them back to England. The Fuegians, given picturesque English names by FitzRoy (Jemmy Button, York Minster, Boat Memory and – the only girl – Fuegia Basket), were educated by church tutors, attired in the latest fashions and even presented at court. Boat Memory soon succumbed to smallpox, and when a lonely York Minster began a relationship with Fuegia Basket, Fitz Roy, fearing scandal, decided it was time to take the Patagonians home.

In December 1831, the *Beagle* sailed out from Portsmouth. Armed with a plentiful supply of Bibles, fine tableware and agricultural tools, the three Fuegians were dropped off back

home. FitzRoy departed, confident that his protégés would immediately set about building the new Jerusalem.

It was not to be. When FitzRoy and Darwin returned in March 1834, they found a ruined settlement and a naked, 'wretchedly thin' Jemmy. York Minster, he told them, had stolen all his possessions and made off with them in a canoe. Paradise had been postponed.

Darwin, meanwhile, was in his element, scribbling down the thoughts and impressions that would later become *The Voyage of the Beagle*. In general, he and FitzRoy got along well, but their friendship would not survive the *Beagle*'s return to England in 1836. Both men became minor celebrities, but while Darwin's fame and influence would wax over subsequent decades, FitzRoy's would inversely wane. FitzRoy retreated into Christian orthodoxy and a literal interpretation of the Bible. He hated *The Origin of Species* (Darwin had sent him a copy) and perhaps felt guilty about having helped the naturalist form his ideas. On 30 April 1865, after enduring years of terrible depression, he cut his own throat with a razor.

Lavish parties were thrown in 2009 to mark the bicentenary of Charles Darwin's birth. By contrast, and despite his significant contributions to the fields of cartography and meteorology, Robert FitzRoy is largely forgotten. History, it seems, is no fairer than life. But no one who sails from Ushuaia through the beautiful channel named after FitzRoy's command, and out into the ferocious seas beyond, will need persuading of the prowess and courage of the man whom writer Peter Nichols has dubbed 'evolution's captain'.

Eat

Ushuaia is one of the few places in Argentina where fish is more highly prized than flesh. The local speciality is *centolla*, or king crab. This delicious decapod is the town's unofficial emblem, and it's a brave restaurateur who chooses to hang a signboard outside their premises depicting something other than an oversized, bristling crustacean.

"Served simply with lemon and freshly ground black pepper, king crab is one of Argentina's great dishes."

Chefs here find seemingly limitless ways to spoil king crab, from putting in on pizza to slathering it in ketchup and mayonnaise, but served simply, with a slice of lemon on the side and some freshly ground black pepper, it is one of Argentina's great dishes. If you're in the mood for excellent Argentinian meat, go for Patagonian lamb, which is lean, tender and quite flavourful.

Chez Manu
4km N of Ushuaia *Avenida Luis Fernando Martial 2135 (02901 432253/www.chezmanu.com). Open noon-3.30pm, 8pm-midnight daily. Closed 15 May-15 June & Mon from July-Sept £££. International.*
Despite the name and the presence behind the stove of French chef Emmanuel 'Manu' Herbin, this delightful hillside eaterie leans more towards Patagonia than Paris. You can, if you like, start with onion soup or moules à la provençal; but far better to tuck into the platter of smoked fish (hake, salmon and herring) prepared on the premises using local lenga wood and Herbin's own secret blend of spices. This is one of the few places in town where the four-legged ingredients are given the same love and attention as the scaly ones, so try the richly flavoured Patagonian lamb, the medallions of *lomo* (fillet steak) with Andean morels or the *conejo Fueguino a la mostaza* (Fuegian rabbit with mustard sauce). The appealing dessert menu includes local forest fruits and a warm chocolate fondant that is gluttony incarnate. The view of the bay is predictably stunning.

Ideal Galway Pub
Avenida San Martín 393 (02901 437860/www. elbarideal.com). Open 9am-midnight Mon-Sat; noon-4pm Sun. ££. Traditional.
With its blonde, lenga-wood walls and corrugated zinc-pitched roof that have been keeping out the unfriendly Fuegian elements for over a century now, this pub is one of the best-known buildings in town (though it's often referred to by its former name, Bar Ideal). Brightly lit and informal – more cantina than restaurant – it's a sure bet for a square meal delivered with a smile, or for simply grabbing a hot chocolate and a bit of shelter when the wind gets up. Ignore the overpriced 'specials' – the king crab drenched in ketchup and mayonnaise is as bad as it sounds – and order some meat 'n' mash from the *minutas* (short-order) menu. Afterwards, go for a pint or two of the locally brewed Beagle beer at one of the 'Irish' pubs along Avenida San Martin.

Kaupé
Avenida Roca 470 (02901 422704/www.kaupe.com.ar). Open Easter-Oct 6.30-11pm Mon-Sat. Nov-Easter noon-2pm, 6.30-11pm Mon-Fri. Closed May. £££. Seafood.
Almost certainly the best restaurant on the 54th parallel, Kaupé screams 'special occasion'; if you don't have a special occasion, make one up. The dining room is a study in traditional elegance, with gleaming wood on all sides setting off the starched table linen. If you can tear your eyes away from the view of the port and Beagle Channel, you'll find a menu dominated by locally netted seafood. Chef-owner Ernesto Vivian has several ways with *centolla* – his king crab and spinach chowder is an original blend of both colours and flavours. If you've had enough of the ubiquitous leggy crustacean, try the *merluza negra a la manteca* (Chilean sea bass in butter) or the light and tangy *ceviche de vieyras* (scallops).

Kuar
Avenida Perito Moreno 2232 (02901 437396/ www.kuar.com.ar). Open Jan-Mar 3pm-4am daily. July-Sept 6pm-1am Mon-Sat. ££. International.
Housed in a striking confection of wood, stone and iron, where the star feature is an enormous window looking over the Beagle Channel, Kuar is Ushuaia's closest approximation to a fashionable nightspot. The fish and meat mains are facsimiles of dishes done better elsewhere, so stick with the seafood tapas and mixed *picadas* (cold cheese and meat platters). The Drake artisanal beer, which is brewed on the premises and comes in three varieties, won't win any real-ale awards, but it makes a pleasant change from chemical Quilmes. The large, crackling fire is a big draw in winter and, if you're looking for an après-ski scene, you'll find a semblance of it here. The live shows are best avoided.

Le Martial
2.5km N of Ushuaia *Las Hayas Resort Hotel, Avenida Luis Fernando Martial 1650 (02901 430710/www.lashayashotel.com). Open noon-2.30pm, 8-11.30pm daily. ££££. Seafood.*
Like most restaurants in five-star hotels, Le Martial is luxurious, well managed and rather dull. Still, if you have someone to impress – preferably a business client or a maiden aunt – or simply want to sink into a padded chair and be fussed over, the dining room at Las Hayas won't let you down. The speciality sea bass is simply presented and perfectly executed; the wine list is by far the best in town; and the service is flawless.

Clockwise from top: Tierra de Leyendas; Ushuaia harbour; local crabs.

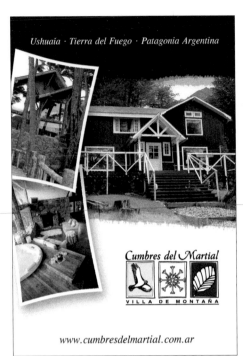

Ushuaïa · Tierra del Fuego · Patagonia Argentina

Cumbres del Martial

VILLA DE MONTAÑA

www.cumbresdelmartial.com.ar

Time Out

timeout.com/travel
Get the local experience

Camel racing in the United Arab Emirates

© Bernardino Testa/HP Images

LOS CAUQUENES
RESORT & SPA - USHUAIA

CANAL BEAGLE, PRIMERA FILA.

INDESCRIPTIBLE.
Probablemente la mejor
palabra para describir
Los Cauquenes Resort & Spa.

INFORMES Y RESERVAS :
+(54) (11) 4735-2648
reservas@loscauquenes.com
www.loscauquenes.com

Tía Elvira

Avenida Maipú 394 (02901 424725/www.tiaelvira.com).
Open Jan-Mar noon-3.30pm, 6.30pm-midnight daily.
July-Sept noon-3pm, 6.30pm-midnight Mon-Sat. £££.
Seafood.
Owner Oscar Sigel and his clan (Elvira was the name of Oscar's late mother) have been boiling crabs and scaling hake on these seafront premises since 1978, and the restaurant is now an Ushuaia classic. As in many of the town's eateries, it's hard to tell where family heirlooms end and interior decor begins, but the madcap blend of sepia-toned local history photos and religious paraphernalia is a visual treat, regardless. Start with a plate of *cholgas en escabeche* (pickled clams) before moving on to one of the star fish dishes, such as garlicky *centolla al ajillo* and the house special of trout fillet in a sauce of king crab and mussels. The menu is a little too long, and the kitchen is occasionally guilty of gilding the lily – king crab in roquefort sauce, for example – but for atmosphere and frontier-town authenticity, Tía Elvira is hard to beat.

Volver

Avenida Maipú 37 (02901 423977). Open Dec-Feb noon-2.30pm, 7-11.30pm daily. Mar-Nov noon-2.30pm, 7-11.30pm Tue-Sun. ££. Seafood.
Occupying a century-old, carrot-coloured building on the seafront, Volver resembles the attic of a fisherman with a taste for pop art and an aversion to clear-outs. Nets and ancient cooking utensils dangle from the ceiling, magazines and football memorabilia cover the walls, and a mannequin of a sou'wester-wearing Che Guevara guards the bathrooms. The food, somewhat surprisingly, is rather good. Order the fish of the day and a side of fries (the pricier, more complex items on the menu are best left alone) and pair it with a crisp, fruity torrontés from the other end of the country. Service is uneven, ranging from sweet and gracious to rude to the point of amusing.

Shop

Ushuaia's duty-free status (initiated in 1972 to encourage investment) makes it one of the best places outside Andorra to buy cigarettes and alcohol. Less hedonistic shoppers are not so fortunate, as most of the retail outlets lining Avenida San Martín are dismal, tacky affairs. Products aimed at tourists (skiing gear, for example) are actually more expensive here than in Buenos Aires, tax breaks notwithstanding, so equip yourself before arriving.

Boutique del Libro

25 de Mayo 62 (02901 432117/www.antartida ypatagonia.com.ar). Open 9am-8pm daily.
Stocking a reasonable range of mainstream English-language paperbacks and lots of publications about local history and culture, this is easily the best bookshop in town. Great for picking up a couple of novels to help kill the long days en route to Antarctica.

Laguna Negra

Avenida San Martín 513 (02901 431144/www.inter patagonia.com/lagunanegra). Open 10am-6pm daily.
Predictably touting itself as 'the most southerly chocolate shop in the world', Laguna Negra is the place to head for instant comfort when the wind whips up. The chocolate-covered figs are particularly tempting, and there are, of course, plenty of treats involving *dulce de leche*.

Stay

Ushuaia's hotel scene isn't quite as good as it pretends to be, but it has, nonetheless, come on in leaps and bounds in the last few years. Room rates are significantly higher than the country average, although you should be able to negotiate a discount on the rack rate in the off-season. Many of the best lodgings are several kilometres out of town. Wi-Fi is poor by international standards, though improving all the time. Unless stated otherwise, your room should come with spectacular views of either the Martial range or the Beagle Channel.

Los Cauquenes Resort & Spa

Reinamora 3462 (02901 441300/www.loscauquenes. com). ££££.
One of the best upmarket hotels in Ushuaia, and a member of the Small Luxury Hotels of the World group, Los Cauquenes mitigates its slick corporate efficiency with charm and style; its prime location overlooking the Beagle Channel doesn't hurt, either. Inside the multi-gabled, Alpine-style property are 54 spacious guest rooms, whose cream and caramel accents are designed to soothe the senses. Where the hotel really shines, however, is in its amenities. The spa offers a long menu of treatments, from anti-cellulite massages to caviar masks. Even better is the private beach by the Channel, where you can enjoy an apple martini at dusk while sucking in lungfuls of briny air. Breakfast, so often a disappointment in Argentina, here resembles more of a banquet than a buffet. Then, come evening, the dining area morphs into the award-winning Reinamora restaurant. The staff combine Fuegian warmth with big-city efficiency, making this place a highly recommended choice.

Cumbres del Martial

7km NE of Ushuaia *Luis Fernando Martial 3560 (02901 424779/ www.cumbresdelmartial.com.ar). £££.*
If the idea of staying in a room called Rhubarb appeals to you, book one of the six superior rooms at this resort at the foot of Glaciar Martial. All rooms come with private balconies and views of the Beagle Channel, and all are named after ingredients used in the hotel's La Cabaña restaurant. The property also includes four discrete wood-and-stone cabins, with deck terraces, jacuzzis, fireplaces and Wi-Fi internet access. Cumbres del Martial is a year-round destination, but one that is particularly well suited to skiers.

Hotel Albatros

Avenida Maipú 505 (02901 423206/
www.albatroshotel.com.ar). ££.
If you're in the market for a reasonably priced three-star lodging in the centre of Ushuaia, look no farther than the Albatros. The rooms aren't going to win any awards for design, but they're reasonably spacious and impeccably maintained. The premises overlook the harbour, so if you're thinking of taking a boat tour, you'll appreciate the location. All in all, a solid budget choice.

Hotel Tolkeyen

4km S of Ushuaia *Del Tolkeyen 2145 (02901*
445315/www.tolkeyenhotel.com). £££.
This sylvan retreat has 11 hectares of private woodland comprising lenga, cohiue and ñire trees. Located four kilometres out of town on the road to the national park, Tolkeyen is a sprawling, gabled lodge containing 50 standard rooms, several suites and a restaurant. All of the rooms are simple, verging on spartan, but Tolkeyen is nonetheless a good choice for people who intend to spend a lot of time exploring the national park.

MII810

25 de Mayo 245 (02901 437710/www.hotel1810.com).
£££.
Three cheers for this new property, which is one of the few hotels in downtown Ushuaia worth recommending. The lobby and other common areas are tastefully decorated, blending contemporary touches with traditional arts and crafts. The fourth-floor café bar, with its stunning view of the port, still looked like a work in progress when we last visited, but should be properly furnished by the end of 2009. Reports suggest that this is one of the more gay-friendly hotels in the area – another new and welcome development. On the downside, the rooms (there are 30 in total) are slightly small, and street noise may be an issue in high season.

Tierra de Leyendas

4km S of Ushuaia *Tierra de Vientos 2448 (02901*
443565/www.tierradeleyendas.com.ar). £££.
Located just outside of town, on the banks of the Beagle Channel, Tierra de Leyendas is that rare bird: an unpretentious boutique B&B. Its welcoming owners Maia and Sebas, who greet their guests with a glass of wine, have prioritised guest comfort and personalised service over contemporary design flourishes; their hands-on hospitality will be particularly appreciated by travellers new to the area. Each spacious guest room is decorated in warm autumnal tones, and has a large bed and – best of all – huge windows, to make the most of the stunning views. The deluxe suite has, in addition, a jacuzzi. The lounge-cum-dining room is a good place to meet other travellers and, in the evening, to sample chef Sebas's excellent cuisine. Look out for special offers in the low season, including a seven-night skiing package.

FURTHER AFIELD

Hostería Kaiken

100km N of Ushuaia *SE shore of Lake Fagnano,*
RN 3, km 2942 (02901 492372/www.hosteriakaiken.
com.ar). £££.
If Ushuaia isn't remote enough for you, try this wonderful lakeside lodge, which truly is in the boondocks. It stands on the reedy banks of Lago Fagnano, whose brilliant blue surface is sometimes whipped up into sizeable waves by the williwaws that come screaming down off the cordillera. (Bring a good anorak.) The complex comprises the main house – which has eight double rooms with terrace balconies overlooking the lake, and an apartment with two bedrooms – and an annex that contains ten rooms with en-suite bathrooms. The range of excursions is top-drawer and includes fishing, sailing on the lake, horse riding, birdwatching, mountain biking, skiing (in winter) and beaver-spotting. Daily transfers leave to and from Ushuaia.

Factfile

When to go

Most people visit Ushuaia between November and March, in what is notionally summer; with an average high of 14°C and an average low of 5°C, there's no need to pack your bikini.

It gets much colder in winter (average high 4°C, average low 2°C), but in recompense, the winds are significantly gentler. It's best to pack plenty of thin layers rather than one or two thick garments. Be prepared for gale-force winds and heavy showers.

Getting there & around

Malvinas Argentinas International Airport (02901 431232) is four kilometres from Ushuaia and is served daily by flights to and from Buenos Aires, Río Gallegos, El Calafate and Trelew. The main operator is Aerolíneas Argentinas (www.aerolineas.com), although LAN (www.lan.com) also runs flights. Bus connections between Ushuaia and the mainland are indirect and extremely limited, and there is no central bus terminal.

Tourist information

Secretaría de Turismo Municipal San Martín 674 (02901 432000, www.tierradelfuego.org.ar). Open 8am-10pm Mon-Fri; 9am-8pm Sat, Sun.

Internet

Café Bar Banana (Avenida San Martín 273, 02901 424201) has several terminals. Most of the high-end hotels offer wireless internet access, though connections are often slow.

Top: Tierra de Leyendas.
Bottom: Los Cauquenes
Resort & Spa (3).

March with the penguins

Ernest Shackleton planned his trip to **Antarctica** in the full knowledge that it might kill him. To ensure that the crew of his 1914 expedition were of a similar mind, he wrote the following on the recruitment poster: 'Men wanted for Hazardous Journey. Small wages, bitter cold, long months of complete darkness, constant danger, safe return doubtful.'

Antarctica has changed little in the century since the great explorer's voyage. It's still bitterly cold, still dark for half the year, still murder for the unprepared. But modern technology, and the rise of an affluent and adventurous leisure class, has made journeying to – and a safe return from – the ice continent almost routine.

Routine, that is, for the cruise-ship operators. The tourist, on the other hand, can start with 'extraordinary' and work up from there. In two weeks (the average trip duration), travellers cross the roughest stretch of sea on the planet, shadow the icy spine of the Antarctic Peninsula, moor in sulfurous lagoons kept warm by active volcanoes, and sink their boots into virgin snow on the world's remotest beaches. Most memorably, they meet the inhabitants of these lucid 'icescapes': penguins, seabirds, elephant seals, whales and the occasional scientist.

Trips usually begin in Ushuaia, where most cruise ships – or 'expedition vessels', as the operators like to call them – dock. Travellers should choose their boat with care. According to the international agreement that regulates tourism activities in Antarctica, only 100 passengers are allowed on shore in any one place at any time. Some cruise ships carry 300 to 400 passengers and use a rota system for excursions; others are more like floating small towns and don't allow for disembarkations. The smallest vessels, which carry only a few dozen passengers, trade lower comfort levels for a greater all-round experience.

The man-made entertainment laid on by most cruises is commendable for being nothing like the kind of entertainment you'd expect to find on a cruise. No bingo, no karaoke, no limbo-dancing nights, no deck skittles. Instead, passengers are offered three or four lectures a day delivered by the on-board scientists, with topics ranging from digital photography to the life cycle of penguins. Food and service tend to be excellent – though at these prices, you'd expect nothing less.

Most preconceptions don't survive first contact with the ice continent proper. Antarctica, many suppose, is pristine, sterile

and untainted, a vast frozen lump of Evian. This, however, is not the case. The sea smells. The ice smells. Elephant seals really smell. As for the stench of penguin guano – it's to chicken dung what chicken dung is to Terre d'Hermès – it will stay with you forever.

The terrain, too, is nothing like the blank slate you might have anticipated. Many of the beaches frame a tableau of outlandish objects, including weirdly inorganic-looking seaweed, bleached whale bones, century-old wooden hulls, abandoned blubber-rendering pots and iridescent shards of ice jutting out from the shingle like frozen yardangs. And what is singular in the late afternoon seems unreal when lit by the midnight sun. (All cruises to Antarctica happen in the southern spring and summer, between October and March.)

Mesmerising as these panoramas invariably are, they rarely claim your full attention when penguins, the natural world's great scene-stealers, are around (as they usually are). There are six species of penguin indigenous to Antarctica; of these, the gentoo, chinstrap and adélie penguins are the ones most commonly encountered by travellers. The

emperor penguin, the largest and most emblematic of the Antarctic species, is the only one that breeds in winter; the chances of spotting it depend on the ship's route, and the month in which it sails. All other species breed in summer, and one of the high points of the trip is getting close to a penguin rookery – a kind of alfresco maternity ward where each couple (penguins are scrupulously monogamous) takes it in turns to shelter their egg or newly hatched chick and collect stones to augment the nest. Those guarding their progeny scan the skies for predatory skuas (for those whose knowledge of biology is entirely gleaned from animated features, these gulls are the bad guys in *Happy Feet*), resembling tuxedoed children at an air show while doing so.

Most excursions last about two hours, which means passengers on smaller vessels might make two landfalls per day. Back on board, snow is kicked off boots, bodies thaw out with a hot chocolate (or something stronger; most ships have well-stocked bars) and the addictive pastime of ice-gazing resumes. In Samuel Taylor Coleridge's *The Rime of the Ancient Mariner*, set in the Southern Ocean,

the ice has a portentous, menacing quality, but it is also hauntingly beautiful: 'And ice, mast-high, came floating by/As green as emerald.' The poet isn't taking any liberties here; that's exactly what happens. And the icebergs just keep floating by. Some are as small as footballs, others as big as football stadiums. They are simultaneously delicate and imperious, and seem to bathe in gently rippling pools of aquamarine or turquoise. Penguins clamber over the smaller bergs; from a distance, they look like ants swarming over a boiled sweet.

At some point – too soon, whenever it is – the captain will point the ship's prow towards Ushuaia, and the return journey will begin. British explorer Aspley Cherry-Garrard famously called his 1910-13 expedition to Antarctica 'the worst journey in the world'. A century on, most people who make this trip will likely feel the exact opposite.

A trip to Antarctica costs from US$8,000 per person. Recommended agents and operators include Cox & Kings, Journey Latin America and Quark Expeditions. For contact details, *see p380* **Need to Know**.

Need to Know

ACCOMMODATION

APARTMENT RENTALS
ApartmentsBA.com 011 4800 1700/+1 646
827 8796 US/www.apartmentsba.com
Apartments Bariloche 02944 425457/
www.apartmentsbariloche.com
Confort Argentina 011 4801 5393/
www.confortargentina.com
International Nest +1 941 306 2115 US/
www.internationalnest.com
Luxury International Living +44 (0) 121 288
5796 UK/www.luxuryinternationalliving.com
Oasis 011 4831 0340/www.oasisba.com

CAMPING
Campingo www.campingo.com
Voy de camping www.voydecamping.com.ar

HOTELS
Buenos Aires Charming Hotels www.buenosaires
charminghotels.com
Best Boutique Hotels www.thebbh.com

ELECTRICITY

Electricity in Argentina and Uruguay runs on 220
volts. Sockets take either two- or three-pronged
European-style plugs. To use US appliances you'll
need a transformer (*transformador*) and adaptor
(*adaptador*); for UK appliances, an adaptor only.

EMBASSIES & CONSULATES

AUSTRALIA
Australian Embassy
Villanueva 1400, Buenos Aires (011 4779 3500/
www.argentina.embassy.gov.au).
Australian Consulate
Cerro Largo 1000, Montevideo (02 901 0743/
www.uruguay.embassy.gov.au).

CANADA
Canadian Embassy & Consulate
Tagale 2828, Buenos Aires (011 4808 1000/
www.international.gc.ca/argentina).
Plaza Independencia 749, office 102, Montevideo
(02 902 2030/www.uruguay.gc.ca).

IRELAND
Irish Embassy
Avenida del Libertador 1068, 6th floor, Buenos

Aires (011 5787 0801/www.embassyofireland.
org.ar). Also serves as diplomatic representation
to Uruguay.

NEW ZEALAND
New Zealand Embassy & Consulate
Carlos Pellegrini 1427, 5th floor, Buenos Aires
(011 4328 0747/www.nzembassy.com).
Miguel Grau 3789, Montevideo (02 622 1543/
www.nzembassy.com).

SOUTH AFRICA
South African Embassy
Marcelo T de Alvear 590, Buenos Aires (011
4317 2900/www.embajadasudafrica.org.ar). Also
serves as diplomatic representation to Uruguay.

UK
British Embassy & Consulate
Luis Agote 2412, Buenos Aires (011 4808
2200/www.britain.org.ar).
Calle Marco Bruto 1073, Montevideo (02 622
3630/www.britishembassy.org.uy).

US
US Embassy & Consulate
Avenida Colombia 4300, Buenos Aires (011
5777 4533/http://buenosaires.usembassy.gov).
Lauro Muller 1776, Montevideo (02 418 7777/
http://uruguay.usembassy.gov).

EMERGENCIES

ARGENTINA
Defensa civil 103 (for gas leaks, power cuts,
floods and other major catastrophes).
Emergencies at sea 106. **Fire service** 100.
Medical emergencies 107. **Police** 101.

URUGUAY
Emergencies 911. **Fire service** 104. **Police** 109.

HEALTH

No vaccinations are required for Argentina or
Uruguay. Tap water in BA and Montevideo is
drinkable. In unpopulated areas, it is best to
drink bottled water. Neither country has reciprocal
health care agreements with other countries, so
take out your own medical insurance policy.
  Farmacity has 24-hour branches throughout
Buenos Aires and in cities across Argentina. In
Uruguay, the big chain pharmacy is San Roque.

ID

By law, everyone must carry photo ID. Checks are rare in bigger cities but more common on the open road. If you get pulled over, you will be expected to show a copy of your passport or (photo) driver's licence.

LANGUAGE

People living and working in tourist areas usually speak some English and welcome the opportunity to practise it with foreigners. However, a bit of Spanish goes a long way, and making the effort to use a few phrases will be greatly appreciated.

As in other Latin languages, there is more than one form of the second person (you) to be used according to the formality or informality of the situation. The most polite form is *usted*, and though it's not used among young people, it may be safer for a foreigner to err on the side of politeness. The local variant of the informal, *vos*, differs from the *tú* that you may know from Spain or other parts of Latin America.

Another quirk in Argentinian and Uruguayan Spanish is the pronunciation of the 'y' and 'll', as 'sh' as in 'shout' or the French 'je'.

GENERAL EXPRESSIONS

hello *hola*
good morning *buenos días*
good afternoon *buenas tardes*
good evening/night *buenas noches*
OK *está bien/dale*
yes *sí*
no *no*
maybe *quizá(s)*
how are you? *¿cómo te va?*
how's it going? *¿cómo andás?*
Sir/Mr *Señor*
Madam/Mrs *Señora*
please *por favor*
thanks *gracias*
you're welcome *de nada*
sorry *perdón*
excuse me *permiso*
do you speak English? *¿hablás inglés?* (informal); *¿habla inglés?* (formal)
I don't speak Spanish *no hablo castellano*
I don't understand *no entiendo*
have you got change? *¿tenés cambio?* (informal); *¿tiene cambio?* (formal)
good/well *bien*
bad/badly *mal*
small *pequeño or chico*
big *grande*
beautiful *hermoso/lindo*
a bit *un poco*
a lot/very *mucho*
with *con*
without *sin*

also *también*
this *este*
because *porque*
if *si*
what? *¿qué?*
who? *¿quién?*
when? *¿cuándo?*
which? *¿cuál?*
why? *¿por qué?*
how? *¿cómo?*
where? *¿dónde?*
where to? *¿hacia dónde?*
where from? *¿de dónde?*
where are you from? *¿de dónde sos?* (informal); *¿de dónde es?* (formal)
I am English *soy inglés* (man); *inglesa* (woman)
Irish *irlandés*
American *americano/estadounidense*
Canadian *canadiense*
Australian *australiano*
New Zealander *neocelandés*
at what time? *¿a qué hora?*
out of order *no funciona/fuera de servicio*
bank *banco*
post office *correo*

GETTING AROUND

airport *aeropuerto*
station *estación*
train *tren*
ticket *boleto*
one way *ida*
return *ida y vuelta*
platform *andén*
bus station *terminal de colectivos/omnibús*
entrance *entrada*
exit *salida*
left *izquierda*
right *derecha*
street *calle*
motorway *autopista*
no parking *prohibido estacionar*
toll *peaje*
petrol *nafta*
unleaded *sin plomo*

ACCOMMODATION

hotel *hotel*
bed and breakfast *pensión con desayuno*
room *habitación*
do you have a room for this evening for two people? *¿tiene una habitación esta noche para dos personas?*
no vacancy *no hay habitación libre*
bed *cama*
double bed *cama matrimonial*
a room with twin beds *una habitación con dos camas*
breakfast *desayuno*
included *incluido*
lift *ascensor*

AT THE RESTAURANT

the menu la carta/el menú
appetiser entrada
main course plato principal
dessert postre
side dish guarnición
still water agua sin gas
sparkling water agua con gas
glass vaso
beer bottle porrón
beer on tap tirada
litre litro
barbeque asado
the bill la cuenta
closed cerrado
open abierto

NUMBERS

0 cero; **1** uno; **2** dos; **3** tres; **4** cuatro; **5** cinco;
6 seis; **7** siete; **8** ocho; **9** nueve; **10** diez; **11**
once; **12** doce; **13** trece; **14** catorce; **15** quince;
16 dieciséis; **17** diecisiete; **18** dieciocho; **19**
diecinueve; **20** veinte; **21** veintiuno; **22** veintidós;
30 treinta; **40** cuarenta; **50** cincuenta; **60**
sesenta; **70** setenta; **80** ochenta; **90** noventa;
100 cien; **1,000** mil; **1,000,000** un millón

LANGUAGE COURSES

Spanish courses geared to foreigners are
common in tourist destinations. In Buenos
Aires and Montevideo there are masses of
options, although there are huge ranges in
price and quality. Many institutions and private
teachers advertise on Craigslist. In Buenos Aires,
see also the classified adverts in the English-
language newspaper *Buenos Aires Herald*.

ARGENTINA

Ayres de Español 011 4834 6340/
www.ayresdespanol.com.ar
Español Andando 011 5278 9886/
www.espanol-andando.com
Road 2 Argentina 011 6379 9391/
www.road2argentina.com
Spanish 4 Foreigners 0387 4214038/
www.spanish4foreigners.com.ar
Spanish in the Mountains 02944 467597/
www.spanishinthemountains.com

URUGUAY

Academia Uruguay 02 9152496/
www.academiauruguay.com
La Herradura 02 4097894/
www.spanish-herradura.com

MONEY

The Argentinian currency is the Argentinian
peso (abbreviated as AR$ in this book). The
peso comprises 100 *centavos*. Notes come in

denominations of 100 (purple), 50 (dark grey),
20 (red), ten (brown), five (green) and two (blue)
pesos, and in every kind of condition. Coins come
in five, ten, 25, and 50 *centavos*, and one peso.
Small change and coins are hard to come by but
are a must for paying taxi and bus fares, and for
use in smaller establishments and at kiosks.

False bills are generally easy to detect, as the
colours tend to lack the precision of authentic
notes, and the texture is plasticky. Fake coins
(predominantly 50 *centavos*) are commonplace;
they're lighter in both colour and weight than
legal tender.

The official Uruguayan currency is the
Uruguayan *peso* (abbreviated as UR$ in this
book). Each *peso* comprises 100 *centavos*.
Pesos are available in ten, 20, 50, 100, 200,
500, 1,000 and 5,000 notes. Coins come in ten,
20 and 50 *centavos*, and one and two *pesos*.

ATMS

Most banks have 24-hour ATMs, indicated by
a 'Banelco' or 'Link' sign. They distribute both
pesos and US dollars, and usually charge a fee.
Look for a machine showing the symbol of your
card company. If withdrawing large sums, do so
discreetly. Some banks only allow you to withdraw
a limited amount per transaction. Generally, you'll
find ATMs in all but the tiniest towns.

CREDIT CARDS

Credit cards are accepted in most outlets,
but photo ID is required. Visa, MasterCard and
American Express are the most accepted cards.
Diners Club is also valid in a number of places,
but check first. For lost or stolen cards, contact
the issuer.
American Express +1 336 393 1111 US
Diners Club Contact the card issuer in your
home country
MasterCard 0800 555 0507 Argentina/
+1 636 722 7111 US
Visa 0800 666 0171 Argentina/
00 0411 940 7915 Uruguay

TRAVELLERS' CHEQUES & BUREAUX DE CHANGE

Travellers' cheques are often refused by
businesses and can be difficult and expensive
to change in banks. Bureaux de change will
change them, and commission is usually around
two per cent, with a minimum charge of US$5.
American Express, Arenales 707, Retiro, Buenos
Aires (011 4310 3000), will change American
Express travellers' cheques without charge. In
Uruguay, Cambio Gales (www.cambiogales.
com.uy) will change American Express travellers'
cheques. The company has offices in Chuy, Punta
del Este and around Montevideo. To find other
locations for exchanging American Express
travellers' cheques, see www.aetclocator.com.

TAX

Local sales tax is called IVA, aka *Impuestos al Valor Agregado*. The current rate in Argentina is 21 per cent; it's 22 per cent in Uruguay. As a rule, it's always included in the bill or price tag, with the exception of hotel rates, which are often listed without IVA in more expensive establishments. If you shop in Argentina, there is a not-entirely-reliable sales tax refund system, claimable at the airport on departure for goods purchased during your stay. Look for the 'Global Refund' sticker and, when you make your purchase, ask for the necessary stamped form, which fully explains the system.

OPENING HOURS

Opening hours are extremely variable and times listed in this book should be taken more as guidelines than gospel. In provincial areas, many businesses close in the afternoon for a siesta. Hours tend to vary from province to province, but in general are: banks 10am-3pm weekdays, some opening an hour earlier or closing an hour later; offices 9am-6pm, with a lunch break from 1pm to 2pm; post offices 8am-2pm; restaurants noon-3pm and again from 8pm until close. Hours vary in summer (from around mid December to early February), when some businesses work shorter hours and can close for weeks at a time. This is not the case if you're visiting a coastal town, where summer working hours can be longer.

PUBLIC HOLIDAYS

Banks, civil-service institutions and most offices close for *feriados* (public holidays), but many shops stay open. Public transport runs a Sunday service in Argentina.

ARGENTINA

The following Argentinian holidays are fixed from year to year: New Year's Day 1 Jan. National Day of Remembrance for Truth & Justice (Día Nacional de la Memoria por la Verdad y la Justicia) 24 Mar. Veteran's Day & Tribute to the Fallen in the Falklands/Malvinas War (Día del Veterano y de los Caídos en la Guerra de Malvinas) 2 Apr. Good Friday (Viernes Santo) 11 Apr. Labour Day (Día del Trabajador) 1 May. Anniversary of the First Independent Argentinian Government (Aniversario del Primer Gobierno Patrio) 25 May. Independence Day (Día de la Independencia) 9 July. Day of the Immaculate Conception (Día de la Inmaculada Concepción de María) 8 Dec. Christmas 25 Dec.

The following holidays move to the prior Monday if they fall on a Tuesday or Wednesday, or to the following Monday if they fall on Thursday to Sunday: Flag Day (Día de la Bandera Nacional) 20 June. San Martín Memorial Day (Aniversario de la Muerte del General José de San Martín) 17 Aug. Columbus Day (Día de la Raza) 12 Oct.

URUGUAY

Uruguay has the following national holidays: Constitution Day (Jura de la Constitución) 18 July. Independence Day (Declaración de la Independencia) 25 Aug. It also shares the holidays of New Year's Day, Good Friday, Labour Day, Columbus Day and Christmas.

SAFETY

With a little common sense and a few basic precautions, visitors to Argentina and Uruguay should be able to avoid trouble. It is always best to avoid pulling out a wallet stacked with bills, and try not to flash expensive jewellery and cameras. Keep a particularly close eye on belongings on public transport, as well as at bus and train stations. To avoid light-fingered pickpockets, don't stash possessions in back pockets or in outside compartments of bags and purses. If you are carrying a backpack, it is recommended you strap it across the front of your body, especially in crowded areas.

Exercise caution when withdrawing money from ATMs, especially on quiet streets. It is best not to withdraw large sums at a time and never get into a taxi waiting just outside an ATM machine.

Forged banknotes abound, so check your notes carefully when you receive change. One trick is for taxi drivers to accept a large note, switch it surreptitiously and hand you back a forged bill saying they can't change your money.

In Buenos Aires, remember that while most central areas are safe to walk around, more care should be taken in the edgier *barrios* of Constitución and La Boca. Touristy San Telmo and leafy Palermo can lull you into a false sense of security; although violent crime is rare, bag snatching is not. If you are threatened, hand over your goods calmly. In Montevideo, be careful in the Ciudad Vieja, especially in the evenings.

If you need to report a crime in Buenos Aires, contact the Comisaria del Turista (Avenida Corrientes 436, 0800 999 2838), where knowledgeable English-speaking staff can assist.

TELEPHONES

If you're looking to make an overseas call, an international phone card is your best bet; buy them from kiosks. Avoid calling from your hotel as rates will be a lot higher than those at *locutorios* (call centres). *Locutorios* are found throughout the country. Public phones take coins or cards; the latter are also available at kiosks.

Argentina's country code is 54. To call overseas, dial 00 plus the country code and then drop the first zero of the area code (if applicable).

In Argentina, mobile phone numbers all begin with the number 15 and need to include the relevant area code when calling from province to province. So if dialling a BA mobile number from another province, you need to dial the city code (011) first. In a confusing twist, if dialling an Argentinian mobile number from overseas, you need to drop the 15, and add a 9 between the country code and the area code (dropping the zero). For example, 15 XXXX XXXX in BA becomes 011 15 XXXX XXXX from elsewhere in Argentina, and +54 9 11 XXXX XXXX if dialled from abroad.

Uruguay's country code is 598. For dialling phone numbers in Uruguay from overseas, use the country code and drop the 0 in the area code. To call mobile phones, dial 9 after the country code.

AREA CODES, ARGENTINA

Barreal 02648
Buenos Aires 011
El Calafate 02902
El Chaltén 02962
Córdoba 0351
Esquel 02945
Esteros del Iberá 03773/03782
Jujuy 0388
Luján 02323
Mar del las Pampas 02255
Mendoza 0261
El Palmar de Colón 03447
Pinamar/Cariló 02254
Puerto Deseado 0297
Rosario 0341
Salta 0387
San Antonio de Areco 02326
San Carlos de Bariloche/El Bolsón 02944
San Luis 02652
San Martín de los Andes/Junín de los Andes 02972
Misiones (El Soberbio, Posadas) 03755/03752
Tafí del Valle 03867
Ushuaia 02901
Villa La Angostura 02944

AREA CODES, URUGUAY

Canelones 33
Carmelo 542
Colonia 52
Fray Bentos 56
Jose Ignacio 48
Montevideo 2
Punta del Este 42
Treinta y Tres 45

TIME

The clocks go back and forward rather arbitrarily, so time differences aren't set in stone. Daylight energy saving means the clocks gain an hour in summer (January to March) and lose one in winter (July to September). Argentina and Uruguay are three hours behind GMT during the southern hemisphere spring and autumn, two hours behind over the southern summer, and four hours behind GMT during the southern winter.

TIPPING

As a rule of thumb, leave ten per cent in a bar or restaurant, or for delivery service; in a cab, round off the fare. In hotels, bell-boys expect about AR$2/UR$12. Luggage handlers on buses expect the same. When checking out of a hotel, it's normal to leave a small tip for the maids.

TOUR COMPANIES

Audley Travel +44 (0)1993 838000 UK/ www.audleytravel.com
Exsus UK +44 (0)20 7337 9010 UK/+1 212 332 4848 US/www.exsus.com
Journey Latin America +44 (0)20 8747 8315 UK/www.journeylatinamerica.co.uk
Plan BA 011 4776 8267 BA/www.planba.com
Say Hueque 011 5199 2517 BA/ www.sayhueque.com
South American Experience 0845 277 3366 UK/www.southamericanexperience.co.uk

TOURIST INFORMATION

ARGENTINA

Argentina National Tourist Office Avenida Santa Fe 883 (0800 555 0016/www.turismo.gov.ar)
London 65 Brook Street W1K 4AH (+44 (0)20 7318 1300)
New York 12 W 56th Street (+1 212 603 0443)

URUGUAY

Uruguay National Tourist Office Rambla 25 de Agosto de 1825, Montevideo (02 188 5100/ www.uruguaynatural.com)
London 140 Brompton Road, 2nd floor SW3 1HY (+44 (0)20 7589 8835)
Washington DC 1913 I Street NW (+1 202 331 1313)

TRAVEL

AIRLINES

Aerolíneas Argentinas www.aerolineas.com
American Airlines www.aa.com
Austral www.austral.com.ar
British Airways www.britishairways.com
Delta www.delta.com
Iberia www.iberia.com
LAN www.lan.com
United Airlines www.united.com

BUSES

More than 80 long-distance bus companies operate out of Buenos Aires' Terminal de Omnibus de Retiro, with services reaching all major destinations in Argentina as well as in neighbouring countries. There are also good services linking regional destinations. Detailed bus company and schedule information is available at the terminal (Avenida Ramos Mejía 1680, 011 4310 0700, www.tebasa.com.ar).

You can usually buy tickets on the day, but it's best to book a few days in advance – and essential to do so during holiday periods. Companies include:

Andesmar 0261 405 4300/www.andesmar.com
Chevallier 011 4000 5255/ www.nuevachevallier.com.ar
Flechabus 011 4000 5200/www.flechabus.com.ar
Plusmar 0810 999 1111/www.plusmar.com.ar
Vía Bariloche 0800 333 7575/ www.viabariloche.com.ar

Bus travel in Uruguay is safe, convenient and inexpensive, with many services running from Montevideo to different towns across the country. The two main bus hubs in Montevideo are Terminal Tres Cruces (Bulevar Artigas 1825, 02 408 8710, www.trescruces.com.uy) and Agencia Central (Bulevar Artigas & Goes, 02 1717, www. agenciacentral.com.uy). Companies include:

COT 02 409 4949/www.cot.com.uy
COPSA 02 1975/www.copsa.com.uy
Turismar 02 409 0999/www.turismarsrl.com

CAR HIRE

You need to be over 21 and hold a driver's licence with a minimum two years of validity, a passport and a credit card to hire a car in Argentina or Uruguay. Major car rental companies in Argentina will allow you to take the car out of the country if you sign a contract four days in advance. This is not permitted in Uruguay. In both Argentina and Uruguay, you can often return the car to a different office within the country. You must have at least third-party insurance (*seguro de responsabilidad civil*), but it's wise to take out fully comprehensive insurance.

Avis www.avis.com.ar/www.avis.com.uy
Baires Rent a Car 011 4822 7361/ www.bairesrentacar.com.ar
Hertz www.hertz.com

DRIVING

Traffic regulations in Argentina and Uruguay don't differ much from the US or Europe. A few basics:
- You have to be 17 to drive (16 with a parent or guardian's permission).
- Front seat belts are mandatory.
- Under-10s must sit in the back in Argentina, while in Uruguay this applies to under-12s.
- Using mobile phones while driving is prohibited.
- Overtake on the left – that's the principle

anyway. The law bends a little to say that if the left-hand lane is moving slower than the right-hand one, you can overtake on the right instead.
- Priority is given to cars crossing other streets from the right.
- Right turns on red lights and left turns at most intersections marked with a stoplight are not permitted.
- On streets (*calles*) the maximum speed allowed is 40kph; avenues (*avenidas*), maximum 60kph; semi-motorways (*semiautopistas*), maximum 80kph; motorways (*autopistas*), maximum 100kph. On main national roads (*rutas nacionales*), signs on different stretches of road indicate minimum and maximum speeds, but the maximum never exceeds 130kph.

FERRIES

Buquebus 011 4316 6500/www.buquebus.com
Colonia Express 011 4317 4100 Argentina/ 0800 8354 Uruguay/www.coloniaexpress.com

TRAINS

Argentina's rail network is very limited, and most long-distance passenger trains operate at a low frequency, with one or two departures weekly. Train fares are very cheap – often about a quarter of the bus fare. Uruguay has no regular, long-distance train services.

Ferrobaires www.ferrobaires.gba.gov.ar
Ferrocentral www.ferrocentralsa.com.ar
TBA www.tbanet.com.ar
Tren Patagónico www.trenpatagonico-sa.com.ar
Trenes Especiales Argentinos www.trenesdellitoral.com

VISAS & IMMIGRATION

Advance visas are not required by members of the European Community or citizens of the USA and Canada for visits of up to 90 days. Immigration grants you a 90-day visa on entry that can be extended by a quick exit out of the country or, in Argentina, via the immigration service for AR$300 (UR $546 in Uruguay). The fine for overstaying is AR$300 (UR$546 in Uruguay); if you do stay longer than the allotted 90 days, arrive at the airport early to pay the fine. American and Australian citizens travelling to Iguazú and planning to cross in to Brazil to see the Brazilian side of the falls need to arrange a visa first; visitors from the UK, Ireland, New Zealand and Canada do not need a visa for Brazil.

WOMEN

It is generally safe for women to travel in Argentina and Uruguay, though all the usual precautions should be taken. No matter what province you are in, men typically flirt, stare, whistle and *piropear* (make a suggestive remark as you pass). Just ignore it.

Festivals & Events

JANUARY

Gualeguaychú, Argentina
Carnaval
A quiet town most of the year, Gualeguaychú is the backdrop for the country's biggest carnival festivities (*see opposite* **Carnival time**).
www.carnavaldelpais.com.ar

José Ignacio, Uruguay
Dotto Models
The Dotto agency's top models slink down an outdoor runway at this annual beachside fashion show.
www.dottomodels.net

Montevideo, Uruguay
Carnaval
Starting in January and finishing in March, this Montevidean celebration is said to be the world's longest-lasting carnival, focusing on street theatre and African-influenced beats (*see opposite* **Carnival time**).
www.turismo.gub.uy

Punta del Este, Uruguay
Festival Internacional de Jazz de Punta del Este
This international jazz festival attracts jazz heavyweights for a series of concerts and collaborations by the beach.
www.festival.com.uy

FEBRUARY

Buenos Aires, Argentina
ATP Buenos Aires, Copa Telmex
For one week in February, male tennis players compete for a cup victory.
www.copatelmex.com

Buenos Aires, Argentina
BA Fashion Week
BA's most stylish come out to see who's wearing what, both on the catwalk and off, at the country's biggest fashion event.
www.bafweek.com

Humahuaca, Jujuy, Argentina
Carnaval de Humahuaca
On the Saturday before Ash Wednesday, this carnival features traditional dance, folklore music and water fights.
www.jujuy.com

MARCH

Buenos Aires, Argentina
Buenos Aires Festival Internacional de Cine Independiente (BAFICI)
Buenos Aires' two-week independent film festival attracts hordes of cinephiles.
www.bafici.gov.ar

Buenos Aires, Argentina
Código País Festival de Música y Diseño
Five days of the latest in local productions, from music and design to technology and gastronomy.
www.codigopais.com

Buenos Aires, Argentina
Copa República Argentina
Teams compete in the final round of the national polo cup over a two-week period.
www.aapolo.com

Buenos Aires, Argentina
Quilmes Rock
A four-date rock festival that takes place over two weeks and features big-name Argentinian and international acts.
www.quilmes.com.ar

Mendoza, Argentina
Fiesta Nacional de la Vendimia
National grape harvest festival, featuring parades, fireworks and a beauty pageant.
www.vendimia.mendoza.gov.ar

Pinamar, Argentina
Pantalla Pinamar
This annual European-Argentinian film festival screens over 50 movies in one week.
www.pantallapinamar.com

Tacuarembó, Uruguay
Fiesta de la Patria Gaucha
Thousands attend this gaucho festival in the Uruguayan interior to witness rodeos, riding competitions and parades.
www.patriagaucha2010.blogspot.com

APRIL

Buenos Aires, Argentina
Feria Internacional del Libro de Buenos Aires
Three-week international book fair.
www.el-libro.org.ar

Carnival time

South America plus carnival means one thing in most people's minds: Brazil. Less known is that Argentina puts on a small-scale version of its own – and one that's remained largely off the radar for international tourists.

Some 230 kilometres north of Buenos Aires, in Argentina's Entre Ríos province and just across the border from Uruguay, the sleepy town of Gualeguaychú is the unlikely centrepoint of the country's festivities. Perched on the western bank of the Río Gualeguaychú, the town bursts into life each summer with a series of colourful and frenzied parades that last for ten consecutive Saturdays, starting at the beginning of January. The 150,000 spectators that descend upon the area are treated to a succession of elaborately decorated floats, accompanied by music and dancing, as women adorned in traditional Bahian skirts and ornate headdresses dazzle the crowd with their samba-influenced moves.

While the festival takes many of its cues from Brazilian traditions, it is also greatly influenced by the *candombe* rhythms that originated among Uruguay's African population, and *chacarera*, a syncopated style of folk music popular throughout Argentina. The highlight of the festivities is the annual competition, when the three main troupes (*comparsas*) are judged on costumes, floats, music and dancing.

Tickets can be purchased on the day of the event at the entrance of the town's open-air *corsódromo*, a former railway station now used as the main concourse of the festival, with seating for over 35,000 spectators.

Across the expansive Río de la Plata, the Uruguayan capital of Montevideo also knows how to put on a good show. The country's largest national festival attracts a multitude of revellers and is best known for its massive *desfile de las llamadas* (literally, parade of calls), inspired by the enslaved Africans' practice of using the *tambor* (a type of snare drum) to communicate during the colonial era. *Candombe* also features prominently in the festivities.

Unlike Gualeguaychú's carnival, the Montevideo festivities occur on Fridays, with important events also taking place on the Monday and Tuesday preceding Ash Wednesday. Montevideo's lengthy carnival season differs from Argentina's as it kicks off towards the end of January and marches on for about 40 days. Although there are celebrations throughout the month of February and into March, if you plan to visit on a weekend, you may find the city surprisingly quiet.

The town of Gualeguaychú makes for an accessible weekend destination from Buenos Aires as the journey there is only three hours 30 minutes by bus. Flecha Bus (011 4000 5200, www.flechabus.com.ar) offers direct service between the two cities. Be sure to book well in advance for the carnival period, as rooms in town fill up quickly. The river-front Posada del Puerto offers attractive, private bungalows as well as an on-site pool and spa (03446 454545, www.posadadelpuerto. com.ar). For accommodation options in Montevideo, *see pp74-75*.

Buenos Aires, Argentina
La Gran Vía de Mayo
On weekends throughout the entire month,
Avenida de Mayo is a backdrop for dance,
theatre and musical performances.
www.bue.gov.ar

Montevideo, Uruguay
**Festival Cinematográfico Internacional
del Uruguay**
This international film festival takes place over
two weeks in the Uruguayan capital.
www.cinemateca.org.uy

Ushuaia, Argentina
Festival Internacional de Ushuaia
A two-week classical music festival, with concerts
by renowned musicians.
www.festivaldeushuaia.com

Villa Carlos Paz, Córdoba, Argentina
Rally Argentina
High altitudes and bumpy terrain characterise
this FIA World Rally Championship race.
www.rallyargentina.com

MAY

Buenos Aires, Argentina
arteBA
This five-day contemporary art fair provides a
great opportunity to spot up-and-coming talent.
www.arteba.com

JUNE

Buenos Aires, Argentina
Ciudad Emergente
A five-day rock and pop music festival featuring
local and foreign bands.
www.ciudademergente.gov.ar

Ushuaia, Argentina
**Fiesta Nacional de la Noche
Más Larga del Año**
This celebration of the longest night of the
year includes musical performances and an
assortment of other activities.
www.tierradelfuego.org.ar

JULY

Buenos Aires, Argentina
**Arteclásica Feria de Arte Moderno
y Contemporáneo**
A five-day classic and contemporary art fair that
includes a series of talks and conferences.
www.arteclasica.com.ar

San Carlos de Bariloche, Argentina
Fiesta Nacional de la Nieve
Winter-sport contests and wacky races are all part
of this national snow carnival.
www.bariloche.org

AUGUST

Buenos Aires, Argentina
Buenos Aires Percussion
Two-week percussion festival.
www.buenosaires.gov.ar

Buenos Aires, Argentina
Festival de Tango
Ten-day tango festival leading up to the
hotly-contested world championship.
www.festivaldetango.gob.ar

SEPTEMBER

Buenos Aires, Argentina
Brandon Fest
A week-long international LGBT film festival.
www.brandongayday.com.ar/brandonfest

Buenos Aires, Argentina
**Feria Internacional de la
Música (BAFIM)**
Four-day international music festival.
www.bafim.buenosaires.gov.ar

Buenos Aires, Argentina
La Semana del Arte
Galleries, museums and cultural centres
participate in a week-long art celebration.
www.lasemanadelarte.com.ar

Buenos Aires, Argentina
South American Music Conference
A one-day celebration of electronic music.
www.samc.net

Buenos Aires, Argentina
Vinos y Bodegas
Four days of all things wine-related.
www.expovinosybodegas.com.ar

Famaillá, Tucumán, Argentina
Fiesta Nacional de la Empanada
National empanada festival (see p133 **The
queen of the empanadas**).
www.famailla.gov.ar

Rosario, Argentina
**El Cruce, Festival de Artes Escénicas
y Contemporáneas**
Dance, theatre and improvisation.
www.festivalelcruce.com.ar

OCTOBER

Buenos Aires, Argentina
Buenos Aires Photo
Five-day photography fair.
www.buenosairesphoto.com

Buenos Aires, Argentina
Festival de Cine y Video Latinamericano de Buenos Aires
Two weeks of Latin American film and video screenings.
www.festlatinoba.com.ar

Buenos Aires, Argentina
Festival Internacional de Teatro de Buenos Aires
This two-week theatre festival showcases the work of local and international talent.
www.festivaldeteatroba.gov.ar

Buenos Aires, Argentina
Personal Fest
Two-day international music festival.
www.personal.com.ar/personalfest

Buenos Aires, Argentina
Buenos Aires Jazz Festival Internacional
Five-day international jazz festival.
www.buenosairesjazz.gov.ar

Rosario, Argentina
Festival de Jazz Santiago Grande Castelli
Seasoned performers and newcomers show off a range of jazz styles.
www.rosario.gov.ar

San Carlos de Bariloche, Argentina
Semana Musical Llao Llao
National and international acts perform at this week-long classical music event.
www.semanamusical.com

Villa General Belgrano, Córdoba, Argentina
Fiesta Nacional de la Cerveza
This Oktoberfest celebration in Córdoba first began in the 1960s and features concerts, dance and, of course, plenty of beer.
www.elsitiodelavilla.com/oktoberfest

NOVEMBER

Buenos Aires, Argentina
Campeonato Argentino Abierto de Polo
The world's fifth-oldest polo competition takes place over the course of a month.
www.aapolo.com

Buenos Aires, Argentina
Creamfields
This well-established electronica festival brings the beats and big-name DJs to BA in a one-day extravaganza.
www.creamfieldsba.com

Buenos Aires, Argentina
Diversa Festival Internacional de Cine Gay, Lésbico, Trans de Argentina
Catch some alternative flicks, from shorts and feature films to documentaries, at this ten-day international LGBT film festival.
www.diversa.com.ar

Buenos Aires, Argentina
Festival Internacional de Tango Queer
Same-sex dance partners dominate this week-long tango fest. Events include classes, workshops and performances.
www.festivaltangoqueer.com.ar

Buenos Aires, Argentina
La Noche de los Museos
Take advantage of free entrance to the city's museums throughout the night.
www.lanochedelosmuseos.com.ar

San Antonio de Areco, Argentina
Fiesta de la Tradición
Horse parades, dancing and games are part of the celebrations of gaucho life in the lead-up to Día de la Tradición on 10 November.
www.sanantoniodeareco.com

DECEMBER

El Bolsón, Argentina
El Bolsón Jazz Festival Internacional
Three days of open-air jazz jam sessions are combined with free talks and exhibitions.
www.elbolsonjazz.com.ar

Buenos Aires, Argentina
Copa Peugeot Argentina de Tenis
Male tennis stars duke it out over four days for a cup title.
www.copapeugeotdetenis.com.ar

Buenos Aires, Argentina
Festival Buenos Aires Danza Contemporánea
Week-long contemporary dance festival.
www.buenosairesdanza.gov.ar

Buenos Aires, Argentina
Gran Premio Internacional Carlos Pellegrini
The biggest horse-racing event of the year, at the only grass track in Argentina.
www.hipodromosanisidro.com.ar

Itineraries

These are suggested itineraries only. They can be used as pick-and-mix guides, depending on your time and budget. Most travellers to Argentina and Uruguay use Buenos Aires as their start and end point, and journey times from the capital to all key destinations featured in this book are listed to the right. Note that these times can vary and should be used only as a guideline.

Internal flights usually go through Buenos Aires, and there are limited direct services between other destinations. The bus networks in both Argentina and Uruguay are highly recommended (*see p221* **Coach class with a difference**) and can be used to link regional destinations together.

If you have one week

If you only have a short time in Argentina, your best bet is to combine unmissable **Buenos Aires** with a visit to one of the country's three other big attractions. Spend three or four nights exploring the city, then travel to either the famous Perito Moreno glacier at **El Calafate**, the wine region of **Mendoza**, or **Iguazú**.

If you have two weeks

In a fortnight, you can pack in **Buenos Aires** and two of the 'big three' out-of-city attractions (*see above*), or you could consider hopping on a bus or plane to spend a week in the lake district surrounding **Bariloche**. Here, you can add side trips to **Villa La Angostura** and **El Bolsón**, and take the famed Siete Lagos (seven lakes) route to **San Martín de los Andes** and **Junín de los Andes**. From Bariloche, you could head further south to **El Calafate** (one hour 45 minutes by plane), before flying back to Buenos Aires. This schedule could comfortably fill two weeks, or you could just visit El Calafate and return to the capital a little earlier to head up to **Iguazú**. If you have energy to burn, you can work your way back to BA overland, stopping off at the marshlands of **Esteros de Iberá** (two nights) and/or the palm forests of **El Palmar de Colón** (one night).

If you have three or four weeks

Those with the luxury of a bit more time can approach the two-week itinerary more leisurely and more extensively. You could also consider adding on a trip way down south to **Ushuaia** or, if the season's right for whale watching (June to mid December), to **Península Valdés**. You could spend extra time up north, venturing further from **Iguazú** into the surrounding rainforests of **Misiones**. Another strong contender for your time is a visit to the north-western provinces of **Salta** and **Jujuy**, which you can get to by bus from Misiones's capital, Posadas, changing in Tucumán (14 hours). Before heading home, try and slot in a relaxing night in an estancia in **San Antonio de Areco**, **Las Sierras de Córdoba** or **El campo** in Uruguay – all just a short hop from BA.

When time is money

If you want to cram as many of Argentina's highlights into your short break as possible, begin with two nights in the capital, then fly to the 'end of the world', **Ushuaia**. Hop back on a plane and head north to **El Calafate** (one hour 15 minutes). From there, fly back to BA, where you can take a day or two to unwind in the pampas around **San Antonio de Areco**. Before heading home, rocket up to the other end of the country to be awed by **Iguazú** falls, which you can reach by plane or bus from BA. If you take the latter option, go overnight and treat yourself to a *cama* (bed) seat.
Time frame: seven to ten days.

Wine and mountains

Load up on culture in **Buenos Aires** and then make your way west to **Mendoza**. If you travel by bus, you can break the journey with a quick hike through the awesome canyons of **Parque de las Quijadas** or an estancia stay in **Las Sierras de Córdoba**. After exploring Mendoza's vineyards and Andean landscapes – perhaps with an adventurous detour to **Barreal** (eight hours by road) – make your way back to the capital.
Time frame: seven to ten days, or two weeks including Barreal.

Northern exposure

Argentina's north is home to indigenous culture and exotic landscapes. Take a bus from **Buenos Aires** to **Salta** and watch the countryside transform as you head towards the Andes. Explore the city of Salta and the wine region of Cafayate (with a possible detour to the grasslands of **Tafí del Valle**, four hours by road), before heading north to **Jujuy**'s multicoloured valleys of Quebrada de Humuhuaca (two hours 30 minutes overland from Salta city).
Time frame: four to ten days.

The big Patagonia circuit

Make no mistake: Patagonia is huge. Most people fly to the key spots, but if you have time and patience, the overland routes will allow you

to truly appreciate the region's size and majesty. Start off by heading from **Buenos Aires** to see the whales and other wildlife around **Península Valdés**. From here, take a bus further south for more sea creatures and remote landscapes in **Puerto Deseado** (11 hours). Truly adventurous types can proceed overland to **El Calafate** (17 hours) and then continue right down to **Ushuaia** (18 hours, changing buses at Río Gallegos), but you'll need to break the journey with some overnight stops (see www.estanciasdesanta cruz.com). When in El Calafate, hikers have the option of heading to the dramatic Parque Nacional Torres del Paine in Chile (10 hours by bus) and/or **El Chaltén** (three hours 30 minutes by bus). Then take a long road trip to **Esquel** for **Parque los Alerces** (24 hours) and on up to **Bariloche** (four hours 30 minutes), where you can take side trips to **Villa La Angostura**, **El Bolsón**, **San Martín de los Andes** and **Junín de los Andes**. Afterwards, make your way by plane or bus back to BA.
Time frame: a month, or highlights in a fortnight.

Beach hopping
Porteños desert the city in droves during the long hot days of summer (January to March) to head to the beaches of either Uruguay or the Argentinian Atlantic coast. A beach-bumming tour could begin with a river crossing to Uruguay's capital, **Montevideo**. Bohemian types can then head straight to **Punta del Diablo** and **Cabo Polonio** (three to four hours by road); fashionistas can make a beeline to **José Ignacio** and **Punta del Este** (two to three hours by road). Take a peek at **El campo** and the pretty riverside towns of **Colonia del Sacramento** and **Carmelo** before crossing back over the Río de la Plata to **Buenos Aires**. From the capital, it's a short hop south to the exclusive end of Argentina's coastal scene in buzzing **Cariló** and **Pinamar**. Then drive an hour further south to laid-back **Mar de las Pampas** before returning to BA.
Time frame: ten days, or one long weekend if you pick one hotspot in Argentina or Uruguay.

Weekend escapes
If you don't have the time or inclination to make a substantial venture outside Buenos Aires, try a day-trip or weekend break. **Tigre** and its Delta is just 30 minutes north of the capital, while Uruguay's **Colonia del Sacramento** and **Carmelo** are just an hour's ride away. Venturing three hours north from Buenos Aires takes you to Argentina's other lovely riverside city, **Rosario**, or, a little further east, the national park of **El Palmar de Colón**. To sample some gaucho traditions and luxury estancias, head to **San Antonio de Areco** and the surrounding pampas, around an hour from BA.
Time frame: one to three days.

Journey times from Buenos Aires

From BA to...	Plane	Road
Bariloche, El Bolsón & Villa La Angostura (p176)	2hrs 20mins	22hrs
Barreal (p280)	1hr 50mins to San Juan	16hrs
Cabo Polonio & Punta del Diablo (p228)	N/A	4-5hrs from Montevideo
Colonia & Carmelo (p138)	N/A	1-3hrs (ferry)
El Calafate (p290)	3hrs	40-45hrs
El Chaltén (p302)	3hrs to El Calafate	44-48hrs
Esquel & Parque Los Alerces (p192)	2hrs 30mins	24hrs
Esteros del Iberá (p148)	2hrs 30mins to Corrientes	10-12hrs
Iguazú (p312)	1hr 45mins	17-19hrs
José Ignacio & Punta del Este (p240)	50mins to Punta del Este	2hrs from Montevideo
Junín de los Andes & San Martín de los Andes (p216)	2hrs 20mins to San Martín de Los Andes	18-22hrs
Mendoza (p200)	1hr 50mins	14hrs
Misiones (p322)	1hr 30mins to Posadas	14hrs
Montevideo (p62)	45mins	3hrs 30mins (ferry)
El Palmar de Colón (p156)	N/A	5hrs 30mins
Parque de las Quijadas (p330)	1hr 50mins to San Luis	8hrs 30mins to San Luis
Península Valdés (p254)	2hrs to Trelew	18-20hrs
Pinamar, Cariló & Mar de Las Pampas (p266)	1hr to nearby Mar del Plata	4-5hrs
Puerto Deseado (p336)	2hrs 30mins to Comodoro Rivadavia	27hrs
Rosario (p78)	2hrs	4hrs 30mins
Salta & Jujuy (p346)	2hrs 15mins	18hrs
San Antonio de Areco (p104)	N/A	1-2hrs
Las Sierras de Córdoba (p116)	1hr 20mins to Córdoba capital	10hrs
Tafí del Valle (p128)	2hrs 15mins to Salta	17-18hrs
El campo (Uruguay, p94)	45mins from Montevideo	1-3hrs (ferry)
Tigre (p164)	N/A	1hr 30mins
Ushuaia (p366)	3hrs 35mins	58-65hrs

Advertisers' Index

Please refer to relevant sections for contact details

Index

Page references in italics indicate illustrations.